걸프 사태

미국 동향 2

걸프 사태

미국 동향 2

한국학술정보

| 머리말

걸프 전쟁은 미국의 주도하에 34개국 연합군 병력이 수행한 전쟁으로, 1990년 8월 이라크의 쿠웨이트 침공 및 합병에 반대하며 발발했다. 미국은 초기부터 파병 외교에 나섰고, 1990년 9월 서울 등에 고위 관리를 파견하며 한국의 동참을 요청했다. 88올림픽 이후 동구권 국교 수립과 유엔 가입 추진 등 적극적인 외교 활동을 펼치는 당시 한국에 있어 이는 미국과 국제 사회의 지지를 얻기 위해서라도 피할 수 없는 일이었다. 결국 정부는 91년 1월부터 약 3개월에 걸쳐 국군의료지원단과 공군수송단을 사우디아라비아 및 아랍 에미리트 연합 등에 파병하였고, 군 · 민간 의료 활동, 병력 수송 임무를 수행했다. 동시에 당시 걸프 지역 8개국에 살던 5천여 명의 교민에게 방독면 등 물자를 제공하고, 특별기 파견 등으로 비상시 대피할 수 있도록 지원했다. 비록 전쟁 부담금과 유가 상승 등 어려움도 있었지만, 걸프전 파병과 군사 외교를 통해 한국은 유엔 가입에 박차를 가할 수 있었고 미국 등 선진 우방국, 아랍권 국가 등과 밀접한 외교 관계를 유지하며 여러 국익을 창출할 수 있었다.

본 총서는 외교부에서 작성하여 30여 년간 유지한 걸프 사태 관련 자료를 담고 있다. 미국을 비롯한 여러 국가와의 군사 외교 과정, 일일 보고 자료와 기타 정부의 대응 및 조치, 재외동포 철수와 보호, 의료지원단과 수송단 파견 및 지원 과정, 유엔을 포함해 세계 각국에서 수집한 관련 동향 자료, 주변국 지원과 전후복구사업 참여 등 총 48권으로 구성되었다. 전체 분량은 약 2만 4천여 쪽에 이른다.

2024년 3월

한국학술정보(주)

| 일러두기

· 본 총서에 실린 자료는 2022년 4월과 2023년 4월에 각각 공개한 외교문서 4,827권, 76만여 쪽 가운데 일부를 발췌한 것이다.

· 각 권의 제목과 순서는 공개된 원본을 최대한 반영하였으나, 주제에 따라 일부는 적절히 변경하였다.

· 원본 자료는 A4 판형에 맞게 축소하거나 원본 비율을 유지한 채 A4 페이지 안에 삽입하였다. 또한 현재 시점에선 공개되지 않아 '공란'이란 표기만 있는 페이지 역시 그대로 실었다.

· 외교부가 공개한 문서 각 권의 첫 페이지에는 '정리 보존 문서 목록'이란 이름으로 기록물 종류, 일자, 명칭, 간단한 내용 등의 정보가 수록되어 있으며, 이를 기준으로 0001번부터 번호가 매겨져 있다. 이는 삭제하지 않고 총서에 그대로 수록하였다.

· 보고서 내용에 관한 더 자세한 정보가 필요하다면, 외교부가 온라인상에 제공하는 『대한민국 외교사료요약집』 1991년과 1992년 자료를 참조할 수 있다.

| 차례

정 리 보 존 문 서 목 록

기록물종류	일반공문서철	등록번호	2012090523	등록일자	2012-09-17
분류번호	772	국가코드	US/XF	보존기간	영구
명 칭	걸프사태 : 미국의 대응, 1990-91. 전6권				
생 산 과	북미과/안보과	생산년도	1990~1991	담당그룹	
권 차 명	V.4 1991.1.3-15				
내용목차					

0001

관리 번호	91-11

원 본

외 무 부

종 별 : 지급

번 호 : USW-0008 일 시 : 91 0103 1704

수 신 : 장관(미북,중근동,미안)

발 신 : 주 미 대사

제 목 : 미-이락 외무장관 회담 제의

연:USW-5665

1. 금 1.3. 백악관 대변인은 주이락 미대사관을 통해 미-이락 양국 외무장관회담을 1.7-1.9 사이에 스위스에서 개최할것을 금일 이락측에 제의하였다는 요지의 부쉬 대통령 성명을 발표하였음.(동 성명 전문 및 FITZWATER 대변인질의 응답 내용은 USW(F)-0022 로 FAX 편 송부)

2. 미측은 이락측에 대해 1.5 까지 전기 제안의 수락여부를 회답하여 줄것을 요청하였다하며, 당초 베이커 국무장관은 1.6. 워싱턴을 출발, 다국적군 참여국과 페만사태 관련 협의를 가질 예정으로 있었다 함.(베이커 장관 여행 일정은 상금 미정)

3. 이락측의 동제안 수락 여부는 상금 알려지지 않고 있으나, 11.30 부쉬 대통령의 미-이락 양국 외무장관 교환 방문 제의시와 마찬가지로 미측은 금일 발표시도 이락과의 여하한 타협이나 교섭이 있을수 없다는 점을 재삼 강조하고 여사한 미-이락간 접촉의 목적이 이락측에 대해 미국의 확고한 의지를 분명히 전달하기 위한 것이라는 점을 부연하였음.(베이커 국무장관은 부쉬 대통령의 후세인 대통령 앞 친서를 휴대할 예정이며, 미측으로서는 회담장소로서 제네바를 상정하고 있다함)

4. 부쉬 행정부로서는, 의회와 여론 일각의 반전론을 인식, 유엔이 제시한 이락군의 철수시한(1.15)직전까지도 금번 사태의 평화적 해결을 위해 노력했다는인상을 심어 주려는 의도를 갖고 있는 것으로 보이며, 또 한편으로는 금명간있을 예정인 EC-이락간 접촉과 관련, 미국나름의 이니셔티브를 계속 유지하기 위한의도도 갖고 있는 것으로 보임.

5. 한편, 이락측으로서는 전기 철수 시한이 불과 며칠 남지 않은점을 고려,일단 금번 미측 제안을 수락할 가능성도 있으며, 연호 2 항으로보고한 지연작전 과 연계작전을 계속 전개하면서 1.15 이후에도 미국이 이락을 공격하지 못하도록 노력할

미주국	장관	차관	1차보	2차보	미주국	중아국	정와대	안기부

PAGE 1 91.01.04 08:02

외신 2과 통제관 BW

0002

것으로 관찰되고 있음.

(대사 박동진-차관)

예고:91.6.30 일반

예고문에 의거 일반문서로
재분류1991 6 30 서명

PAGE 2

0003

원 본

외 무 부

종 별 :

번 호 : USW-0048 일 시 : 91 0104 1918

수 신 : 장 관(미북,중근동,미안)

발 신 : 주 미 대사

제 목 : 페만사태 관련 세미나

1. 금 1.4. 당지 소재 CSIS 는 학계, 언론계, 재계등 각계인사 다수가 참석한 가운데, 페만사태관련 세미나를 개최하였는바, JAMES SCHLESINGER 전 국방장관의 세미나 기조 연설요지를 하기 보고함.(당관 김영목,임성남 서기관참석)

가.현재 실시중인 대이락 경제 봉쇄가 실질적인 효과를 거두기 위해서는 보다 더 많은 시간이 소요될것으로 예상되는바, 90.11. 부쉬 행정부의 걸프지역 주둔 미군 병력 배증 결정을 계기로 무력사용에 의한 금번 사태의 해결 가능성이 보다 더 가시화한 것으로 봄.

나. 미측이 이락군의 쿠웨이트로 부터의 완전철수를 계속 강력히 요구해 왔고, 금번 사태 종결후의 새로운 걸프지역 안보장치 수립문제를 검토해온점및 후세인 대통령으로서도 쿠웨이트로부터의 철수결정을 내릴만한 특별한 인센티브가 없는점등을 고려할때, 결국은 전쟁이 발발할것으로 봄 (WAR IS THE LIKELY OUTCOME)

다. 미측으로서는 가능한한 단기간내에 전쟁을 종료시키기 위해 노력할 것으로 보이며, 전장을 쿠웨이트 영토로만 국한할것인지, 아니면 이락 영토까지 확대하여야할것인지를 심사 숙고하여야 할것임.

(전쟁 기간은 기본적으로 이락군의 사기가 어느정도 오래동안 유지될 지에 달려 있는 것으로 봄.)

라. 한편 일단 전쟁이 발발케되면 이락측으로서는 각종 테러 공격 및 대이스라엘 공격을 통해 전쟁의 확산을 꾀할것임.

마. 또한 미측으로서는 일단 전쟁을 통해 사태가 종결된후,이란의 세력 확장가능성 및 다국적군에 참여하고 있는 시리아의 영향력 증대등을 염두에 두고 중동지역의 새로운 질서를 모색하여야할 것이며, 아랍인들의 대미 적대감에 대해서도 관심을 가져야 할것임.

미주국 1차보 미주국 중아국 정문국 안기부

PAGE 1 91.01.05 09:46 WG

외신 1과 통제관

0004

한편 미국내적으로는 금번 사태가 국방예산 감축정책, 국내산업의 경쟁력 향상 추진정책, 마약퇴치정책등 각종 국내 현안의 해결노력에 끼친 부정적 영향 (국민적 관심의 상대적 감소등)에 대해서도 적절한 시정 조치를 취하여야 할것임.

2. 한편, 동 장관의 기조연설후, CROWE 전합참의장을 비롯 CSIS 의 연구원등 학계 및전문가의 PANEL 토론이 있었으나, 발표의 대부분은 그간 언론 및 청문회를 통해 보도된 내용과 동일하였음.

3. 다만, 금일 세미나를 통해 일반적으로 요약된결론은 다음과 같음.

- 일단 군사행동시 미군의 능력은 상당히 짧은 기간내에 이락군은 쿠웨이트로부터 몰아낼 능력이 있음.

- 다만, 미국으로서는 전략적목표를 단순히 하여 쿠웨이트 해방만을 추구하는것이 현명하며, 이락자체에 대한 공격 또는 이락군의 파괴를 위한 추가적 군사조치는 바람직하지 않음.

- 이락군의 생.화학.핵무기 능력에 대한 과장된 보도가 있는바, 동위협은 현시점에서 심각히 우려할 대상은 아님.

- 미국은 최후까지 평화적 해결을 모색하여야함 (금일 세미나 도중, 미측의 1.9 제네바 회담에 대한이락의 동의 보도가 전달된바,발표자들은 이에 대한 상세한 답변을 회피하였으나 일단 미국의 대이락공격이 당장 강행되지는 않을 것이라는 견해를 표시함.)

(대사박동진-국장)

PAGE 2

0005

관리번호	91-78

원 본

외 무 부

종 별 : 지급

번 호 : USW-0049 일 시 : 91 0104 1918

수 신 : 장관(미북,중근동,미안)

발 신 : 주 미 대사

제 목 : 미-이락 외무장관 회담

연 USW-0008

1. 금 1.4 부시 대통령은 백악관에서 기자 회견을 갖고, 이락측이 표제 회담을 1.9 제네바에서 개최하는데에 대해 동의하여왔다고 공식 발표하였음(기자 회견 전문은 USWF-0034 로 FAX 편 송부)

2. 부쉬 대통령은 금일 회견시도 이락의 쿠에이트 침공을 반대하는 국제 사회의 확고한 결의를 이락측에 전달하는것이 표제 회담의 목적임을 거듭 강조하였는바, 동 회담을 계기로 금번 사태의 평화적 해결을 위한 획기적 전기가 마련되지는 못할것이라는것이 당지의 일반적 견해임.

(대사 박동진-차관)

91.6.30 일반

예고문에 의거 일반문서로 재분류 1991.6.30. 서명

미주국	장관	차관	1차보	2차보	미주국	중아국	청와대	안기부

PAGE 1

91.01.05 10:11

외신 2과 통제관 BW

0006

이라크와의 전쟁은 필요한 것인가 ?

(91.1.6.자 Paul Nitze 및 하바드대 Michael Stafford의

W.P. 공동 기고문 내용 요약)

1. 폐만사태 관련 미국의 정책 목표

ㅇ 가장 중요한 목표

- 냉전 종료 이후시대 국제사회에서 어느 누구도 침략, 강압 또는 무력에 의해서는 득을 볼 수 없다는 선례 확립

ㅇ 부수적인 목표

- 중동 지역에서의 세력 균형 파괴 방지 및 우호적인 국가내 내부 붕괴 기도 세력 부추김 방지
- 세계 원유 시장의 안정성 유지
- 사담 후세인의 핵무기등 대량 학살무기 보유방지 및 기타지역에서의 핵무기등 확산 방지

2. 미국의 정책 목표 달성을 위해 선택 가능한 수단

가. 이라크와의 전면전

ㅇ 지상전을 포함한 전면전을 수행할 경우 최대 6개월의 기간과 약 500-600억불의 전비 소요 예상

ㅇ 사담 후세인을 제거하거나 이라크 점령을 위해서 추가 비용 소요

중동아국장

공람	북미과	담당	과장	심의관	국장	차관보	차관	장관

0007

나. 이라크에 대한 현 제재조치 계속 및 선택적 공중공격 실시

o 해상 봉쇄 및 금수조치 계속 실시
  - 현재 이라크의 민간부문 생산 능력은 사태 이전에 비추어 40% 감소
  - 시간이 경과함에 따라 부품등 부족으로 이라크 군사력 감소 예상

o 사우디 방어를 위해 현 수준보다 적은 미군 병력 계속 사우디 주둔

o 향후 6-12개월간 현 제재조치 계속후 소기의 성과가 없을 경우, 이라크내 전략 목표물에 대한 공중공격 실시
  - 전략 목표물 파괴로 경제 제재조치 효과 증대
  - 경제 제재조치 계속후 무력사용시 정당성 획득 용이

3. 결 론

o 전면전은 다음과 같은 이유에서 미국의 정책 목표 달성에 가장 부적합
  - 전면전에서의 승리가 향후의 잠재적 침략자를 억제하는 효과를 반드시 가져온다는 보장 없음.
    · 미군의 사상자수가 증가함에 따라 미국내 여론이 보다 고립 주의화할 가능성
    · 이경우 장차 유사 사례 발생시 미국의 개입이 어렵게 됨.
  - 전면전에서의 승리 하더라도 중동지역 세력 균형 파괴 및 혼돈화로 인해 동 지역 정세 불안정은 더욱 악화될 전망
    · 이라크 패배시 시리아, 이란의 지역 패권 추구를 부추길 가능성
  - 시리아나 이란이 이라크를 대체할 경우, 세계 원유 공급은 또 다시 위협 받을 가능성
  - 중동지역의 세력 균형 파괴될 경우, 사우디등 국가들의 군비경쟁 촉발 가능성 농후

0008

o 따라서 현 시점에서 가장 바람직한 선택 수단은 현 제재조치 계속 및 선택적 공중공격 실시

- 세계정세 안정 파괴 위협 최소화 가능
- 중동지역의 세력 균형의 급격한 파괴 방지
  - 이라크의 군사력 유지시 사우디나 쿠웨이트에 다국적군 주둔을 통해 대처
- 현 세계 원유 공급이 불확실하긴하나 현 제재조치 지속이 전면전시의 원유 공급 중단 사태보다는 바람직
- 핵무기등 대량 살상무기의 확산 방지는 지속적인 국제적 노력에 의해 보다 효과적으로 달성될 수 있으며 이라크 1국을 패퇴 시킴으로써 달성될 수 있는 것이 아님.

0003

Baker Faces Mighty Diplomatic Challenge

Aziz Meeting Will Differ From Situations in Which the Secretary of State Has Thrived

By David Hoffman
Washington Post Staff Writer

Secretary of State James A. Baker III departs today on a mission to Europe and the Middle East that could prove far more challenging to his skills as a negotiator and persuader than anything he has yet attempted in domestic politics or international affairs.

His planned meeting Wednesday in Geneva with Iraqi Foreign Minister Tariq Aziz will be the first direct high-level contact between the United States and Iraq since the invasion of Kuwait five months ago. It also may be the last such contact before the Jan. 15 United Nations deadline for Iraq to vacate Kuwait.

NEWS ANALYSIS

The meeting is expected to be the centerpoint of the Baker mission during which the secretary of state will be trying to head off any last-minute flurry of third-party diplomacy that might encourage Iraq to keep its troops in Kuwait.

In many ways, the meeting with Aziz is different from other pressure-filled environments in which Baker has always thrived. He will not enjoy the kind of leeway that he has had in the past as a negotiator because this time he has been instructed not to negotiate. He also may find it necessary to throw open the curtains on his discussions rather than operate in the secrecy that he prefers as a tactician.

"This has got to be kind of a nightmare for him," said an associate who has worked closely with Baker in both diplomacy and domestic politics. "It is a no-win situation. He can't make any secret deals, but everyone will suspect that he has."

Moreover, Baker's possible avenues for progress in the talks were somewhat narrowed Friday when President Bush announced that Baker could not go on to Baghdad to see Iraqi President Saddam Hussein if the opportunity should arise. Bush said that option was no longer open because Saddam had refused to agree to the dates that Bush had proposed earlier for such a visit.

The president's statement in effect puts even more importance on the meeting with Aziz, who has been regarded by U.S. officials as more a messenger than a decision-maker in the Iraqi leadership.

In earning his reputation as a negotiator, Baker has always relied on a similar pattern of tactics. He believes in staking out a series of positions, sometimes at the outer boundary of what he really wants, then working, often in complete secrecy, to convince his adversary that Baker's positions are really in the adversary's best interests, too. Baker then makes concessions toward his opponent in an effort to close a deal, only going public with the terms when all the details have been agreed.

He did this, for example, when representing Ronald Reagan in the bargaining with Jimmy Carter's team over the climactic debate before the 1980 election. Baker opened with a preposterous position, that the debate be held on the eve of the election; he finally settled for a few days before the election, but close enough to suit the purposes of the Reagan campaign.

Even as secretary of state, Baker has tried to employ these tactics. He worked over many months, for example, to convince the Soviet leadership that a unified Germany within the North Atlantic alliance was really in the Soviet Union's interests. Over and over he looked for concessions that would allow the Soviets to accept this reasoning and make it easier for them to sell the concept to skeptical audiences at home. Ultimately, with generous offers of cooperation from West Germany, Soviet President Mikhail Gorbachev agreed.

But Baker goes into the talks with Aziz carrying a different kind of brief.

Bush and the other leaders of the coalition against Iraq already have ruled out any serious negotiations over the basic terms of the 12 United Nations resolutions calling for Iraq's complete and unconditional withdrawal from Kuwait. Baker has no license to make concessions to Aziz on the central demands, and this instruction effec-

Jan. 6, 1991
WP

0043-5

0010

: USW(F) -

: 장 관　　　　발신 : 주미대사

:

보안	
통제	

(매)

tively will be made clear in the letter from Bush to Saddam that Baker is expected to deliver.

Second, Baker is not sitting across the table from a real interlocutor who is in a position to make concessions. Aziz is not considered by U.S. intelligence agencies to be part of Saddam's inner circle but rather a reliable funnel back to Baghdad.

Thus, Baker has been limited in advance to the task of presenting, not negotiating, and doing it to an intermediary, not a principal.

Furthermore, officials said they do not think Iraq has reached the point where it is serious about negotiating an end to the crisis, but rather is looking for a way to forestall any attack by the international coalition arrayed against it. This calculation, if borne out, would seem to restrict further the scope of the discussion, suggesting that the talks would not address such delicate but important topics as how to begin a de-escalation of the massive armies facing each other on the Arabian Peninsula.

However, Baker's hands are not completely tied. Perhaps relying on his familiar approach of trying to articulate his opponents' "best interests," Baker is expected to tell Aziz that the coalition will not attack if Iraq pulls out. And if Iraq does not withdraw, Baker will stress, Saddam and Aziz will lose all in a war against a superpower and its partners. Baker may well emphasize anew that Bush is not bluffing about the use of military force.

Baker also is not proscribed from talking to Aziz about life after the crisis—assuming Iraq quits Kuwait and providing Baker does not link the withdrawal to other issues. The United Nations resolutions contemplate Iraqi negotiations with Kuwait over disputed territory, and Baker has said the alliance anticipates the creation of new security structures in the region afterward. Although Baker cannot truly negotiate these matters in Geneva, a discussion of them may be significant in unlocking a diplomatic solution.

Finally, Baker often has used secrecy to avoid public pressure while he is negotiating, but in this case, officials said, he may find he is better served by staying in the open, thus insulating himself against any suspicion that he has made or suggested any private deals. "This is going to be very open diplomacy," said a senior official familiar with Baker's thinking.

0043-6　　　　Jan. 6, 1991 WP

0011

: USW(F) -

: 장 관 발신 : 주미대사

:

보안 통제	

(매)

War Whether We Need It or Not?

A Blockade—Plus Bombs—Can Win

By Paul H. Nitze and Michael F. Stafford

WE ARE rushing headlong into all-out war in the Persian Gulf. There is an alternative to this painful course. Continued reliance on the United Nations embargo—possibly augmented by air strikes—promises a much more favorable result.

If this week's last-minute round of diplomacy fails and the United States applies its new military doctrine of overwhelming force, the carnage will be severe—probably thousands of American casualties, as well as widespread death and destruction in Kuwait and Iraq. A massive clash with Saddam Hussein's well-entrenched forces on the ground as well as in the air also will have severe long-term impact on U.S. public opinion, U.S. standing in the Middle East and other key American interests.

One of the most dangerous forms of human error is forgetting what one is trying to achieve. In the gulf crisis, it is crucial that we look beyond our anger at Saddam and remind ourselves of precisely what U.S. interests are in the crisis and what we seek to accomplish. Underlying our support for the United Nations' resolutions calling for Saddam to withdraw from Kuwait and allow the restoration of the Kuwaiti government are several important objectives.

See GULF, C2, Col. 1

Paul H. Nitze most recently served in the Reagan administration as special adviser on arms control to the president and secretary of state. Michael F. Stafford is executive director of the Center for Science and International Affairs at the John F. Kennedy School of Government at Harvard.

GULF, From C1

Our main goal should be to establish a precedent for a new post-Cold War era, in which the community of nations, working through the United Nations and other organizations, can insure that would-be aggressors do not profit from invasion, coercion and force.

Subordinate goals should be:

- To avoid major disruptions in the regional balance of power in the Middle East, and at the same time to avoid encouraging internal foes of friendly regimes;
- To maintain stability in the world oil market, which has adjusted to the loss of Iraqi and Kuwaiti oil, (8 percent of pre-crisis world supply), by insuring that Saddam cannot follow up his aggression against Kuwait *so as to* eventually gain leverage over Saudi oil (9 percent of world supplies) or of the entire Middle East's (30 percent);
- To deny Saddam the ability to field weapons of mass destruction, including an atomic bomb, and to prevent the spread of such weapons elsewhere in the region.

To achieve these goals, the United States and its international partners have available a choice among two general courses of action:

The first is all-out war, including heavy reliance on the prompt offensive use of ground forces. U.S. gulf commander Gen. H. Norman Schwarzkopf has said it could take up to six months to win such a conflict. If we get bogged down, it could take longer. In addition to troop losses, such a campaign would cost about $50-60 billion, plus that much or more in indirect expenditures such as future medical and other care for the casualties. Efforts to eliminate Saddam or occupy Iraq could take longer and cost more.

The second is continued sanctions, possibly augmented by air strikes. This course would balance power with restraint; it would measure out sufficient force to make unmistakable to Iraq and the rest of the world the adverse consequences of aggression.

We would continue the international embargo, including its enforcement by the naval blockade. To defend Saudi Arabia, we would retain and rotate a sustainable de-

0043-9

Jan. 6, 1991
WP

0012

: USW(F) -

: 종 국

발신 : 주미대사

보안
통제

(매)

ployment of ground forces, a level lower than the forces there now.

Under the current international embargo, only a trickle of goods is getting in or out of Iraq; oil exports and earnings are nil and civilian production is estimated to be down by about 40 percent. In time, lack of spare parts will erode Iraq's military capabilities, and civilian and military production will fall further.

But over the next six to 12 months, it may become evident that a blockade by itself will not do the job. In that case, we would favor supplementing the naval blockade with selected but powerful air strikes.

Before this step was taken, however, it would be important that our allies and the American people be convinced that sanctions alone had been given a full chance to work and had failed. It would also be important that the public be better convinced that the interests at stake justified use of military force.

While the shortcomings of strategic air campaigns are well known, modern air delivery systems can inflict great damage on the Iraqi war machine and the economy. Combined with the naval blockade, a well-directed air assault could force Iraqi capitulation. And if, over months, it did not achieve its goal, there remains the possibility of a later ground attack against greatly weakened Iraqi forces.

In our view, all-out war promises the least success in achieving the objectives we have outlined.

First, it would not necessarily discourage other potential aggressors. Defeating Saddam Hussein promptly in an all-out war would send an unequivocal signal that *this* aggression had not been tolerated. But if casualties were high, U.S. sentiment probably would be driven toward a more isolationist posture. Many Americans would be dismayed by the carnage and resentful that our allies were not paying a similar price. (The seeds of such resentment already exist.) They could be expected to oppose any comparable U.S. role in the future. The message would be that the United States had neither the inclination to work in concert with other nations nor the stomach to repeat the anti-Iraq action. Many of our current collaborators, who are ambivalent at best about the war option, might also lose interest in future cooperation with us. A world of growing brutality and chaos would become a likely prospect.

Second, Middle East instability has already been exacerbated by the rallying of Moslem extremists toward Iraq, and no option is likely to be very successful at the delicate task of restoring a balance while shoring up friendly but shaky regimes.

But even a successful all-out war could throw the Middle East into chaos. With the destruction of much of Iraq's military capability, Syria and Iran could be expected to vie for regional domination. Other nations—including Saudi Arabia, Jordan and Egypt—could be destabilized, with strong internal forces rising in opposition, enraged by their governments' collaboration with Americans who had killed thousands of their Arab brothers. In all this ferment, U.S. influence could be reduced to shoring up friendly regimes, if we had the stomach for it. All these troubles would be exacerbated if Saddam were to succeed in drawing Israel into the war.

Third, with instability in the Middle East, oil supplies would remain quite uncertain. If Syria or Iran replaced Iraq as the potentially dominant regional power, or if friendly governments in Saudi Arabia and other oil-producing countries were overthrown by hostile, fundamentalist groups, supplies would be threatened once more.

Finally, a well-executed attack on Iraq could sharply set back its efforts to acquire weapons of mass destruction but also could create problems elsewhere in the region. The crisis has already had this effect: the Saudis, for example, are reported to be newly seeking to buy a nuclear weapon. The increased regional instability we can expect after a war can only heighten these incentives.

In sum, the all-out war option seems highly counterproductive in the long term and certainly not worth the thousands of lives it would cost.

Much more promising is continued reliance on sanctions.

First, successful sanctions would be most likely to produce a stable world order. Critical to this outcome is that a substantially lower level of violence would be more likely to result in continued public support for an active U.S. international role.

Second, this option would likely be less disruptive to regional stability. But any approach that left much of Iraq's military capability intact would produce a need to retain a peacekeeping force on the front lines, either in Kuwait or Saudi Arabia, and perhaps elsewhere. While internal destabilization in other countries of the region would remain a concern, this threat would be lower than that produced by all-out war, especially if the

Jan. 6, 1991
WP

0043-10

0013

: USW(F) -

: 종 권 발신 : 주미대사

보안 통제	

(매)

:

peacekeeping force were primarily Arab.

Third, although oil supplies would remain uncertain, we would be better able to reduce our vulnerability to disruption of those supplies. The key is the strategic petroleum reserve, which provides us an assured source of oil which we can use to make up supply shortfalls or dampen price hikes an unfriendly nation might seek to impose. The reserve already holds almost 600 million barrels, enough for us to increase market supply by over 3 million barrels a day (more than we import from all Arab OPEC nations) for as long as six months. For about $15 billion, or a fraction of the estimated cost of a prompt, all-out war, we could increase the reserve to the 1 billion barrels recommended by most experts. In the longer term, we could impose an oil tariff to induce conservation (while also generating revenues) and reverse cutbacks in development of alternative energy sources.

Finally, the key to halting proliferation in the region lies not merely with what we do in this immediate crisis but rather in a sustained campaign among potential suppliers to cut off sources of critical materials and technical cooperation. Successful sanctions would be most likely to encourage such a campaign, but they must be supplemented by provisions for continued International Atomic Energy Agency inspections and additional U.N. inspections to insure supplies remain stemmed.

On all counts, therefore, the sanctions-air strikes approach promises to serve U.S. interests better than a prompt, all-out war.

Some argue that the threat of all-out war is the key element in the U.S. approach—a weapon in itself—and that Saddam must be convinced that the use of overwhelming force is imminent before he will back down. Arguments that question the all-out war option, they contend, undermine that strategy. But the momentum toward such a war, whose results threaten to be so costly, may have become dangerously irreversible. War may occur whether it serves our purposes or not.

For the past generation, Americans have regretted that in Vietnam, we let the passions of the moment and a lack of healthy skepticism toward presidential claims obscure a clear-headed assessment of our national interests. The result was that we were driven into a costly, divisive, and ultimately counterproductive expansion of a war that lacked adequate public support. Let's not spend the next generation wondering how we came to repeat that mistake.

Jan. 6, 1991
WP

0014

관리 번호	A-32

원 본

외 무 부

종 별 : 지급

번 호 : USW-0079 　　　　　　　　일 시 : 91 0108 1834

수 신 : 장관(미북,중근동,미안)

발 신 : 주 미 대사

제 목 : 페만 사태 관련 부쉬 대통령및 퀘일 부통령 연설

연 USW-0049

1. 금 1.8 주재국 공보처(USIA)는 자체 국제 방송망인 WORLDNET 를 통해, 우방국가들을 대상으로 행한 부쉬 대통령연설(ADDRESS TO THE COMMUNITY OF NATIONS UNITED AGAINST IRAQI AGGRESSION)을 방송한바, 동 대통령은 이락의 무조건 철수 및 유엔 안보리 결의안 이행을 재차 강조한바, 요지 하기 보고함(연설문전문 USW(F)-0061 로 FAX 편 송부)

가. 이락군의 쿠웨이트 철수 시한(1.15)을 앞둔 향후 며칠간이 금번 페 만 사태의 향방을 가름할수 있는 가장 결정적 시기(THE MOST CRITICAL PERIOD)가 될것임.

나. 유엔 안보리가 상기 철수 시한을 제시한 목적은, 이락군이 동 시한까지무조건 전면 철수치 않는 경우 다국적군 참여국들이 향후 언제라도 무력을 사용할수 있다는점을 사전 경고키 위한것이었는바, 동 일자에 반드시 전쟁이 발발 한다는 의미는 아님.

다. 현재, 국제 여론의 일각에서는 훗세인의 체면을 어느정도는 살려 주어야 하고, 따라서 이락군의 조건부 철수도 받아들여야 한다는 주장이 대두하고 있으나, 여사한 미봉책은 훗세인의 정복욕을 억제하지 못할것이며 향후 이락의 핵무기 보유가 현실화 되는 경우 보다 더 어려운 상황이 도래할것임.

라. 즉, 탈 냉전 시대의 국제 평화를 위해서는, 다국적군 참여국간의 결속을 계속 강력하게 유지함으로서 이라군의 무조건 전면 철수를 유도하는것이 긴요한바, 특히 앞으로 남은 며칠간(IN THE DAYS AHEAD)여사한 결속을 유지해 나가는것이 중요함.

2. 상기 부쉬 대통령 연설은 명 1.9 제네바 개최 예정인 미-이락 외무장관 회담을 목전에 두고, 페 만 사태의 부분적 해결에 반대하는 미국의 입장을 분명하게 천명하뭄로서 명일 회담에 임하는 베이커 장관의 입장을 지원하고, 프랑스등 구라파

미주국 장관 차관 1차보 2차보 미주국 중아국 정문국 청와대
총리실 안기부

91.01.09 09:35
외신 2과 통제관 BW

0015

[redacted] [redacted]

일각에서 대두하고 있는 조건부 철수론등에 쐐기를 박음으로서 이락의지연 작전을 봉쇄키 위한 의도에서 비롯된것으로 보임.

3. 한편, 전기와 같이 금일 부쉬 대통령이 국제적 AUDIENCE 를 대상으로 한연설을 통해 다국적군 참여국간의 결속 유지를 호소한 반면, 퀘일 부통령은 라성 WORLD AFFAIRS COUNCIL 에서의 연설을 통해 금번 사태가 평화적으로 해결되기위해서는 미 의회등 국내 정치적 차원의 대행정부 지지가 긴요하다는점을 중점강조하고 최근 의회및 일부 여론의 반전론 또는 키통령의 군사 통수권 제한 주장에 반격을 가했음.

4. 이처럼 미 행정부 수뇌부가 대내외적으로 적극적인 홍보전을 전개하고 있는 주 목적은 지금까지 이락에 대해 구사해온 -극한 전략(BRINKMANSHIP)-의 막바지에서 마지막 피치를 올림으로서, 국민적 지지와 국제적 결속을 계속 강력하게 유지, 이락군의 자진 철수를 유도하려는것으로 보이는바, 진전 사항 추보 예정임.

(대사 박동진-차관)

예고:91.6.30 일반

예고문에 의거 일반문서로
재분류 1991 6.30 서명

번호 : USW(F) - 0061

수신 : 장 관(미북, 중근동, 미안) 발신 : 주미대사

보안 통제

제목 : "페"만 사태 관련 부쉬 대통령 연설 (3 매)

ADDRESS OF PRESIDENT BUSH TO THE COMMUNITY OF NATIONS UNITED AGAINST IRAQI AGGRESSION/ WASHINGTON, DC/ TUESDAY, JANUARY 8, 1991

PRESIDENT BUSH: More than five months ago, in the early morning hours of August 2nd, Iraqi forces rolled south and the rape of Kuwait began. That unprovoked invasion was more than an attack on Kuwait -- more than the brutal occupation of a tiny nation that posed no threat to its large and powerful neighbor. It was an assault on the very notion of international order.

My purpose in speaking to you, the people of countries united against this assault, is to share with you my view of the aims and objectives that must guide us in the challenging days ahead.

From the center of the crisis in the Middle East, to people and countries on every continent -- to the families with loved ones held hostage, to the many millions sure to suffer at the hands of one man with a stranglehold on the world's economic lifeline -- Iraq's aggression has caused untold suffering, hardship and uncertainty.

In the more than five months since August 2nd, Iraqi troops have carried out a systematic campaign of terror on the people of Kuwait -- unspeakable atrocities against men and women, and among the maimed and murdered, even innocent children.

In the more than five months since August 2nd, Iraq's action has imposed economic strains on nations large and small, among them, some of the world's newest democracies, at the very moment they are most vulnerable.

And yet, Iraq's aggrression did not go unchallenged.

In the five months since August 2nd, the world has witnessed the emergence of an unprecedented coalition against aggression. In the United Nations, Iraq's outlaw act has met a chorus of condemnation in 12 resolutions with the overwhelming support of the Security Council. At this moment, forces from 27 nations -- rich and poor, Arab and Muslim, European, Asian, African and American -- stand side by side in the Gulf, determined that Saddam's aggression will not stand.

We are now entering the most critical period of this crisis. For the past five months, Saddam has held the world and the norms of civilized conduct in contempt. In the next few days, Iraq arrives at a deadline that spells the limit of the civilized world's patience.

Let me be clear about the upcoming deadline. January 15 is

0061-1

0017

01/09/91 18:51 ☎202 797 0595 EMBASSY OF KOREA --- WOI 2 ☎001/003 not a 'date certain" for the onset of armed conflict -- it is a deadline for Saddam Hussein to choose - to choose peace over war.

The purpose of declaring this deadline was to give Saddam fair warning: withdraw from Kuwait, without condition and without delay, or -- at any time on or after that date -- face a coalition ready and willing to employ "all means necessary" to enforce the will of the United Nations.

Everyone of us, each day of this crisis, has held out hope for a peaceful solution. Even now, as the deadline draws near, we continue to seek a way to end this crisis without further conflict. That is why, back on November 30, I offered to have Secretary Baker travel to Baghdad to meet with Saddam Hussein. That is why, even after Saddam failed to respond -- failed to find time to meet on any of the 15 days we put forward -- I invited Iraq's foreign minister to meet with Secretary Baker in Geneva on January 9th.

In Geneva, we will be guided by the will of the world community, expressed in those 12 UN resolutions I mentioned a moment ago.

I didn't send Secretary Baker to Geneva to compromise, or to offer concessions. This meeting offers Saddam Hussein a chance -- possibly the final chance -- before the UN deadline to resolve by peaceful means the crisis he has created.

Saddam may seek to split the coalition, to exploit our sincere desire for peace to secure for himself the spoils of war. He will fail -- just as he has failed for more than five months.

I know that pressures are now building to provide Saddam some means of saving face -- or to accept a withdrawal that is less than unconditional. The danger in this course should be clear to all. The price of peace now on Saddam's terms will be paid many times over in greater sacrifice and suffering. Saddams's power will only grow -- along with his appetite for more conquest. The next conflict will find him stronger still -- perhaps in possession even of nuclear weapons -- and far more difficult to defeat.

That is why we simply cannot accept anything less than full compliance with the UN dictates: Iraq's complete and unconditional withdrawal from Kuwait.

I began by saying that Iraq's action was more than an attack on one nation -- it is an assault on us all, on the international order we all share. We who have witnessed in this past year an end to the long years of cold war and conflict -- we who have seen so much positive change -- stand now at a critical moment, one that will shape the world we live in for years, even decades, to come.

The key now in meeting this challenge is for this remarkable

0061-2

0018

coalition to remain steadfast and strong. If we remain in the days ahead nations united against aggression, we will turn back not only the actions of an ambitious dictator -- we will, as partners, step forward toward a world of peace.

Thank you, and may God bless all of you.

END

0019

관리번호	91/1080

외 무 부

종 별 : 지급

번 호 : USW-0097 일 시 : 91 0109 1837

수 신 : 장관(미북,미안,중근동,정이,연기)

발 신 : 주 미 대사

제 목 : CARL FORD 부차관보 접촉

당관 이승곤 공사는 금 1.9 이임을 앞두고 CARL FORD 국방부 부차관보와 오찬을 가졌음. 동 오찬 석상에서 FORD 부차관보는 한미 양국간의 몇가지 공동 관심사에 대해 언급하였는바, 요지 다음과같이 보고함.

1. 페만 사태

가. 미국의 입장에 대한 각국의 협조

0 현재까지 미국이 사우디, 이집트 및 걸프 제국등 전선국가들과 지속적인 결속을 유지하는데에는 아무런 문제점이 없음. 오히려 이들 국가들은 경제 제재 조치가 효력을 발휘하지 못한데 대해 실망하여 강경한 군사 조치를 취할것을 미국에 요구하여왔으며 오히려 미국이 이를 저지하고 있는 실정임.

0 EC 국가들은 최근 유화적인 입장을 취하여 이락측과 타협하는듯한 태도를보이고 있으나 미국으로서는 이를 수용할수 없는 입장임. 특히 불란서는 가장 타협적인 입장을 취함으로서 미국의 정책 수행에 지장을 주고 있는것이 사실임.미국으로서는 불란서가 페만 사태에 있어 연합국으로부터 이탈하여 독자적인 노선을 취하는 경우가 있더라도 이에 무관 할것임.

0 소련은 대체적으로 미국의 입장을 지지하여 왔으며, 이러한 태도는 쉐 외상의 사임에도 불구하고 변화가 없음. 다만 소련이 경제 제재 조치를 위반하여 물자 수송을 시도하다가 미국에 적발된적이 있으나 동 제재 조치 실시에 협조하고 있음. 이락 주재 소련인은 대부분 이미 귀국하였거나 귀국중에 있음.

0 중국은 초기부터 페만 사태 해결에 미온적이었으며 유엔등 국제 기구에서중립적 입장을 취하였음. 중국은 페만 사태를 미국과의 접촉에 있어 LEVERAGE 로 사용하려하고 있으나 미국으로서는 이를 수용할수 없는 입장임.그러나 미국은중국을 페만 사태 해결에 방해되는 국가로 생각하지는 않고 있음.

미주국	장관	차관	1차보	2차보	미주국	중아국	정문국	외연원
청와대	총리실	안기부						

PAGE 1

91.01.10 09:40

외신 2과 통제관 BW

0020

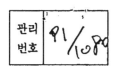

나. 페만 사태 지원 증가 문제

0 페만 사태 관련 소요 경비는 현재 미국이 약 50 프로(병력, 인건비, 수용비, 유지비등포함), 사우디, 쿠웨이트 및 걸프 제국이 약 40 프로, 그리고 기타 우방국이 나머지 10 프로를 부담하고 있음. 그러나 이는 동 사태 발생 초기인 작년 8-9 월에 결정된것이며, 그후 병력의 대폭 증가등 많은 변화가 있었으므로 더많은 경비가 소요되고 특히 미 의회가 우방국의 지원 증액을 요청하는 실정이므로 미 행정부로서는 부득이 우방국에 지원 증가를 요청해야 할 입장에 있음.

0 상기 지원 증가 요청안은 초안 작성 단계에 있어 정확한 액수를 알수 없으나 한국의 경우 사태 초기에 요청한 정도가 될 가능성이 있음. 지원 내역에 있어서는 각국 사정에 따라 다르나 일본에 대해서는 경제 지원 보다는 현금을, 그리고 한국에 대해서는 현금, 수송, 군수 물자 및 기타 지원(물자등)의 순위로 요청할것으로 보임.

0 요청 시기와 관련, 현재 미측으로서는 우선 1 월 하순경에 액수를 제시하지는 않고 개괄적인 추가 지원 요청을 한후, 구체적 액수 및 내역을 결정 각국에제시할것으로 고려하고 있음.

다. 의회 반응에 대한 행정부 입장

0 페만 사태에 대한 의회의 입장은 전반적으로 호전되고 있으나, 행정부로서는 의회가 취하고 있는 입장이 사태 해결에 장애가 된다고 보지는 않고 있음.

0 사견으로서는 일단 무력 행사가 개시되면 의회및 국민이 행정부 결정을 지지할것으로 기대하며, 다만 무력 사용 경과및 결과에 대해 국민이 비판 또는 반대를 할수 있다고 생각함.

[redacted]

PAGE 2

0021

[redacted]

(대사 박동진-국장)
91.12.31 일반

검 토 필(1991. 6. 30.) 서명

PAGE 3

0022

김

원 본

외 무 부

종 별 :

번 호 : LAW-0024 일 시 : 91 0109 1110

수 신 : 장 관(미북)

발 신 : 주 라성 총영사

제 목 : D.QUAIL 부통령 연설

1. DQUAIL 부통령은 1.8(월) LOS ANGELES WORLDAFFAIRS COUNCIL 주최로 당지 CENTURY PLAZA HOTEL에서 개최된 오찬에서 중동사태에 관한 미국입장에 관하여 연설하였음.

2. D.QUAIL 부통령은 1.9(화) 제네바에서 개최되는 미국의 BAKER 국문장관과 AZIS 이락 외상간의 회담은 어떤 협상을 위한것이아니며, 사담후세인 군대가 무조건 KUWAIT 에서 철수해야하고, KUWAIT 의 합법적인 정부가 회복되어야한다는 UN 안보리의 결의와 동결의를 준수하지 않을때는 필요한 제반조치를 취할것이라는 미국정부의 입장을 통보하기 위한 회담이며 그외의 협의사항은 없다고 말함.

3. 동 오찬 연설에는 약 1,500명이 참석하였으며 HOTEL 밖에서는 약 30명의 반전데모가 있었고, 연설시작시 어떤 부인이 전쟁을 반대한다는 고함이 있었고, 연설중간에 흑인남자가 또다시 전쟁을 반대한다는 고함으로 약간의 소동이 있었음.끝.

(총영사 박종상-국장)

미주국 1차보 정문국 안기부

PAGE 1 91.01.10 09:12 WG

외신 1과 통제관

0023

관리 번호 91-37

원 본

외 무 부

종 별 :

번 호 : USW-0100 일 시 : 91 0109 1905

수 신 : 장관(미북,중근동,미안,마그) 사본:주유엔 대사-직송필

발 신 : 주 미 대사

제 목 : 미-이락 외무장관 회담

연: USW-0079,0049

1. 금 1.9 제네바 개최 표제 회담 종료 직후, 회담장인 INTERCONTINENTAL 호텔에서 베이커 국무장관은 기자 회견을 통해 약 6 시간반에 걸쳐 진행된 금일 회담시 미측으로서는 이락측에 대해 쿠웨이트로 부터 철수치 않는 경우 무력이 사용될것이라는 메세지를 분명히 전달하였으나, 이락측은 부쉬 대통령의 친서 접수 자체를 거부하는등 아무런 융통성(FLEXIBILITY)도 보이지 않았다고 발표함. 베이커 장관의 기타 주요 언급 요지 다음임(베이커 장관 기자 회견 전문은 USW(F)-79 로 FAX 송부)

가. 기본적으로 이락측은 현재 주변 상황을 부정확하게 판단하고 있는바, 다국적군 참여국간의 공동 보조는 와해 되지 않을것임.

나. 1.15 까지 앞으로 남은 며칠동안 유엔 사무총장의 중재 노력등 금번 사태의 외교적 해결 노력이 계속 진행될것으로 기대함.

불란서, 알제리아등의 외교적 해결 노력등 금번 사태를 평화적으로 해결하기 위한 모든 노력을 미측은 환영함.

다. 이락의 쿠웨이트 침공 문제와 팔레스타인 문제간에 여하한 연계도 있을수 없다는 미측의 입장에는 변함이 없음.

여사한 연계 조건이 수락되는 경우, 이락측이 쿠웨이트로 부터 철수할수도 있다는점을 금일 회담시 아지즈 이락 외상이 암시하기는 하였으나, 이를 분명히 언급치는 않았음.

라. 아지즈 외상은 현재 주이락 미국 대사관에 잔류하고 있는 5 명의 미국 외교관에 대해 1.12 부 출국 허가를 발급하겠다고 약속하였음 (동건 관련, 당관 임성남 서기관이 국무부 이란-이락과 JOSEPH MCGHEE 부과장으로부터 확인한바에

미주국 안기부	장관	차관	1차보	2차보	미주국	중아국	중아국	총리실

PAGE 1

91.01.10 10:45

외신 2과 통제관 BT

0024

의하면 금일 현재 주이락 대사관 직원의 철수 여부를 공식으로는 결정치 못한 상태이나, 실무선에서는 금명간 철수 결정을 내릴것으로 예상하고 있다함. 한편 작일 주이락 독일 대사관 직원 전원이 현지 고용원만을 잔류 시킨채 이락측에 공식통보도 하지 않고, 모두 바그다드를 떠났다함)

2. 미측과 이락측의 합의에 따라 아지즈 이락 외상은 전기 베이커 국무장관에 이어 동일 장소에서 기자 회견을 가졌는바, 동 외상은 -쿠웨이트로 부터의 철수-등과같은 직접적 표현을 전혀 사용하지 않으면서, 금번 사태와 팔레스타인 문제간의 연계 해결을 강력 주장함. 동 외상의 주요 언급요지 다음임(동 외상의 기자 회견 전문 USW(F)-80 으로 FAX 송부)

가. 이락은 중동 지역의 - COMPREHENSIVE, LASTING AND JUST PEACE- 를 위해 협력할 용의가 있는바, 팔레스타인 문제의 해결 없이는 아랍권의 안정을 확보키 어려움.

나. 이락은 미국의 위협에 굴복하지 않을것인바, 미국은 지금까지의 이중기준(DOUBLE STANDARDS)을 버리고 이스라엘의 핵무기 보유등에 대해서도 우려를가져야할것임 (미국은 이락의 핵보유 문제만을 공박하고, 이스라엘에 대해서는침묵한다고 지적)

다. 부쉬 대통령의 친서는 그 용어에 있어서 정상간 친서가 가져야할 외교 관행상의 정중함 (POLITENESS)을 결하고 있기 때문에 접수를 거부한것임.

라. 금번 사태를 위요한 전쟁 발발 여부는 미국의 태도에 달려 있는바, 이락으로서는 다국적군의 공격을 받게 되는 경우 이스라엘을 공격할것임.

3. 한편, 부쉬 대통령도 표제 회담 종료후 백악관에서 기자 회견을 갖고 이락측의 전기 비타협적 입장을 강력한 어조로 비난하는 한편, 금번 사태가 외교적으로 해결되기에 너무 늦은것은 아니라는점을 강조함. 여사한 평화적 해결 노력을 포기하지 않을것이라고 언급하였는바, 주요 언급 요지는 다음임(부쉬 대통령 기자 회견 전문 USW(F)-81 로 FAX 송부)

가. 금일 외무 장관 회담시 이락측의 반응은 본인의 친서 접수 거부등에서 나타난바와같이 -TOTAL REBUFF- 였으나, 미측으로서는 외교적 해결 노력을 포기치 않을것임.

나. 금번 사태의 초점은 이락의 쿠웨이트 침공 사태에 있는바, 팔 문제와의연계를 반대하는 미측의 입장에는 변함이 없음 (이락측이 자국의 영향 증대를 위해

[redacted] [redacted]

쿠에이트를 침공한것이지 팔 문제 해결을 위해 쿠웨이트를 침공한 것이 아니라는점은 명약 관화 함)

4. 당관 관찰

가. 연호 보고와같이 표제 외무장관 회담은 별다른 성과없이 종료 되었는바, 금일 기자 회견시 부쉬 대통령은 마지막까지 외교적 해결 노력을 포기하지 않겠다는 점을 강조하고, 베이커 국무장관은 유엔 사무총장의 중재 노력에 대해 기대감을 표시한점이 주목됨.

금번 회담이 무산되고 유엔 안보리가 제시한 철수 시한인 1.15 까지 남은 기일이 며칠되지 않는데에도 불구, 미측이 이처럼 외교적 해결 노력을 계속 중시하는 입장을 표명한데에는 다음 의도가 포함되어 있는것으로 보임.

-설사 대이락 공격 결정을 내리는 경우라도, 미측으로서는 금번 사태의 평화적 해결을 위해 끝까지 노력했다는 인상을 줄수 있는점.

-프랑스등 일부 구주 국가의 대이락 접촉이 곧 이어서 진행될 전망이므로, 여사한 제 3 국 주독의 외교적 해결 노력에 대해서도 미국 나름의 영향력을 행사하기 위해서는 사태의 평화적 해결 우선 입장을 포기할수 없는점.

-특히 유엔 사무총장의 경우는 유엔 안보리 결의안의 내용에 구속을 받을수밖에 없으므로, 대이락 직접 접촉에 나선다 하더라도 미국의 입장(이락군의 쿠웨이트로부터의 전면 철수등)에서 크게 일탈하지 않을것으로 예상되는점.

나. 한편, 금일 당지 일부 언론에서는 전문가들의 견해를 인용, 이락측이미국측에 굴복한다는 인상을 주는것은 후세인에게 치명적 정치적 손실이 될뿐아니라, 오히려 끝까지 미국에 대항하는 자세를 보일경우는 미.이락간 무력 충돌시의 군사적 패배를 상쇄할수 있는 효과도 기대할수 있기때문에 비타협적 자세를 보인것으로 분석하고, 금번 회담이 줄다리기 외교의 최종점은 아니라는 견해도제시하였음.

(대사 박동진-차관)

91.12.31 일반

검 토 필 (1991.6.30.)

일반문서로 재분류(1991.12.31.)

PAGE 3

0026

걸프事態 關聯

美 行政府와 議會間 戰爭 遂行 權限 論議

1991. 1.

美 洲 局

0027

目　　次

0028

Ⅰ. 美 憲法 條項

1. 關聯 規定

가. 美 憲法 第1條 第8項

ㅇ 美 議會는 다음 權限을 가진다
"戰爭을 宣言하고 捕獲 認許狀을 授與하고 陸上 및 海上의 捕獲에 관한 規則을 정하는것"
(ArticleⅠ Section 8
To declare War, grant Letter of Marque and Reprisal, and make Rules concerning Captures on Land and Water)

나. 美 憲法 第2條 第2項

ㅇ 大統領은 合衆國의 陸軍, 海軍 및 現在 合衆國의 軍役에 복무하는 각주 민병의 총지휘관이 된다 ......
(Article Ⅱ, Section 2)
The President shall be Commander in Chief of the Army and Navy of the United States, ...)

2. 論爭 沿革

가. 美 憲法 制定 當時 論議

ㅇ 制憲 議會에서는 당초 戰爭 遂行 權限을 당시 여타국 예에 따라 行政府에 부여키로함.

ㅇ 필라델피아 立憲會議(1987.8.17)시 절충끝에 戰爭 遂行權(to make war)을 戰爭 宣布權(to declare war) 으로 수정, 戰爭 宣布 權限 만을 議會에 부여함.

0023

- 牽制와 均衡의 原則 適用
- 經驗, 先例 및 당시 時代 狀況등이 고려 요소로 작용

나. 議會의 宣戰 布告 事例

ㅇ 1812년 戰爭(1812-14), 멕시코 戰爭(1846-48), 미.스페인 戰爭 (1989), WWI 및 WWII 등 5차례에 불과함.

다. 宣戰 布告 없는 戰爭에 대한 論難

ㅇ 1950-53 韓國戰, 1958 레바논 事態, 1965 도미니카 共和國 事態 및 1965-73간 越南戰 등 이후 宣戰 布告 없는 戰爭에 대한 論議가 시작됨.
  - 行政府는 과거 전례 원용(1946-75간 議會 宣戰 布告 없이 政治的 目的으로 美 軍事力 使用 事例는 215건)
  - 宣戰 布告 方式은 奇襲 攻擊 대비 必要 및 核武器의 登場등으로 時代 錯誤的 制度라고 主張

라. 大統領의 戰爭 遂行權

ㅇ 大統領의 戰爭 遂行權의 背景으로서
  - 軍 統帥權者로서의 責任
  - 憲法을 保存, 保護 및 防禦한다는 就任 宣誓
  - 緊急 攻擊으로 부터 國家를 保護해야 할 義務
  - 行政府의 수반으로서의 固有 權限등을 主張

마. 議會內 決議案 通過 方式

ㅇ 合同 決議案(Joint Resolution) : 法案과 同一한 拘束力
  - 통킹만 決議案(1964)

0030

· 軍 統帥權者인 大統領에게 美軍에 대한 攻擊 격퇴 및 추가 侵略 沮止를 위한 權限을 부여함.

· 1970.12. 議會는 동 決議案 폐기

o 一般 決議案 및 共同 決議案(Concurrent Resolution) : 上.下院內 특정 行政府 政策에 대한 찬.반 의견 또는 분위기 전달에 이용됨.

- 이란 人質 抑留 非難 決議案(1979)

- 리비아산 原油 輸入 禁止 贊成 決議案(1982)

- 越南戰 탈주자 사면 반대 決議案(1977) 등

0031

Ⅱ. 戰爭 授權法

1. 立法 背景

o 제2차 世界大戰 이후 大統領이 議會의 승인없이 美 軍事力을 사용하는 事例 增加에 따라, 특히 越南戰 이후 美 議會内에서는 '美 國民의 安全과 利益에 影響을 미치는 결정에 대한 議會의 参與權 侵害' 라는 批判 여론이 增大됨.

o 특히 越南戰의 長期化에 따라 닉슨 行政府의 軍事力 사용에 대한 재량권 확대 및 對議會 協議 소홀 사례 빈발로 1973.6. War Power Resolution을 통과시켜 軍事力 사용에 대한 議會의 統制 增大를 도모함.

- 1973.10. 닉슨 大統領은 同 決議案이 위헌이며 最善의 美 國家 利益에 배치됨을 이유로 拒否權 행사
- 1973.11. 上.下院은 상기 大統領의 拒否權을 무효화(override) 함으로써 確定 通過

나. 戰爭 授權法 要旨(原文 別添 #1)

(大統領의 對議會 協議 및 報告 義務)

o 大統領은 가능한한(in every possible instance) 軍事力 使用前 議會와 협의해야 하며 軍事力 使用後에는 終了時까지 議會와 정기적으로 協議해야 함.

o 大統領은 美軍이 宣戰布告 없이 ①敵對行爲 또는 임박한 敵對行爲에 돌입하거나 ②戰闘態勢로 他國 領内에 投入된 경우, 軍事力 使用을 必要케한 상황, 軍事力 使用의 法的根據 및 軍事力 使用 範圍와 時期에 대해 議會에 書面(in writing) 報告해야 함.

0032

(軍事力 使用 中止)

- 議會가 軍事力 使用 報告 接受後 60일 이내에 ①宣戰 布告 決議 ②軍事力 使用을 許可하는 法的 措置, 또는 ③美 領土에 대한 공격으로 議會의 召集이 물리적으로 不可能한 경우가 아니면 大統領은 軍事力 사용을 중단하여야 함.

  단, 大統領이 불가피한 사유를 議會에 서면 통보하면 위60일 시한을 30일 연장 가능

- 議會의 承認없이 美軍이 領土밖에서 발생한 敵對 行爲에 개입된 경우, 上下院이 共同 決議(Concurrent Resolution)로 철수를 요구하면 大統領은 軍隊를 撤收하여야 함.

다. 美 行政府의 W.P.R. 規定 履行 事例

- 美 行政府가 W.P.R. 상 規定된 48시간내 보고 의무를 이행한 사례는 아래 5가지 경우임.
  - 1975.4. 포드 大統領은 다낭, 프놈펜 및 사이공으로 부터의 美國人 및 난민 철수시 3차례 보고
  - 1975.5. 포드 大統領은 캄보디아군에 억류된 마야게즈호 乘務員 39명 釋放을 위한 武力 使用時 報告
  - 1980.4.26. 카터 大統領이 이란내 人質 救出 作戰時 報告

라. 軍事 作戰의 秘密 유지 必要性과 國民의 '알 權利'間 相衝

- 軍事 作戰의 基本 性格上 전격전의 필요성 등으로 W.P.R. 규정상 事前 協議 義務 이행에는 문제가 많다고 行政府側은 不平함.
  - 民主 國家에서 國民의 알 權利 保障과 軍事 作戰의 기밀 유지 必要間의 相衝은 最近 제기된 딜레마
  - 파나마, Grenada 侵攻時 및 리비아 事態時등은 W.P.R.상 事前 協議 義務 불이행

0033

Ⅱ. 페灣 事態 關聯 最近 戰爭 遂行 權限 論議

1. 페灣 派兵의 法的 根據

- ㅇ 페灣 派兵 自體에 대해서는 90.10. 上.下院의 派兵 支持 決議案 採擇으로 法的 問題는 없음
  - 美 上.下院은 90.10.1. 및 10.2. 美 行政府가 취한 措置를 支持하는 決議案(Joint Resolution) 通過
  - 現在 論難이 되고 있는 대이라크 軍事力 사용 문제도 議會의 사전 承認 事項이 아님.

2. UN 安保理 決議의 性格

- ㅇ 73년 W.P.R. 등과 이후 先例가 없어 UN 軍事力 사용 허가의 美 國內 法的 效果를 단정키는 곤란함.
  - UN 武力 使用 決議案 (別添 # 2)
- ㅇ 그러나 대이라크 軍事力 使用에 대한 行政府의 法的.政治的 立場은 크게 強化될 것으로 展望

3. 中間 選擧 前後 美 議會內 動向

- ㅇ 中間 選擧 以前 부쉬 行政府의 페灣 政策에 대한 높은 지지도에 따라 民主黨側은 同 問題를 선거 이슈로 이용하는데 실패함.
  - 대 UN 긴밀 協調 體制에 비해 對議會 및 國民들과의 진지한 논의 결여에 노골적 不滿 表示
- ㅇ 특히 中間 選擧 직후 부쉬 大統領의 페灣 駐屯 병력 증강 결정(90.11.8) 시 증파 目的에 대한 對國民 설명 부족을 지적함.
  - 行政府의 페灣 戰略에 疑問 제기
  - 美國의 中東地域에서의 具體的 利益 設定 促求

0034

o 즉 中間選擧 以後 議會 휴회중 行政府가 議會의 承認없이 戰爭에 돌입할 可能性에 대해 깊은 우려를 표명함.

- 90.11.20. Dellums 議員(CA) 등 45명의 民主黨 下院議員들은 대이라크 武力使用時 의회 承認 必要 與否 決定을 요구하는 소송을 워싱턴 D.C. 聯邦 地方 法院에 提起
- 90.11.27-12.3.간 美 上院 軍事委 聽聞會 開催
- 90.12.4.-12.5.간 및 12.6. 美 上.下院 外交委 聽聞會 開催

o Lugar, Dole 上院議員등 共和黨 중진의원들은 상기와 같은 민주당내 반발 움직임에 대처하고 11.29. UN 安保理의 무력 사용 허가 決議案과 동일한 決議案 채택을 위한 의회 특별회기 소집 필요성을 강조함.

- 부쉬 大統領 및 民主黨 지도부의 미온적 반응으로 90년내 소집은 무산

4. 最近 動向

o 부쉬 大統領은 91.1.8.자 의회앞 서한을 통해 이라크가 1.15. 이전 철수 결정치 않을 경우 武力使用을 포함한 모든 수단 사용을 지지하는 決議案을 美 議會가 통과시켜 줄 것을 정식 요청함.

- 이라크군의 쿠웨이트로 부터의 撤收를 관철시키려는 美國의 결연한 의지 傳達 目的
- 1964. 존슨 大統領의 통킹만 決議案 통과 요청 이래 두번째 요청

o 同 決議案이 통과될 경우, 이라크에 대한 공격 개시 이전 의회의 간접적인 宣戰布告로 간주될 가능성이 높음

- 美 行政府는 전쟁 수권법과 관련한 미 의회내 논란 종식에 이용 豫想
- 91.1.10.-1.12. 간 上.下院 特別會議를 통해 審議 豫定
- 民主黨側은 문안 희석을 위한 지도부간 협의 계속

0035

o 1.9(수) Baker-Aziz 간 미.이라크 外務長官 會談 결렬과 관련, 美 行政府의 대이라크 武力 制裁를 위한 최종 법적 보장 장치가 될 것으로 예상됨.

o 民主黨內 일부 인사들 조차도 전쟁이외에는 事態 解決을 위한 현실적 대안이 없으며 經濟 制裁 措置에의 의존은 커다란 전략적 실패를 가져다 줄 수 있다는 주장(Haig 전 국무장관등)에 동조하고 있어 부쉬 大統領 요청 決議案 통과는 낙관시됨.

- Foley 下院議長(민주, WA)도 1.12.이전 決議案 通過 豫想
- Les Aspin 下院 軍事委員長(민주, WIS) 등도 호의적

0036

Ⅳ. 展 望

1. 最近 輿論 調査 結果

가. NYT/CBS News 輿論 調査(1.5-1.7 간 미 전역 1,348명의 성인을 대상으로 전화 조사, 오차 ± 3%)

o 1.15. 이전 이라크가 쿠웨이트로 부터 撤收치 않을 경우 美國은 軍事 行動을 개시해야 하는가 ?

贊成 : 46%

反對 : 47%(경제 제재 조치 효과 계속 기대)

* 90.12월 輿論 調査 結果는 贊成 45% : 反對 48%

다. Times지/CBS News 輿論 調査

o 응답자의 57% 가 이라크와의 戰爭 勃發 可能性을 믿고 있음.

- 90.12월의 경우 44%

o 응답자의 60%가 美軍 攻擊 개시전 의회는 宣戰布告를 해야 한다고 응답함.

o 1.9(수) 美.이라크 外務長官 會談과 관련해서는 51%가 實質 問題 討議를 기대하고, 36%는 쇼에 불과하다고 답변함.

2. 展 望

o 부쉬 大統領이 의회에 요청한 武力使用 승인 決議案이 통과될 경우, 1973년 전쟁 수권법 제정 이후 美 軍事力 사용에 議會의 사전 승인을 받은 선례도 없으므로 戰爭 授權法을 위요한 議會내 論難은 종식될 것으로 예상됨.

0037

o 問題의 본질은 民主黨 중심의 議會와 共和黨 行政府間 對外 政策 決定에 관한 주도권 다툼으로 政治的 解決이 모색될 것임.

- 司法府도 상기 民主黨 下院議員들의 소송 제기에 대해서 동 문제를 政治的 問題로 간주, 判決 留保 豫想

o 武力 使用 이후 結果에 따라 사태의 양상이 변하거나 武力 대치 상황이 장기화될 경우, 戰爭 授權法에 대한 論議 再開 可能性이 있음.

添附 : 1. War Power Resolution 1 부

2. U.N. Resolution 678 1 부. 끝.

0038

첨부 # 1

War Powers Provisions

The 1973 War Powers Resolution :

o Stated that the president could commit U.S. armed forces to hostilities or situations where hostilities might be imminent only pursuant to a declaration of war, specific statutory authorization or a national emergency created by an attack upon the United States.its territories or possessions, or its armed forces.

o Urged the president "in every possible instance" to consult with Congress before committing U.S. forces to hostilities or to situations where hostilities might be imminent, and to consult Congress regularly after such a commitment.

o Required the president to report in writing within 48 hours to the Speaker of the House and president pro tempore of the Senate on any commitment or substantial enlargement of U.S. combat forces abroad, except for deployments related solely to supply, replacement, repair or training ; required supplementary reports at least every six months while such forces were being engaged.

o Authorized the Speaker of the House and the president pro tempore of the Senate to reconvene Congress if it were not in session to consider the president's report.

0039

o Required the termination of a troop commitment within 60 days after the president's initial report was submitted, unless Congress declared war, specifically authorized continuation of the commitment, or was physically unable to convene as a result of an armed attack upon the United States ; allowed the 60 day period to be extended for up to 30 days if the president determined and certified to Congress that unavoidable military necessity respecting the safety of U.S. forces required their continued use in bringing about a prompt disengagement.

o Allowed Congress at any time U.S. forces were engaged in hostilities without a declaration of war or specific congressional authorization by concurrent resolution to direct the president to disengage such troops.

o Set up congressional procedures for consideration of any resolution or bill introduced pursuant to the provisions of the resolution.

o Provided that if any provision of the resolution was declared invalid, the remainder of the resolution would not be affected.

0040

첨 부 # 2

U.N. Resolution 678

Following is the text of the resolution the U.N. Security Council adopted Nov. 29, 1990:

THE SECURITY COUNCIL,

RECALLING, AND REAFFIRMING its resolutions 660(1990) of 2 August, 661 (1990) of 6 August, 662(1990) of 9 August, 664(1990) of 18 August, 665(1990) of 25 August, 666(1990) of 13 September, 667(1990) of 16 September, 669(1990) of 24 September, 670(1990) of 25 September, 674(1990) of 29 October, and 677(1990) of 28 November,

NOTING THAT, despte all efforts by the United Nations, Iraq refuses to comply with its obligation to implement resolution 660(1990) and the above-mentioned subsequent relevant resolutions, in flagrant contempt of the Security Council,

MINDFUL of its duties and responsibilities under the Charter of the United Nations for the maintenance and preservation of international peace and security,

DETERMINED to secure full compliance with its decisions,

ACTING under Chapter VII of the Charter,

1. DEMANDS that Iraq comply fully with resolution 660(1990) and all subsequent relevant resolutions, and decides, while maintaining all its decisions, to allow Iraq one final opportunity, as a pause of good will to do so;

0041

2. AUTHORIZES Member States cooperating with the Government of Kuwait, unless Iraq on or before 15 January 1991 fully implements, as set forth in paragraph 1 above, the foregoing resolutions, to use all necessary means to uphold and implement resolution 660(1990) and all subsequent relevant resolutions and to restore international peace and security in the area;

3. REQUESTS all States to provide appropriate support for the actions undertaken in pursuance of paragraph 2 of the present resolution;

4. REQUESTS the States concerned to keep the Security Council regularly informed on the progress of actions undertaken pursuant to paragraphs 2 and 3 of the present resolution;

5. DECIDES to remain seized of the matter.

0042

長官報告事項

報告畢

1991. 1.10.
中近東課

題目 : 제네바 會談 決裂과 걸프事態 展望

o 美.이락 外務長官間의 1.9. 제네바 會談은 6時間 半에 걸쳐 열리는 중에 各其 本國과의 協議를 위해 두차례나 休會를 함으로써 어느정도 進展이 있을 것으로 期待 되었으나, 結果的으로는 決裂된 것으로 判明 되었는바,

o 會談後 兩國 外務長官의 記者會見과 關聯 各國의 反應을 綜合하여 볼때 今後 展望은 아래와 같습니다.

1. 平和的 解決 可能性

가. 베이커 長官은 記者 會見에서 兩國間의 再協商 可能性이 없음을 示唆하고 부쉬 大統領도 이점을 確認 하였으나 平和的 解決에 대한 期待를 完全히 抛棄하지는 않았다고 함으로써 關聯諸國의 平和 努力에 期待를 表示하였음.

나. 西方의 仲裁 努力으로 가장 눈에 띄는것은 미테랑 佛蘭西 大統領의 노력인바, 佛蘭西는 일단 美國의 立場과 努力을 支持하는 EC 諸國과 同一한 步調를 취하면서도 中東問題의 包括的 解決을 위한 國際會議에 대해 同情的인 立場을 示唆하면서 中東平和會議를 積極 推進해온 알제리등 今番 事態에 비교적 中立的인 아랍國家들과 함께 積極的인 仲裁 意思를 表明하고 나서고 있음. 實際로 제네바 會談이 決裂된 直後 미테랑 大統領은 記者會見에서 이러한 仲裁 立場을 分明히 하고 會見 直前 부쉬 大統領과도 通話 했다고 밝힘으로써 美國도 佛蘭西의 仲裁를 諒解 했음을 示唆함. 다만 미테랑 大統領은 이락이 1.15.전 撤軍하지 않으면 佛蘭西도 대이락 武力行事에 參與하게 될 것이라고 함으로써 이락의 伸縮性 있는 協商 姿勢를 公開的으로 促求한 것으로 볼수 있겠음.

0043

다. 佛蘭西 以外에 蘇聯도 바그다드에 特使를 派遣 고르바쵸프의 親書를 전하겠다고 하였으며 外信의 報道 傾向을 綜合 判斷하면 이에 대해 큰 期待를 거는 것 같지는 않음

라. 한편 케야르 유엔 事務總長도 今明間 바그다드를 訪問할 것이라고 하는바 會談 決裂後 부쉬 大統領이 發表한 것으로 보아 수일전 부쉬가 케야르를 休養地에 招待했던 事實로 보아 이것은 美側의 이니시어티브에 의한것이 分明하며 따라서 이락이 이에 呼應하리라고 期待하기는 어렵다고 보겠음. 美國이 이것을 알면서도 推進하는 것은 開戰이 不可避할때 美國으로서 最大限의 外交努力을 傾注했다는 것을 對內外에 誇示하기 위한 것으로 봄.

2. 戰爭 勃發 可能性

가. 따라서 現在 마지막 期待는 결국 佛蘭西와 中道 아랍國을 代表하는 알제리의 共同 努力인바 이것도 일단은 1.15. 까지의 時限的인 努力으로 보아야 하며, 그렇기 때문에 美國이 이를 諒解한 것으로 추측됨.

나. 미국은 제네바 會談 決裂 直後 징발권에 관한 명령을 내림으로써(내용은 확실치 않음) 開戰이 한발짝 다가왔다는 印象을 강하게 주었으나 이는 실제로 戰爭 遂行을 위한 準備와 同時에 이락에 대한 美國의 決意를 재과시 하고 미테랑등의 仲裁 努力을 支援코자 하는 의도도 있는 것으로 보임.

다. 일단, 會談 決裂로 戰爭 可能性은 높아졌다고도 볼수 있으나 불란서가 아랍권에 歷史的으로 오랜 緣故를 가지고 있고 그중에서도 특히 깊은 관계를 가지고 있는 알제리가 마침 今番 事態에 中道的 立場을 취함으로써 仲裁에 유리한 위치에 있어 兩國이 共同으로 努力한다면 어느정도 성과가 있을 수 있겠다는 期待를 가질수도 있겠음. 끝.

0044

제네바 美. 이락 外務長官 会談結果에 대한
베이커 長官의 口頭 報告

1991. 1. 10

外　　務　　部

0045

1.9 美. 이락 제네바 會談이 끝난후 會談 結果에 대한 베이커 長官의 口頭報告中 主要事項을 아래와 같이 報告합니다. 同 報告는 그레그 駐韓 美國大使가 1.10 外務部에 傳達해 온 것임을 첨기 합니다.

"부시 대통령을 만나" 라는 내용이 누락된
- 번역내용은 요약한 [illegible]

ㅇ 이라크가 撤軍하고 威脅이 減少된다면 美國 걸프地域에 現 兵力 駐屯을 維持할 意圖가 없다는 것은 우리가 이미 公言한 바임

ㅇ 이라크가 撤收한 後에는 유엔 安保理 決議 660號에 따라 이라크와 쿠웨이트가 紛爭을 平和的으로 解決하는 것을 支持한다는 立場도 이미 公言한 바임

ㅇ 아직도 平和的 解決이 可能한 것을 분명히 하고 우리는 이락이 유엔 安保理의 再決議를 完全히 그리고 條件없이 履行하지 못하면 破局的 結果를 招來할 것임을 전하려 努力 하였음.

ㅇ 우리는 또한 化學. 細菌 武器를 使用할 경우에는 가차없는 報復을 받을 것임을 警告하고 美國人에 대한 테러나 쿠웨이트 油田 破壞도 용서 받을수

0046

없을 것임을 警告 하였음

ㅇ 아지즈는 會議 初盤에 우리가 傳達한 사담 후세인 앞 부쉬 大統領의 親書의 表現이 國家 元首間의 書信에는 適合하지 않다고 이야기 하고 이의 接受를 拒絶하였으며, 美國이 원하면 그 內容을 公表해도 좋다고 對應 하였는바 우리는 그 便紙를 혼자서 읽고 接受를 拒否한다면 엄청난 責任을 지게되는 것이며 아지즈가 그러한 責任을 감당하기를 원한다면 接受하지 않아도 無妨하다고 말 하였음

ㅇ 會談이 끝날 즈음에 아지즈는 外相間 相互訪問을 提議했지만 從前과 마찬가지로 아지즈의 워싱턴 訪問 日程은 우리가 정하고 本人의 바그다드 訪問 日程은 자기가 정한다는 식으로 말하면서 날자는 具體的으로 提議하지 않았음. 우리는 1.15 時限을 불과 6日 앞두고 그러한 提議를 하는 것은 時限을 어기고 時間을 벌려는 企圖일 뿐이라고 指摘 하였음.

ㅇ 우리는 美國이 1.12 바그다드에 있는 우리 大使館 職員 5名을 撤收시킬 것이라고 말하였음. 우리는 大使館 職員들이 지체없이 아무 妨害없이 그날까지 出國할 수 있도록 아지즈의 保障을 두번 要求하였음. 첫번째는 아무 對答이 없었고 두번째 "우리도 國際法을 지킬 것"이라고 말하였음.

0047

우리는 이말을 그들이 妨害받지 않고 出國할수 있다는 것을 뜻하는 것으로 理解할 것이라고 말하였음.

添 附: 美國大使 傳達 구두 메시지 全文

0048

미북(미일)

베이커 국무장관의
Aziz 이락 외무장관과의
회담결과.

3. BEGIN TEXT OF ORAL MESSAGE:

-- WANTED TO PROVIDE YOU QUICKLY WITH MY IMPRESSIONS OF MEETING TODAY WITH FM AZIZ.

-- I EMPHASIZED AT OUTSET THAT I HAD COME NOT TO NEGOTIATE, BUT TO COMMUNICATE, TO LISTEN AS WELL AS TALK.

-- THE MESSAGE THAT I CONVEYED FROM PRESIDENT BUSH AND OUR COALITION PARTNERS WAS A SIMPLE ONE: IRAQ MUST EITHER COMPLY WITH THE WILL OF THE INTERNATIONAL COMMUNITY AND WITHDRAW PEACEFULLY FROM KUWAIT, OR BE EXPELLED BY FORCE.

-- THE IRAQI LEADERSHIP MUST HAVE NO ILLUSIONS AND NO MISUNDERSTANDINGS. ONE WAY OR ANOTHER, IRAQ WILL

0043

-- I EMPHASIZED REPEATEDLY TO FM AZIZ OUR STRONG GENUINE PREFERENCE FOR A PEACEFUL RESOLUTION. THE ROAD TO THAT OUTCOME HAS BEEN MADE CLEAR IN TWELVE UNSC RESOLUTIONS:

- IMMEDIATE, UNCONDITIONAL WITHDRAWAL OF ALL IRAQI FORCES FROM KUWAIT.

- RESTORATION OF KUWAITI SOVEREIGNTY AND THE LEGITIMATE GOVERNMENT OF KUWAIT.

-- I REITERATED THAT THE UNITED STATES WILL NOT ATTACK IRAQ OR ITS MILITARY FORCES IF IRAQ COMPLIES FULLY WITH THE UNSC RESOLUTIONS AND MAKES NO FURTHER PROVOCATION.

-- I NOTED THAT THE LARGE US FORCES IN THE GULF ARE THERE BECAUSE OF THE THREAT CREATED BY IRAQI ACTIONS. AS WE HAVE STATED PUBLICLY, AND DISCUSSED WITH OUR FRIENDS IN THE REGION, WE HAVE NO INTENTION OF MAINTAINING SUCH FORCE LEVELS THERE ONCE IRAQ WITHDRAWS AND THE THREAT RECEDES.

-- AND AS WE HAVE ALSO SAID PUBLICLY, WE SUPPORT UNSCR 662'S CALL ON IRAQ AND KUWAIT TO SETTLE THEIR DIFFERENCES PEACEFULLY AFTER REPEAT AFTER IRAQI WITHDRAWAL.

-- HAVING MADE CLEAR THAT THE PATH TO PEACE IS STILL OPEN, I ALSO TRIED TO CONVEY THE CATASTROPHIC CONSEQUENCES FOR IRAQ OF FAILURE TO COMPLY FULLY AND UNCONDITIONALLY WITH THE UNSC RESOLUTIONS.

-- I OUTLINED IN DETAIL FOR FM AZIZ THE CAPABILITIES OF THE MULTINATIONAL FORCES ARRAYED AGAINST IRAQ. PUT BLUNTLY, IF IRAQ CHOOSES TO CONTINUE ITS BRUTAL OCCUPATION OF KUWAIT, IT WILL CHOOSE A MILITARY CONFRONTATION WHICH IT CANNOT WIN, AND WHICH WILL HAVE DEVASTATING RESULTS FOR IRAQ.

-- I WARNED FM AZIZ THAT, IN THE EVENT OF WAR, IRAQ COULD EXPECT NO BREATHING SPACE OR PREMATURE CEASEFIRE. THERE WILL BE NO STALEMATE; IF A WAR BEGINS, IT WILL BE FOUGHT TO A SWIFT, DECISIVE CONCLUSION.

-- I ALSO WARNED OF THE HARSH CONSEQUENCES OF ANY IRAQI USE OF CHEMICAL OR BIOLOGICAL WEAPONS. NOR WILL WE TOLERATE TERRORISM DIRECTED AGAINST AMERICANS OR THE DESTRUCTION OF KUWAIT'S OIL INSTALLATIONS.

0050

AND I DID SO WITH N[illegible]NSE OF SATISFACTION, FOR [illegible]
SINCERELY WANT A PEA[illegible]UL OUTCOME AND THE PEOPL[illegible]
THE UNITED STATES HAVE NO QUARREL WITH THE PEOPLE OF
IRAQ.

-- I SIMPLY WANTED TO LEAVE AS LITTLE ROOM AS POSSIBLE
FOR YET ANOTHER TRAGIC MISCALCULATION BY THE IRAQI
LEADERSHIP.

0051

CAN STILL AVOID. [redacted] THE CHOICE IS IRAQ'S TO [redacted].

-- REGRETABLY, FM AZIZ GAVE NO INDICATION DURING OUR MORE THAN SIX HOURS OF DISCUSSIONS OF ANY FLEXIBILITY OR READINESS TO COMPLY WITH RELEVANT UNSC RESOLUTIONS.

-- AZIZ REFUSED THE LETTER FROM PRESIDENT BUSH TO SADDAM HUSSEIN THAT I GAVE HIM AT THE OUTSET OF THE MEETING. HE DESCRIBED THE LETTER'S LANGUAGE AS INAPPROPRIATE FOR A COMMUNICATION BETWEEN HEADS OF STATE. HE DECLINED TO ACCEPT IT AND COMMENTED THAT THE U.S. WOULD BE FREE TO PUBLISH IT. I TOLD HIM THAT IN BEING THE ONLY IRAQI TO READ THE LETTER AND THEN REFUSE TO ACCEPT IT, HE WAS ACCEPTING A LARGE RESPONSIBLITY, BUT IF HE WANTED TO ACCEPT THE RESPONSIBILITY, SO BE IT.

-- AZIZ SAID IRAQ HAD MADE NO MISCALCULATIONS. IRAQ UNDERSTANDS FULLY THE FORCES ARRAYED AROUND IRAQ AND THE EFFECTIVENESS OF THE WEAPONS WHICH COULD BE EMPLOYED BY THE COALITION FORCES.

-- AZIZ SAID THE IRAQI LEADERS KNOW THE U.S. CONGRESS, READ OUR PRESS, AND WATCH U.S. TELEVISION, SO THEY HAVE NO ILLUSIONS REGARDING AMERICAN INTENTIONS.

-- HE SAID IRAQ HAS EXPECTED MILITARY ACTION AGAINST IT SINCE THE BEGINNING (I.E., AUGUST 2).

-- AZIZ MAINTAINED THAT THE PRESENT IRAQI LEADERSHIP WILL CONTINUE NOW AND IN THE FUTURE AND THAT IRAQ WILL EMERGE FROM A WAR VICTORIOUS.

6. AZIZ ARGUED AT LENGTH THAT PRIOR TO AUGUST 2 IRAQ HAD BEEN FACED WITH ECONOMIC STRANGULATION. HE NOTED THAT AT THE BAGHDAD SUMMIT IN MAY, SADDAM HUSSEIN HAD SPOKEN ABOUT OIL OVERPRODUCTION AND SAID THAT ANY NATION WHICH DID NOT MEAN WAR BY THIS ACTION, SHOULD REFRAIN.

-- AZIZ SEVERAL TIMES DESCRIBED ALLEGED KUWAITI ECONOMIC AGGRESSION AGAINST IRAQ.

-- HE THUS DESCRIBED IRAQ'S AUGUST 2 ACTION AS A "DEFENSIVE MOVE."

-- AZIZ SPOKE AT GREAT LENGTH ABOUT THE PALESTINIAN ISSUE AND ARAB-ISRAELI DIFFERENCES. HE ARGUED THAT IRAQ'S ACTION "IN THE GULF" PROVIDED A "GOLDEN OPPORTUNITY FOR THE PALESTINIAN LEADERSHIP."

-- I REBUTTED THAT IRAQ HAD NOT INVADED KUWAIT TO PROMOTE THE CAUSE OF PALESTINIANS AND THAT IRAQ'S AGGRESSION HAD PRODUCED CONTRARY RESULTS.

-- I TOLD HIM HIS JUSTIFICATION OF THE AGGRESSION AGAINST KUWAIT AS "DEFENSIVE" WAS LUDICROUS AND THAT

0052

NO ONE BELIEVED IT.

-- I TOLD HIM THE WAY TO CREATE OPPORTUNITIES FOR PEACEFUL SETTLEMENT OF THE PALESTINIAN ISSUE WAS NOT THROUGH AGGRESSION BUT THROUGH WITHDRAWAL.

-- AZIZ COMPLAINED BITTERLY THAT U.S. MAGAZINES IN JUNE OF 1990 HAD DESCRIBED SADDEM HUSSEIN AS THE "MOST DANGEROUS MAN IN THE WORLD" AND AS "PUBLIC ENEMY NO. ONE." I RESPONDED THAT IRAQ'S SUBSEQUENT AGGRESSION PROVED THAT THOSE DESCRIPTIONS WERE CLOSE TO THE MARK.

-- AZIZ MAINTAINED THAT SADDAM HUSSEIN HAD NEVER TOLD KING FAHD, KING HUSSEIN, OR PRESIDENT MUBARRAK THAT IRAQ WOULD NOT ATTACK KUWAIT IN THE DAYS PRECEDING AUGUST 2. HE DESCRIBED THIS AS DISINFORMATION BY PRESIDENT MUBARAK AND OTHER MEMBERS OF THE ARAB COALITION. HE DENIED THAT ANYONE TOLD THE U.S. IRAQ WOULD NOT MOVE MILITARILY. IN REBUTTAL WE QUOTED FROM TWO TELEPHONE CONVERSATIONS THAT KING HUSSEIN HAD WITH PRESIDENT BUSH ON JULY 28 AND JULY 31, STATING CLEARLY KING HUSSEIN'S "ASSURANCES" THAT THERE WOULD BE NO CONFLICT.

-- AZIZ STATED THAT IN THE EVENT OF WAR, ALL COUNTRIES IN THE REGION WILL BE INVOLVED INCLUDING ISRAEL.

-- AZIZ ARGUED THAT UN SECURITY COUNCIL RESOLUTION 660 WAS SOMEHOW INVALID BECAUSE THE IRAQI PERMANENT REPRESENTATIVE TO THE UN WAS NOT PRESENT. I POINTED OUT THAT THE IRAQI CHARGE WAS INDEED THERE. AZIZ ARGUED THAT RESOLUTION 678 AUTHORIZING THE USE OF FORCE AFTER JANUARY 15 WAS INVALID BECAUSE THERE WAS NO PRECEDENT.

-- I RAISED WITH AZIZ IRAQ'S BRUTALITIES IN KUWAIT AND THE AMNESTY INTERNATIONAL REPORT DESCRIBING THESE. AZIZ BELITTLED THE REPORT.

[illegible] IMPORTANT TO POLITICIANS, IPLOMATS, [illegible], AND JOURNALISTS, H[illegible]ID THAT THE FIGHTERS IN WAR WILL NOT REMEMBER TH[illegible] RESOLUTIONS.

-- AZIZ ALLOWED THAT WAR MAY BE "DESTINY" OR "FATE."

-- AZIZ ARGUED THAT THE ARAB LEAGUE RESOLUTIONS AGAINST IRAQ'S AGGRESSION ARE NULL AND VOID BECAUSE THEY WERE NOT UNANIMOUS.

-- IN THE LAST HOUR OF OUR MEETING AZIZ PROPOSED THAT HE COME TO WASHINGTON AND THAT I VISIT BAGHDAD, BUT USING THE SAME FORMULA WE HAD HEARD FROM THEM BEFORE (YOU PICK A DATE FOR WASHINGTON; WE PICK A DATE FOR BAGHDAD) HE SPECIFIED NO DATES. I POINTED OUT THAT RESOLUTION 678 WAS PASSED 40 DAYS AGO. PRESIDENT BUSH HAC PROPOSED SUCH MEETINGS IN A STATEMENT ON DECEMBER 1. THE U.S. HAD OFFERED 15 DIFFERENT DATES FOR MY TRIP TO BAGHDAD BETWEEN DECEMBER 20 AND JANUARY 3 INCLUDING CHRISTMAS DAY AND NEW YEAR'S DAY. IRAQ HAD REJECTED THEM ALL.

-- I POINTED OUT THAT PRESIDENT BUSH HAD ALREADY STATED THAT I WOULD NOT NOW BE GOING TO BAGHDAD. TO PROPOSE SUCH MEETINGS ONLY SIX DAYS BEFORE THE JANUARY 15 DEADLINE IS A CLEAR ATTEMPT TO MANIPULATE THE DEADLINE AND TO EXTEND THE PROCESS BEYOND.

-- I TOLD AZIZ THAT THE U.S. WOULD WITHDRAW ITS FIVE REMAINING AMERICAN PERSONNEL FROM OUR EMBASSY IN BAGHDAD ON JANUARY 12. I ASKED HIM TWICE FOR HIS ASSURANCE THAT THEY WOULD BE PERMITTED TO DEPART WITHOUT DELAY OR HINDRANCE ON THAT DATE. THE FIRST TIME AZIZ PASSED OVER ANY RESPONSE. THE SECOND TIME HE STATED THAT "WE WILL ABIDE BY INTERNATIONAL LAW AND LIVE UP TO IT." I SAID WE UNDERSTOOD THIS TO MEAN THEY COULD LEAVE UNIMPEDED.

-- I CLOSED BY CALLING AGAIN FOR IRAQ TO OBSERVE THE SECURITY COUNCIL RESOLUTIONS. I STRESSED THAT JANUARY 15 IS A REAL DEADLINE. I SAID THAT WE HAVE HAD FIVE AND ONE HALF MONTHS FOR DIPLOMATIC STEPS AND NOW IS THE TIME FOR ACTION: IRAQ'S IMMEDIATE WITHDRAWAL FROM KUWAIT. I SAID THAT IRAQ TOOK ONLY TWO DAYS TO MOVE A HUGE FORCE INTO KUWAIT AND IT SHOULD REVERSE THAT DEPLOYMENT NOW. END OF SECRETARY'S ORAL MESSAGE.

0054

4

관리번호	H-40

외 무 부

종 별 : 지 급

번 호 : USW-0136 일 시 : 91 0111 1824

수 신 : 장관(중근동,미북)

발 신 : 주 미 대사

제 목 : 페만 사태(EAGLEBURGER 부장관 이스라엘 방문 계획)

1.BOUCHER 국무부 부대변인은 금 1.11 정례 브리핑에서 EAGLEBURGER 부장관이 금주말 이스라엘을 방문할 계획임을 밝혔음.

2. 동 대변인은 EAGLEBURGER 부장관의 구체적 방문 목적 및 의제에 대해 언급을 회피했으나, 당지 전문가들의 견해에 따르면 미국 행정부로서는 이스라엘이현 페만 사태에 개입하게되는 경우 사담 후세인의 의도대로 금번 사태가 이스라엘-아랍 분쟁화될것임을 우려, 이스라엘로 하여금 가능한 직접 개입을 자제해 줄것을 요청할것으로 보임.

3. 이와는 별도로 부쉬 대통령은 1.10 SHAMIR 수상과의 전화 통화를 통해 동일한 요지의 요청을 한것으로 알려졌음.

4. 상기 국무부 브리핑 내용 별첨 FAX 송부함(USW(F)-0117)

(대사 박동진-국장)

91.12.31 일반

일반문서로 재분류(1991.12.31.)

검 토 필(1991.6.30.)

중아국 1차보 미주국 총리실 안기부

PAGE 1

91.01.12 09:23

외신 2과 통제관 FE

0055

호 : USW(F) - 0117

신 : 장 관 (중동1, 미북)　　발신 : 주미대사

보안 통제

목 : (첨부 4)　　(/ 매)

STATE DEPARTMENT REGULAR BRIEFING/ BRIEFER: RICHARD BOUCHER
1:10 PM/ FRIDAY, JANUARY 11, 1991

Q Also, on this Eagleburger trip, do you have anything on that?

MR. BOUCHER: Yeah. Deputy Secretary Eagleburger will be traveling this weekend to Israel for consultations with senior Israeli leaders. He expects to discuss the situation in the region, as well as bilateral matters. The trip has been planned for several days.

Throughout the crisis in the Gulf, we've consulted frequently with the Israeli government. This includes President Bush's recent meeting, and a phone -- and the President's phone contact with Prime Minister Shamir.

Q Since Mr. Baker is right in that area right now, why isn't he going?

MR. BOUCHER: Mr. Baker, I think, has been three different places today, three different places tomorrow, and four different places on Sunday. Mr. Eagleburger's going to Israel.

Q Yes, is it concerned mostly with the present Gulf situation, or would it be -- would the question of Soviet emigration to Israel come up?

MR. BOUCHER: He expects to discuss the situation in the region and bilateral matters. That's my only answer.

Q Is he going to ask Israel to continue to lay low?

MR. BOUCHER: I -- he expects to discuss the situation in the region and bilateral matters.

Q Oh.

MR. BOUCHER: I'm afraid that's how we're describing the visit, and I'm not going to talk any more about agendas.

Q How long will he be there?

MR. BOUCHER: I don't have that information for you. I'm sorry.

Q Will he be out there the 15th?

MR. BOUCHER: Again, I don't have any information for you. I said he will be traveling this weekend to Israel.

Q -- mention any other stops?

MR. BOUCHER: None that I'm aware of.

0056

원 본

외 무 부

종 별 :

번 호 : USW-0139 일 시 : 91 0111 1946

수 신 : 장 관(미북,중근동,동구일)

발 신 : 주 미 대사

제 목 : 페만 사태 등 관련 미.소 협의

1. 백악관 FITZWATER 대변인은 금 1.11정례 브리핑을 통해 부쉬 대통령과 고르바쵸프 대통령이 페만 사태와 박틱 사태를 협의하기 위해 금일 아침 전화 통화를 가졌고, 이어서 BESSMERTNYRH주미 쏘련 대사가 백악관으로 부쉬 대통령을 방문하였다고 발표함.

2.동 협의를 통해 고르바쵸프 대통령은 국제사회의 대 이라크 제재에 대한 쏘련의 협조를 재다짐하였으며,부쉬 대통령은 발틱 사태와 관련 고르바쵸프에게 무력 사용 자제를 요청하였다고 발표됨.

3.기자 회견 내용 FAX 송부함(USW(F)-0118

미주국 1차보 구주국 중아국 정문국 안기부 고차원

PAGE 1

91.01.12 09:54 WG

외신 1과 통제관

0057

수신 : 장 관 (미북, [redacted]주1) 발신 : 주미대사

제목 : "페"만 관련 미쏘협의 (첨부물) (/ 매)

USW-0139

Q Are you going to, as you tick through, give a feel on the Gorbachev talk?

MR. FITZWATER: Yeah, let me -- the President talked about his phone call with President **Gorbachev.** I really can't add much to what he said in terms of the description of the phone call, but let [illegible] spoke at about 8:00 this morning for approximately 25 minutes. As the President said, the discussion focused primarily on the Persian Gulf. President Gorbachev reiterated Soviet support for the position of the international coalition. And President Bush did raise the -- our concern about the Baltic situation. He urged President Gorbachev to avoid the use of force and to seek a political solution. President Gorbachev said he would like Ambassador Bessmertnykh to visit with the President personally to discuss the matter with him.

Q Which matter?

MR. FITZWATER: Both. The matter in the Baltics as well as the Gulf. The President in his interview, which was just shown in its entirety on CNN, said that the Bessmertnykh meeting dealt primarily with the Persian Gulf. The Ambassador was in about 10:00, and I don't have how long that meeting lasted although I think it was in the range of 20 minutes. We continue to monitor the Baltic situation. The NSC Deputies Committee, chaired by Deputy NSC Advisor Robert Gates, met this morning on the situation. Our US consular officer in Vilnius met this morning with President Landsbergis to also review the situation from his perspective. We continue to view this matter very seriously.

Pascal?

0058

외 무 부

종 별 : 지 급

번 호 : USW-0140 일 시 : 91 0112 1606

수 신 : 장관(중근동,미북,미안)

발 신 : 주미대사

제 목 : 페만 사태 관련 언론 논조

페만 사태 관련, 금 1.12 당지 언론은 케야르 유엔 사무총장의 최후 중재 노력에도 불구,미.이락 야측은 점차 전쟁 발발에 대비한 제반조치들을 진행시키고 있어 상황이 급박해지고 있다고 보도하고 있는바, 주요 기사 내용 아래 보고함.(상세는FAX 참조)

1.의회 무력 사용 결의안 채택 예정

0 미 의회는 금 1.12 부표 예정인바, 무력 사용 결의안의 채택을 통해 부쉬 행정부의 입장을 강화시켜 줄것으로 전망함.(금일 표결 결과는 별전 참조)

2.무력 행사를 위한 사우디측 통의 확보

0 베이커 장관은 FAHD 사우디 국왕과의 회담을 통해 무력 공격 개시를 위한 원칙적 동의를 사우디측으로부터 확보 했다고 밝히면서 미-이락 양측은 전쟁 발발 일보 직전 상태에 돌입했다고 언급함.

3.미국 외교관및 미국 시민 철수

0 미국 정부는 이락 주재 미국 외교관을 전원 철수시켰을뿐만 아니라, 이스라엘을 포함 중동 제국에 체류중인 미국인들에게 전쟁 발발에 대비 조속 철수할것을 권고하고 있음.

4.주미 이락 대사관 인원 감축

0 미국 정부는 금 1.12 주미 이락 대사관 인원을 4명으로 감축할것을 요청했음.

(별전 참조)

5.후세인, 대미 전쟁 준비 완료 주장

0 사담 후세인 대통령은 1.11 밤 INTERNATIONAL ISLAMIC CONFERENCE(바그다드) 에서의 연설을 통해 이락측의 요구가 수용되지 않는 한 미측의 무조건 철수 요구에굴복할 의사가 없음을 분명히 하고 이락군은 미군의 공격을 분쇄 할수 있는 만반의태세를 갖추가 있다고 언급했다함.

(대사 박동진 - 국장)

중아국 1차보 미주국 미주국 정문국

장관 차관 2차보 중아국 대책반 청와대 안기부

PAGE 1 91.01.13 08:36 DQ

외신 1과 통제관

0053

가6

美 議会 페灣事態 武力 使用 承認

1991. 1.

外 務 部

0060

美 上.下 兩院은 1.12(土) 페灣事態 關聯 行政府의 武力使用을 承認하는 上.下 兩院 合同 決議案을 上院 52:47, 下院 250:183으로 通過시켰읍니다. 한편, 民主黨側이 提案한 現 對이라크 經濟制裁 措置 및 外交的 努力을 繼續할 것을 促求하는 決議案은 上.下院에서 共히 否決 되었는 바, 關聯事項 아래 報告드립니다.

武力使用承認 決議 要旨

* 提案 議員

. 上院 : 도울(共和, 캔자스) - 워너(共和, 버지니아)

. 下院 : 솔라즈(民主, 뉴욕) - 마이클(共和, 일리노이)

ㅇ 페灣事態 關聯, 武力使用을 許容한 유엔 安保理 決議 第678號에 依據, 美 軍事力을 使用하는 權限을 大統領에게 附與함

- 금번 決議案 通過에 따라 大統領은 戰爭 授權 法上의 權限을 附與 받은 것으로 간주

- 大統領은 軍事力 使用前 外交的 手段을 포함한 모든 平和的 努力에도 不拘, 이라크측이 유엔 安保理 決議를 遵守토록 하는데 失敗하였음을 下院 議長 및 上院 臨時 議長에게 通報 必要

0061

o 大統領은 60日 마다 最小 1回以上 이라크의 유엔 安保理 決議 履行을 위해 취한 措置를 議會에 報告해야함

今後 節次

o 同 合同 決議는 大統領의 署名을 위해 즉시 行政府에 移送될 豫定이며 부쉬 大統領은 同 決議에 즉시 署名할 것으로 豫想됨

- 同 決議는 署名과 동시 法律과 동일한 效力 發生

評価 및 展望

o 금번 表決 結果는 부쉬 大統領에 대한 信任 投票의 性格을 가진 것으로서 부쉬 大統領의 페灣政策에 대한 議會의 超黨的인 支持를 明確히 하는 重要한 轉換点을 마련함

- 부쉬 行政府의 페灣事態 政策에 대한 美國民의 支持度를 反映

o 부쉬 大統領은 금번 決議 通過로 武力使用에 대한 國內 政治的인 障碍를 除去함으로써 對이라크 軍事 攻擊을 포함한 페灣事態 解決을 위한 政策을 보다 強力히 推進할 수 있게됨

0062

○ 向後 페灣事態 關聯 友邦國에 대한 分擔金 追加 支援 및 兵力 派遣 要請이 增加될 展望임

- 決議案 贊反 討議時 日本 및 獨逸의 微溫的 支援 態度를 批判하는 議員 多數(韓國에 대해 言及한 議員은 없었음)

参考事項

○ 금번 武力使用承認 決議는 1964年 존슨大統領이 要請한 통킹灣 決議 通過以來 첫번째임

○ 上記 決議와는 별도로 下院은 議會의 戰爭 宣布權을 再確認하는 決議案을 302:131로 通過시켰는 바, 이는 法的 拘束力이 없는 勸告的 性格임

끝.

0063

관리번호	91-1318

원 본

외 무 부

종 별 : 지 급

번 호 : USW-0141 일 시 : 91 0112 1607

수 신 : 장관(중근동,미북,미안)

발 신 : 주 미 대사

제 목 : 미국정부,워싱턴 주재 이락 공관원 감축 요청

1. 미 국무부는 1.12 워싱턴 주재 이락 외교관의 인원을 4 명(대사 포함)으로 감축할것을 이락측에 요청하였다고함.

2. 이와 관련, 당관이 국무부 이란-이라크과에 확인한 내용은 다음임.

0 JAMES COVEY 국무부 중동 담당 차관보 대리는 금 1.12 이락 대사를 국무부로 초치, 외교 공한을 수교하면서 상기 미측 결정 내용을 설명하였음.

0 미 국무부는 현재까지 주미 이락 대사관에 16 명의 공관원 주재를 허용하여왔으나, 페만 사태로 인해 이락 주동의 테러 행위 시도 가능성이 고조됨에 따라 부득이 상기 조치를 취하게되었음.

0 상기 잔류 인원 4 명(가족은 포함되지 않음)을 제외한 전 직원및 가족은1.15 자정까지 철수해야하며, 잔류자 4 명은 25 마일 활동 지역 제한을 받게됨.

0 상기 조치로 미.이락간의 외교 관계를 단절하는것은 아니며, 미국은 이락측과 최소한의 접촉 채널을 계속 유지할것임.

(대사 박동진-국장)예고: 91.12.31 까지

검 토 필 (1991. 6. 30.)

중아국 차관 1차보 2차보 미주국 미주국 청와대 안기부

PAGE 1

91.01.13 08:45

외신 2과 통제관 DG

0064

외 무 부

종 별 : 지 급

번 호 : USW-0144 일 시 : 91 0112 2057

수 신 : 장관(중근동,미북,미안)

발 신 : 주 미 대사

제 목 : 페만 사태(부쉬 대통령 기자 회견)

1. 부쉬 대통령은 금 1.12 의회 상하원에서 무력사용에 관한 권한을 대통령에게 부여 하는 결의안이 통과된 직후 가진 기자회견을 통해 미군의 대이락 공격 시기가 임박했음을 암시하고, 이락군의 무조건적인 철수를 재촉구 했는바, 부쉬 대통령의 언급 내용 요지 아래 보고함.

0 현 싯점이 페만 사태의 평화적 해결을 위한 마지막 기회인바, 이락군의 대규모적인 철수가 즉각 실시되어야 할 것임.

0 미군의 무력 공격 시점과 관련, 만약 이락군이 철수 하지 않을 경우 대이락 공격이 조만간 (SOONER RATHER THAN LATER) 개시될 수 있을 것임.

0 그러나 후세인의 태도 변화에 따라 아직도 전쟁을 피할수 있다고 생각함 (WARIS NOT INEVITABLE)

0 만약 금번 사태와 관련된 테러 행위가 발생할 경우 이는 전적으로 후세인이 책임져야할 것임.

2.동 기자 회견 내용 별첨 FAX 송부함.

첨부: USW(F)-0126

(대사 박동진-국장)

중아국	장관	차관	1차보	2차보	미주국	미주국	중아국	정문국
상황실	청와대	안기부		대책반				

0065

PAGE 1

91.01.13 11:23 CG

외신 1과 통제관

WUS(F)-0126 KORE[redacted]WASHINGTON DC P.001

수신: 장관 (중동, 미북, 미안)

발신: 주미대사

제목: 페만 사태 (부시 대통령 기자 회견)

USW-0144 외신 (10 매)

PRESS CONFERENCE WITH PRESIDENT BUSH/WHITE HOUSE BRIEFING ROOM
Z-6-1 page# 1 SATURDAY, JANUARY 12, 1991

dest=swh,mwh,mme,notvme,mideast,pergulf,fns20611,fns13126,fns10000
dest+=fns13677,iraq,kuwait,armfor,warpower,un,forpolus,defense,arab
data

PRESIDENT BUSH: I have a brief statement, and then I'll be glad to take a few questions.

First, let me just say that I am gratified by the vote in the Congress supporting the United Nations Security Council resolution. This action by the Congress unmistakably demonstrates the United States commitment to the international demand for a complete and unconditional withdrawal from Kuwait. This clear expression of the Congress represents the last best chance for peace. As a democracy, we've debated this issue openly and in good faith, and as President, I have held extensive consultation with the Congress.

We have now closed ranks behind a clear signal of our determination and our resolve to implement the United Nations resolutions. Those who may have mistaken our democratic process as a sign of weakness now see the strength of democracy. And this sends the clearest message to Iraq that it cannot scorn the January 15th deadline. Throughout our history, we have been resolute in our support of justice, freedom and human dignity.

The current situation in the Persian Gulf demands no less of us and of the international community. We did not plan for war, nor do we seek war. But if conflict is thrust upon us, we are ready and we are determined. We've worked long and hard as have others, including the Arab League, the United Nations, the European community, to achieve a peaceful solution. Unfortunately, Iraq has thus far turned a deaf ear to the voices of peace and reason.

Let there be no mistake, peace is everyone's goal. Peace is in everyone's prayers. But it is for Iraq to decide.

Laurie (sp).

Q Mr. President, does this mean now that war is inevitable --

PRESIDENT BUSH: No.

Q -- and have you made the decision in your own mind?

PRESIDENT BUSH: No, it does not mean that war is inevitable. And I have felt that a statement of this nature by both Houses of the United States Congress

CONTINUED

0066

PRESS CONFERENCE WITH PRESIDENT BUSH/WHITE HOUSE BRIEFING ROOM
Z-6-2 page# 1 SATURDAY, JANUARY 12, 1991

dest=swh,mwh,mme,notvme,mideast,pergulf,fns20611,fns13126,fns10000
dest+=fns13677,iraq,kuwait,armfor,warpower,un,forpolus,defense,arab
dest+=syria,france,egypt,dod
data

was, at this late date, the best shot for peace. And so let us hope that that message will get through to Saddam Hussein.

Q Have you made the decision in your own mind?

PRESIDENT BUSH: I have not because I still hope -- hope -- that there will be a peaceful solution.

Q Mr. President, there's only three days left until the deadline which isn't enough time for Saddam Hussein to pull out his troops. In fact, you, yourself, wouldn't let Jim Baker go to Baghdad on this date because there wouldn't be enough time.

Do you see a possibility of anything happening in these last few days that could avert war or any chance for -- that he will pull his troops out?

PRESIDENT BUSH: Well, in terms of the chance, I'd have to say I don't know, and in terms of what could avert war, you might say an instant commencement of a large scale removal of troops with no condition, no concession, and just heading out could well be a -- the best and only way to avert war, even though it would be at this date I would say almost impossible to comply fully with the United Nations resolutions.

Q Sir, as a followup, have you heard from the UN Secretary -General Perez de Cuellar today, and is there any hope on that front?

PRESIDENT BUSH: No, I'm -- well, I don't know whether there is hope on it because I haven't heard from him today.

Q Mr. President, are you satisfied that countries in the international coalition like France, Syria and Egypt will take part in offensive operations in the event of hostilities in the Gulf?

PRESIDENT BUSH: Yes.

Q The second part of that question, Sir, you've said that if hostilities come, it will not be another Vietnam. What kind of assumptions are you making about the duration of the conflict, and can you assure the American people that hostilities would not expand beyond the current period of operations?

PRESIDENT BUSH: Well, I am -- I am not making any assumptions in terms of numbers of days. But I have said over and over again that the differences
between what is happening in the Gulf and what happened in Vietnam are enormous in terms of the coalition aligned against the Iraqis,

126-2

0067

PRESS CONFERENCE WITH PRESIDENT BUSH/WHITE HOUSE BRIEFING ROOM
Z-6-2 page# 2 SATURDAY, JANUARY 12, 1991

in terms of the demographics, in terms of the United Nations action and I am convinced, in terms of the force that is arrayed against Iraq. So I just don't think there is a parallel.

But I would like to say that I have gone over all of this with our Secretary of Defense and with the Chairman of the Joint Chiefs and all three of us, and all -- everybody else involved in this, are determined to keep casualties to an absolute minimum. And that's one of the reasons that I authorized Secretary Cheney to move the additional force several weeks ago.

Q What about a firebreak to keep the war from expanding --

PRESIDENT BUSH: Well, I don't think -- I don't worry too much about the war expanding. I have said very clearly, and I'd like to repeat it here, that we will -- we will hold Saddam Hussein directly responsible for any terrorist action that is taken against US citizens, against citizens of others in the coalition. So I must confess to some concern about terrorism. It's not just that it relates to this -- this crisis, because I've always felt that way. But if it is related to the crisis -- if the terrorist acts are related to it, Saddam Hussein will be held directly responsible for that. And the consequences will be on him.

Q Mr. President, a pendulum of hope has swung back and forth, and you, yourself, have said you didn't hold out tremendous hope for the last-minute diplomatic efforts. What do you do on midnight on January 15th?

PRESIDENT BUSH: Well, Ann, I can't tell you I know what I'll do on midnight, but I do feel that the action taken by the United States Congress today is a very important step in hopefully getting Saddam Hussein to realize what he's up against, the determination of the American people. I have felt that the support is there from the people, but I think now with the Congress, the representatives of the people on record, it makes it much, much clearer to Saddam Hussein.

Q The polls have shown peoples' support moving fairly quickly after the 15th. Would that be your intention?

PRESIDENT BUSH: Well, I have said and without trying to pin it down, or in any sense go beyond what I'm about to say, sooner rather than later. And I got into a discussion, and I know that's perhaps not of much help. But I think the worst thing you'd want to do is if a determination was made to use force to signal when you might be inclined to act. That would not be -- that would -- that would, in my view, put the lives of coalition forces needlessly at risk.

Yeah, John?

Q Sir, I'm sure you're hearing all these scenarios that are coming out, the various peace scenarios. One has it that Saddam Hussein will wait until after the 15th -- to get into this

126 - 3

0068

PRESS CONFERENCE WITH PRESIDENT BUSH/WHITE HOUSE BRIEFING ROOM
Z-6-2 page# 3 SATURDAY, JANUARY 12, 1991

face-saving again -- wait till the 16th or the 17th, possibly, and then start to withdraw, say, "Look, I stood up to George Bush, but I'm moving enough in order to avoid war, to pull my troops out now." Is that the type of thing that will go into your calculations? Would that be important to you? Would you say, "Well, let's give the guy a couple of days and see if indeed that scenario is true."

PRESIDENT BUSH: I -- I don't want to give any indication to Saddam Hussein that we will be interested in anything that looks like delay or trying to claim victory. It isn't a question of winning or losing, it's a question of his getting out of Kuwait rapidly without concession.

And so I -- I -- I -- I can't -- I'd have to know a lot more about the situation, the scenario, as you say, before I could give you a more definitive response. But I don't want anything here to be interpreted by him as flexibility on our part. We have not been flexible, we have been determined. And we are still determined to see that this is -- that he is -- complies fully with the resolutions.

Now Rita raised the question, is it -- is it logistically

CONTINUED

126-4

0069

PRESS CONFERENCE WITH PRESIDENT BUSH/WHITE HOUSE BRIEFING ROOM
Z-6-3 page# 1 SATURDAY, JANUARY 12, 1991

dest=swh,mwh,mme,notvme,mideast,pergulf,fns20611,fns13126,fns10000
dest+=fns13677,iraq,kuwait,armfor,warpower,un,forpolus,defense,arab
data

possible to fully comply? At this moment, I am not sure that you could -- logistically possible to fully comply, that if he started now to do that's what -- that what he should have done weeks ago, clearly that would make a difference -- and I'm talking about a rapid, massive withdrawal from Kuwait. But I still worry about it because it might not be in full compliance. So, the standard full compliance with all these resolutions.

Now, some can't be complied with fully before the 15th; one of them relates to reparations, and reparations is a very important part of this -- it's a very important part of what the United Nations has done. So, I don't think the whole question of reparations can be resolved before the 15th.

Q Sir, can you explain why sooner is better than later?

PRESIDENT BUSH: Yes, because I think -- well, that's been a major part of the debate on the Hill, and I think it's very important that he knows that the United States and the United Nations are credible. I don't want to see further economic damage done to Third World economies or to this economy. I don't want to see further devastation done to Kuwait. This question of when was debated in the United Nations, and these countries came down saying, this is the deadline. And I don't want to veer off from that for one single iota. And I certainly don't want to indicate that the United States will not do its part in the coalition to fulfill these resolutions.

Yes.

Q Mr. President, you spoke of the debate. It was a very somber day up there --

PRESIDENT BUSH: Yes.

Q -- and people talked about the costs of war. I wondered if you watched it and what effect it had on you?

CONTINUED

126-5

0070

PRESS CONFERENCE WITH PRESIDENT BUSH/WHITE HOUSE BRIEFING ROOM
Z-6-4 page# 1 SATURDAY, JANUARY 12, 1991

dest=swh,mvh,mme,notvme,mideast,pergulf,fns20611,fns13126,fns10000
dest+=fns13677,irac,kuwait,armfor,warpower,un,forpolus,defense,arab
dest+=dod,eurcom,ussr
data

PRESIDENT BUSH: That's a good question. On the parts of it I saw, I couldn't agree more. It was somber, properly somber. It was, I thought, with very little rancor. I thought it was conducted, for the most part -- not entirely -- by -- in a very objective manner in terms of the subject, and yet subjective in terms of the individual speaking. The compassion, and the concern, the angst of these members, whether they agreed with me or not, came through loud and clear.

And so I guess I shared the emotion. I want peace. I want to see a peaceful resolution, and I could identify with those, whether they were on the side that was supporting of the administration or the other, for those who were really making fervent appeals for peace.

But I think it was historic; I think it was conducted in the best -- showing the best of the United States Congress at work, and I keep feeling that it was historic because what it did and how it endorsed the President's action to fulfill this resolution, when you go back and look at war and peace, I think historians will say this is a very significant step.

I am pleased that the Congress responded. I am pleased that they have acted, and therefore, are a part of all of this. But I didn't sense -- you know when you win a vote on something you work hard for, sometimes there's a sense of exhiliration and joy, pleasure. I didn't sense that at all here. I was grateful to the members that took the lead in -- in supporting the positions that I'm identified with. I could emphathize with those who -- who didn't vote for us. So I guess my emotion was -- was somber itself. I mean it was -- I didn't watch the whole thing; I didn't watch the whole debate. But what I saw I appreciated because there was very little personal rancor or assigning motives to the other person or something of that nature. So it was quite different than some of the debates that character -- that properly characterize the give and take of competitive politics.

Yeah?

Q On the question --

Q Sir? Sir, the crackdown was still going on today in Lithuania. What is your answer to those who say that you putting the Lithuania and the Baltics under the rug because of the Persian Gulf?

PRESIDENT BUSH: Well I don't think that's true. I've had an opportunity to express myself directly to President Gorbachev on that. We had a statement on it. I have talked to him not just this

126 - 6

0071

PRESS CONFERENCE WITH PRESIDENT BUSH/WHITE HOUSE BRIEFING ROOM
2-6-4 page# 2 SATURDAY, JANUARY 12, 1991

-- this last phone call but in others, and the Soviets know our position clearly. So I don't -- I don't think that's a fair charge at all.

Yeah? A couple of more. I think I've been -- I've been a little lengthy here and we didn't get as many as we want.

Q How about in the back of the room?

PRESIDENT BUSH: Not this time, Sarah. Not this time, okay?

Q Mr. President, it must now be absolutely clear to Saddam Hussein, perhaps for the first time, that you've got the domestic and the international support you need to use force to drive him out of Kuwait. Wouldn't this be a prudent time to give him an avenue out of this mess, perhaps through something Perez de Cuellar could offer him today or tomorrow?

PRESIDENT BUSH: Well, let's wait and see what -- I talked -- what Perez de Cuellar, how those talks go. I talked to him beforehand and he is properly -- properly -- I would say confined to operating within the UN resolutions. He must do that. We are talking about the United Nations Security Council and indeed at the General Assembly the will of the entire world against Saddam Hussein. But I have always felt, Jerry, that the best way, the best way is to make Saddam Hussein understand that we have the will to do what the Congress I think has now suggested what I should do, or can do. And secondly, that if force is used Saddam Hussein simply cannot prevail.

And I -- my hope is that the mission of the Secretary General, added to what the Congress has done here today, added to the many other initiatives taken by Arab League people or by EC people, or -- will convince him.

So if your question is should we now compromise, give him something in order to do that which he should have done long ago, the answer is absolutely not.

I'm going to take two more here and then I really do have to leave.

Q Mr. President, let me follow Jerry's question because the reports persist that the UN Secretary General, when he meets with Saddam Hussein

CONTINUED

126 - 7

0072

PRESS CONFERENCE WITH PRESIDENT BUSH/WHITE HOUSE BRIEFING ROOM
Z-6-5-E page# 1 SATURDAY, JANUARY 12, 1991

dest=swh,mwh,mme,notvme,mideast,pergulf,fns20611,fns13126,fns10000
dest+=fns13677,iraq,kuwait,armfor,warpower,un,forpolus,defense,arab
dest+=pal,israel
data

will layout steps beyond compliance with the resolutions to include a US peacekeeping force, to include an eventual Mideast peace conference. Given the demand for absolute compliance, are those within the Secretary General's mandate to advance further steps?

PRESIDENT BUSH: What were the two?

Q Well, the two -- two of several that are out there are a UN peacekeeping, also a timetable for your withdrawal, and then a Mideast peace conference.

PRESIDENT BUSH: Well, my view is that a withdrawal to the status quo ante is not satisfactory, and thus there will have to be a peacekeeping force of some kind. In other words, we just can't -- Saddam Hussein will not simply be able to go back to square one if he started that today. There would be a -- there would have to be further compliance with other resolutions, and there would have to be a peacekeeping force.

Secondly, I have said I don't want US ground forces to stay there a day longer than necessary. So, I am not troubled with that. On the other question, I simply want to see us avoid what is known as linkage, and I think the American people more clearly see now what I mean by linkage because they watched the Aziz press conference where the whole question was shifting -- trying to shift the onus away from the aggression and brutality against Kuwait and move it over and try to put the blame on Israel, or try to shift the onus to the Palestinian question.

So, we have, along with the United Nations -- other participants in the UN Security Council process have avoided linkage. And so I think -- I guess I'd say it depends how it's -- how it's put forward. I myself, at the United Nations, when I presented the US position this fall, spoke up against eventually wanting to see this question solved. And indeed, everyone knows that Jim Baker tried very hard to -- to have us be catalytic in bringing that age old question to a solution.

So I think -- I think it's -- I just think whatever is done it has to be done in a way to preserve the US position that there be no linkage.

Q Would it be fair to extrapolate then, that you have discussed these additional steps with Mr. Perez de Cuellar and endorsed them?

PRESIDENT BUSH: No, Charles, I read before this meeting here with you all, some -- some five-point proposal. And I can tell you

(6 - 8

0073

that was not discussed. And I'm not sure it is a proposal, because I -- in this -- in this -- in this complicated situation in which all -- all countries that want to see peace come about, we hear a lot of things that eventually prove not to have been correct. And I don't know of any five-point proposal. And just to clear the record, Perez de Cuellar did not discuss with me any five-point proposal.

This is the last one, Dan.

Q Mr. President, you have said on a number of occasions there is no secret diplomacy, no backroom diplomacy, no side door diplomacy. Are you prepared at this
avoided linkage. And so I think -- I guess I'd say it depends how it's -- how it's put forward. I myself, at the United Nations, when I presented the US position this fall, spoke up against eventually wanting to see this question solved. And indeed, everyone knows that Jim Baker tried very hard to -- to have us be catalytic in bringing that age old question to a solution.

So I think -- I think it's -- I just think whatever is done it has to be done in a way to preserve the US position that there be no linkage.

Q Would it be fair to extrapolate then, that you have discussed these additional steps with Mr. Perez de Cuellar and endorsed them?

PRESIDENT BUSH: No, Charles, I read before this meeting here with you all, some -- some five-point proposal. And I can tell you that was not discussed. And I'm not sure it is a proposal, because I -- in this -- in this -- in this complicated situation in which all -- all countries that want to see peace come about, we hear a lot of things that eventually prove not to have been correct. And I don't know of any five-point proposal. And just to clear the record, Perez de Cuellar did not discuss with me any five-point proposal.

This is the last one, Dan.

Q Mr. President, you have said on a number of occasions there is no secret diplomacy, no backroom diplomacy, no side door diplomacy. Are you prepared at this
point, given the conversations you had yesterday with Mr. Gorbachev and the meetings you had with the Soviet ambassador, that there is now still nothing else out there other than the Perez de Cuellar mission that might lead to a diplomatic solution to this?

PRESIDENT BUSH: Well, I'd say that is the main initiative out there right now, and the only one that I know of, although you hear rumors that others may go. President Gorbachev may want to send somebody. The EC may decide after the Perez de Cuellar mission to send somebody. But I don't know of that for a fact certain. And if Perez de Cuellar finds no flexibility and indeed, is faced with the

126 - 9

0074

PRESS CONFERENCE WITH PRESIDENT BUSH/WHITE HOUSE BRIEFING ROOM
2-6-5-E page# 3 SATURDAY, JANUARY 12, 1991

rhetoric that we heard coming out of Iraq as recently as a few hours ago, that, I think will be a sign of -- I'll put it this way -- a discouraging sign, and I think it will frustrate the understandably noble intentions of countries all around the world that would like to think that at the last minute this man would come to his senses.

Q If I could follow that: If the Soviets or the EC or someone else decides they want to send someone to Baghdad after the Perez de Cuellar mission, does that in any way tie your hands in the use of military force after the 15th if these are bumping up against the 15th deadline or slightly thereafter?

PRESIDENT BUSH: Well, I -- I would not leave the door open on "slighty thereafter." I think we have sent out an advisory to -- certainly to American citizens, and I would enlarge that to everybody to -- to -- that the 15th is a very real deadline. And so, I wouldn't -- your question -- if I answer it -- I want to be sure I don't answer it in leaving the door open for any activity after midnight on January 15th, because that is what is called for under the UN -- the UN resolutions set that date. And so, I don't want to -- don't want to suggest that one last visit could take place after that and have the approval of the United Nations Security Council which has stood against -- solidly against -- that kind of, some would say, "flexibility," but I would say a breach of the United Nations resolutions.

So, please, to anyone who might be listening in countries around the world, let me simply say, there is no flexibility on our part, and I have sensed none on the part of the other members of the coalition that is arrayed against Saddam Hussein, nor have I found any flexibility -- and I'm glad about that -- on the part of other members of the Security Council or other countries -- other countries whose leaders I have spoken to. So, the coalition is together. The United Nations is strongly together. I think the vote in the United States Congress today shows that the United States position is strongly firmed up by what happened in Congress today and by what appears to be the will of the American people. And it's in keeping with how -- my will and how I feel about this.

So let us just pray that -- that this -- that we will make the necessary contribution, through the action that was taken today, to bring this man to his senses because it is a critical moment in history. And what the Congress did today was indeed historic.

And I will conclude here by once again thanking them, thanking them for coming to grips to the question, obviously thanking them for backing the position that is so strongly held by so many countries around the world.

Thank you all very much.

END

1-6-10

0075

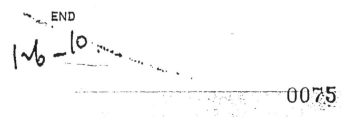

외 무 부

종 별 : 지 급

번 호 : USW-0145 일 시 : 91 0112 2057

수 신 : Y장관(중근동,미북,미안)

발 신 : 주미대사

제 목 : 페만 사태 (부쉬 대통령의 후세인 앞 서한)

금 1.12 백악관 대변인은 베이커- 아지즈 회담 (1.9 제네바)시 이락측에서 접수를 거부한바 있는부쉬 대통령의 후세인 대통령앞 서한을 공개하였는바, 동 서한 별첨훽스 송부함.

첨부: USW(F)-0127

(대사 박동진-국장)

중아국 장관 차관 1차보 2차보 미주국 미주국 중아국 상황실 청와대 안기부

PAGE 1

91.01.13 11:25 CG

외신 1과 통제관

0076

번호: USWF-127

수신: 장관 (중근동, 미북, 미안)

발신: 주미대사

제목: 페만 사태 (부시 대통령의 후세인 대통령앞 서한)

배부처	장관실	차관실	1차보	2차보	외정실	분석관	아주국	미주국	구주국	중아국	국기국	경제국	통상국	정문국	영교국	총무과	감사관	공보관	외연원	청와대	안기부
	/	/	/	/				2		2				/						/	/

(2매)

USW-0145 첨부

THE WHITE HOUSE

WASHINGTON

JANUARY 5, 1991

Mr. President:

We stand today at the brink of war between Iraq and the world. This is a war that began with your invasion of Kuwait; this is a war that can be ended only by Iraq's full and unconditional compliance with UN Security Council Resolution 678.

I am writing you now, directly, because what is at stake demands that no opportunity be lost to avoid what would be a certain calamity for the people of Iraq. I am writing, as well, because it is said by some that you do not understand just how isolated Iraq is and what Iraq faces as a result. I am not in a position to judge whether this impression is correct; what I can do, though, is try in this letter to reinforce what Secretary of State Baker told your Foreign Minister and eliminate any uncertainty or ambiguity that might exist in your mind about where we stand and what we are prepared to do.

The international community is united in its call for Iraq to leave all of Kuwait without condition and without further delay. This is not simply the policy of the United States; it is the position of the world community as expressed in no less than twelve Security Council resolutions.

We prefer a peaceful outcome. However, anything less than full compliance with UN Security Council Resolution 678 and its predecessors is unacceptable. There can be no reward for aggression. Nor will there be any negotiation. Principle cannot be compromised. However, by its full compliance, Iraq will gain the opportunity to rejoin the international community. More immediately, the Iraqi military establishment will ...

0077

THE WHITE HOUSE OFFICE OF THE PRESS SECRETARY
For Immediate Release January 12, 1991
STATEMENT BY THE PRESS SECRETARY
ZA-6-1-E page# 2

escape destruction. But unless you withdraw from Kuwait completely and without condition, you will lose more than Kuwait. What is at issue here is not the future of Kuwait -- it will be free, its government will be restored -- but rather the future of Iraq. This choice is yours to make.

The United States will not be separated from its coalition partners. Twelve Security Council resolutions, 28 countries providing military units to enforce them, more than one hundred governments complying with sanctions -- all highlight the fact that it is not Iraq against the United States, but Iraq against the world. That most Arab and Muslim countries are arrayed against you as well should reinforce what I am saying. Iraq cannot and will not be able to hold on to Kuwait or exact a price for leaving.

You may be tempted to find solace in the diversity of opinion that is American democracy. You should resist any such temptation. Diversity ought not to be confused with division. Nor should you underestimate, as others have before you, America's will.

Iraq is already feeling the effects of the sanctions mandated by the United Nations. Should war come, it will be a far greater tragedy for you and your country. Let me state, too, that the United States will not tolerate the use of chemical or biological weapons or the destruction of Kuwait's oil fields and installations. Further, you will be held directly responsible for terrorist actions against any member of the coalition. The American people would demand the strongest possible response. You and your country will pay a terrible price if your order unconscionable acts of this sort.

I write this letter not to threaten, but to inform. I do so with no sense of satisfaction, for the people fo the United States have no quarrel with the people of Iraq. Mr. President, UN Security Council Resolution 678 establishes the period before January 15 of this year as a "pause of good will" so that this crisis may end without further violence. Whether this pause is used as intended, or merely becomes a prelude to further violence, is in your hands, and yours alone. I hope you weigh your choice carefully and choose wisely, for much will depend upon it.

(signed) George Bush

His Excellency
Saddam Hussein
President of the Republic of Iraq
Baghdad

END

127-2

0078

외 무 부

종 별 : 지 급

번 호 : USW-0146 일 시 : 91 0113 1620

수 신 : 장 관(중근동,미북)

발 신 : 주 미대사

제 목 : 중동 사태 (케야르 사무총장 중재 노력)

1. 케야르 유엔 사무총장이 금 1.13 후세인 대통령과의 회담을 마쳤으나 상금 구체적 회담 결과가 밝혀 지지 않고있음.

당지 언론은 동 사무총장이 지난 1.11 유럽 지도자 와의 회담에서 협의 한바와 같이 이락군의 쿠웨이트 철수가 이루어진후 중동 문제의 포괄적 해결을 위한 국제 회의 소집에 관한 제안을 했을 가능성이 있는것으로 관측하고있음.

2.한편, 후세인 이락 대통령은 이락 국회의 긴급회의를 유엔 안보리의 이락군 철수 시한을 하루 앞둔 1.14에 개최한다고 발표 했는바, 당지 언론은 외국인 인질의석방등 중요한 정책 결정시동 의회 소집이 있었던점을 감안 중대한 변화가 기대 된다고 보도함.

그러나 CNN 방송은 후서인 대통령이 금 1.13 쿠웨이트가 이락 영토의 일부임을 재주장, 강경 입장을 계속 고수하고 있다고 보도함.

3.관련 기사 별첨: USW(F)-129

(대사 박동진-국장)

중아국 장관 차관 1차보 미주국 안기부

PAGE 1

91.01.14 08:04 CT

외신 1과 통제관

0079

(F) - 129

권 (중근동. 비북) 발신 : 주미대사

동 사태 (유엔사무총장 중재 노력) (3 매)

USW-0146의 첨부

U.N. Chief in Baghdad With 'Substantive' Proposals

By PATRICK E. TYLER

Special to The New York Times

BAGHDAD, Iraq, Jan. 12 — United Nations Secretary General Javier Pérez de Cuéllar arrived here tonight carrying what an aide described as "substantive" proposals to prevent the outbreak of war in the Persian Gulf as the last major evacuation of foreign diplomats flew out of the country at midday on an American-chartered Iraqi Airways flight.

Arriving on a United Nations executive jet this evening, Mr. Pérez de Cuéllar was greeted by Foreign Minister Tariq Aziz and escorted to what was expected to be the first of two meetings tonight and Sunday with President Saddam Hussein.

Before the talks started, Mr. Hussein announced an emergency session of the National Assembly on Monday in a move that could signal the Iraqi leader's intention to reveal his final diplomatic maneuver a day before the deadline expires. Mr. Hussein has used the consultative body to affirm key national decisions, such as last month's announcement that it was freeing all foreign hostages.

> As the deadline nears, the last foreign diplomats leave Iraq.

Mr. Pérez de Cuéllar told reporters that he was not carrying "any specific proposals," but an aide said later that he was bringing "something substantive, otherwise he would not have come."

'Important to Talk'

Without addressing reports that he would discuss how United Nations peacekeeping forces might play a role in an Iraqi withdrawal from Kuwait, Mr. Pérez de Cuéllar said, "I am bringing the will of the international community for a peaceful solution" to the crisis and added that it was "important to talk to the Iraqis" about compliance with United Nations resolutions that call for Iraq's withdrawal from Kuwait by midnight Tuesday, or face eviction by the American-led forces in the Persian Gulf. The talks were to begin tonight after another day of somber departures by diplomats representing many of the more than 70 nations here.

The senior American diplomat, deputy chief of mission Joseph C. Wilson 4th, ordered the lowering of the American flag over the United States Embassy compound at 8 A.M. today to prevent what he later termed was the "possible desecration of our national symbol" after he closed the mission. He said he was carrying the flag that has flown over the Baghdad mission since Aug. 2 to present to President Bush in a few days.

Mr. Wilson, 41 years old, led a group of 44 diplomats and foreign nationals from 13 nations who are abandoning their embassies here three days before the United Nations deadline that demands Iraq's withdrawal from Kuwait under threat of military force.

The departure heightened the sense of impending war in the Iraqi capital, but did not signify an end to international diplomatic efforts to construct a last minute formula under which Mr. Hussein would agree to pull his occupation army out of Kuwait.

Most formulations have sought to link Iraq's withdrawal from Kuwait with guarantees for Iraqi security and with the convening of an international conference to address the plight of Palestinians living under Israeli occupation in the West Bank and Gaza Strip. The Bush Administration has said any such linkage would be a reward for aggression and has demanded unconditional withdrawal and a restoration of Kuwait's legitimate Government.

Bush Opposes Linkage

Mr. Bush has vehemently opposed any agreement linking withdrawal with a conference. But in a speech to the United Nations General Assembly in September, he said Iraq's withdrawal might pave the way for additional efforts to resolve the overall Arab-Israeli dispute and, last month, the United States supported a Security Council resolution calling for the protection of Palestinians living under occupation. The resolution was accompanied by a nonbinding statement by the Security Council president calling for an international conference to address the Palestinian question at the proper time.

Iraq's official English-language newspaper, The Baghdad Observer, later said Iraq deserved the credit for

91.1.13
NYT

0080

the United States decision to support the resolution, which the newspaper said still was inadequate.

At a news conference at Saddam International Airport, Mr. Wilson expressed his regret about the termination of United States diplomatic efforts through the embassy in Baghdad, which has served as an important point of contact between Washington and the Iraqi leadership during months of tense efforts to free thousands of Americans and other foreign nationals in hiding in Kuwait or held hostage by Iraq as so-called human shields to protect Iraqi facilities from preemptive American attacks.

More than 2,500 Americans and other foreign nationals were evacuated from Kuwait and Iraq on a series of charter

Hussein calls an emergency session of his Assembly for Monday.

flights under the supervision of Mr. Wilson and his consular staff, which he praised today. About 100 American passport holders remain in Iraq, many of them married to Iraqis.

Tearful Final Exchanges

As the diplomatic evacuation formed up at the airport, many Iraqi and other foreign nationals on the local staffs of embassies accompanied their employers and the departure lounge was filled with emotional embraces and tearful final exchanges.

Mr. Wilson was embraced by a 78-year-old German peace worker, Eva Boremann of Hanover, who gave the envoy a bouquet of roses, which Mr. Wilson distributed to acquaintances throughout the departure area.

Many embassies that are locking their doors will continue to pay local staffs and fly their national flags. About 100 Iraqi nationals will remain on the salary of the American embassy, but will perform only maintenance functions at the American compound.

Mr. Wilson, who became the ranking diplomat in Baghdad when Ambassador April Glaspie was called back to Washington for consultations the days before Iraq's invasion, also said he personally was saddened by his forced departure, after laboring unsuccessfully for weeks to help arrange a visit to Baghdad by Secretary of State James A. Baker 3d for talks with Mr. Hussein.

The American envoy had told colleagues in the diplomatic corps in recent weeks that he thought such a meeting was important because Mr. Hussein was the only Iraqi official who could make concessions on Kuwait.

"Despite this crisis," he said, "at some point we will want to repair our relationship with Iraq and I would like to be part of that effort."

The American charter flight of the Iraqi Airways Boeing 727 also carried Canadian Ambassador, J. Christopher Poole, along with the ranking diplomats from Norway, Switzerland, Austria, Finland, Belgium, Brazil and The Netherlands. Most of the 126 seats on the plane were empty as many embassies opted for driving overland to Jordan.

The last British diplomat, Chris Segar, was due to leave today, while France was planning to evacuate its chargé d'affaires, André Janier, on Monday. China abruptly changed its plans to keep its its embassy open, and Friday evacuated all of its diplomats. Turkey, which earlier said it would keep its embassy open, said today it was closing the mission and brining home its ambassador and remaining diplomats.

The Soviet Union, which has the largest foreign mission here, also was said by diplomatic sources to be reconsidering its decision to keep more than 150 diplomatic personnel in residence during after the deadline.

Most Embassies Closing

It appeared today that most of the 70 foreign missions represented here would be closed by the Jan. 15 deadline. Japan's Ambassador, Kunio Katakura, said he would take his staff out on the 15th at the completion of a visit here by a delegation of Japanese members of Parliament led by the Socialist Party leader, Takako Doi.

Mr. Poole said the mass exodus of diplomats was both a security precaution and a political statement to Iraq.

"The departure of all these embassies signifies the fact that everyone's life is at risk, but it also sends a strong signal to Saddam Hussein that there are no more diplomatic moves and good will has come to an end."

The Canadian envoy said he did not think there would be a speedy return of diplomats even if a breakthrough occurred between now and the Jan. 15 deadline. "Once you pull the plug, you close a lot of options," he said, "I don't think we would come back at the first sign of an opening on the diplomatic side. It will take some time."

Six hours after the evacuation flight Mr. Pérez de Cuéllar arrived at Saddam International Airport, where he told news reporters that "all I bring is not only my good will but my determination to find a peaceful solution" to the crisis.

12P-2

0081

Perez de Cuellar Expected to See Saddam Today

By Tod Robberson
Washington Post Foreign Service

BAGHDAD, Iraq, Jan. 12—U.N. Secretary General Javier Perez de Cuellar arrived here today in an urgent attempt to avert war in the Persian Gulf, as the United States pulled out its diplomatic staff and closed its embassy in Baghdad three days before the U.N. deadline for Iraq to leave Kuwait.

Perez de Cuellar told reporters on arrival that he hoped "to convey possibly good news" at the end of his visit, although he was not specific about the agenda and duration of his trip. He was greeted at the airport by Foreign Minister Tariq Aziz and the two men met twice later in the day. The U.N. chief was expected to meet with President Saddam Hussein on Sunday.

"As you know very well, I come here as a messenger of peace," Perez de Cuellar told reporters. "I am not bringing any specific proposal. All I bring is . . . my good will" and "the wish of the international community for a peaceful solution" to the crisis in the Persian Gulf, where U.S.-led multinational forces are massed for possible attack against Iraq should it refuse to honor the U.N. deadline.

While Perez de Cuellar said he did not come with a peace plan, he had met in Geneva Friday with European Community foreign ministers and discussed a multi-stage process to end the crisis. The ministers said Perez de Cuellar would tell Saddam that Iraq would not come under military attack if it withdraws, and he would cite the strong European backing for an international conference on the Middle East, two issues believed important to the Iraqi leader.

Saddam today called for the rubber-stamp National Assembly to meet on Monday, according to Iraqi television. No reason for the session was given, although in the past, Saddam has used the assembly to ratify significant moves, such as in early December when he decided to release thousands of foreigners he had been holding hostage here and in Kuwait. The timing of the session—on the eve of the U.N. deadline—suggested Saddam might make an announcement regarding his plans on Kuwait.

"I would think that we're fairly close to the brink," U.S. Embassy charge d'affaires Joseph C. Wilson IV said at his residence today before his departure aboard a chartered Iraqi Airways plane that flew him, his five American staff members and 38 other passengers to Frankfurt.

Among the passengers were an unidentified Iraqi citizen and diplomats from Canada, the Netherlands, Belgium, Brazil, Norway and Ireland. Three Swiss Embassy officials also were aboard, including the ambassador, despite earlier Swiss statements that they would remain here as a symbol of Switzerland's desire for peace and to symbolize its neutrality in the crisis.

Western diplomats said the rush to evacuate the embassies was prompted by rumors that the United States plans to bombard Baghdad heavily after expiration of the U.N. deadline.

Wilson said he had no comment on U.S. military plans after the deadline expires, and he cautioned, "If you portray this as a U.S.-Iraqi confrontation, you're all wrong." He said any military action against Iraq would occur under a U.N. umbrella and involved a coalition of international forces that "remains firm."

As the U.N. deadline approached, new calls were made for a diplomatic solution to the crisis. Syrian President Hafez Assad, who joined the U.S.-led coalition against Iraq, appealed in a radio address for Saddam, his archenemy, to leave Kuwait before a war erupted that, he said, would benefit Israel.

Assad, who met with U.S. Secretary of States James A. Baker III in Damascus today, told Saddam to "take the courageous decision to spare Iraq a major catastrophe in order not to enable the enemies of the Arab nation to gain benefit from the present situation." In the message, broadcast over Damascus radio, Assad said the enemy was Israel.

Meanwhile in Moscow, the Soviet parliament called on President Mikhail Gorbachev to pursue new efforts with Iraq and the United States aimed at finding a peaceful settlement, although it did not specify what actions might be taken, Reuter reported. The parliament appealed to all sides in the conflict to avoid a military conflict, saying it would have "catastrophic consequences." In a related development, Baker today praised Gorbachev for pursuing new efforts to avert war.

Yemen, an Arab state that has been sympathetic to Iraq in the crisis, today urged Baghdad to leave Kuwait and moved to repair fractured relations with Egypt, a leader in the U.S.-led coalition against Iraq. Yemen and Cuba were the only two countries on the 15-member U.N. Security Council to vote against the Nov. 29 resolution authorizing the use of all necessary means to free Kuwait.

Today, Yemen's foreign minister, Abdul Karim Iryani, arrived in Cairo unannounced and met Egyptian President Hosni Mubarak for talks, Reuter reported. Diplomats said Yemen's move indicates that it does not want to be too isolated in the Arab world by backing Saddam.

Here in Baghdad, the American flag was taken down from atop the U.S. Embassy early this morning, an action Wilson said he ordered "to avoid the desecration of our national symbol." Earlier this week, Wilson took down the flag that had flown atop the embassy throughout the ordeal that began with Iraq's Aug. 2 invasion of Kuwait, and replaced it with a reserve flag. Wilson said he plans to present a flag to President Bush after his arrival in Washington early Sunday.

12P-3

91.1.13. WP

0082

원 본

외 무 부

종 별 : 지 급

번 호 : USW-0147 일 시 : 91 0113 1625

수 신 : 장 관(중근동,미북)

발 신 : 주미대사

제 목 : 페만 사태(시리아 및 이집토 입장)

1. 베이커 장관은 1.12 ASSAD 시리아 대통령과의 회담에서 무력 사용에 대한시리아측의 협조를 요청했으나, ASSAD 대통령은 시리아군의 공격작전 가담은 거부하고, 방어적 역할만 수행할 방침임을 밝힌것으로 알려 졌는바, 이는 이스라엘의 대규모 보복을 우려하기 때문인것으로 당지 언론은 분석하고 있음.

한편 ASSAD 대통령은 베이커 장관과의 회담이 개시 되기 직전 방송된 라디오 연설에서 후세인 대통령에게 이락군의 쿠에이트 철수를 호소 하였다함.

2. 이보다 앞서 베이커 장관은 무바라크 이집트 대통령과의 회담에서는 대 이락 공격시 이집트군의 적극적 참여를 보장 받은것으로 알려졌음.

3. 관련기사: USW(F)-130

(대사 박동진-국장)

중아국 장관 차관 1차보 미주국 안기부 2차보 정문국 언론국

 91.01.14 08:07 CT

외신 1과 통제관

(F) - 129

권 (중동. 미북) 발신 : 주미대사

중 사태 (유엔사무총장 중재 노력) (3 매)

보안 통제

USW-0146의 첨부

U.N. Chief in Baghdad With 'Substantive' Proposals

By PATRICK E. TYLER

Special to The New York Times

BAGHDAD, Iraq, Jan. 12 — United Nations Secretary General Javier Pérez de Cuéllar arrived here tonight carrying what an aide described as "substantive" proposals to prevent the outbreak of war in the Persian Gulf as the last major evacuation of foreign diplomats flew out of the country at midday on an American-chartered Iraqi Airways flight.

Arriving on a United Nations executive jet this evening, Mr. Pérez de Cuéllar was greeted by Foreign Minister Tariq Aziz and escorted to what was expected to be the first of two meetings tonight and Sunday with President Saddam Hussein.

Before the talks started, Mr. Hussein announced an emergency session of the National Assembly on Monday in a move that could signal the Iraqi leader's intention to reveal his final diplomatic maneuver a day before the deadline expires. Mr. Hussein has used the consultative body to affirm key national decisions, such as last month's announcement that it was freeing all foreign hostages.

As the deadline nears, the last foreign diplomats leave Iraq.

Mr. Pérez de Cuéllar told reporters that he was not carrying "any specific proposals," but an aide said later that he was bringing "something substantive, otherwise he would not have come."

'Important to Talk'

Without addressing reports that he would discuss how United Nations peacekeeping forces might play a role in an Iraqi withdrawal from Kuwait, Mr. Pérez de Cuéllar said, "I am bringing the will of the international community for a peaceful solution" to the crisis and added that it was "important to talk to the Iraqis" about compliance with United Nations resolutions that call for Iraq's withdrawal from Kuwait by midnight Tuesday, or face eviction by the American-led forces in the Persian Gulf. The talks were to begin tonight after another day of somber departures by diplomats representing many of the more than 70 nations here.

The senior American diplomat, deputy chief of mission Joseph C. Wilson 4th, ordered the lowering of the American flag over the United States Embassy compound at 8 A.M. today to prevent what he later termed was the "possible desecration of our national symbol" after he closed the mission. He said he was carrying the flag that has flown over the Baghdad mission since Aug. 2 to present to President Bush in a few days.

Mr. Wilson, 41 years old, led a group of 44 diplomats and foreign nationals from 13 nations who are abandoning their embassies here three days before the United Nations deadline that demands Iraq's withdrawal from Kuwait under threat of military force.

The departure heightened the sense of impending war in the Iraqi capital, but did not signify an end to international diplomatic efforts to construct a last minute formula under which Mr. Hussein would agree to pull his occupation army out of Kuwait.

Most formulations have sought to link Iraq's withdrawal from Kuwait with guarantees for Iraqi security and with the convening of an international conference to address the plight of Palestinians living under Israeli occupation in the West Bank and Gaza Strip. The Bush Administration has said any such linkage would be a reward for aggression and has demanded unconditional withdrawal and a restoration of Kuwait's legitimate Government.

Bush Opposes Linkage

Mr. Bush has vehemently opposed any agreement linking withdrawal with a conference. But in a speech to the United Nations General Assembly in September, he said Iraq's withdrawal might pave the way for additional efforts to resolve the overall Arab-Israeli dispute and, last month, the United States supported a Security Council resolution calling for the protection of Palestinians living under occupation. The resolution was accompanied by a nonbinding statement by the Security Council president calling for an international conference to address the Palestinian question at the proper time.

Iraq's official English-language newspaper, The Baghdad Observer, later said Iraq deserved the credit for

91.1.13

NYT

0084

the United States decision to support the resolution, which the newspaper said still was inadequate.

At a news conference at Saddam International Airport, Mr. Wilson expressed his regret about the termination of United States diplomatic efforts through the embassy in Baghdad, which has served as an important point of contact between Washington and the Iraqi leadership during months of tense efforts to free thousands of Americans and other foreign nationals in hiding in Kuwait or held hostage by Iraq as so-called human shields to protect Iraqi facilities from preemptive American attacks.

More than 2,500 Americans and other foreign nationals were evacuated from Kuwait and Iraq on a series of charter

Hussein calls an emergency session of his Assembly for Monday.

flights under the supervision of Mr. Wilson and his consular staff, which he praised today. About 100 American passport holders remain in Iraq, many of them married to Iraqis.

Tearful Final Exchanges

As the diplomatic evacuation formed up at the airport, many Iraqi and other foreign nationals on the local staffs of embassies accompanied their employers and the departure lounge was filled with emotional embraces and tearful final exchanges.

Mr. Wilson was embraced by a 78-year-old German peace worker, Eva Boremann of Hanover, who gave the envoy a bouquet of roses, which Mr. Wilson distributed to acquaintances throughout the departure area.

Many embassies that are locking their doors will continue to pay local staffs and fly their national flags. About 100 Iraqi nationals will remain on the salary of the American embassy, but will perform only maintenance functions at the American compound.

Mr. Wilson, who became the ranking diplomat in Baghdad when Ambassador April Glaspie was called back to Washington for consultations the days before Iraq's invasion, also said he personally was saddened by his forced departure, after laboring unsuccessfully for weeks to help arrange a visit to Baghdad by Secretary of State James A. Baker 3d for talks with Mr. Hussein.

The American envoy had told colleagues in the diplomatic corps in recent weeks that he thought such a meeting was important because Mr. Hussein was the only Iraqi official who could make concessions on Kuwait.

"Despite this crisis," he said, "at some point we will want to repair our relationship with Iraq and I would like to be part of that effort."

The American charter flight of the Iraqi Airways Boeing 727 also carried Canadian Ambassador, J. Christopher Poole, along with the ranking diplomats from Norway, Switzerland, Austria, Finland, Belgium, Brazil and The Netherlands. Most of the 126 seats on the plane were empty as many embassies opted for driving overland to Jordan.

The last British diplomat, Chris Sagar, was due to leave today, while France was planning to evacuate its chargé d'affaires, Andre Janier, on Monday. China abruptly changed its plans to keep its its embassy open, and Friday evacuated all of its diplomats. Turkey, which earlier said it would keep its embassy open, said today it was closing the mission and brining home its ambassador and remaining diplomats.

The Soviet Union, which has the largest foreign mission here, also was said by diplomatic sources to be reconsidering its decision to keep more than 150 diplomatic personnel in residence during after the deadline.

Most Embassies Closing

It appeared today that most of the 70 foreign missions represented here would be closed by the Jan. 15 deadline. Japan's Ambassador, Kunio Katakura, said he would take his staff out on the 15th at the completion of a visit here by a delegation of Japanese members of Parliament led by the Socialist Party leader, Takako Doi.

Mr. Poole said the mass exodus of diplomats was both a security precaution and a political statement to Iraq.

"The departure of all these embassies signifies the fact that everyone's life is at risk, but it also sends a strong signal to Saddam Hussein that there are no more diplomatic moves and good will has come to an end."

The Canadian envoy said he did not think there would be a speedy return of diplomats even if a breakthrough occurred between now and the Jan. 15 deadline. "Once you pull the plug, you close a lot of options," he said, "I don't think we would come back at the first sign of an opening on the diplomatic side. It will take some time."

Six hours after the evacuation flight Mr. Pérez de Cuéllar arrived at Saddam International Airport, where he told news reporters that "all I bring is not only my good will but my determination to find a peaceful solution" to the crisis.

12p-2

0085

Perez de Cuellar Expected to See Saddam Today

By Tod Robberson
Washington Post Foreign Service

BAGHDAD, Iraq, Jan. 12—U.N. Secretary General Javier Perez de Cuellar arrived here today in an urgent attempt to avert war in the Persian Gulf, as the United States pulled out its diplomatic staff and closed its embassy in Baghdad three days before the U.N. deadline for Iraq to leave Kuwait.

Perez de Cuellar told reporters on arrival that he hoped "to convey possibly good news" at the end of his visit, although he was not specific about the agenda and duration of his trip. He was greeted at the airport by Foreign Minister Tariq Aziz and the two men met twice later in the day. The U.N. chief was expected to meet with President Saddam Hussein on Sunday.

"As you know very well, I come here as a messenger of peace," Perez de Cuellar told reporters. "I am not bringing any specific proposal. All I bring is . . . my good will" and "the wish of the international community for a peaceful solution" to the crisis in the Persian Gulf, where U.S.-led multinational forces are massed for possible attack against Iraq should it refuse to honor the U.N. deadline.

While Perez de Cuellar said he did not come with a peace plan, he had met in Geneva Friday with European Community foreign ministers and discussed a multi-stage process to end the crisis. The ministers said Perez de Cuellar would tell Saddam that Iraq would not come under military attack if it withdraws, and he would cite the strong European backing for an international conference on the Middle East, two issues believed important to the Iraqi leader.

Saddam today called for the rubber-stamp National Assembly to meet on Monday, according to Iraqi television. No reason for the session was given, although in the past, Saddam has used the assembly to ratify significant moves, such as in early December when he decided to release thousands of foreigners he had been holding hostage here and in Kuwait. The timing of the session—on the eve of the U.N. deadline—suggested Saddam might make an announcement regarding his plans on Kuwait.

"I would think that we're fairly close to the brink," U.S. Embassy charge d'affaires Joseph C. Wilson IV said at his residence today before his departure aboard a chartered Iraqi Airways plane that flew him, his five American staff members and 38 other passengers to Frankfurt.

Among the passengers were an unidentified Iraqi citizen and diplomats from Canada, the Netherlands, Belgium, Brazil, Norway and Ireland. Three Swiss Embassy officials also were aboard, including the ambassador, despite earlier Swiss statements that they would remain here as a symbol of Switzerland's desire for peace and to symbolize its neutrality in the crisis.

Western diplomats said the rush to evacuate the embassies was prompted by rumors that the United States plans to bombard Baghdad heavily after expiration of the U.N. deadline.

Wilson said he had no comment on U.S. military plans after the deadline expires, and he cautioned, "If you portray this as a U.S.-Iraqi confrontation, you're all wrong." He said any military action against Iraq would occur under a U.N. umbrella and involved a coalition of international forces that "remains firm."

As the U.N. deadline approached, new calls were made for a diplomatic solution to the crisis. Syrian President Hafez Assad, who joined the U.S.-led coalition against Iraq, appealed in a radio address for Saddam, his archenemy, to leave Kuwait before a war erupted that, he said, would benefit Israel.

Assad, who met with U.S. Secretary of States James A. Baker III in Damascus today, told Saddam to "take the courageous decision to spare Iraq a major catastrophe in order not to enable the enemies of the Arab nation to gain benefit from the present situation." In the message, broadcast over Damascus radio, Assad said the enemy was Israel.

Meanwhile in Moscow, the Soviet parliament called on President Mikhail Gorbachev to pursue new efforts with Iraq and the United States aimed at finding a peaceful settlement, although it did not specify what actions might be taken, Reuter reported. The parliament appealed to all sides in the conflict to avoid a military conflict, saying it would have "catastrophic consequences." In a related development, Baker today praised Gorbachev for pursuing new efforts to avert war.

Yemen, an Arab state that has been sympathetic to Iraq in the crisis, today urged Baghdad to leave Kuwait and moved to repair fractured relations with Egypt, a leader in the U.S.-led coalition against Iraq. Yemen and Cuba were the only two countries on the 15-member U.N. Security Council to vote against the Nov. 29 resolution authorizing the use of all necessary means to free Kuwait.

Today, Yemen's foreign minister, Abdul Karim Iryani, arrived in Cairo unannounced and met Egyptian President Hosni Mubarak for talks, Reuter reported. Diplomats said Yemen's move indicates that it does not want to be too isolated in the Arab world by backing Saddam.

Here in Baghdad, the American flag was taken down from atop the U.S. Embassy early this morning, an action Wilson said he ordered "to avoid the desecration of our national symbol." Earlier this week, Wilson took down the flag that had flown atop the embassy throughout the ordeal that began with Iraq's Aug. 2 invasion of Kuwait, and replaced it with a reserve flag. Wilson said he plans to present a flag to President Bush after his arrival in Washington early Sunday.

12P-3 91.1.13. WP

0086

원 본

외 무 부

종 별 : 지 급

번 호 : USW-0149 일 시 : 91 0113 2107

수 신 : 장관(중근동,미북)

발 신 : 주미대사

제 목 : 페만 사태(후세인 연설)

당지 CNN 방송은 금 1.13 19:30 뉴스를 통해 후세인 대통령이 이락 의회에서 행한 연설 내용을 보도하였는바, 요지 아래 보고함.

1. 이락은 미국이 주도하고 있는 무력 공격 위협에 결코 굴복하지 않을 것임. 이락은 이번 사태가 평화적 으로 해결될 것을 바라고 있으나 상금 부쉬 대통령으로부터 진정한 평화 제의가 없었음.

2. 이락은 미국의 침공을 격퇴시킬수 있는 만반의 준비를 갖추어 놓았는바, 미국은 파나마 침공에서와 같은 속전 속결에 의한 승리를 기대할수 없을 것임.

3. 쿠에이트 영토는 이제 아랍 세계 전체의 상징물로 되었으며, 팔레스타인 문제를 포함 중동 문제에 대한 포괄적 해결책이 마련되지 않고는 결코 타협하지 않을 것이라는 이락의 기존 입장에는 아무런 변화가 없음.

(대사 박동진-국장)

현지 1.14. 10시 (관저) 776-1881

(대사관) 776-5486

중아국	장관	차관	1차보	2차보	미주국	정문국	청와대	안기부
					중아국	대책반		

PAGE 1

91.01.14 14:37 CG

외신 1과 통제관

0087

관리 번호	91-486

원 본

외 무 부

종 별 : 지 급

번 호 : USW-0150 일 시 : 91 0113 2107

수 신 : 장관(중근동,미북,미안)

발 신 : 주 미 대사

제 목 : 페만 사태 관련 미국내 동향

연: USW-0142,0144

연호 관련, 작일, 미 의회에서의 무력 사용 결의안 통과 이후, 금 1.13 당지의 주요 동향을 하기 요지 보고함.

1. 언론 보도 동향

가.WP 지는 금일자 신문의 머리 기사를 -분열된 의회(DIVIDED CONGRESS)가 대통령에게 대 이락 전쟁 수행 권한 부여- 라고 하고 NYT 지도 찬반 양론간의 득표 차이가 상원의 경우 5 표에 불과하고, 하원의 경우도 67 표로서, 부쉬 대통령의 대의회 설득 노력은 제한적 승리(LIMITED VICTORY)를 걷우었다는 요지로 보도함.

나. 즉, 당지 언론은 작일의 결의안 통과로 부쉬 행정부가 대이락 전쟁을 수행할수 있는 법적 요건은 구비한셈이지만, 전쟁 수행에 긴요한 -튼튼한 정치적기반(SOLID POLITICAL BASE)- 까지 확보한것으로 보기는 어렵다는 논조를 보이고 있음.

다. 특히, NYT PUBA - MEN PLANBATTLE HAS A MIND OF ITS OWN- 이라는 논평기사를 통해 일반론적인 관점에서 전쟁 결과의 불가측성에 대한 우려를 표명하고,WP 지도 -중동 지역 일기의 불순함, 미군과 다국적군간의 작전 지휘 체계 혼란, 이스라엘의 적극적 군사 개입 가능성-등으로 인해, 미측이 속전 속결 작전이예상외의 어려움을 겪을수 있다고 보도하는등 비교적 조심스런 태도를 취함.

2. 기타 관련 동향

가. 한편 전기 결의안 통과를 계기로, 미국내 반전론자들도 보다 더 적극적인 활동을 전개할 것으로 예상되고 있는바, 작일 당지에서 있었던 반전 데모에는 종교계 인사, 걸프 지역 주둔 미군 가족등을 중심으로 약 2,000 명이 참여한것으로 알려짐.

나. 그 밖에 당지 중동 전문가들은, 작 1.12 바그다드에 도착한 유엔 사무총장의 교섭 결과와 명 1.14 개최될 것으로 알려진 이락 국회 긴급 회기등이어떠한 방향으로

중아국	장관	차관	1차보	2차보	미주국	미주국	청와대	총리실
안기부								

PAGE 1 91.01.14 12:28

외신 2과 통제관 BT

0088

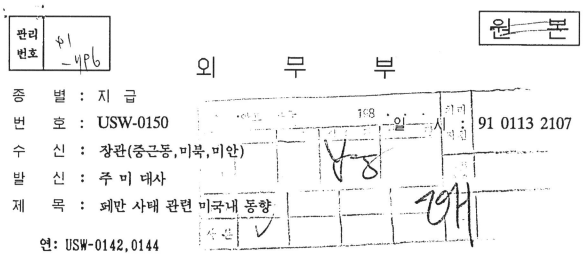

진행될지 등에 대해 관심을 모으고 있으며, 특히 금일 새벽 소련군에 의한 리투아니아인 시위 유혈진압이 미소간의 협조를 바탕으로 유지되어온 그간의 대이락 경제 봉쇄등 국제적 협력에 어떠한 영향을 미칠지에 대해서도많은 관심을 갖고 있는것으로 알려지고 있음.

3. 당관 관찰

가. 전기와같이, 미 언론이 작일의 결의안 통과에 대해 비교적 조심스런 평가를 내리고 있는것은 미 언론이 전통적으로 행정부의 독주를 가급적 견제하려는의도에도 기인하고 있는것으로 보이며, 또 한편으로는 무력 사용에 의해서라도금번 사태를 해결하겠다는 미국민의 확고한 의지를 훗세인에게 인식키기에는 표결 결과가 다소 미흡한 것으로 보는 여론도 있기 때문것으로 관찰됨.

나. 그러나 기 통과된 유엔 안보리의 대이락 무력 사용 허용 결의안과 연호미 의회 결의안으로 부쉬 행정부는 일단 대이락 공격을 위한 국제및 국내적으로 허가증을 공히 확보한 셈인바, 전기 유엔 사무총장의 이락 방문 결과및 불란서등에 의한 외교적 해결 노력 추이등을 보아 가면서 무력 사용 여부를 최종결정할것으로 보임.

다. 다만 대 이락 무력 공격시는 상술한 바와 같이 부쉬 행정부에 대한 국내외의 지지가 완벽하게 확고하지는 않은점을 감안 미측은 가능한한 단기간내에 전쟁의 승패를 가름짓기 위해 최대의 노력을 경주할 것으로 보임 (당지 언론에서도 전쟁의 기간이 승패에 직결될 것이라는 견해를 빈번히 보도 하고 있음)

라. 한편, 당지 언론은 리투아니아 사태의 악화로 인해, 부쉬 행정부가 역사의 진로를 결정지을 두개의 중대한 사태를 동시에 처리해야 하는 상황에 처하게 되었으며, 또 리투아니아 사태가 부쉬 행정부의 대 -페-만 사태 관련 정책 결정 과정 상의 중요 변수로 작용할수도 있다고 보도 하고 있는바, 관련 진전 사항계속 추보 예정임.

(대사 박동진-차관)

검 토 필 (1991 . 6 . 30 .)

91.12.31 까지

PAGE 2

0089

United States Information Service

Embassy of the United States of America
63, 1-ka, Ulchiro, Choong-ku
Seoul 100-191
Tel. 732-2601~18
Fax No. 774-6775

USIS

January 14, 1991

Dear Friends:

Given the importance of developments in the Middle East to all of us these days, we thought you might find of interest the enclosed text of an article by Representative Stephen Solarz, which appeared in the January 7-14 edition of The New Republic. While not a member of the Bush administration or even of the President's political party, Representative Solarz provides some excellent background and insights into U.S. policy in the Persian Gulf. We hope that you find it useful and interesting.

0090

BACKGROUNDER
배 경 설 명

Press Office
United States Information Service (USIS)
United States Embassy, Seoul, Korea

駐韓美國公報院 公報室
Tel. 732-2601 Ext. 4368, 4389

1991년 1월 14일

페르시아灣에 걸린 利害관계

스티븐 솔라즈
(美國 下院議員)

아이러니는 때로는 고통스러울 수도 있다. 나는 1966년에 이 나라 최초의 反戰(越南戰)議会議員 후보의 한 사람을 위한 선거운동 사무장으로서 나의 政治 생애를 시작했었다. 그로부터 4半世紀가 지난 오늘날 나는, 또 하나의 越南戰爭이 될 수도 있다고 많은 사람들이 믿고 있는 戰爭으로 이끌지도 모를 페르시아灣政策을 지지하고 있는 나 자신을 발견한다. 그러한 입장은 民主党 내에서는 차츰 変則的인 것으로 보인다는 것을 나는 알고 있다. 하지만 나는 越南 사태와의 유사성을 받아들일 수 없고, 또 그로해서 行政府의 페르시아灣 정책을 지지하지 말도록 설득당하지 않을 것이다.

越南에서는 미국의 절대적인 利害관계가 걸려있지 않았었다. 그러나 페르시아灣의 위기는 비단 미국의 근본적인 이익 뿐아니라, 미국의 필수적 価値觀에 대해서도 挑戰을 가한다. 인도차이나에서는 우리가 쏟은 피와 財貨의 代価가, 越南의 성공적인 방위로부터 얻을 수 있을 것으로 기대되었던 성과에 비해서 너무나도 컸었다. 페르시아灣에서는 미국의 介入의 잠재적 부담은, 쿠웨이트로부터의 이라크 철수를 요구하는 유엔決議案을 행동으로 옮기는 성공적인 노력이 가져올 혜택에 비하면 훨씬 적은 것이다. 越南戰爭은 여러 해 동안 질질 끌다가 미국의 패배로 끝났다. 페르시아灣에서의 전쟁이 피할 수 없는 것이라면, 이 전쟁은 數週日은 아니라도 數個月동안에 미국의 결정적인 승리로 끝날 것같다. 우리가 만약 과거를 기억하게 된다면, 다시 말해서 과거로부터 그릇된 교훈을 얻어낸다면, 그리하여 과거에 대한 기억으로해서 현재를 잘못 보게 된다면 때로는 과거의 잘못을 되풀이할 수밖에 없는 것이다.

미국은 분명히, 사담 후세인이 쿠웨이트를 침공하여 병탄하고나서도 무사하지는 못하도록 이를 막는데 절대로 중요한 이해관계를 가지고 있다. 이웃 나라를 흡수하는데 血眼이 되어 있는 이라크는 미국의 이해관계에 대한 심각한 경제적 위협이 되고있다. 化学무기, 生物学무기 그리고 마침내는 核무기로 무장하게 될 敵対的인 이라크는 미국의 安保에 대한 "분명하고, 현실적인 위험"을 나타낸다. 無法的인 이라크는 새롭고, 보다 평화로운 세계질서에 대한 우리의 희망에 직접적인 도전을 가하게 된다. 이러한 이유들 중 그 어느 하나만으로도 이 挑發받지 않은 잔인한 침략행위에 대한 미국의 굳건한 対應을 正當化시키기에 충분하다. 이 이유들을 합치면 쿠웨이트로부터의 이라크의 철수를 확실케 하고, 세계에서 가장 불안전하고 戰略的으로 중요한 지역들중의 하나에서의 보다 안정된 힘의 균형을 이룩하기 위해 우리와 제휴하고 있는 국가들과 힘을 합쳐, 해야 할 필요가 있는 일은 무슨 일이나 할 수 있는 강력한 論據가 된다.

0091

먼저 石油문제가 있다. 만약 사담 후세인이 쿠웨이트를 합병하는데 성공하게되면 그는 위협이나 침공으로 페르시아湾 전체의 石油 자원을 장악할 수 있는 입장에 서게 될 것이다. 그렇게 되면 그가, 오직 그만이, 알려진 世界石油 매장량의 半 정도의 価格 뿐아니라 生産 수준까지도 독단적으로 결정할 수 있게 될 것이다. 이는 단순히 注油所에서의 휘발유 가격의 문제 만이 아니다. 그것은 우리와 세계의 우리 盟邦들이 집을 덥히고, 工場을 돌리고, 우리의 經濟를 활발하게 유지하는데 필요한 필수적 에너지를 調達할 수 있느냐의 문제인 것이다.

미국은 페르시아湾 石油에 대한 우리의 依存度를 줄이게 될 종합적인 에너지 정책을 필요로 한다. 이는 1973년의 石油禁輸 때에도 명백히 드러났었고, 오늘날도 역시 명백하다. 그러나 페르시아湾 石油에 대한 우리의 依存度를 줄이지 못했던 일을 후회하고, 장차 그 依存度를 줄이기로 결심한다고해서 그것 만으로 현재 우리가 당면한 문제를 해결할 수는 없다. 우리가 이제는 石油를 수입할 필요가 없다해도 대부분의 다른 나라들은 페르시아湾 石油에 여전히 依存하게 될 것이다. 그리고 우리의 경제적 복지가 그들의 經濟的 복지와 연결되어 있는 만큼 우리는 이 필수불가결한 공급원의 단절이 가져올 결과로부터 초연할 수는 없는 것이다.

사담이 페르시아湾의 石油 매장량을 장악한다고 해도, 그는 자기의 邪惡한 목적을 위한 収入을 갖기 위해 石油를 팔고자 할 것이기 때문에 그가 미국의 이익에 대해 받아들일 수 없는 위협이 될 수는 없다고 주장한 사람도 있었다. 그러나 사담은 石油생산을 극적으로 줄일 수 있는 위치에 서게 될 것이고, 그렇게 되면 생산 감소로 가능해질 引上된 油価로 적절한 収入을 안전하게 유지하면서 餘他세계에 대한 상당한 견제수단을 행사할 수 있게 될 것이다. 따라서 사담과 같은 狂暴한 독재자가 세계의 經濟의 숨통을 쥘 수 있도록 내버려둔다는 것은 미국으로서는 생각조차 할 수 없는 일이다.

그러나 石油문제보다 훨씬 중요한 것은, 미국의 憲法上의 用語로, 사담이 "명백하고, 현실적인 위험"이라는 사실이다. 사담은 지난 10년 동안에 자기 나라를 두 번이나 전쟁으로 몰고갔던 인물이다. 처음은 1980년 이란과의 전쟁을 일으켰으며, 다음은 1990년 쿠웨이트를 침공했다. 억제할 수 없는 權力욕에 사로잡혀, 그리고 아랍民族을 이라크의 지배하에 통일할 것을 다짐하고 있는 바트党의 理念的 명령에 따라 사담은 中東 전체를 지배하려고 결심하고 있다. 물론 부시 大統領이 사담과 히틀러를 비슷한 사람으로 보는 것은 도가 지나치다 할 수 있다. 그러나 사담과 히틀러 사이에 근본적인 차이가 있다면 教訓的으로 비슷한 점도 있다. 히틀러와 마찬가지로 사담도 목적을 달성하기 위해서 필요한 모든 수단을 기꺼이 동원할, 무자비한 의지와 합쳐진, 억누를 수 없는 權力욕을 가지고 있다.

超强大國들, 유엔安保理事会 및 아랍聯盟의 단합된 반대에 맞서서도 무사할 경우 사담의, 자기는 無敵이라는 의식은 틀림없이 부풀어오를 것이며, 그리하여 征服과 병탄을 위한 보다 많은 싸움을 하기 위한 무대가 마련될 것이다. 뿐만 아니라 만약 現危機에서 사담이 이기게 될 경우 그는 마침내 미국 자체에 대해서 직접적인 위협을 가하게 될 것이다. 合理性을 잃은 인간이 가진 核무기의 그늘 아래에서 산다는 것은, 그 核무기가 우리의 核무기보다 훨씬 작은 것이라 할지라도 결코 받아들일 수 없다. 이라크는 어떤 합당한 防衛필요에 의해서도 正當化될 수 없는 각종 長거리 무기계획을 가차없이 추진해왔다. 核무기 계획 뿐아니라 이라크는 지금 大陸間彈道유도탄체제 계획도 추진하고 있다. 사담은 아마 앞으로 1년 이내에 核무기를 생산할 수 있는 위치에 있지 않을 것이나 5년 내지 10년이면 생산할 수 있을는지 모른다. 지금 우리가 그를

0092

막지 않으면 장차 그와 対決해야 할 상황이 틀림없이 올 것이다—그 때는 그는 섬찍할 정도로 훨씬 가공할 상대가 될 것이다.

페르시아湾 危機의 정치적 해결이라는 맥락에서 우리는 안정을 깨뜨리는 이라크의 대량파괴무기의 위협을 어떻게 다룰 수 있을 것인가? 戰爭을 하게 될 경우 이라크의 化学, 生物学 및 核무기 시설은 우선순위가 높은 표적이 될 것이고, 따라서 이 가공할 파괴력을 가진 무기들을 사용할 수 있는 그들의 능력은 앞으로 오랫동안 '절름발이'가 되고 말 것이기 때문에 아이러니칼하게도 이 무기들은 큰 문제가 되지 않을 것이다. 하지만 이 危機가 평화적으로 해결되면 사담이 가진 가공할 무기는 무사하게 남고, 核무기를 가지려는 그의 노력은 급속도로 진행될, 현실적인 위험이 있다. 그러한 결과는 막대한 희생을 치르고 얻는 승리가 될 것이다. 부시行政府는 지금까지는 이 문제에 마땅히 부여해야 할 우선순위를 부여하지 않고 있다.

우리는 그러한 무기를 가진 다른 나라들과 수십년 동안 함께 살아왔다고, 그러면서도 그런 무기들의 解体를 요구할 필요를 느끼지 않았다고 말하는 사람도 있을 것이다. 파키스탄, 印度, 브라질, 아르헨티나 또는 南아프리카도 있는데 왜 유독 이라크가 核무기를 갖는 것을 더 우려해야 하는가? 그 물음에 대한 대답인즉, 이들 나라들의 核무기 계획도 의당 우려해야 할 사항이지만 이들 어느 나라도 대량파괴 무기를 사용한 일이 없다는 사실이다. 이라크의 입장을 옹호하는 사람들은 한 걸음 나아가, 이라크는 核무기 확산금지조약의 가맹국이기 때문에 우리의 걱정은 거기에 해당되지 않는다고 주장해왔다. 그러나 이라크는 化学무기 사용금지조약의 가맹국이면서도 化学무기를 사용했었다. 條約에 관한 限 이라크는 믿을 수 없는 나라이다. 사담과 같은 능숙한 犯法者는 약속을 어기는 일을 그다지 괴로와하지 않을 것이다.

그럼에도, 다른 사람들은 制裁조치에 의해 단절되어 온 형태의 원조 없이는 이라크가 核武器를 개발할 수 없을 것이라고 시사해왔다. 이 주장은 몇몇 관점에서 그 논거가 타당하지 않다. 첫째, 이 주장은 제재 조치가 영원히 실시될 것으로 가정하고 있다. 둘째, 이는 우리가 파키스탄이 核武器 제조를 위한 部品을 획득하지 못하도록 막는데에 실패한 것이, 技術拒否戰略이 성공할 가능성이 없음을 보여준다는 사실을 무시하고 있다. 셋째, 이는 이미 이라크의 兵器廠에 저장되어 있는 化学무기와 生物学的 藥劑를 도외시하고 있다. 넷째, 비록 외부의 원조가 없다고 할지라도, 이라크가 앞으로 10년 안에 몇 개의 核무기를 제조하기에 충분한 核分裂 물질을, 현재 가동할 수 있는 原子爐와 파괴된 오시라크 원자로로부터 이미 획득했다는 데는 의심의 여지가 없다. 이라크의 核계획은 경제적 禁輸조치에 의해 이를 멈추게 할 수 없을 정도로 크게 진척되어 있는 것이다.

만약 이스라엘이 1981년 오시라크 원자로를 공격하지 않았더라면, 이라크가 십중팔구 이미 核무기를 보유했을 것이다. 당시 이스라엘의 공격을 비판했던 사람들 중 많은 사람들이 이스라엘이 매우 단호하게 행동한 것이 그 지역 전체를 위해 얼마나 다행한 일이었던가를 이제는 인식하고 있다. 만약 이스라엘이 겁많은 사람들의 충고를 따랐더라면, 이라크가 対이란戰에서 아마도 核무기를 사용했을 것이다. 노골적으로 말해서, 이라크의 大量파괴 무기들이 철거되거나 파괴되지 않는 限, 페르시아湾 地域에는 장기적 安定의 전망이 없다. 유일한 문제는 이를 위한 수단의 하나를 선택하는 일이다.

만약 미국과 그 聯合同伴國들이 이라크의 대량학살무기 철거가 危機의 外交的 해결책의 필수적 구성 요소임을 명백히 한다면, 사담이 이들 武器를 철거하도록 설득될 수 있다는 것은 있을법한 일이다. 國際社会는, 바그다드政權이 이들 武器를 철거하는

0093

데에 동의할 때까지는, 비록 이라크가 쿠웨이트로부터 철수하고 각종 유엔決議의 기타 조건들에 순응한다할지라도, 制裁조치를 계속 시행·유지하겠다는 決意를 명시해야 할 것이다. 그래도 우리는 이 戰略이 실패할지도 모른다는 점을 인식해야만 하는데 —실패할 경우 미국은 이들 무기의 생산 중심 시설들과 이들 무기의 장거리 운반체제를 다같이 제거하기 위해 힘을 행사하는 선택권을 留保해야만 한다. 이 정책은 몇몇 아랍國家들을 포함하는 우리의 많은 同伴國들의 강력한 지지를 받을 것이다. 이 지역을 최근에 두 번 방문하고나서 나는 이 지역 사람들이 이라크의 대량파괴 무기를 크게 두려워하고 있으며, 이 非在來式 위협을 무슨 수단을 써서라도 제거해야하는 필요성을 인식하고 있다는 사실에 감명받았다.

사담의 야심을 좌절시켜야 하는 셋째 이유는, 우리가 새로운 世界秩序의 수립을 희망하고 있다는 사실에 있다. 우리가 冷戰後의 첫 위기를 어떻게 해결하는가는, 世界에 심대한 역사적 결과를 안겨줄 것이다. 이 세계가, 국가간의 관계가 法의 支配에 의해 다스려지는 세계로 될 것인가, 그렇지 않으면 (충분한 통제를 위한 유일한 수단으로서의 강력한 政府를 창도한 英國 哲学者 토머스) 홉즈式 세계로 될 것인가? 强者가 계속해서 弱者를 지배하는 세계로 될 것인가, 아니면 正義의 존중이 힘의 現実을 극복할 것인가? 日本이 滿洲를 침공했을 때, 이탈리아가 아비시니아를 침공했을 때, 또 히틀러가 라인江 (西쪽) 지방을 점령했을 때, 만약 세계가 집단행동으로 이에 대응했더라면, 우리는 역사상 최악의 공포의 일부를 겪지 않았을 수도 있었을 것이다. 만약 우리가 협조적 국제행동을 통해, 이라크軍隊의 철수와 쿠웨이트의 合法政府의 회복을 확실히 실현시키려는 노력에 성공한다면, 우리는 훨씬 더 평화로운 앞날의 세계를 위한 강력한 先例를 창조한 것이 될 것이다. 그러나 만약 사담이 이기게 된다면, 세계는 도처에서 暴君들에게 애착을 갖게 되어, 계속 옛날의 규칙들이 적용되고, 침략이 득을 볼 것이다.

쿠웨이트는 우리 눈앞에서 침략자에게 삼켜지고 있다. 인큐베이터(早産児 保育器)를 바그다드의 병원으로 끌고가기 위해, 갓 태어난 아기들이 인큐베이터로부터 끌어내려져, 죽도록 방치되고 있다. 수천명의 쿠웨이트人들이 살해되었다. 임신한 여인들이 총검에 찔렸다. 많은 남자들의 眼球가 담뱃불로 지져졌다. 쿠웨이트人들이 학살당하거나 추방당하고 있으며, 이 나라의 物質的 下部構造가 해체당하거나 파괴당하고 있기 때문에, 쿠웨이트는 몇 달 안가서 존재하지 않게 될 것이다. 미국과 國際社会가 이전에 있었던 침략행위들에 대응하지 못했던 사실이, 이같은 침략의 죄를 범한 자에게 용감히 맞서지 않는 이유가 되지는 못한다. 쿠웨이트를 휩쓴 모진 운명은 또한 쿠웨이트를 수호하기 위해 궐기한 나라들의 聯合을 가져와, 이라크가 자신이 저지른 약탈에 대한 완전한 배상금을 지불하지 않으면 안되도록 만들 것이다. 바그다드政權의 침공은 또한 역사상 최대의 은행강도 사건이었는데, 만약 이라크가 배상금을 지불하도록 강요당하지 않는다면, 이 강탈은 사담에게는 멋진 하루의 일거리가 될 것이다.

이 위기는, 國際社会가 기존하는 국경의 神聖性과, 나라들이 약한 그들의 隣接國들을 침공하고 合併하도록 허용되어서는 안된다는 원칙을 받드는 世界秩序를 창조하기 위한 드문 그리고 어쩌면 現代의 여명 이래 처음인 기회를 제공한다. 유엔安全保障理事会에서의 압도적인 票들은, 적어도 이같은 목표에 찬성하는 국제적 의견 일치가 있다는 것을 증명해 보인다. 이 압도적 票들은 또한, 이 世界機構가 평화의 保全을 위해 列强들에 의해 사용될 수 있으리라는, 프랭클린 루스벨트와 기타의 유엔 創設者들의 꿈이 실현되고 있음을 시사해 준다.

0094

우리는 이들 목표를, 우리의 권익과 일치하고, 우리의 가치관과 양립하는 방식으로 어떻게 달성할 것인가? 미국 下院과 上院의 일련의 청문회에 의해 자극받아, 전국에 걸쳐 토론이 이미 벌어졌다. 대체로 말해서, 쿠웨이트로부터의 이라크軍隊 철수, 쿠웨이트의 合法政府의 회복, 이 침략의 희생자들에 대한 배상금 지불, 그리고 이 지역내의 보다 안정된 힘의 均衡 수립 등이 성취될 수 있는 3개 방안이 있는 것같다.

첫째는 계속된, 어쩌면 오래 지속되는 제재 조치의 적용을 통한 방안이다. 美國 合同參謀本部議長이었던 윌리엄 크로우提督과 데이비드 존슨將軍 같은 사람들은 우리는 制裁조치를 적극 시도해봐야 한다고 주장해 왔다. 만약 우리가 6개월, 12개월 또는 18개월을 앞으로 더 기다린다면, 제재 조치는 이라크를 쿠웨이트로부터 철수하지 않을 수 없게 만들 가능성이 있다고 그들은 주장한다. "왜 서두르는가?"라고 뉴욕 타임스紙 社說은 묻고 있다. 좀더 오래 기다림으로써 우리는 戰爭을 하지 않고서도 우리의 목표를 달성할 수 있다고 大統領의 정책을 비판하는 사람들은 주장한다.

만약 제재조치가 이라크를 철수하게 만들 그 어떤 합당한 가능성이 있다면, 제재조치가 실효를 거두도록 더 많은 시간을 이에 부여하는 것이 우리 軍隊를 전쟁에 투입하는 것보다 물론 더 좋다. 무력 충돌이 빚어내는 人命 손실을 편안한 마음으로 바라보는 사람은 아무도 없다. "徐行"정책의 지지자들은 제재조치가 국제사회로부터 전례없는 정도의 지지를 받아왔다는 점을 올바로 지적했다. 이라크의 外貨稼得의 90%를 차지했던 이라크의 모든 石油輸出이 단절되었고, 이라크는 자신의 국제적 고립의 경제적 결과를 느끼기 시작하고 있음이 분명하다. 이라크의 공장들은 폐쇄되었다. 이라크의 生產能力은 손상되었다.

하지만 제재조치의 성공을 樂觀視하기는 어렵다. 國際經濟研究所가 실시한, 제재조치가 이라크에 미치는 있음직한 영향에 관한 세부적 분석에 따르면, 禁輸조치는 이라크의 국민총생산(GNP)의 약 40%를 감소시킬 것이다. 이는 틀림없이 이라크의 經濟에 대한 매우 심각한 타격이 될 것이다. 그러나 이로 인해 이라크가 쿠웨이트로부터 철수하는 결과가 빚어질 것인지의 여부는 또다른 문제이다. 上院軍事委員会에서의 증언을 통해 "徐行"戰略에 정치적 타당성을 부여했던 크로우提督조차도, 제재조치의 효능에 대한 그의 판단은 "전적으로 추측적인" 것이라고 말한 바 있다.

이라크는 비옥한 나라이고, 국민에게 식량을 공급할 수 있을 것이다. 그러나 이란, 요르단, 터키 및 시리아와의 국경을 통한 식품과 기타 필수품목의 密輸入이 이미 일어나고 있으며, 이라크는 경제적 고통이 심화됨에 따라 이에 조절해나갈 수 있을 것이다. 만약 이 분석이 정확하다면 이라크의 人口 1人當 所得은 연간 약 2,600 달러에서 1,600 달러로 감소될 것이다. 하지만, 이처럼 40%가 감소되더라도, 이라크의 人口 1人當 所得은 계속해서, 예를 들면 이집트의 2배가 넘는, 그리고 前線國家들의 하나인 터키보다 상당히 많은 액수를 유지할 것이다. 어찌되었든, 비록 이라크 국민들은 분량과 영양이 충분치 못한 식사를 할 수밖에 없을지라도 사담과 그의 軍隊는 충분한 식량을 갖게 될 것이 확실하다. 이 사람은 100만의 이라크人 死傷者가 생겼음에도 불구하고 対이란戰爭을 계속해나가려 했던 사람이다. 그가 쿠웨이트로부터 선뜻 撤収하리라고는 믿기 어렵다. 왜냐하면 그렇게 되면 이라크 국민들이 칼로리 섭취량을 낮추거나, 생활 수준의 저하를 받아들이지 않을 수 없기 때문이다.

軍事面에서, 制裁가 효과가 있을 것임은 의심할나위가 없다. 윌리엄 웹스터 CIA 局長이 의회에서 말했듯이, 국제적인 경제적 보이콧은 90일 내에 이라크 空軍에게 격심한 타격을 주게되고, 기타 이라크軍에게는 9개월 내지 12개월의 기간에 걸쳐서 그 質

0095

이 떨어지게 만들 것같다. 그렇다 할지라도, 軍事전문가들 간의 일치된 견해인즉, 만 1년 동안의 制裁조치 후에도 쿠웨이트駐屯 이라크軍의 防衛능력은 그리 크게 줄어들지 않을 것이라는 것이다. 미국과 그리고 미국과 손잡은 국가들이 가지고 있는 막강한 空軍力 優位를 감안해서, 사담은 이라크空軍이 없는 것으로 생각하고 있다고 대부분의 분석가들은 믿고 있다. 그의 힘의 핵심을 이루는 軍事力의 構成要素들, 즉 쿠웨이트에 이미 배치되어 있는 步兵隊, 砲兵隊, 戰車隊, 裝甲車隊 등은 분명히 연장된 禁輸조치의 영향을 가장 적게 받는 것들일 것이다. 더욱이 長期化된 制裁조치들은 이라크에게 참호를 파서 자기들의 防衛陣을 구축하고, 이라크에서 쿠웨이트에 이르기까지의 도로와 送水管들을 보다 많이 건설할 수 있는 시간을 줌으로써, 이라크軍에 대한 공격으로 해서 발생될 美國측 人命被害를 보다 많아지게 만들 것이다.

武力 사용 없는 制裁조치로 이라크 측의 쿠웨이트 撤收를 강요하기에 충분할 것이라고 주장하는 사람들은 禁輸조치가 어떻게 이러한 결과를 낳게 될 것인가를 결코 명백히 설명한 적이 없다. 그들은 制裁조치의 분명한 經濟的 영향과 쿠웨이트로부터 철수하기로 하는 정치적 결정 간의 관계를 확립하지 못했다. 制裁조치가 이라크의 쿠웨이트로부터의 철수와 아울러 페르시아湾 위기를 만족스럽게 끝내기 위해 필요한 기타 讓步사항을 만들어낼 수 있는 방법은 두 가지 뿐인 것같다. 즉, 사담이 쿠웨이트로부터 철수하기로 결정하게 되든가, 아니면 그의 휘하의 軍部가 그를 打倒하고, 이러한 결정(쿠웨이트로부터의 철수)을 하게 될 지도자(또는 徒党)가 그를 대신하게 되든가이다.

그러나 制裁조치가 앞으로 6개월 내지 12개월, 아니면 그보다 더 장기간 계속된다고 假定해 볼 때, 사담이 쿠웨이트로부터 기꺼이 철수하려고 들 가능성은 어떠한가? 결국, 그는 再選을 위한 出馬나, 시끄러운 議会나, 비판적인 言論이나, 여론조사에서의 下降一路의 評點 등을 걱정할 필요가 없다. 그리고 사담이 자기의 힘의 極大化보다도 自國民의 安寧에 더 관심을 가지고 있다고 진지하게 믿을 수 있는 사람은 아무도 없다. 사담은 感傷的인 인간이 아니다. 사담은 聯合세력이 무너지고, 制裁조치들이 사그러지기 시작하는 것은 時間문제라고 계산하고 있는 것같다. 만약 그가 걱정해야 할 일이 계속적인 制裁조치 뿐이라면, 그가 그것을 견뎌낼 수 있을 것같은 가능성은 훨씬 더 많다.

이로 해서 이라크軍部에 의한 사담 打倒 가능성 만이 남는다. 이라크 軍部内에는 사담이 자기들을 사막의 모래 언덕들로 이끌어, 재난으로 몰고 가고 있음을 알고 있어 그를 정말 제거하고 싶어하는 장교들이 많이 있음에 틀림없다. 그러나 사담은 그의 국민들 사이에서 뿐만 아니라 그의 軍部内에서의 불만의 어떠한 움직임도 교묘히 질식시켜 왔다. 이라크軍은 提報者들 투성이이며, 사담은 자기에게 謀反하고 있는 것으로 의심되는 者에게는 누구를 막론하고 무자비한 조치를 할 것이라고 거듭 설명해왔다. 그의 과대망상증에 저항하여 말썽을 빚는 사람들은 살아 남지 못한다.

그러므로 우리가 制裁조치가 효과를 나타내도록 시간 여유를 더 주고 기다린다면, 制裁조치가 成功하기보다는 聯合세력이 붕괴할 展望이 더 클 것같다. 부시大統領이 능란한 外交솜씨로 모아놓은 聯合세력은 다루기 힘들고, 깨지기 쉬운 집단이다. 그 중에서 특히 아랍圈 국가들은 우리와는 다른 利害관계를 가지고 있다. 금년(1990년)가을의 예루살렘의 마운트寺院 사건은 세계의 이 지역의 可燃 가능성에 대한 명백한 경고였다. 정치적인 사건들의 文化的 反響은 聯合세력을 쉽사리 깨뜨릴 수 있다. 그리고

0096

분명히 그것이야 말로 인간과 사건들을 마키아벨리式으로 조종하는 책모가인 사담 후세인이 달성해보려고 드는 일이다.

聯合세력에 대한 압력은 해외로부터만 오지는 않을 것이다. 부시 대통령이 長期化된 制裁조치를 선택했음이 일단 명백하게 되면, 우리가 사우디 아라비아로 파견한 군대의 대부분을 철수시키기 시작하라는 요구가 강력히 대두될 것이다. 우리의 유일의 目的이 사우디 아라비아의 수호에 있다면, 40만명의 兵士들은 필요하지 않다. 그리고 이러한 配置로 해서 생기는 兵站요구를 감안해 본다면, 사우디 아라비아에서의 이러한 대규모의 군대 주둔을 무기한으로 유지시키기는 매우 힘들 것이다. 일단 우리가 페르시아灣 지역으로부터 군대를 철수시키기 시작하면, 대부분이 制裁조치 만으로는 사담을 쿠웨이트로부터 철수하게 만들 수 없다고 믿고 있는 우리 聯合세력 국가들은 사담이 우세하게 되는 것은 단지 시간 문제라고 斷定할 것같다. 그 時點에 이르면 그들은 새로 전개될 地域 現實을 예상하고서 그들 자신의 실속만을 챙기기 시작할 것이다.

설사 制裁조치의 효과가 나타나기를 우리가 기다리는 동안, 聯合세력 국가들이 결속한다 할지라도 예컨대, 지금부터 1년이나 2년이 지난 후 우리가 그것이 사담에게 철수하도록 유도하기에 충분하지 않았다고 斷定할 때쯤해서 이미 우리는 武力을 사용할 意志를 잃게 될 가능성이 크다. 부시 대통령에게, 制裁조치가 효과를 나타낼 수 있는 시간 여유를 더 주도록 촉구해 온 일부 人士들은 制裁조치가 실패할 경우에는 武力 使用을 지지할 용의가 있다고 말해왔지만, 制裁조치가 이라크의 쿠웨이트 철수를 달성시키지 못할 경우에도 기다리기를 찬성하는 대다수의 人士들은 여전히 対이라크戰에 반대할 것이다. 그리고 制裁조치가 줄어들게 되고, 武力使用이 이제 더 이상 정치적으로 存続가능한 선택안이 되지 않게 되면, 사담은 그의 탄탄대로를 걸어서 승리로 이르게 될 것이다. 그렇다면, "徐行"戰略은 사담을 반대하여 모여든 聯合세력의 手中으로 사담을 넘기는 것보다 사담 후세인에게 말려들어갈 가능성이 더 크다.

國家들 사이에서 外交的으로 해결될 수 없는 견해 차이란 없다고 믿고 있는 人士들에게는 언제나 協商에 의한 해결의 희망이 있다. 그러나 우리는 우리 자신이 좋아하는 規範에서 일반적 결론을 導出해서는 안된다. 현재까지 사담은 그가 이라크의 19번째州라고 부르는 쿠웨이트로부터 완전히 그리고 무조건 철수할 用意를 나타내는 아무런 징후도 보이지 않았다. 케야르 유엔事務總長과 쿠르트 발트하임, 요르단의 후세인王, 아라파트 팔레스타인解放機構議長, 소련의 예프게니 프리마코프, 빌리 브란트, 나까소네야스히로 前日本首相, 무하마드 알리, 그리고 제시 잭슨牧師 등을 비롯한 각종 國際的인 순회 설교자들이 모두 바그다드에 쇄도했다가 (사담이 이 人質들이 공격에 대한 방패用으로 더 이상 쓸모가 없다는 결론을 내렸을 경우에 어쨌든 석방되었을 약간의 人質들을 제외하고는) 그들의 노력에 대한 아무런 代価도 얻지 못하고 되돌아왔었다. 나는 제임스 베이커國務長官이 설사 바그다드를 방문한다 할지라도 양보를 많이 얻어내고서 미국으로 돌아올 것이라고는 생각하기 어렵다.

더 정곡을 찔러서 말하자면, 정확히 協商해야 할 점은 무엇인가? 일부 人士들은 우리가 이라크측의 쿠웨이트 철수의 代価로, 페르시아灣과 그리고 이라크 國境 남쪽의 루마일라 油田들에 대한 사담의 무제한한 接近을 가로막고 있는 쿠웨이트領의 두 섬(島)인 부비얀島 및 와르바島를 제공하라고 示唆해왔다. 그러나 쿠웨이트, 사우디 아라비아, 아랍聯盟의 대다수 국가들, 유엔安全保障理事会, 그리고 부시行政府는 모두 그것이 침략행위에 대한 보상이 될 뿐만 아니라 추가적인 강탈행위를 위한 무대를 만들어 줄 것이라는 이유로 이 아이디어를 거부했다.

0097

사담 자신은 이라크 측의 쿠웨이트 철수 문제를 이스라엘 측의 요단江 西岸 및 가자 地區로부터의 철수나, 아니면 적어도 팔레스타인 문제를 해결하기 위한 國際会議의 개최에 연결시키려고 시도해왔다. 이것이 그에게 반대하여 모인 나라들 사이에 不和의 씨를 뿌리려는 시도임은 분명하다. 이 두 가지 문제들은 전혀 別個의 문제들이다. 이스라엘은 1967년 아랍國家들의 聯合공격을 받은 후에야 그 領土를 차지하게 되었던 것인데 반하여, 1990년의 이라크의 쿠웨이트 침공은 아무런 도발도 받지 않은 침략행위였다. 사담은 팔레스타인 사람들을 돕기 위해서가 아니라 자기 자신의 힘을 극대화하기 위해서 쿠웨이트를 침공했다. 그는 팔레스타인 사람들의 困境이나, 아니면 어느 다른 사람의 困境을 생각하고서 움직인 것이 아니었다. 그는 단지 그것을 이용하고 있을 뿐이다. 그런데 팔레스타인 사람들은 그들 자신을 이용하는 행위를 도와줌으로써 행복한 것같다.

逆說的인 일로, 이 危機를 평화적으로 해결할 진정한 가능성이 존재한다면, 그것은 侵略에 대한 보상을 해주는 양보로 이르는 協商에 있지 않고, 사담이 유엔安保理決議의 조건을 준수하지 않을 경우, 우리가 開戰할 태세가 되어 있다는 사실을 그에게 확신시키는 데에 있다. 나는 우리가 그의 최근의 人質 석방 배후에 있는 그의 큰 野心을 필요하다면 武力에 의해서라도 꺾을 것을 진지하게 생각하고 있음을 그가 차츰 깨닫기 시작하고 있지나 않았는가 하고 생각한다. 그런데 분명히 그것은 아니었다. 왜냐하면 그는 갑자기 축제 기분으로 가득차 있었기 때문이다.

그러나 人質들이 그들의 가족들과 再結合하는 것을 기뻐하는 나머지, 이라크가 미국의 절대로 중요한 國益에 아직도 가하고 있는 위협을 잊어서는 안된다. 사담이 쿠웨이트 駐屯과 죽음 아니면, 쿠웨이트 철수와 살기 간의 兩者擇一을 하지 않을 수 없다는 것을 마침내 설득당할 때까지는, 그에게 쿠웨이트 철수를 종용할 수 있는 진정한 가망은 없을 것이다. 그러나 이러한 최후통첩이 그에게 전달된다면—武力使用을 승인하고 있는 유엔安保理 決議案에 그것이 분명히 함축되어 있기 때문에—우리는 그가 철수를 거부할 경우 武力을 사용할 태세를 갖추어야 한다.

그러면 이는 위기종결의 세번째 길로 이어지게 된다. 무력의 사용은 물론 심대한 정치적, 도덕적 그리고 헌법상의 문제들을 제기한다. 전쟁은 의심할나위 없이 많은 사상자들을 낼 것이고—우리는 局部공격에 따르는 개념의 자기幻想에 빠져서는 안되겠지만—이런 전쟁에 뒤이어 어떤 결과가 일어날지 아무도 확신을 가지고 말할 수 없는 것이다. 무력은 최종적인 수단이어야 한다. 그러나 마지막 수단이 때로는 필요한 수단이 될 때도 있다. 마지막 수단이라해서 결코 써서는 안되는 수단이라는 뜻은 아니다.

군대의 무력사용에 반대하는 일부 사람들은 전쟁이 中東에서의 불안정성과 反美주의를 증가시킬 것이라고 주장해오고 있다. 이러한 분석에는 어느 정도의 진실이 담겨 있다. 그렇기는 하나 연합세력에 대한 사담 후세인의 평화時의 승리는 연합세력이 戰時를 통해 사담 후세인에게 승리하는 것 이상으로 그 지역의 안정에 대해 보다 큰 위협을 가하게 됨을 틀림없이 뜻하게 될 것이다. 아랍세력의 急進化에 가장 물들기 쉬울 것으로 생각되는 中東국가들이 바로 우리를 가장 강력하게 지지하고 있는 국가들이라는 사실을 想起하는 것이 중요하다. 왜냐하면 이들 국가의 지도자들은 사담 후세인을 억제하지 않고 내버려둘 경우의 결과에 대해 이야기를 해줄 필요가 없을 것이기 때문이다.

물론 미국의 무기들이 이라크의 兵士들에게 겨누어져 사용될 경우 아랍 세계에서 미국에 대한 敵対感이 어느 정도 표출될 것이다. 그러나 아랍의 다른 국가들이 이라크에 반대하는 전쟁에서 우리와 나란히 싸우고 있다는 것으로 하여, 특히 우리의 의도가 이

0098

라크의 점령에 있는 것이 아니라 쿠웨이트의 解放에 있다는 것이 천명된다면, 이러한 감정 표출은 어느 정도까지는 확실히 相殺될 것이다. 최근의 역사는 중동에서 美軍이 실력을 행사한다해도 이 때문에 이 지역이 미국으로부터 물러서지는 않을 것이라는 것을 보여주고 있다. 몇 년 전에 미국 군인들에 대한 테러공격에 가담했다하여 미국이 가다피에 징벌을 가하려 할 경우 대규모의 反美시위가 일어날 수 있는 가능성에 관해 우리는 경고를 받은 바 있으나, 1986년 우리가 리비아에 대한 공중공격을 가했을 때 아랍세계에서는 이렇다 할 부정적인 반응이 없었으며, 오히려 미국에 대한 존경심이 증가된 결과를 가져왔던 것처럼 보인다.

전쟁에 따르는 예기치 못한 결과에 대해 걱정하고 있는 사람들은 비교적 단기간의 결정적인 전투에서조차 일어날 수 있는 사상자들에 대해 그들의 관심을 집중시키고 있다. 나는 미국인들의 생명에 대한 配慮에 있어서는 어느 누구에게도 뒤지지 않을 것이나, 우리가 어떠한 사상자들의 희생을 치르든간에, 사담 후세인이 그가 현재 보유하고 있는 화학 및 생물학 무기에 核무기를 추가하게 될 때까지 우리가 결정적인 시기를 연장하는 경우에 우리가 입게 될 사상자들의 규모보다는 훨씬 적을 것이라는 엄연한 사실을 우리는 直視해야 한다. 사담에게 核전쟁의 수단을 강력히 거부한다는 것은 그 자체가 미국인들의 생명에 대한 배려를 표명하는 것이다. 또한 설사 페르시아湾에서의 미군의 대규모 주둔 유지 때문에 財政的 및 정치적 우려가 따르게 된다해도 우리는 쿠웨이트를 解放시키는 과정에서 사담이 보유하고 있는 대량파괴의 군사장비나 무기들의 대부분을 파괴하는 경우보다도, 우리가 사담이나 그의 군대의 쿠웨이트 잔류를 허용하게 되는 경우에 이 지역에 보다 큰 규모의 抑止軍을 주둔시키지 않을 수 없게 될 것이다.

어떤 사람들은 우리가 사담을 쿠웨이트로부터 몰아내지 못한다 하더라도 우리는 그의 팽창주의적인 경향을 봉쇄하고, 페르시아湾에 미군을 영구히 주둔시킴으로써 그 지역의 남은 부분을 그의 약탈적인 야욕으로부터 절연시킬 수 있다고 말하고 있다. 그들은 우리가 40년 동안 소련이나 북한을 봉쇄했는데, 中東에서 이 봉쇄정책이 성공하지 못할 이유가 없는 것이 아닌가라고 말한다. 이런 論者들은 中東의 현실에 관해서는 극단적인 낙관론자들이라고 말하지 않을 수 없다. 유럽이나 韓半島에서는 미군의 존재가, 우리가 수호하려던 국가들의 안정에 기여했다. 아랍 세계에서는 많은 미군의 장기적인 주둔은 거의 틀림없이 안정을 깨뜨리는 요소가 될 것이다.

더욱이 세계에서 가장 보수적인 回敎사회인 사우디아라비아가 어떤 특정 기간 동안 自國에서의 상당 규모의 외국군대 유지를 허용할 것인지도 의심스럽다. 미국이 中東에서 미군을 유지한다면 우리가 수호하려고 나섰던 모든 정권의 몰락에 本意아니게나마 기여하게 되는 결과를 빚게 된다는 사우디 측의 주장은 옳은 말이다. 우리가 쿠웨이트로부터 이라크를 몰아내기 위해 40만의 미군을 사우디 아라비아에 파견했고, 그리고나서 이라크에 의한 쿠웨이트 합병을 기정사실로서 받아들이게 된다면 사우디는 그들을 수호하겠다는 우리의 의지를 그다지 신임하지 않게 될 것이고, 이라크에 대한 主從관계를 통해 그들의 安保를 찾으려는 가능성이 더 많아질 것이다. 우리가 유럽의 핀란드化에 저항했던 것처럼 우리는 中東의 사담化에 저항해야 한다.

만일 부시 대통령이, 봉쇄의 제재조치가 성공할 것같지 않고, 수락될 만한 정치적 해결의 현실적인 전망이 전혀 없으며, 우리에게 무력사용 이외의 다른 대안이 없다는 결론을 내린다면, 그로서는 一方的인 방법에 의해서보다도 多辺的인 방법으로 전쟁에 임하는 것이 필수적인 일일 것이다. 쿠웨이트의 解放과 이라크의 위협 제거는 미국의

0099

책임만은 아니다. 연합세력에 참여하고 있는 아랍 국가나 유럽 국가들도—사실 그들 가운데 일부는 우리보다도 더 많은—책임을 같이 나누어 지니고 있다. 범죄적인 국가로부터 그들의 침략행위에 따르는 戰利品을 빼앗으려는 국제적인 방위隊의 隊長이 되는 일과, 미국이 세계의 警察의 역할을 떠맡으려 나서는 것과는 서로 별개의 일이다. 前者는 미국국민이 이해하고 받아들일 수 있는 과업이나, 後者는 미국국민이 추구하지 않으려는 역할이다.

그러나 일단 전쟁이 일어난다면, 우리는 혼자가 아닐 것이다. (아마도 시리아를 예외로 하고) 이 연합세력에 참여하고 있는 우리의 아랍 提携國들은 일단유사시에는 우리와 함께 전쟁에 임할 충분한 태세를 갖추고 있다. 영국도 무력사용의 용의에 있어서는 강력하고, 한때 일방적인 군축을 지지했던 勞動党 당수 닐 킨노크까지도 사담이 쿠웨이트로부터의 철수를 거부할 경우 무력사용에 찬성한다고 발언한 바 있다. 프랑스의 미테랑 대통령은 연합세력이 전쟁에 임한다면 프랑스는 함께 참전하겠다고 시사하고 있다. 페르시아灣에 배치되어 있는 兵力의 과반수가 미군인 것은 사실이지만 다른 나라들도 상당한 기여를 하고 있다. 연말(1990년)까지 영국과 이집트 및 시리아는 사우디아라비아에 있는 그들의 병력을 倍加시킬 것이고, 전투에 투입될 수 있는 외국군의 총병력은 22만 5천명이 될 것이다. 28개국으로부터 온 兵力은 연합세력에 正統性을 부여할 뿐아니라, 군사력의 상당한 증가를 보증해주는 것이다.

우리는 연합세력에 참여한 우리의 제휴국들이 앞으로 더 많은 부담을 지게 되기를 바라게 될 것인가. 물론이다. 그러나 다른 나라들이 제공한 군사적 기여도가 상당히 증가했는데도 연합세력 내의 유럽이나 아랍 국가들의 노력에 대해 비판적인 거의 모든 사람들은 그래도 미국정책에 대한 반대를 계속할 것이다. 어떻든 사담에 의한 쿠웨이트의 합병을 白紙化시키는 것이 우리의 이익이라면, 우리가 받을 수 있을 지원을 다른 나라들로부터 받지 못했다는 이유만으로 우리의 이익에 反하는 행동을 취하기보다는 이 목적의 성취를 위해 요구되는 어떤 일이라도 할 수 있는 준비를 우리는 갖추어야 할 것이다. 무력 사용에 관한 결정은 전략적인 필요성에 따라야지 計算을 위한 公式에 따를 것은 아니다.

부시 대통령이 무력사용의 결정을 내릴 경우, 그로서는 우리의 연합세력 제휴국들뿐 아니라 議会의 지원을 받는 것이 중요한 일일 것이다. 한 국가로서, 전쟁에 돌입함으로써 그 나라 국민의 희생을 각오하는 것만큼의 중대한 결정도 없을 것이다. 대통령으로서, 議会의 同意 없이(이라크에 의한 先制공격처럼 不意의 挑發이 없는 경우) 自國군대를 전투에 투입하게 되는 일이 있다면, 이는 그로서는 헌법상으로나 정치적으로 심각한 실책이 될 것이다. 대통령이 議会의 지지를 얻어야 하는 또하나의 이유가 있다. 우리가 전쟁을 하게 되고, 현재의 짐작으로는 신속하고 결정적인 승리를 거두게 되는 경우, 대통령이 議会의 승인을 얻으려 하지 않았다는 사실은 역사가들이나 컬럼 집필자들 간의 논쟁의 주제는 될 수 있을지 모르나, 議会나 또는 미국국민과의 대통령의 관계에 크게 손상을 줄 것같지는 않다. 그러나 전쟁이란 예측을 불허하는 것이다. 이런 여러 상황 속에서 사상자들의 數가 늘어나기 시작할 때 대통령이 敵対행위에 돌입하기 전에 議会의 동의를 얻는데 실패한다면 그는 전쟁에 대한 지지를 지속시킬 수 있는 능력에 있어 심각한 타격을 입게 될 것이다.

半世紀 전 히틀러가 폴란드에 침공했을 때 영국 下院은 영국의 대응책을 논의하기 위해 모였었다. 네빌 쳄벌렌이 정부정책을 머뭇거리며 변호하고 난 후 野党의 한 議員

0100

이 일어서서 "勞動党을 대표해서 발언하자면..."이라는 서두로 발언하려하자 즉각 議席의 뒷자리에서 "영국을 대표해서... "라는 고함소리가 터져나왔다. 지금이야말로 이 忠告의 말을 想起할 때이다. 페르시아灣의 위기는 민주당의 문제도 아니고, 공화당의 문제도 아니다. 이는 바로 미국의 문제이다.

전쟁돌입의 결정은 어떤 경우에라도 派党的인 고려에서 이루어져서는 안된다. 민주당은 무력사용에 대한 고려조차도 이를 反射的으로 거부하는데 따르는 결과를 熟考해야 한다. 민주당은 미국 자체에 대한 직접적인 공격 이외의 거의 어떤 상황하에서도 무력을 사용하기를 절대적으로, 그리고 감정적으로도 원치 않고 있다는 일반대중 간의 인식 때문에 너무나 많은 전국선거에서 패배를 맛보아왔다. 침략이라는 사실이 의심할 나위가 없고, 국제사회가 그토록 단결되어 있으며, 위기에 따르는 이해관계가 그렇게 큰 데도 민주당이 이러한 상황하에서 무력사용을 지지할 용의를 갖추지 못한다면 혼란과 애매성, 불확실성이 이보다 훨씬 더 큰 상황하에서 민주당이 미국의 근본적인 이익수호를 위해 무력사용을 지지하게 되리라고 누가 기대할 수 있겠는가.

나는 페르시아灣에 대한 행정부의 정책들이 비판으로부터 면제되어야 한다고 주장하는 것은 아니다. 대통령과 그의 부하들이 아무리 슬기롭게 지난 8月부터 이 위기를 관리해왔다하더라도, 이라크와의 우리의 관계는 그전까지는 이처럼 슬기롭지는 못하게 처리되어왔다. 우리의 対이라크 정책을 이라크-이란전쟁이 끝난 후 끄박 2년 동안이나 自動조종식으로 처리해온데 대해서는 변명의 여지가 있을 수 없다. 바로 행정부가 취해온 정책이 이런 것이었지만, 사실 행정부는 이라크에 대해 제재를 가하려던 議会의 노력을, 우리가 사담에게 고개를 숙이게되면 그의 행동에 영향력을 미칠 수있는 우리의 입장이 더 나아질 것이라는 계산에서 이에 반대했었던 것이다. 우리가 쿠웨이트를 수호해야 할 아무런 의무가 없다는 것을 천명하고, 쿠웨이트와 이라크와의 국경분쟁에 대해 아무런 입장도 취하지 않음으로써 행정부 代辯人들은 페르시아灣에서의 무력행사시 미국이 이에 항거하지 않을 것이라는 인식을 사담 측에 심어주는데 기여했던 것이다.

이런 문제의 발생 경위를 事後에 검토해볼 수 있는 시간의 여유는 많다. 이런 침공이 일어날 수 있는 환경을 만들어낸데 대해 책임이 있는 사람들은 그에 따르는 책임을 마땅히 져야 할 것이다. 그러나 우리는 즉각적인 위험에 관한 논의가 토론자들이 제기하는 문제점들 속에 파묻히도록 해서는 안된다. 지금의 과제는 우리가 이라크의 쿠웨이트 침공의 결과를 白紙化시킬 수 있는 정책을 만들어내는 일이다.

우리가 사담의 야욕을 봉쇄하고, 쿠웨이트의 독립을 회복시키는데 성공한다면 우리는 석유의 안정공급을 위한 계속적인 통로를 보존할 수 있게 될 것이다. 사담에 반대하여 우리와 함께 同參한 아랍政府들의 안정은 크게 강화될 것이다. 우리는 사담이 가지고 있는 대량파괴 무기들을 제거하고, 核무기를 보유하려는 이라크의 노력은 상당기간 동안—아니 어쩌면 영구히 逆轉시킬 수 있는 가능성을 갖게 될 것이다. 이스라엘과 아랍인들간의 평화를 위한 과정에서 진전이 있을 수 있는 전망이 크게 열리게 될 것이다. 우리는 그럴 경우 엄청난 규모의 不正義를 逆轉시켰고, 세계에서 가장 잔혹한 팽창주의자들 가운데의 하나를 敗退시켰으며, 새로운 국제질서를 위한 기반을 구축했다는 업적을 남기게 될 것이다.

이것이 싸울만한 가치가 있는 일이 아니라면, 나는 미국민의 한 사람으로서 그리고 民主党員의 한 사람으로서 무엇이 우리가 싸울만한 가치가 있는 일인지를 알지못한다.

0101

관리번호	91/1081

분류번호	보존기간

발 신 전 보

번 호 : WUS-0131 910114 1646 FC 종별 : 지급

수 신 : 주 수신처 참조 대사. 총영사

발 신 : 장 관 (중근동)

제 목 : 패만사태 비상 대책

WJA -0173 WUK -0087
WSV -0117 WFR -0062
WUN -0071 WIT -0079
WSB -0084 WCA -0043

연 : WUS-0107

연호와 같이 패만사태 비상 대책 수립에 참고코자 하니 1.13. 케야르 유엔 사무총장의 사담 후세인 대통령 회담, 결과 및 1.14. 이라크 비상의회 소집, 기타 유엔이 정한 이라크의 철군 시한을 앞두고 일련의 움직임에 주재국 정부, 언론계, 학계등의 관찰, 정세전망, 입장등을 파악 지급 보고 바람. 끝.

(안보리 소집, 관련국가의 중재노력 등)

유엔이 정한 철군시한을 앞두고, 중동문제해결을 위한 국제적노력이 금후 48시간이내에 적극화 될것으로 보이는바, 귀주재국 당국, 연구소들과 긴밀히 접촉, 이러한 동향을 수시로 지급 보고바람.

1991. 6. 30. 에 예고문에 의거 일반문서로 재분류됨

(차 관 유종하)

예 고 : 91.6.30. 까지

수신처 :

주미, 일, 영, 소, 불, 독일, 이태리, 사우디, 이집트 대사

보 안 통 제	

앙 고 재	91년 1월 14일	중근동과	기안자 성 명	과 장	국 장	차 관	장 관

외신과통제

0102

관리번호 91-244

원 본

외 무 부

종 별 : 지 급

번 호 : USW-0156 일 시 : 91 0114 1655

수 신 : 장관(미북,중근동,미안)

발 신 : 주 미대사

제 목 : 페만 사태 관련 동향

검토필(1991.6.30.)

1991.12.31에 예고문에 의거 일반문서로 재분류됨

연 USW-0150

연호 관련 당관이 각계 접촉및 당지 언론등을 통해 파악한바 금 1.14 오후 현재의 표제 동향을 하기 보고함.

1. 평화적 해결을 위한 국제적 노력

가. 작 1.13 바그다드에서 있었던 유엔 사무총장과 훗세인 대통령간의 약 2 시간반에 걸친 회담이 별다른 성과없이 끝나고 불란서및 EC 측도 대이락 교섭 추진 계획을 포기한것으로 알려짐에 따라, 당지 언론등은 전쟁 발발 이전 시행 가능한 대이락 대화 노력이 대부분 종료된것으로 간주하고 있음.

나. 그러나 일부 친 이락계 성향의 아랍권 국가들(예멘, 알제리아등)을 중심으로한 마지막 대화 노력은 계속 진행되고 있는것으로 알려지고 있는바, 금 1.14 백악관측도 대변인실을 통해 여사한 제 3 국 주도의 평화적 해결 노력에 반대하지 않는다는 기본 입장을 밝히고 있으며, 국무성 관계관(정무차관 보좌관)도이를 시인하고 있음. 한편 백악관 NSC 의 PAAL 보좌관은 이러한 마지막 노력이어떠한 성과를 가져오기에는 시기적으로 너무 늦어 비관적으로 본다고 말함.

다. 전기 관련, 예멘측은 사우디 주둔 다국적군의 철수를 전제로한 이락군의 쿠에이트로부터의 철수와 중동 평화 회의 개최등을 주 내용으로 하는 금번 사태 해결 방안을 이락측과 논의하고 있는것으로 알려지고 있으나, 여사한 노력이 금번 사태를 평화적으로 해결할수 있을지 여부는 극히 불투명한 실정임(국무부측은 이락측의 소위 -연계 전략-에 반대해온 미측의 기본 입장에 따라 전기 예멘측구상에도 반대한다는 입장임)

2. 이락내 동향

가. 한편, 금일 개최된 이락 국회는 후세인 대통령의 대미 성전을 전폭 지지키로

미주국	장관	차관	1차보	2차보	미주국	중아국	청와대	총리실
안기부								

PAGE 1

91.01.15 09:58

외신 2과 통제관 BW

0103

결의하는등 계속 강경 입장을 고수하고 있으며, 또 후세인 대통령도 언론을 통해 공개한 사우디 국왕앞 서한에서 이락측은 당초부터 사우디 공격 의사가 없다는 점을 강조하고 사우디측의 다국적군 주둔 허용 결정을 비난하는등 유화적인 변화 조짐을 전혀 나타내지 않고 있음.

나. 그 밖에 금일 후세인 대통령은 아라파트 PLO 의장 면담및 리비아 혁명 위 대표단 접수등 나름의 외교 활동을 통해 강경 아랍권내의 결속을 강화하고 아랍권 지도자로서의 자신의 위치를 고양하기 위해 계속 노력하고 있는것으로 알려짐.

3. 당관 관찰

가. 금번 사태의 평화적 해결을 위한 마지막 실질적 노력이라 할수 있는 유엔 사무총장의 이락 방문이 별다른 성과없이 종료됨에 따라 당지의 분위기는 무력 사용 불가피론으로 기울어가고 있는것으로 관찰됨.

나. 다만, 유엔 측이 제시한 철수 시한 직후의 이라군 부분 철수 예상이 언론계등 당지 일각에 의해 계속 제기되어 왔고, 미측도 공식적으로는 1.15 이 자동적으로 공격 개시일이 아니라는점을 누차 강조해온점등을 감안할때 대 이락 무력 사용 시기를 예측하기는 아직 어려운 실정임.

(대사 박동진-차관)

91.12.31 까지

PAGE 2

0104

원 본

외 무 부

종 별 : 지 급

번 호 : USW-0177 일 시 : 91 0114 2039

수 신 : 장 관(중근동,미북,국연)

발 신 : 주 미 대사

제 목 : 불란서 제의 평화안

1.당지 언론 보도에 의하면 UN 안보리5개 상임 이사국은 불란서가 제의한 막바지 평화안을 놓고 협의중인 것으로 알려짐.

2.동 평화안은 1) 이락이 쿠웨이트에서 철수하는 조건으로, 2) 유엔 안보리가 중동 평화에 대한 국제 회의를 소집한다는것인바, 불란서는 금일저녁 안보리에 동 평화안을 제출할 예정이라함.

3.독일은 동 평화안을 지지하고,이락도 비교적 호의적인 반응을 보이고 있으나 미국은 조건부 철수에는 응할수 없다는 입장을 고수하고 있는 것으로 알려짐.

(대사 박동진-차관)

중아국 차관 1차보 미주국 중아국 국기국 정문국 안기부

PAGE 1

91.01.15 11:09 WG

외신 1과 통제관

0105

관리 번호	91-66

	분류번호	보존기간

발 신 전 보

WUS-0155

번 호 : WJA-0203 외 별지참조 종별 : 910115 1927

수 신 : 주 수신처 참조 ~~대사, 총영사~~

발 신 : 장 관 (미북)

제 목 : UN 안보리 철군 시한 경과 관련 성명 발표

1. 페만 사태와 관련 UN 안보리가 설정한 1.15. 이라크군 철수 시한이 임박함에 따라 독일 정부는 상기 시한전 이라크군의 철군을 촉구하는 수상실명의 성명을 1.14. 발표하였음.

2. 본부 조치 결정에 참고코자 하니, 1.15. 시한을 전후하여 주재국 정부의 여사한 입장 표명이 있을 경우 발표 즉시 지급 보고 바람. 끝.

(미주국장 반기문)

검토필 (1991. 6. 30.)

예고 : 91.12.31. 일반

수신처 : 주일, 주영, 주불, 주카나다, 주이태리, 주벨지움, 주 덴마크, 주그리스, 주터어키, 주호주대사, 주카이로총영사, 주파키스탄, 주사우디, 주방글라데시, 주모로코, 주세네갈, 주체코, 주소대사

(사본 : 주미대사)

일반문서로 재분류(1991.12.31.)

중동아국장 대변인

보안 통제	

앙 고 재	91년 1월 15일	북미과	기안자 성명		과 장	심의관	국 장		차 관	장 관
							전결			

외신과통제

0106

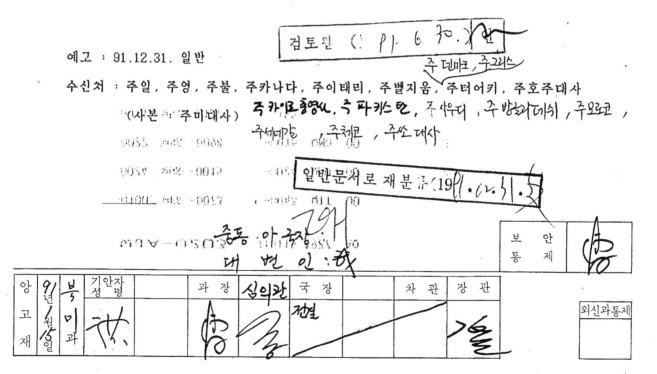

유엔 안보리 철군 시한 경과후

~~대한민국 정부~~ 외무부 대변인 성명(안)

1991. 1. 16.

1. 대한민국 정부는 유엔 안보리 결의가 설정한 1.15. 철수 시한이 지났음에도 불구하고 이라크 정부가 쿠웨이트에 불법 주둔중인 이라크군을 아직 철수치 않고 있음을 유감스럽게 생각합니다.

2. 이에 따라 페르시아만 지역정세가 전쟁 발발 일보 직전으로 치닫고 있어 페르시아만 인근지역 전체는 물론 전세계인들을 공포와 불안에 떨게하고 있는데 대해 우리는 깊은 우려를 갖고 있습니다.

3. 우리 정부는 이라크 정부가 지금이라도 전세계 평화 애호인의 염원에 부응하여 유엔 안보리 결의가 요구하고 있는 바와 같이 쿠웨이트로부터 즉각 철군할 것을 거듭 촉구하는 바입니다.

4. 대한민국 정부는 이 기회를 빌어 페르시아만 지역에 파견된 미국을 비롯한 다국적군의 헌신적인 평화유지 노력에 깊은 경의와 찬사를 보내고자 합니다.

끝.

중동아국장
대변인

앙 고 재	북미과	91년 1월 15일	담 당	과 장	심의관	국 장	차관보	차 관	장 관

0107

폐만 사태 관련 미국의 입장

(비상 대책회의 자료)

91. 1. 15.

1. 부쉬 대통령의 미국 입장 표명

o 부쉬 미 대통령은 1.12. 상.하원에서 무력사용 권한을 대통령에게 부여하는 합동 결의안(Joint Resolution)이 통과된 직후 기자회견을 통해 다음과 같이 미군의 대이락 공격시기가 임박했음을 암시하고 이라크군의 무조건적 철수를 거듭 촉구함.

- 현 싯점이 페만 사태의 평화적 해결을 위한 마지막 기회이므로 이라크 군의 대규모적인 철수가 즉각 실시되어야 할 것임.
- 미군의 무력공격 시점과 관련, 만약 이라므군이 철수하지 않을 경우 대이라크 공격이 조만간(SOONER RATHER THAN LATER) 개시될 수 있을 것임.
- 그러나 후세인의 태도 변화에 따라 아직도 전쟁을 피할수 있다고 생각함. (WAR IS NOT INEVITABLE)
- 만약 급번 사태와 관련된 테러 행위가 발생할 경우 이는 전적으로 후세인이 책임져야 할 것임.

0108

* 기타 부쉬 대통령 동정

- 1.11 고르바쵸프 대통령과 약 20분간 전화통화, 동 통화시 고르바쵸프 대통령은 국제사회의 대이라크 제재에 대한 쏘련의 협조 재다짐.
- 1.11. 카이후 수상은 부쉬 대통령에게 전화, 한국 방문 결과에 대해 설명하고, 페만 사태에 관해 우방국에 대한 지원 다짐.
- 1.14. 베이커 국무, 체니 국방, 스코우크로프트 안보보좌관, 파우웰 합참의장 등을 비롯한 모든 안보 관계자들이 참석하는 고위 안보관계관 회의 개최

2. 미 국무부, 워싱톤 주재 이라크 공관원 감축요청

o 미 국무부 James Covey 중동담당 차관보 대리는 1.12. 주미 이라크 대사를 초치, 이라크 주도의 테러행위 시도 가능성이 고조됨에 따라 주미 이라크 대사관원을 1.15 자정까지 현재의 16명에서 대사포함 4명으로 감축할 것을 요청하고 다음과 같이 통보함.

- 잔류자 4명은 활동지역이 25마일로 제한됨.
- 금번 조치가 미-이라크간 외교관계 단절을 의미하는 것은 아니며, 미국은 이라크와 최소한의 접촉 채널을 계속 유지할 것임.

o 이와관련, 주한 미 대사관측은 1.14(월) 이라크의 대규모 테러활동 전개 가능성을 감안, 아국과의 정보 교환등 긴밀한 협조 체제 유지를 요청해 옴.

0109

3. 의회 동향

ㅇ 1.12. 합동결의안 통과후 Thomas Foley 하원의장은 의회의 의사가 명확히 표명된만큼 찬반 표차 등은 아무 의미가 없다고 언급.

ㅇ 또한 1.14. Sam Nunn 상원 군사 위원장등 민주당 지도부는 부쉬 대통령이 무력 사용을 결정할 경우 전선에 나가있는 미군을 지원할 것이라고 발언.

- 예산 삭감 등 조치를 취하지 않을 것임을 언명

* 1.12. 의회 표결 성향 분석

- 소속당별 : 공화 98% 찬성, 민주 70% 반대

- 지 역 별

(단위 : 명)

구 분 지역별	찬 성	반 대	비 고
남부 출신 의원	86	32	남부출신 민주당 상원의원의 찬성이 상원에서의 결의안 통과에 결정적 역할
남서부 출신 의원	35	13	
산악지역 출신의원 (Mountain States)	16	8	
New England 지역 출신 의원	13	23	
중서부지역 출신의원	63	74	
Mid Atlantic 출신 의원	51	45	
태평양 연안지역 출신의원	38	35	

0110

4. 언론보도 및 기타 동향

o W.P.지 및 N.Y.T.지 등은 1.12. 의회의 결의안 통과에 대하여 부쉬 행정부가 대이라크 전쟁을 수행할 수 있는 법적 요건은 구비한 셈이지만 찬반 양론 간의 표차가 상원의 경우 5표, 하원의 경우 76표에 지나지 않아 전쟁 수행에 긴요한 튼튼한 정치적 기반(solid political base)까지 확보한 것으로 보기는 어렵다는 기사를 게재.

o 그러나, 상기 양대 신문은 1.13자 사설에서 금번 결의안 통과는 아무런 정보도 없는 상태에서 갑작스레 통과됐던 1964년 TonKin 만 결의와는 전혀 다른 것으로 평가하면서, 의회는 그간 5개월여에 걸쳐 전쟁과 평화의 문제에 대하여 솔직하고 신중하며 심도깊은 논의를 거쳐 금번 결정을 내렸음을 강조하고 사담 후세인은 "쿠웨이트에서 나가라"라는 미국의 명백한 멧세지를 오인하지 말도록 경고.

o 한편, 미국내 중동문제 전문가들은 쏘련군의 리투아니아 시위 유혈진압이 미.쏘간 협조관계에 미칠 영향에 대해 지대한 관심 표명

0111

관리 번호 91-25

원 본

외 무 부

종 별 : 지 급

번 호 : USW-0197 일 시 : 91 0115 1846

수 신 : 장관(미북,중근동,미안,국연)

발 신 : 주 미 대사

제 목 : 페 만 사태 관련 동향

1991.12.31. 에 예고문에 의거 일반문서로 재분류됨

검토필(1991.6.30.)

연: USW-0177

유엔 안보리가 제시한 철수 시한(당지 시간 1.15 자정)을 불과 수시간 앞둔금 1.15 오후 현재, 부쉬 대통령을 포함, 백악관, 국무부, 국방부등의 금번 사태 관련 고위 당국자들은 별다른 공개적 움직임은 보이지 않고 있는바, 당관이 파악하 표제 동향등을 하기 요지 보고함.

1. 유엔 안보리를 중심으로한 평화적 해결 노력

가. 이락군 철수와 중동 평화 국제 회의 개최를 연계코자 하는 연호 불란서측 제안외에도, 안보리 회원국 명의로 이락군 철수를 재촉구하는 요지의 성명을 발표하자는 영국측 제안및 불란서 제안과 유사한 내용의 유엔 사무총장 명의 성명을 발표하자는 구상등 금번 사태를 평화적으로 해결하기 위한 각종 노력이 유엔 안보리에서 활발히 전개되고 있기는 하나, 현재 아무런 구체적 진전도 이루어지지 않은것으로 알려지고 있음.

(특히 미측은 금일 국무부 정례 브리핑을 통해 팔레스타인 문제와의 연계에반대하는 입장을 재확인하는 한편, 페 만 사태 관련 기 통과된 유엔 안보리 결의안 내용을 사실상 수정하는 내용의 전기 불란서측 제안을 수용할수 없다는점을공식 천명함)

나. 한편, 이락측은 현재까지 전기 불란서측 구상등에 대해 공식적으로는 아무런 관심도 표하고 있지 않다함.

2. 미국내 동향

가. 당지 CNN 방송에 따르면 최신예 MIAI 탱크 수송 작전이 상금 완료되지 안는등 미 지상군 병력의 배치는 현재도 계속 진행되고 있는 상황이나, 미측은 현재 사실상 무력 사용 태세를 완비하고 있다함(금일 현재 페 만 지역에 배치된 미 병력 총수는 약

미주국	장관	차관	1차보	2차보	미주국	중아국	국기국	청와대
총리실	안기부							

PAGE 1 91.01.16 09:41

외신 2과 통제관 BT

0112

415,000 명이라 하는바, 미 병력 배치 현황에 대해서는 USW(F)-168 로 송부한 국방부 PETE WILIAMS 대변인 발표 내용 참조)

나. 또한 실제 무력 충돌이 발생하는 경우, 미국과 이락중 어느쪽이 선제 공격을 가할지에 대해서도 당지의 관심이 집중되고 있는바, 다수의 당지 전문가들은 미측이 먼저 무력을 사용할것으로 예상하고 있으나, 이락측이 여사한 미국의 선제 공격 의사를 감지하는 경우, SCUD 미사일등으로 이스라엘과 사우디 동부의 미군 주둔 지역등을 먼저 공격할 가능성도 배제할수 없는것으로 보임 (금일당관 임성남 서기관이 국무부 근동국 지역총괄과 EUGENE DORRIS 부과장으로부터 탐문한바로는, 금번 사태의 해결을 위해 무력 사용이 불가피한것으로 보는것이 금번 사태 담당 국무부 실무선의 전반적 견해라함)

다. 현재 미 국방부는 완전 임전 태세에 돌입해 있다하며, 테러 공격의 가능성을 사전 봉소비키 위해 출입자 검문 검색을 강화 하는 한편, 관광객들을 위해 매일 시행해왔던 페타곤 시찰 프로그램도 현재 중단 하고 있다함.

라. 당지 국방 전략 문제 관련 실무자들은 당관 관계관들과의 접촉시 가급적 조속한 공격 개시가 바람직한 것으로 본다는 견해를 표시하고 있음.

3. 이락내 동향

가. 바그다드에서는 금일 후세인 대통령의 대미 성전을 지지하는 시위가 계속되는등, 이락측은 전혀 철군의 움직임을 보이고 있지 않다함.

나.JASSIM 이락 공보 장관도 금일 방송된 CNN 과의 인터뷰시 이락측의 불철수 의사를 계속 강력히 표명함.

(대사 박동진-차관)

91.12.31.까지 고문에 의거 일반문서로 재분류됨

: USW(F) - 0162
: 종 군(미북,미안,중근동) 발신 : 주미대사
: "페"만 사태 관련 각종 현황 자료 (9 매)

보안 통제	외	검

FACING OFF:
The Balance Of Forces

THE MULTINATIONAL FORCE IN THE GULF

- 28 nations have sent ships, aircraft or personnel to the gulf.
- Biggest such force assembled since the Korean War.
- Total force (U.S. and allies) estimated at 615,000 to 660,000 troops.

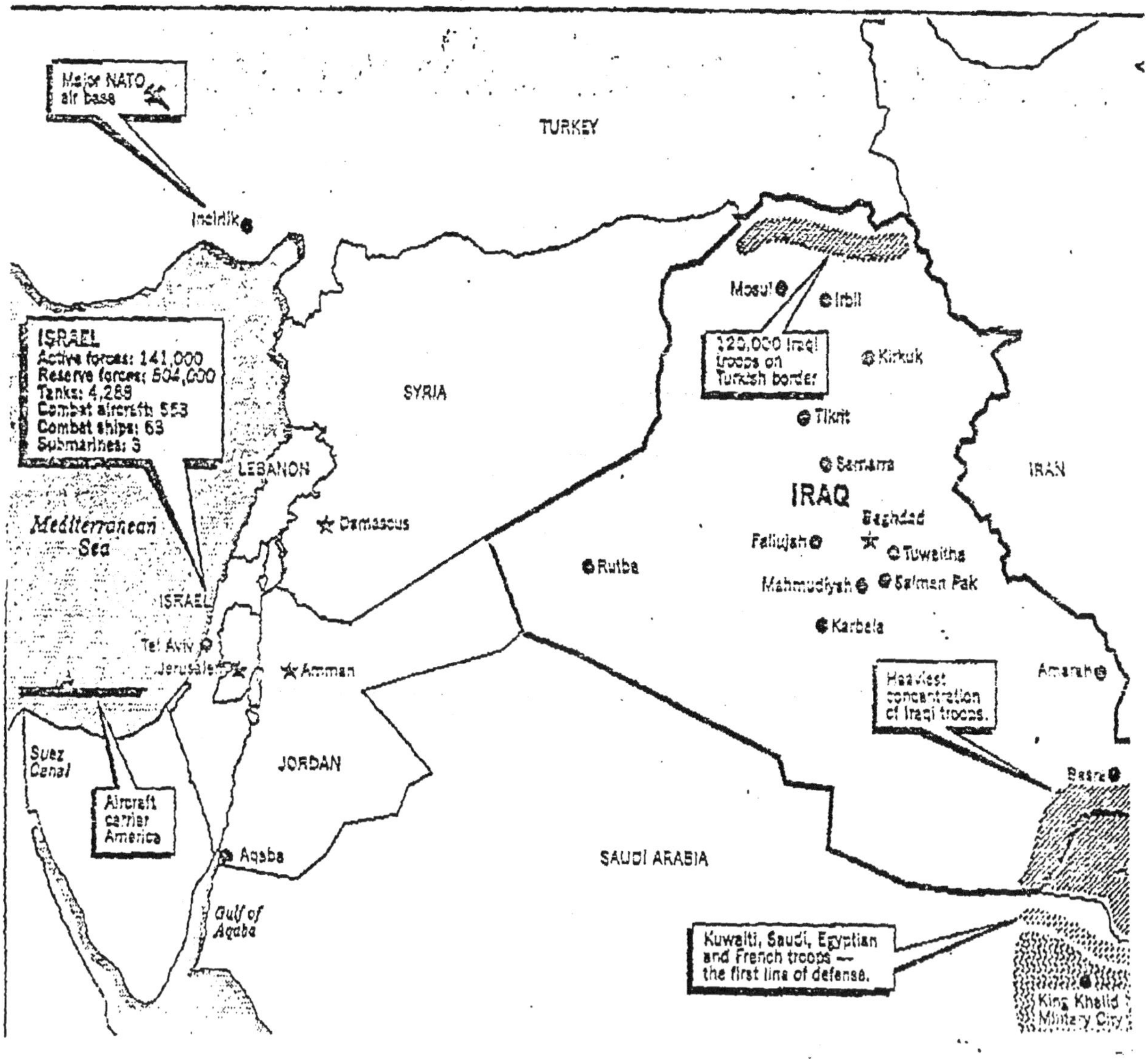

0162-1

Jan. 15, 1991
WP

01/15/91 17:10 ☎202 797 0595 EMBASSY OF KOREA 010

0114

수 : USW(F) -
신 : 장 관 발신 : 주미대사
제 :

보안
통제

(매)

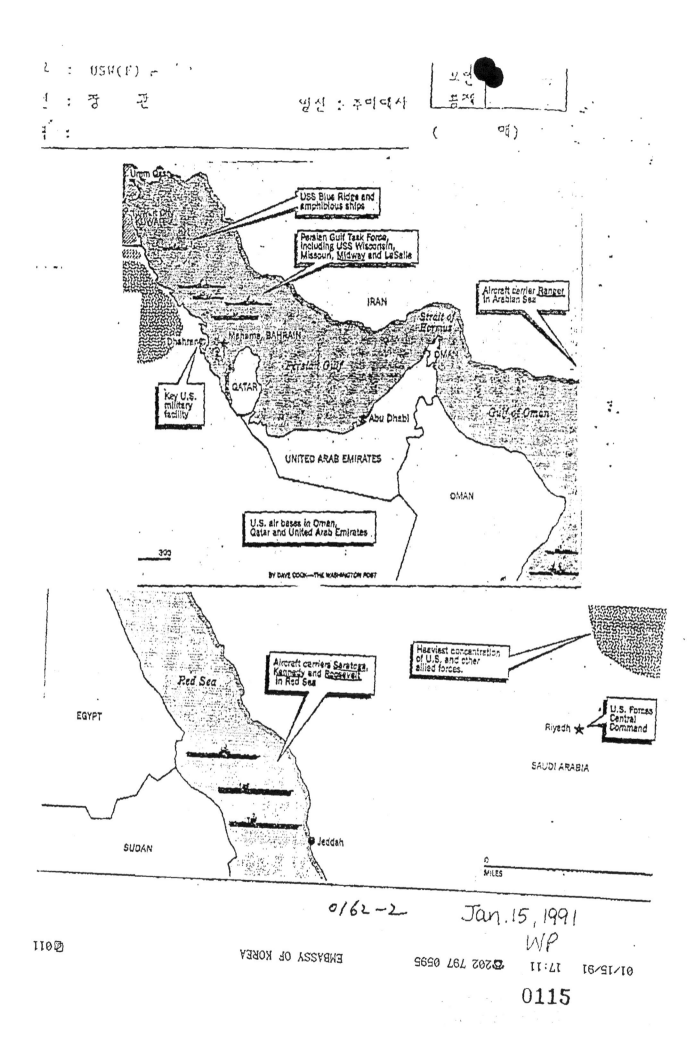

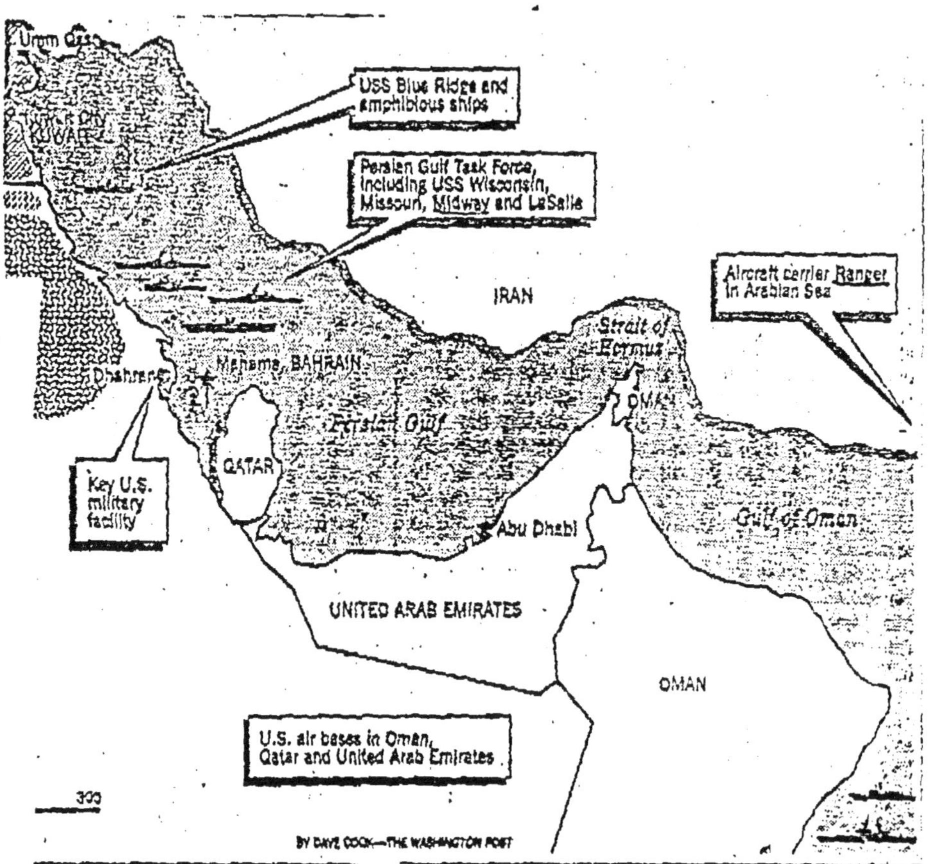

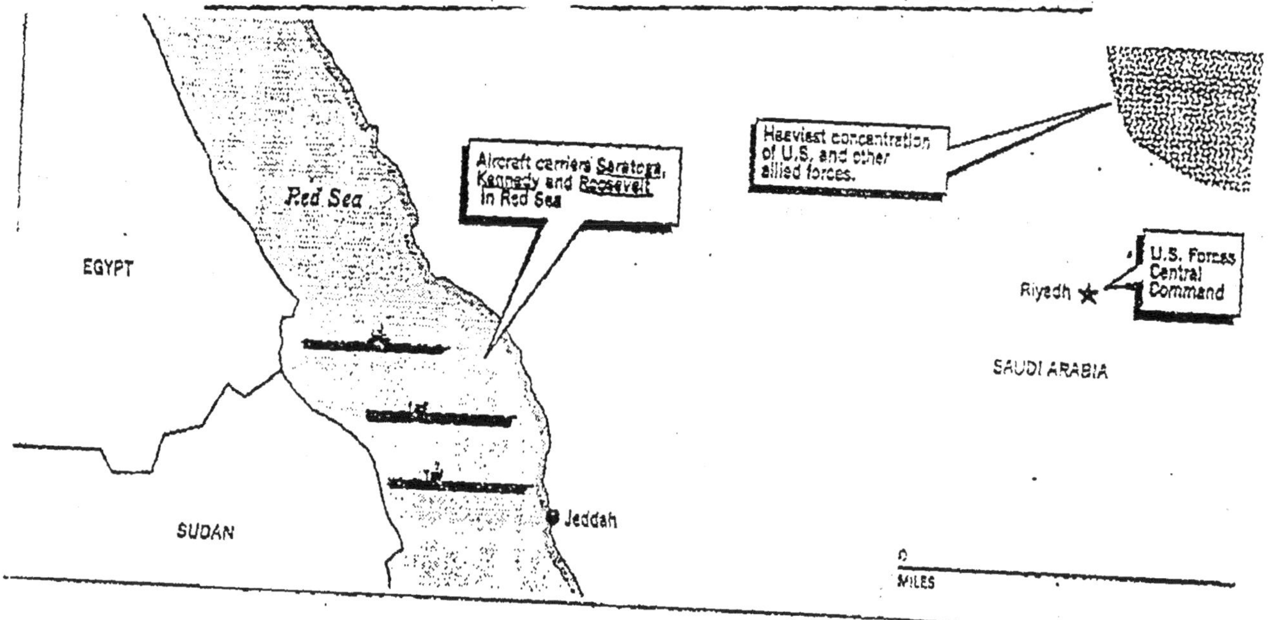

0162-2 Jan. 15, 1991
WP

01/15/91 17:11 ☎202 797 0595 EMBASSY OF KOREA 011

0115

수신 : 장 관 발신 : 주미대사

제목 : (매)

THE BREWING CONFRONTATION

February 24, 1990: Iraqi President Saddam Hussein, at Arab Cooperation Council meeting in Jordan, warns of American dominance in the Persian Gulf as Soviet world power wanes. He suggests Arabs withdraw money from the West and reinvest it in the Soviet Union. Egypt's President Hosni Mubarak leaves in protest.

April 26: John Kelly, undersecretary of state for Middle Eastern affairs, opposes a congressional move to impose economic sanctions on Iraq, arguing it would hamper President Bush's ability to be a "restraining influence" on Iraq.

July 17: Saddam makes a Revolution Day speech, blasting Kuwait and the United Arab Emirates as stooges for America by keeping oil prices low. He accuses Kuwait of stealing oil from border oil fields.

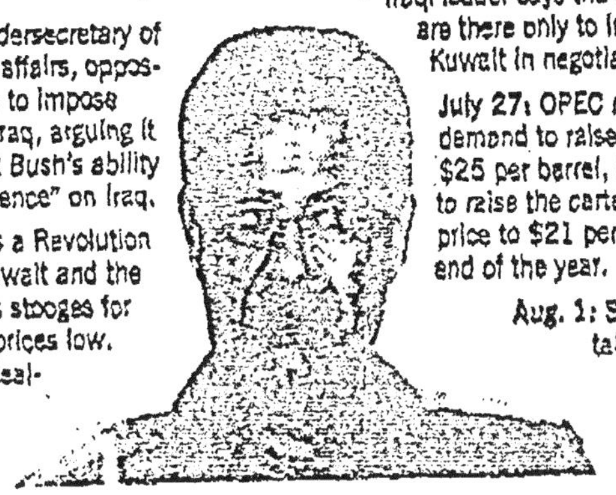

Saddam Hussein

July 24: Two Iraqi armored divisions mass on the Kuwait border, but Arab diplomats say Iraq has given its neighbors assurances it will not attack Kuwait.

July 25: April C. Glaspie, U.S. ambassador to Iraq, tells Saddam the United States will not take sides in his dispute with Kuwait. The Iraqi leader says the border tanks are there only to intimidate Kuwait in negotiations.

July 27: OPEC refuses Iraq's demand to raise oil prices to $25 per barrel, but does decide to raise the cartel's reference price to $21 per barrel by the end of the year.

Aug. 1: Saudi-mediated talks between Iraq and Kuwait collapse.

Aug. 2: Iraq invades Kuwait. Bush freezes Iraqi and Kuwaiti assets and bans all trade and financial relations with Iraq. U.N. Security Council condemns the invasion and demands the immediate, unconditional withdrawal of Iraqi forces from Kuwait.

Aug. 3: Americans and Soviets issue joint statement in Moscow condemning Iraq. Arab League issues declaration denouncing invasion, with Jordan, Libya and Palestine Liberation Organization abstaining. Iraq says it will withdraw troops from Kuwait within two days.

Aug. 4: European Community imposes broad sanctions against Iraq.

Aug. 6: U.N. Security Council approves resolution imposing comprehensive trade and financial sanctions against Iraq and Kuwait. Several hundred Westerners, including 28 U.S. nationals, are detained in Kuwait and taken to Baghdad.

Aug. 7: Bush orders U.S. military aircraft and troops to Saudi Arabia to defend it against Iraqi attack in an operation code-named Desert Shield.

Aug. 8: Iraq announces annexation of Kuwait.

Aug. 9: U.N. Security Council declares that Iraq's annexation of Kuwait "has no legal validity and is null and void." Iraq seals its borders, barring departure of all foreigners except diplomatic personnel. About 2,500 Americans are trapped in Kuwait, another 500 in Iraq.

Aug. 10: At an emergency summit in Cairo, Arab leaders vote 12 to 3 to send troops to Saudi Arabia to help defend against possible invasion by Iraqi forces. Iraq orders foreign governments to close their embassies in Kuwait City and move diplomatic functions to Baghdad by Aug. 24.

Aug. 12: Bush administration adopts a policy of "interdiction," including use of force to stop ships attempting to circumvent the U.N. embargo. Saddam says he would withdraw from Kuwait as part of a settlement of "all issues of occupation," including Israeli withdrawal from the West Bank and Gaza Strip and Syrian pullout from Lebanon.

Aug. 15: Saddam offers peace proposal to Iran.

Aug. 18: U.N. Security Council votes to demand that Iraq release all detained foreigners.

Aug. 19: United Arab Emirates and Bahrain allow deployment of Arab and "friendly" (including U.S.) forces on their territory. Following reports that French nationals have been "displaced" from their hotels to unknown locations, France authorizes its ships in the Persian Gulf to use force if necessary to ensure compliance with U.N. sanctions.

Aug. 22: Bush authorizes the first call-up of reserves in two decades. The initial mobilization is expected to number about 40,000.

Aug. 23: As deadline for closing embassies in Kuwait nears, the United States and most other Western embassies reduce staffs to minimum and vow to remain open. Oil prices continue to soar to new highs on spot and futures markets, and stock prices post broad losses.

Aug. 24: Iraqi troops surround U.S. embassy in Kuwait and those of other nations defying Iraq's order to close.

Aug. 25: U.N. Security Council approves resolution that, in effect, authorizes military action to enforce the trade sanctions against Iraq.

Aug. 28: Iraq declares Kuwait to be its 19th province. Saddam says all foreign women and children will be free to leave Iraq and Kuwait.

Aug. 29: Bush proposes a plan under which wealthy U.S. allies would share the cost of the U.S. deployment in the gulf and help those countries adversely affected by enforcement of the embargo.

Sept. 1: About 550 American, European and Japanese women and children are allowed to leave Iraq.

Jan. 15, 1991
WP

0162-3

01/15/91 17:12 ☎202 797 0595 EMBASSY OF KOREA 012

0116

수신 : 장 관 발신 : 주미대사

제목 : (매)

Sept. 2: Iraq limits consumer purchases of basic foods, calling the measure "rationalization of consumption" rather than rationing.

Sept. 9: Bush and Soviet President Mikhail Gorbachev meet in Helsinki and issue a joint declaration condemning the invasion and stating that both countries will take unspecified further steps if sanctions fail to force an Iraqi withdrawal.

Sept. 10: Iran and Iraq resume diplomatic ties.

Sept. 14: Iraqi soldiers forcibly enter French, Canadian, Australian and Belgian embassies in Kuwait City, holding five Western consuls for several hours and taking four French hostages.

Sept. 17: Saudi Arabia and the Soviet Union reestablish diplomatic ties after a 52-year break. In response to "very grave illegal acts" by Iraqis who raided Western embassies, 12 European Community governments expel Iraqi military attaches and restrict the movements of other Iraqi diplomats.

Sept. 23: Saddam threatens to attack Saudi oil fields and Israel if Iraq is "strangled" by economic sanctions.

Sept. 25: U.N. Security Council votes to bar all air traffic to and from Iraq and Kuwait save for humanitarian purposes.

Sept. 28: The exiled emir of Kuwait tells Bush that Iraq is pillaging his country and repopulating it with outsiders, jeopardizing the prospects of restoring the former government even if Iraqi forces withdraw. After the emir's two-hour session at the White House, U.S. officials say the timetable for possible military action against Iraq is shortening.

Oct. 13: Kuwait's exiled rulers promise a meeting in Jeddah of more than 1,000 Kuwaiti exiles to restore a democratic parliament if their country is freed from Iraqi occupation.

Oct. 19: Iraq announces gasoline rationing, indicating that the international embargo has curtailed supplies of chemicals needed in refining crude oil.

Oct. 23: Iraq says it will free all 400 French hostages. Thirty-three Britons fly out with former prime minister Edward Heath. His visit, followed by Japan's Yasuhiro Nakasone and Germany's Willy Brandt, turns Baghdad into what the State Department calls a "hostage bazaar."

Oct. 28: Saddam rescinds gasoline rationing and fires his oil minister; government radio

THE BREWING CONFRONTATION

explains that rationing had been introduced "on the basis of erroneous information."

Oct. 29: U.N. Security Council votes to demand that Iraq resupply beleaguered Western embassies in Kuwait, establishes a framework for financial claims against Iraq for its invasion and urges states to collate information about Baghdad's human rights violations.

Nov. 5: Secretary of State James A. Baker III and Saudi Arabia's King Fahd reach a new military command and control agreement, guaranteeing that American troops will be under the command of American officers if an offensive operation against Iraq is launched.

Nov. 8: Bush orders a new wave of U.S. troops to the Persian Gulf to create an "adequate offensive military option should that be necessary." Pentagon officials say the reinforcements could number 200,000, which would bring the total American deployment to about 430,000.

Nov. 9: Pentagon officials confirm that they have postponed plans to begin rotating any of the U.S. troops already in the gulf in order to keep American forces at maximum strength.

Nov. 19: Iraq says it will pour 250,000 more troops into Kuwait in response to the American buildup, which would bring the Iraqi total to about 680,000.

Nov. 20: Saddam proposes the release of all German hostages.

Nov. 22: Bush spends Thanksgiving Day visiting troops in Saudi Arabia and warns that Iraq's progress in developing nuclear weapons gives the soldiers' mission a sense of urgency.

Nov. 23: Bush, declaring he would "work with" any nation willing to oppose Iraqi aggression, meets with Syrian leader Hafez Assad in Geneva.

Nov. 28: Two former joint chiefs of staff, retired Gen. David C. Jones and retired Adm.

Jan. 15, 1991
WP

0162-4

01/15/91 17:14 ☎202 797 0595 EMBASSY OF KOREA ☎013

0117

수신 : 장 관 발신 : 주미대사 [redacted]

제목 : (예)

The Bushes with troops at Thanksgiving.

William J. Crowe Jr., tell Congress that the United States should refrain for now from military action and allow sanctions more time to work.

Nov. 29: U.N. Security Council approves a resolution effectively authorizing the use of force against Iraq if it does not withdraw from Kuwait by Jan. 15.

Nov. 30: Bush invites Iraqi Foreign Minister Tariq Aziz to Washington and offers to send Baker to Baghdad before Jan. 15 to meet Saddam to discuss a possible peaceful solution to the gulf crisis. Easing a four-month siege of the U.S. embassy in Kuwait, Iraqi troops deliver fruit, vegetables and cigarettes to diplomatic personnel inside the mission.

Dec. 6: Saddam asks Iraq's Parliament to free all foreign hostages.

Dec. 7: State Department announces the U.S. Embassy in Kuwait City will be abandoned once all Americans who want to leave Kuwait and Iraq have gone.

Dec. 8: Iraq proposes that Baker come to see Saddam on Jan. 12. U.S. officials insist instead that the meeting take place no later than Jan. 3.

Dec. 12: Saddam replaces his defense minister with a younger general who fought in the war against Iran.

Dec. 19: Deputy commander of U.S. forces in the gulf, Lt. Gen. Calvin A.H. Waller, tells reporters that American troops will not be ready to attack Iraq by Jan. 15.

Jan. 2: NATO announces that Germany, Belgium and Italy will send 42 jet fighters to Turkey to reinforce defenses along the border with Iraq.

Jan. 3: Bush, saying he is making "one last attempt" to avoid a war in the gulf, proposes that Baker meet Aziz between Jan. 7 and 9 in Geneva to try to settle the crisis peacefully.

Jan. 4: Aziz agrees to meet Baker in Geneva on Jan. 9. Bush rules out any future meeting between Baker and Saddam in Baghdad.

Jan. 6: Saudi King Fahd reviews U.S. and other troops in his country, and says that

U.S. Ambassador to Kuwait W. Nathaniel Howell, left, returns home.

Saddam could escape "any further punishment" by pulling his troops out of Kuwait, adding that Saudi Arabia would then support any negotiated agreement on territorial and financial disputes between Iraq and Kuwait.

Jan. 8: Bush asks Congress to approve a resolution authorizing the use of "all necessary means" to drive Iraq out of Kuwait.

Jan. 9: Baker and Aziz meet in Geneva, but more than six hours of talks fail to break the diplomatic impasse as Iraq shows no sign of buckling to international demands.

Jan. 10: U.S. Congress begins debate on the gulf crisis.

Jan. 11: U.N. Secretary General Perez de Cuellar, en route to Baghdad for talks with Saddam, suggests a neutral peacekeeping force could be deployed to preserve peace along Iraq's borders with Kuwait and Saudi Arabia if Iraq withdraws. The State Department recommends Americans living in Israel consider leaving, the latest in a series of advisories cautioning U.S. citizens around the world about threats to their safety in case of war.

Jan. 12: A divided and solemn Congress grants Bush the authority to wage war against Iraq. The vote in the Senate is 52-to-47; the House vote is 250-to-183.

Jan. 13: Perez de Cuellar ends talks in

Reps. Michel and Fascel after the debate in Congress.

Baghdad without any report of progress, saying that "only God knows" if there will be war.

Yesterday: Perez de Cuellar says he does not "see any reason to have real hope" that war will be averted in the gulf. Iraq's National Assembly calls for a "holy war" to defend the occupation of Kuwait. Bush spends his day in conversations with international leaders and in White House sessions devoted to the gulf crisis.

0162-5

Jan. 15, 1991 WP

01/15/91 17:15 ☎202 797 0595 EMBASSY OF KOREA 014

0118

: USW(F) -

: 장 관 발신 : 주미대사

:

보안
통제

(매)

THE IRAQI FORCE

- More than 540,000 troops in occupied Kuwait and southern Iraq.
- Estimated 120,000 troops near the border with Turkey.
- Tens of thousands more mobilized.

U.S. FORCES

- Current troop strength is 415,000, of whom 370,000 are considered combat ready. The total is expected to reach 430,000 by the end of January.
- The last official breakdown by service was issued when troop strength was 325,000. The breakdown then was:

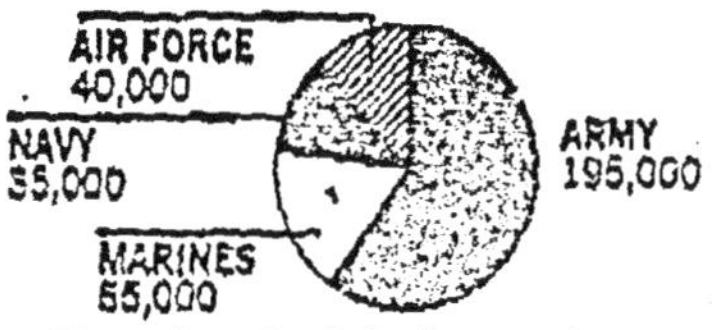

- More than 152,000 reservists have been called up.
- The troops are supported by roughly 2,000 tanks, 1,300 aircraft, more than 100 ships.
- The U.S. fleet in the region includes battleships Wisconsin and Missouri, command ships LaSalle and Blue Ridge, aircraft carriers America, Kennedy, Midway, Ranger, Roosevelt and Saratoga.

IRAQI FORCES

- Army has seven corps totalling 55 to 60 divisions. 555,000 regular troops and 480,000 reserves, all of whom are believed mobilized.
- Regular forces include six divisions of elite Republican Guards. Iraq claims its militia, the Popular Army, has 8 million men, but true strength is estimated at around 850,000.
- Forces are supported by 4,000 tanks, 2,700 armored personnel carriers, 3,000 artillery pieces and 500 combat aircraft. Iraq's navy is tiny and considered negligible.
- The country reportedly has more than 200 missiles of four types, all either Soviet-made or modified versions of Soviet weapons. They are code-named Frog, Scud-B, Hussein and Abbas. The Abbas has the greatest range, about 500 miles.

Jan. 15, 1991
WP

0162-6

01/15/91 17:16 ☎202 797 0595 EMBASSY OF KOREA 015

0119

수 : USW(F) -

신 : 장 관 발신 : 주미대사

제 :

보안	
통제	

(매)

THE U.S.-LED MULTINATIONAL FORCE

Flags denote countries with greatest number of troops in the region.

ARGENTINA
Two warships in the Red Sea, two transport planes in the region. A 100-man army unit has also been committed.

AUSTRALIA
One destroyer, one guided missile frigate and one supply ship interrogating vessels in approaches to the Strait of Hormuz.

BANGLADESH
6,000 troops in Saudi Arabia.

BELGIUM
Two minesweepers, one supply ship in the region, three more ships deployed. Six C-130 transport planes in the region.

BRITAIN

The second-largest Western contingent in the region with about 35,000 men, at least 50 combat jets and a naval armada of more than 18 ships, including four destroyers.

CANADA
Two destroyers, one supply ship and about 30 transport and fighter aircraft have been deployed to the region. Total forces number about 1,700.

CZECHOSLOVAKIA
Has sent a 200-man chemical defense unit and more than 150 volunteer medical personnel.

DENMARK
One ship in the region. Danish merchant vessels are helping in the U.S. sealift.

EGYPT

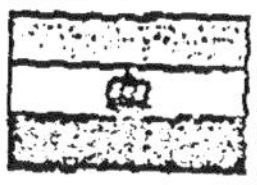

At least 30,000 have been sent to the region, supported by about 400 tanks. Another roughly 2,500 troops are in the United Arab Emirates.

FRANCE

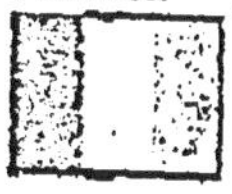

17,000 men in the region, 10,000 in Saudi Arabia alone—the biggest French military deployment overseas since the Algerian War. The troops are supported by 350 tanks, 12 ships and 40 combat aircraft.

GREECE
Frigate in the Red Sea. Greece also has supplied merchant ships for the U.S. sealift.

GULF COOPERATION COUNCIL (Saudi Arabia, Bahrain, Oman, United Arab Emirates, Qatar and Kuwait)
"Peninsular Force" of roughly 10,000 troops based in northern Saudi Arabia, near the Kuwaiti border. They and allied Arab-Islamic forces form the first line of defense. GCC force is supported by 7,000 soldiers of Kuwait's 20,000-man army.
The GCC and other gulf Arab forces total about 150,500 men, 330 combat aircraft, 800 tanks and 36 major naval units, although not all are likely to be involved in Desert Shield.

HONDURAS
Sent 150 troops and may send 350 more.

ITALY
No ground force deployment planned. Six ships deployed to the gulf and eastern Mediterranean. Four minesweepers sent to the Gulf of Aqaba. Squadron of eight Tornado fighters based in U.A.E., to provide air cover.

MOROCCO
1,500 troops in Saudi Arabia. Has 500 permanently stationed in U.A.E.

NETHERLANDS
Two frigates and one combat supply ship in the gulf. Squadron of 18 F-16A/B fighters has been readied for deployment.

NEW ZEALAND
Has deployed two C-130 transports and combined support, medical teams.

NIGER
Has sent 480 troops to guard the holy shrines of Mecca and Medina in Saudi Arabia.

NORWAY
One Coast Guard cutter in the gulf supporting the Danish ship. Norway has offered anti-chemical warfare equipment and provided ships to carry Egyptian troops to Saudi Arabia.

PAKISTAN
About 2,000 troops in Saudi Arabia, 2,000 in the U.A.E. with 1,000 advisers. Pakistan began sending another 3,000 troops to Saudi Arabia in December.

PORTUGAL
Naval support ship is carrying equipment and supplies to the British force. Portugal

0162-9

Jun. 15, 1991
WP

01/15/91 17:17 ☎202 797 0595 EMBASSY OF KOREA ☑016

0120

: USW(F) -

: 경 권 발신 : 주미대사

보안 통제

(매)

OTHER COUNTRIES' EFFORTS

has allowed U.S. aircraft to refuel at its air-bases.

SENEGAL
About 500 troops in Saudi Arabia.

SAUDI ARABIA

About 20,000 troops on the front line. At full strength, the kingdom will contribute 200 tanks. Has committed over 500 combat aircraft.

SOVIET UNION
Guided missile destroyer on patrol in the Persian Gulf. Moscow has indicated it would send ground forces only under U.N. command.

SPAIN
Three frigates patrolling near the Bab al Mandab Strait, gateway to the Red Sea.

SYRIA

Has pledged 20,000 troops. About 19,000, including 3,200 Special Force paratroopers, are in Saudi Arabia, another 2,000 in the U.A.E. Fifty thousand troops are deployed along the Iraq-Syria border.

TURKEY

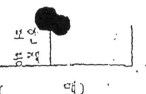

Two frigates in the gulf. About 100,000 Turkish troops, two squadrons of F-16s and 42 jet fighters sent by NATO are defending border with Iraq. Has allowed the U.S. to base bombers, fighters, fighter-bombers at Incirlik Air Base. Sent five ships and two submarines to the eastern Mediterranean earlier this month.

AFGHANISTAN
Mujahadeen leaders have pledged up to 2,000 troops if transportation is provided.

BULGARIA
Will send military medical personnel, army engineers.

GERMANY
Has sent five minesweepers, two support ships and one destroyer to eastern Mediterranean. Providing merchant ships to the sealift, ammunition to allied forces and billions of dollars in equipment, assistance and contributions. Germany's constitution prohibits committing military forces outside NATO areas.

HUNGARY
40-man army medical team is being readied for service in the gulf.

JAPAN: Sending vehicles, equipment, food, medical supplies. Sent medical personnel, who have since returned home. Contribution of supplies and services will total $2 billion, plus $2 billion in aid to allied states in the region.

POLAND
Medical team, hospital ship and rescue ship are expected to arrive late this month.

Compiled by James Schwartz, The Washington Post

SOURCES: The Washington Post; Department of Defense; Associated Press; Center for Defense Information; International Institute for Strategic Studies; the Naval Institute.

0162-A

Jan. 15, 1991
WP

01/15/91 17:18 ☎202 797 0595 EMBASSY OF KOREA 017

0121

호 : USW(F) -

신 : 장 관　　　　　　발신 : 주미대사

목 :

보안	
통제	

(매)

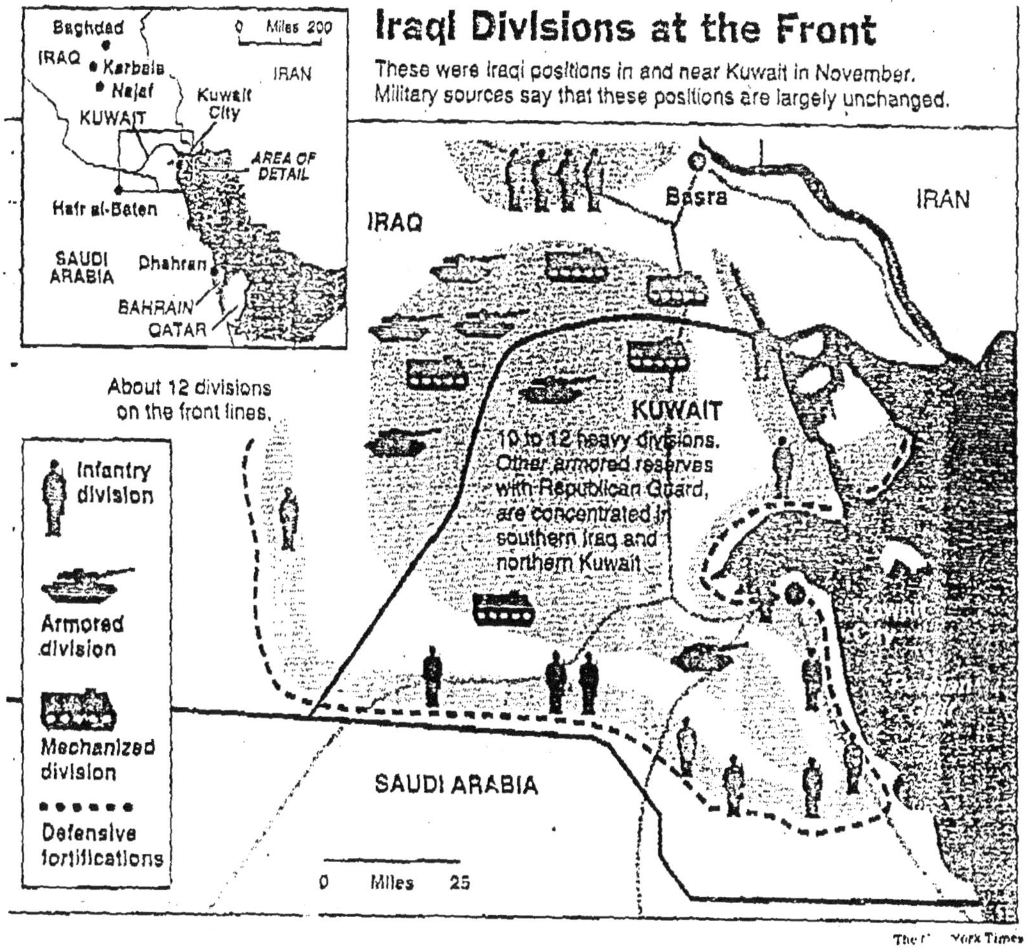

The N. York Times

0162-9

Jan. 15, 1991
NYT

01/15/91 17:18 ☎202 797 0595 EMBASSY OF KOREA 018

0122

번호 : USW(F) - 0168

수신 : 장 관 (미북, 중근동, 미안) 발신 : 주미대사

제목 : "페"만 지역 이 병력 배치 현황 (3 매)

보안 통제	0h

DEFENSE DEPARTMENT/REGULAR BRIEFING, BRIEFER: PETE WILLIAMS
12:04 P.M., EDT, TUESDAY, JANUARY 15, 1991

All right, let me go through the usual sorts of things that we discuss in terms of numbers. First of all, in the theater of operations there are now more than 415,000 US troops. That's up from the last briefing we had here last Thursday, when the number was 370,000. The number of allied troops in the coalition in the theater of operations is now more than 265,000. That number is up from 245,000 at our last briefing.

In terms of service-by-service for US personnel, let me give you some round numbers here, which is about as specific as I'm going to be able to be. This is for the United States forces in the Persian Gulf region, by service: Army, 245,000; Marines, 75,000; Navy, 50,000; and Air Force, 45,000.

In terms of Iraqi forces, our current estimates are that in terms of troops, the Iraqis have more than 545,000 troops in what we call the Kuwaiti theater of operations. That's up 5,000 from our last briefing last Thursday.

Tanks, we estimate the Iraqis have 4,200 tanks; that's up 200 from last Thursday. Armored personnel carriers and infantry fighting vehicles, our estimate is 2,800; that's up 100 from our last briefing. And artillery pieces, we estimate 3,100; that's up 100 from our last briefing.

And in terms of how I would characterize the Iraqi forces, I would say, first of all, that this increase in forces, tanks, armored personnel carriers, artillery pieces, and so forth, is consistent with what we've been saying here the last few days, a westward expansion of their defensive lines -- I don't know how many miles; I can't get into specifics -- but generally a westward expansion of their defensive lines and our current assessment of their forces in the Kuwaiti theater of operations.

There is no evidence that we can detect of their change in their fundamental posture, which is, they're in a defensive posture, although they retain the capability to go on the offensive on very short notice; which is what we've been saying here for quite some

We don't see any evidence that they are in any way pulling out of Kuwait; quite the contrary, from our last briefing the number of forces, tanks, artillery pieces, and so forth, has gone up, which is certainly not consistent with their withdrawal.

배부처	장관실	차관실	一차보	二차보	기획실	의전장	아주국	미주국	구주국	중아국	국기국	경제국	통상국	정문국	영공관	총무과	감사관	공보관	외연원	청와대	총리실	안기부	[illegible]
	/	/	/	/				2		/2				/	/					/	/	/	

13 01 26

0168 - 1

0123

In terms of what our forces are doing today. They are doing what they've been doing for the last several weeks. They continue their training. Among the training activities of ground forces are landing zone operations, trench line clearings, Stinger missile training, platoon battle drills. This is a, again, more or less what our troops have been doing there for the last several weeks. Marine units conducted some helicopter operations, some mine and counter mine exercises, and various live fire exercises with ammunition ranging from 50 caliber to 120 millimeter.

Air Force units flew routine patrols and various types of training ranging from dissimilar air combat training -- that's when two planes engage each other with different kinds of planes -- and other kinds of practice. Additional Navy battle groups are coming into the area, and I'll go into that in a little more detail here in a moment. But in terms of the other carriers that are there, there were routine air operations from the decks of those other aircraft carriers. And of course, our intercept operations continued in both the Red Sea and the Arabian Gulf. So, obviously the forces can read the calendar, they know what the date is, but their training continues as it has been going on for the last several weeks.

Now, I have had some -- several questions down the hall here in the last couple of days about, are our troops on an increased state of alert or a higher level of readiness. And those of you who are regular Pentagon correspondents know that the Department has a history of not discussing alert status or readiness. But I guess I could say that as a general matter, we are taking prudent actions, we are giving due consideration to the current climate in that area,

and we have taken appropriate defensive measures in anticipating the impending deadline of the UN Security Council resolution. But I can't get into specific readiness conditions, I can't talk about specific security measures that we might have undertaken.

Let's see. In terms of other information, in terms of the ship dispositions coming into the Persian Gulf -- just to go down these numbers for it, I realize this is a lot of statistical information but that's kind of the best way to give you the picture of what's going on over there.

In the Arabian Gulf, 34 ships -- well, let me give you the big picture first and then go on down to the detail. All six carriers are there and there's two battleships in terms of the Navy force.

Now more specifically, in the Arabian Gulf we have 34 ships. They consist of the carrier Midway, the battleships Wisconsin and Missouri, and then two command ships, which are the Blue Ridge and the LaSalle, four cruisers, five destroyers, three frigates, four mine warfare ships, seven amphibious ships and six auxiliary ships. And then not included in that would be the non-combatant ships, the two hospital ships -- the Comfort and the Mercy -- and Midway, which is the latest carrier to enter the Persian Gulf went in last Friday.

0162-2

0124

In the Northern Arabian Sea, including the Gulf of Oman, [there are] 35 US ships. That includes the carrier Ranger and its battle group. Ranger and its group arrived in the central area -- the central command area of responsibililty over the weekend. But in the northern Arabian Sea, the Ranger, a cruiser, a destroyer, 24 amphibious ships and eight auxiliary ships.

Twenty-six ships are currently in the Red Sea, and that would include four US aircraft carriers. The America, the Teddy Roosevelt -- I should say the Theodore Roosevelt --
the Saratoga and the John F. Kennedy. And then in addition to those four carriers, there are eight cruisers, four destroyers, two frigates, and eight auxilliary ships.

Now, the Teddy -- the Theodore Roosevelt battle group entered the Red Sea last weekend, and the America battle group came through the Suez Canal today.

In the Mediterranean, 13 ships. They consist of three cruisers, two destroyers, two frigates, five amphibious ships, and one auxiliary ship.

0168-3

0125

관리 번호	91-1513

외 무 부

종 별 : 지 급

번 호 : USW-0201 일 시 : 91 0115 2030

수 신 : 장관(아일,미북,중근동)

발 신 : 주 미 대사

제 목 : 나까야마 외상 방미

연 USW-0154

당관 안 호영 서기관은 금 1.15 국무부 일본과 MOLLOTT 과장과 면담, 표제건에 관해 문의한바 동인 발언 내용 하기보고함. 91.6.30.

1. 나까야마 외상은 어제 부쉬 대통령, 베이커 국무장관이외에 HILLS USTR 대표, BRADY 재무장관과 면담한바, 주요 의제는 페 만 사태에 대한 협력과 UR 문제였음.

2. 페만 사태에 대해서는 나까야마 외상이 난민 지원을 위한 3.8 억불 이외에는 뚜렷한 약속을 하지 못하였으나, 미국으로서는 일본이 추가 지원을 약속하였다는 사실 자체를 큰 진전으로생각함.

단, 일본의 추가 지언은 재정 지원 이상은 불가능할것임.UR 에 대해서는 UR의 성공적 타결에 대한 원칙적인 의견 교환이외에 구체적인 협의는 없었던것으로 알고 있음.

3. 부쉬 대통령 면담시에 배석하였던 솔로몬 차관보가 작성한 면담록에는 한국 관계 논의가 안들어 있으나, 이것은 한국관계 논의가 사진 촬영(PHOTO OPPORTUNITY)전후의 어수선한 분위기하에서 이루어진 때문인것으로 봄.

4. 베이커 장관과의 면담시에는 페 만 토의에 좀더 많은 시간을 할애하기 위해 우선 일본이 관심있는 의제에 대해 나까야마 외상이 약 10 분간 이야기하고베이커 장관은 주로 듣기만 하였는바, 한국문제는 이기회에 거론되었음.

5. 나까야마 외상은 최근 자신도 동행하였던 가이후 수상의 방한이 매우 성공적이었다고 평가하고, 일.북한 관계 정상화를 위한 회담이 1 월말 시작될 예정인바, 일본은 1) 이과정에서 미국및 한국과 긴밀히 협의하고 2) IAEA 문제에 대해서는 한및의 양보도 하지 않겠다(JAPAN WILL NOT CONCEDE ONE INCH TO NORTHKOREA)는 입장을 보였다함.

아주국	장관	차관	1차보	2차보	미주국	중아국	국기국	정문국
청와대	안기부							

PAGE 1 91.01.16 11:39

외신 2과 통제관 BW

0126

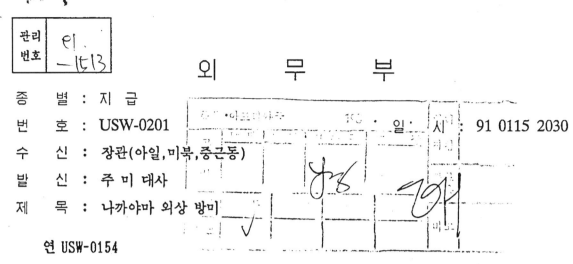

6. 이와 관련 MALLOTT 과장은 본인이 지난 12 월 일본을 방문 가와시마 아주국 심의관과 면담시 동 심의관은 일.북한 관계 진전 문제가 이제 외무성으로 넘어 와 잇으므로 일.북한 관계가 졸속으로 서둘러질 염려가 없다는 의견이었다고 첨언함.

7. 금번 동 외상 방미와 관련 미 국무부 동 아태국이 발표한 언론 발표문과일본측 기자 회견 전문을 별도 FAX(USW(F)-171) 송부함.

(대사 박동진-국장)

91.12.31 일반

長 官 報 告 事 項

報 告 畢

1991. 1 . 16.
美 洲 局
北 美 課(1)

題 目 : 페灣 事態 武力使用 關聯 最近 輿論調査 結果

> 91.1.15자 NYT지는 91.1.11(금)-13(일)간 미 전역 1,512명의 성인을 대상으로 NYT/CBS 뉴스가 합동으로 실시한 페만 사태 무력사용 관련 여론조사 결과를 보도하였는 바, 동 요지 아래 보고드립니다.

1. 부쉬 대통령의 전쟁 회피 노력 및 사태 대처 신뢰도

   o 부쉬 행정부는 전쟁 회피를 위해 가용한 모든 조치를 다했는지 ?

   - 55%(긍정) : 36%(추가노력 필요) : 9%(모르겠음)
   - 59%의 응답자는 1.15 시한 직전 후세인과의 마지막 협상 시도 희망

   o 사태 대처 신뢰도

   - 58%(만족) : 33%(불만)

2. 전쟁발발 가능성

   o 66%가 전쟁 불가피성 인정

   - 개전 시기 ~~관련~~ 이견 노출
   다만, 에 관해서는

앙고재	북미과	91년 1월 16일	담 당	과 장	심의관	국 장	차관보	차 관	장 관
			(서명)	(서명)	(서명)	(서명)			

0128

3. 부분적 사태 해결

o 56%가 이라크군의 쿠웨이트 철수를 전제로한 중동평화 국제회의 개최 지지

o 47%는 이라크군의 쿠웨이트 철수를 조건으로 2개 도서등 양보 조건 해결을 용인

4. 미군 파병 명분

o 주변 중동국에 대한 침략 저지(42%) : 원유 수송로 보호(29%) : 쿠웨이트 정부 회복(11%)

5. 전쟁지속 예상 기간

o 수주(29%) : 수개월(42%) : 1년 이상(21%)

6. 예상되는 미군 사상자 수

o 1,000명 미만(11%) : 1,000명-5,000명(27%) : 5,000명 이상(48%)

7. 전투 양상

o 공습 위주(28%) : 치열한 지상전(67%)

8. 참고 사항

o 흑인 및 여성 응답자들은 백인 또는 남성 응답자에 비해 부쉬 행정부의 강경정책에 대해 비판적 태도를 표명함(15% 차이)

- 장기전에 대한 우려 표명 및 전쟁수행 필요성에 대한 회의 표시

0129

제목 : "파"만 사태 관련 미국내 여론 조사 결과 (2 매)

1304

Americans Don't Expect Short War

By ANDREW ROSENTHAL

A majority of Americans say they are satisfied that President Bush has done everything he should to prevent war in the Persian Gulf. But the country remains deeply divided over whether fighting Iraq is the right policy, and most people do not expect the short war with relatively low casualties that Mr. Bush and his officials have talked about, the latest New York Times/CBS News poll shows.

While the poll suggests that Mr. Bush has been able to maintain public approval for his handling of the crisis, with 55 percent saying they approve and 33 percent saying they disapprove, it also shows where his political vulnerabilities may lie. And it provides the most detailed view to date of Americans' gloomy expectations about what a war in the gulf would be like.

Most of the 1,512 people who were questioned from Friday through Sunday said they expected the war to last several months to more than a year, to require heavy combat on the ground, produce thousands of American deaths and make a major attack by Iraqi agents within the United States likely.

Fear of Another Vietnam

In the end, the greatest political threat to Mr. Bush could come from precisely what he has tried to counter in his public statements: the fear of many Americans, as expressed in follow-up interviews conducted after the survey was completed, that war in the gulf could bring about a repetition of the United States' bitter experience in Vietnam.

"Basically, I guess we're hoping that it's not a Vietnam, not going in nudging and pushing, but going full force and getting it over with minimal loss of lives," said Drew A. Collins, an Ohio banker.

Even among those who say Mr. Bush should give economic sanctions more time, four out of ten said they would consider a short war with low casualties worth fighting. But at the same time, the poll showed that nearly half of those who said Mr. Bush should act now expressed the view that the price for getting Iraq out of Kuwait would not be worth paying if a war dragged on with heavy casualties.

The nationwide telephone survey, which carried a possible sampling error of three percentage points one way or the other, was conducted after the failure of the Iraqi-American talks in Geneva last Wednesday and while Congress debated and then voted for a resolution authorizing Mr. Bush to use force in the gulf.

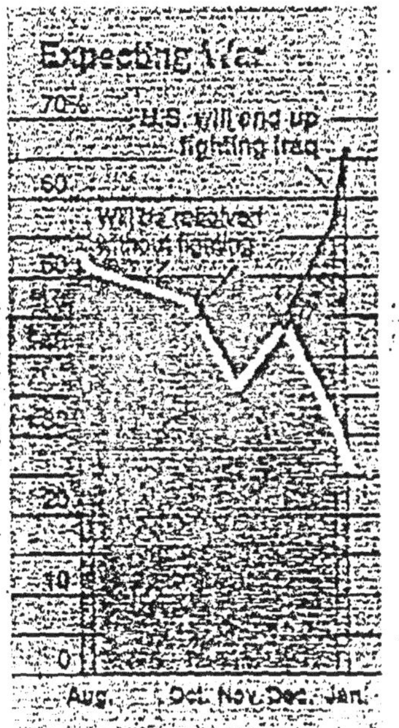

Based on one New York Times Poll and six New York Times/CBS News Polls; the most recent one interviewed 1,512 adults nationwide Jan. 11-13.

The New York Times

A solid majority, 66 percent, said they expected that the country would end up in a war, an increase of nine percentage points from a poll conducted a week earlier. But they were evenly split on whether Mr. Bush should immediately begin hostilities or wait to give economic sanctions more time.

The Congressional vote had little effect on how Americans answered this second question. People interviewed on Friday, before Congress voted, were equally divided between the use of force and continuing sanctions, as were those interviewed on Saturday or Sunday, after the votes in the Senate and the House.

The follow-up interviews suggested that some of those who called for action soon were expressing a desire to get it over with rather than registering enthusiastic support for Mr. Bush's position.

"We should be real sure we're going to get this thing done or not do it at all," said Robert T. Grindle, a 58-year-old Korean War veteran from Blue Hill, Me. "Bush opened his mouth and we have to back him up. We appointed him President and have to back him but Bush — he said too much, got himself in trouble."

Majorities for Conflicting Views

Fifty-five percent of Americans said Mr. Bush had done "everything he should to avoid war." But 59 percent continued to say that Mr. Bush should seek a meeting with President Saddam Hussein before midnight tonight.

The sample was evenly divided between those who said they thought that Mr. Bush had already made up his mind to have a war and those who thought he might still be trying to call Mr. Hussein's bluff. "It's a poker hand," said Randy Fisher, 35, of Grand Rapids, Mich. "If Hussein doesn't back down, you show him your aces, all four of them. Make it fast and sweet."

Although Mr. Bush has said he rules out any negotiation or compromise with Iraq, a majority of Americans — 56 percent — said it would be acceptable for the United States to first agree to an international conference on Arab-Israeli problems if Iraq would then withdraw from Kuwait. Forty-seven percent said it would be acceptable to them if the ousted leadership of Kuwait offered to trade a piece of the country's territory in return for Iraq's withdrawal from most of Kuwait.

Although the Bush Administration has devoted much attention in recent weeks to its attempts to explain the reasons for sending troops to Saudi Arabia, Americans remained divided on why those forces are there.

Forty-two percent said it was mainly to stop Iraq from attacking its neighbors, 29 percent said it was mainly to protect oil supplies, and 11 percent said it was mainly to restore the leadership of Kuwait.

But when it came to deciding whether those reasons were "good enough to go to war," the poll showed an even split overall. Only among those who said American troops were sent to stop attacks by Iraq did a majority say that was a good enough reason for a war.

The groups most polarized by the gulf crisis were blacks and whites and men and women. By margins of 15 percentage points or more, blacks and women were more opposed to early action, more disapproving of Mr. Bush and his handling of the gulf crisis, and more inclined to say that a war of any duration was not worth fighting.

0163 - 1

Jan. 15, 1991
NYT

01/15/91 17:21 ☎202 797 0595 EMBASSY OF KOREA ☑019

0130

수신 : 장 관 [redacted] 발신 : 주미대사 [redacted]

제목 : (매)

The New York Times | CBS NEWS Poll

The Split on Iraq: Sanctions vs. War

If Iraq does not withdraw from Kuwait by Jan. 15, do you think the United States should start military actions against Iraq, or should the United States wait longer to see if the trade embargo and other economic sanctions work?

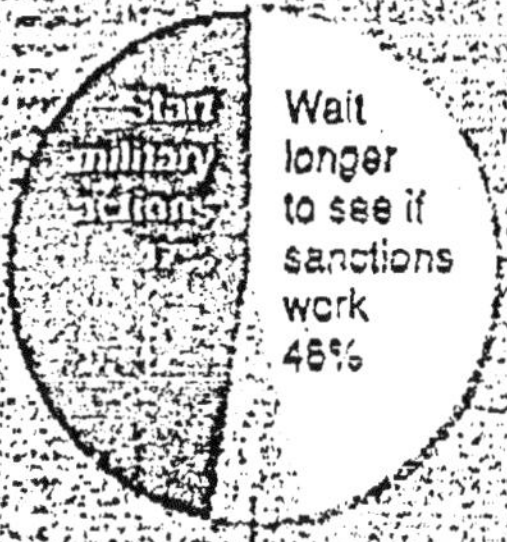

Don't know/no answer 6%

Percent of Each Group Who Say:

Size of Each Group		Start Military Actions	Wait Longer on Sanctions
EXPECTED DURATION OF WAR			
29%	A few weeks	64	33
42	Several months	48	47
21	A Year or longer	30	64
EXPECTED LOSS OF LIFE OF AMERICAN SOLDIERS			
11%	Under 1,000	62	34
27	From 1,000 to 5,000	56	40
46	Over 5,000	41	53
EXPECTATION FOR BOMBING VS. GROUND COMBAT			
28%	Mainly bombing by air	62	31
67	Heavy combat on ground	44	52

Based on 1,512 adults nationwide, interviewed by telephone Jan. 11-13.

The New York Times

The New York Times
CBS NEWS Poll

Do you think that George Bush has done everything he should to avoid war, or should he be doing more?

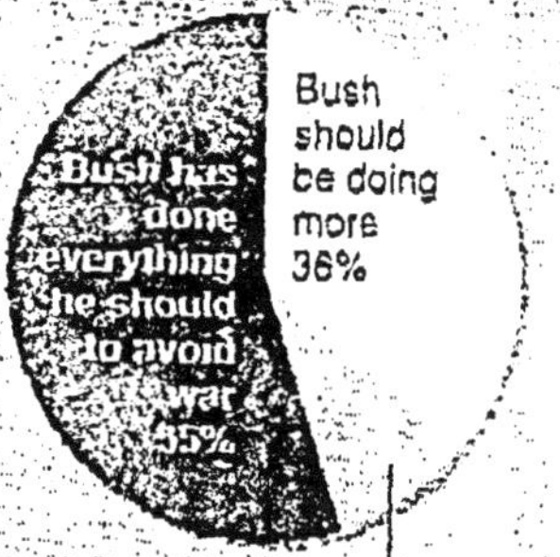

Don't know/no answer 9%

Based on a survey of 1,512 adults nationwide interviewed Jan. 11-13.

The New York Times

Jan. 15, 1991
NYT

0163-2

01/15/91 17:22 ☎202 797 0595 EMBASSY OF KOREA ☑020

0131

정 리 보 존 문 서 목 록					
기록물종류	일반공문서철	등록번호	2012090524	등록일자	2012-09-17
분류번호	772	국가코드	US/XF	보존기간	영구
명 칭	걸프사태 : 미국의 대응, 1990-91. 전6권				
생 산 과	북미과/안보과	생산년도	1990~1991	담당그룹	
권 차 명	V.5 1991.1.16-31				
내용목차	* 1.16 다국적군, 대이라크군 군사작전 개시(걸프전 발발)				

0001

관리번호	91-70

원 본

외 무 부

종 별 : 지 급

번 호 : STW-0016 일 시 : 91 0116 1630

수 신 : 장관(미북, 중동)

발 신 : 주 시애틀 총영사

제 목 : 폐만사태

대 AM-0012

1. 금 16 일(수) 오후 당지 방송들은 일제히 이락에대한 다국적군의 공격이시작되었음을 보도하고있음

2. 당관은 대호 필요한 조치를 취하고있음

(총영사-국장)

예고 일반 91.12.31

일반문서로 재분류(1991.12.31.)

검 토 필 (1991.6.30.)

미주국 중아국

PAGE 1

91.01.17 10:00

외신 2과 통제관 BT

0002

갈

외 무 부

종 별 :

번 호 : USW-0205 일 시 : 91 0116 1029

수 신 : 장 관(통일, 중근동,미북,해운 항만청)

발 신 : 주 미대사

제 목 : 페만 항행 선박에 대한 특별 주의

연: USW-3810

이락의 쿠웨이트 철수 시한이 경과, 무력 사용이 농후해짐에 따라 미국무부는 페만, 아라비아 해 및 홍해지역 통항 선박에 대한 연호 해상 검색 강화 및 이의 준수를 재 강조한 별첨 특별 주의문을 발표 하였음.

첨부: USW(F)-0173 (1매)

(대사 박동진- 국장)

통상국 미주국 중아국 해항정 1차보 2차보 동자부

PAGE 1

91.01.17 07:34 CT

외신 1과 통제관

0003

SW-
0173

장관 (통일, 중근동, 미북, 해운항만청) 발신 : 주미대사

USW-0206 첨부 (1매)

SPECIAL WARNING NUMBER 64.
PERSIAN GULF - ARABIAN SEA - RED SEA.
<TEXT>
1. UNITED NATIONS SECURITY COUNCIL RESOLUTION 678 (1990), ADOPTED 29 NOVEMBER 1990, AUTHORIZED MEMBER STATES CO-OPERATING WITH
UNCLASSIFIED

UNCLASSIFIED
PAGE 04
THE GOVERNMENT OF KUWAIT, UNLESS IRAQ ON OR BEFORE 15 JANUARY 1991 FULLY COMPLIES WITH RESOLUTION 660 (1990) AND ALL SUBSEQUENT RELEVANT RESOLUTIONS, TO USE ALL NECESSARY MEANS TO UPHOLD AND IMPLEMENT SUCH RESOLUTIONS AND TO RESTORE INTERNATIONAL PEACE AND SECURITY IN THE AREA.
2. ALL MERCHANT SHIPS ARE ADVISED THT, SHOULD IRAQ FAIL TO COMPLY FULLY WITH REOLUTION 678, THEN, AFTER 0500 (GMT) 16 JANUARY 1991, ARMED FORCE MAY BE USED IN THE WATERS BORDERING THE NATIONS OF IRAQ AND KUWAIT AND THE ARABIAN PENINSULA, INCLUDING THE PERSIAN GULF, NORTH ARABIAN SEA. AND RED SEA.
3. ALL PROCEDURES OF THE MULTINATIONAL INTERCEPTION FORCE, DESCRIBED IN SPECIAL WARNING NO. 80 REMAIN IN EFFECT.
4. FAILURE OF A SHIP TO PROCEED AS DIRECTED BY THE
PAGE 06 RUCKSGG6461 UNCLAS
INTERCEPTING SHIP WILL RESULT IN THE USE OF THE MINIMUM LEVEL FORCE NECESSARY TO ENSURE COMPLIANCE.
5. ALL SHIPS, INCLUDING WATERBORNE CRAFT AND ARMED MERCHANT SHIPS OR AIRCRAFT, WHICH THREATEN OR INTERFERE WITH THE MULTINATIONAL INTERCEPTION FORCE WILL BE CONSIDERED HOSTILE AND COULD BE FIRED UPON.
UNCLASSIFIED
NNNN

END

0004

HO[redacted]E UNITED STATES ENT[redacted] WAR

In its 224-year history, the United States has used its armed forces outside its borders 215 times. Only five of these situations were formally declared wars. Following is a brief analysis of how the U.S. has entered war. First are several general principles describing how America enters into war. Next, historical examples of the five declared wars and other major undeclared wars are used to illustrate these general principles.

<u>BASIC PRINCIPLES</u>

To understand how the United States enters into and conducts a war, and how public support for war has developed, the following general principles are useful.

* The U.S. has not historically entered wars through deliberate consideration by the Congress and the President of all relevant factors, including public opinion. U.S. entry has usually been provoked by prior hostile acts by foreign powers. Wars have also been pushed on the country by a determined President ordering military actions or by a determined Congress. American wars, at their start, have sometimes lacked popular support.

* There is a strong feeling against use of force by Americans, with a few historical exceptions. In recent times Americans have been very skeptical of long-lasting or costly military commitments. But even during unpopular, prolonged, and costly wars, Congress has never

0005

used its budget power to end American participation in a war while shooting continued.

* Public attitudes towards the question of war at the start of American participation are not necessarily any guide to opinion as it will develop during a war. Also, dissent has sometimes ended or declined with the beginning of fighting even after initial popular disagreement over war aims. Dissent tends to increase with the length of hostilities, unless countered by military successes and progress towards clear victory. Wars or other uses of force have been initiated by the President and Congress with great public support, by the President over badly divided public opposition, and amidst public apathy or ignorance.

THE DECLARED WARS

The War of 1812 was possibly America's least popular war. It was supported by the South and West of the country but not by New England or New York, and it arose from unresolved conflicts with Britain. Popular support for the war was so mixed that Congress failed to take several actions requested by the President to prepare the country to fight, and the government was unable to raise its desired army. American forces won no significant victories, and Britain made peace because of distractions elsewhere. The declaration of war passed the Senate by only 4 votes, 19-13. This war was an example of a determined President leading the country into war against a divided Congress and strong regional opposition. That popular opposition, by discouraging volunteers from entering the army, eventually denied the President the forces he needed to fight.

0006

World War I the U.S. into it fully 3 ye[illegible]er it had begun. President Wilson was elected partly on the basis of keeping America out of the war. Popular opinion was not strongly in favor of entering the war, although U.S.-German relations were poor and Americans sympathized with the Allies. But Germany's unrestricted submarine warfare against American seamen on unarmed merchant ships in the Atlantic provided the provocation that eventually allowed President Wilson to obtain a declaration of war from Congress. Americans thought that a fresh American force could help bring the prolonged European contest to a quick end. In this case the U.S. entered war with expectations of quick success, after serious provocation by Germany, and without the fear of heavy casualties. The shocking casualties and disappointing political results of the war were major factors that drove the country into its isolationist mood of the 1920s and 1930s. Only the Japanese attack on Hawaii changed this isolationist condition. A substantial anti-war element campaigned against U.S. participation in World War I and against a war declaration, but these opponents supported U.S. policy after the U.S. entered the war on the side of the Allies.

World War II is usually considered to be the most popular and successful American war. But the country was dragged into the conflict through horrible provocation by Japan and terrible enemy misjudgment, and might never have played the role it did without these factors. As Secretary Cheney has pointed out, less than 3 months prior to Pearl Harbor, the House passed by a single vote a law to lower the draft age to 18 from 20 and extend the service period to 18 months. Only the Japanese attack on Hawaii changed the political atmosphere. President Roosevelt got a declaration of war on the day he requested it. But even after Pearl Harbor, many Americans hoped the U.S. would fight only Japan in the Pacific, while Britain fought Hitler in Europe. The Nazis

0007

The Mexica[redacted]erican War of 1846 was als[redacted]pular. President Polk ordered an American military movement that provoked an alleged Mexican attack, and Polk used this to request a declaration of war from Congress. The war was essentially based on the desire of Polk and others to promote expansion of the U.S. to the West, which required pushing back Mexico. But the war proved more and more unpopular, and members of Congress attempted to limit the war effort. Mexico was so militarily weak that Polk did not need much from Congress, however. Even though the U.S. was victorious, the war attracted congressional criticism even after it ended. None of the acts by Congress directly affected the military campaign. The Mexican War survived popular opposition because it was short, successful, and because the President needed no extraordinary measures, such as a draft, to conduct it. It was begun by a determined President who ordered the initial military provocation against Mexico.

The Spanish-American War of 1898 was a war pushed on a reluctant President by public hysteria encouraged by the press. Despite repeated concessions by Spain, popular sympathy created by the rebellion of Cuba against Spanish rule eventually forced President McKinley to ask Congress for a declaration of war. The war was short and successful, which maintained its popularity, and only became controversial when the peace treaty to end it gave the U.S. control of the Philippines, since many Americans had supported the war as a struggle against colonialism. Of all American declared wars, this one began with broad and strong popular support, and without real foreign provocation -- that is, it was a war that America chose to start. This can be explained in part by the energetic and confident American popular mood of the time, which saw the war as a moral crusade against European colonialist domination.

0008

solved this problem for President Roosevelt by declaring war on the U.S. to fulfill their duties under the Axis alliance with Japan. Here again, the U.S. did not enter a war after a process of prolonged deliberation. As in World War I, a large number of opponents to American participation in the war quickly lined up behind the war effort once Japan had involved the U.S. in the war.

UNDECLARED WARS AND LIMITED ACTIONS

Current American attitudes towards war have been set much more by the undeclared **Korean War** and especially the **Vietnam War** than by the World Wars or the conflicts of the 19th century. This is also true of patterns of interaction between the President and Congress on issues of war. But certain historical patterns persist. Limited military actions in the **Dominican Republic** (1965), **Grenada** (1983), and **Panama** (1989) demonstrate again that conflicts of short duration, with limited casualties, and immediate success, are either genuinely popular with the American people or are over before dissent and can become serious. In each of these three cases the use of force proved popular after the fact. In the first two cases the actions were brief and came as a surprise to most Americans. In Panama, a long-building resentment towards General Noriega's government helped make the relatively light casualties of the operation acceptable to American public opinion.

Vietnam had several characteristics that must be kept in mind. First, U.S. objectives there were never seen by the public as relating to a vital interest or to self-defense. Second, popular opposition to the war was not significant until after many years, thousands of American deaths in action, the institution of a draft, and a series of events that seemed to show a tough prolonged fight was likely. The main event was the

0009

communists' Tet Offensive of 1968, which badly damaged the Vietcong forces but shocked Americans, who did not expect any more major fighting.

Actual U.S. entry into Vietnam was not unique. In the pattern of the post-World War II period, Congress had authorized presidential action in broad terms to defend American forces and interests. Similar authorizations had accompanied crises in the Middle East, Cuba, Berlin, and the Formosa Straits. Unlike those crises, Vietnam blossomed into a full-scale conventional military commitment with major American casualties.

Even in Vietnam, which grew to be very unpopular, Congress never used its budgetary authority to stop the war or limit American war actions. The Senate adopted such restrictions, but the full Congress never went beyond non-binding statements of opposition to the war. So while Vietnam represents a break in the historical pattern of dissent ending once the shooting starts, it continued the important tradition of Congress never actually denying a President the tools of war when the conflict had already started.

The struggle between Congress and the President over the war power is partly based on an institutional conflict that comes from the U.S. Constitution, which gives both branches of government important power over military matters. It is also based on the a political fact: members of Congress find it difficult to support a policy that will result in the sons of some voters being killed or wounded. Historically, only Presidents have had the political strength and national stature to lead the country into wars. Congress has usually cooperated, but normally plays a minor role once fighting begins.

0010

관리 번호	91/273

외 무 부

종 별 : 지 급

번 호 : USW-0218 일 시 : 91 0116 1806

수 신 : 장관(아일,미북,중근동)

발 신 : 주 미 대사

제 목 : 나까야마 외상방미 종합 보고

연:USW-0201

나까야마 외상의 금번 방미목적, 미측의 태도, 언론보도등을 종합, 하기 보고함.

1. 방문 배경 및 목적

0 일본의 안보 무임승차 및 미.일 무역역조에 대한 미국 조야의 불만은 폐만 사태 이후에 특히 고조되어, 의회에서 폐만 사태 논의시 마다 일본및 독일의 무성의(FAIR-WEATHER ALLY) 가 성토되고, 급기야는 일본이 주일 미군경비 전액을부담하지 않으면 주일 미군을 매년 5,000 명씩 삭감한다는 극단적 내용의 수정안 (BONIOR AMENDMENT) 까지 통과하게됨.

0 일본은 폐만 사태로 인한 긴장과 이에 따라 점증하는 반일감정을 무마시킬 필요가 있었고 미국으로서는 유엔 결의안 678 호가 지정한 이락군 철군 시한인 15 일이 임박한 시점에서 주요 우방인 일본 외상이 방미, 미국의 대 폐만 노력에 지원을 보여주는것이 대국민 및 대외 홍보에 효과가 있다는 이익이 일치하여 금번 방문이 서둘러 이루어진 것으로 관찰됨. (주미 일본대사관 나까무라 참사관에 의하면, 일본은 지난 12 월말 금번 방문을 미측에 제의하여 이루어진것이라 함.)

2. 미국의 태도

0 미 정부는 상기 목적을 충족시키고, 아울러 언론과 의회의 대일본 감정을완화 시킴으로써 중요한 우방인 일본과의 관계 증진을 꾀한다는 취지에서 폐만사태는 물론이고, 주일 미군주둔 경비, UR 등 주요한 문제 전반에 대해 미.일간에 긴밀한 협조가 이루어지고 있다는 인식을 극대화하기 위해 노력한 것으로 보임.

0 미 국무부는 정례 기자회견 이외에 별도로 동.아태국이 성명을 발표하여 일본이 (1)대 폐만 지원을 위해 추가 지원을 약속하였으며, (2) 일본이 부담하는주일 미군 주둔 비용을 40 % 에서 50 % 로 인상하는 협정에 서명 하였음을 부각시키고자

아주국	장관	차관	1차보	2차보	미주국	중아국	청와대	안기부

PAGE 1

91.01.17 09:06

외신 2과 통제관 BT

0011

노력하였음.

3. 한국관계 협의

0 나까무라 외상- BUSH 대통령 면담시 PHOTO OPPORTUNITY 를 통해 이루어진짧은 기자회견 (USW-0154 로 기보고)을 통해 나까무라 외상이 가이후 수상 방한, 일. 북한 협상등에 대해 발언한 것과 관련, 일본이 동북아에서 일본이 차지하는 역할을 부각 시키기 위해 의도적으로 동기회를 이용했을 가능성을 상정해 볼수있으나, 30 분간에 걸쳐 BUSH 대통령 예방을 하는 중간에 동 PHOTO OPPORTUNITY가 있었음에 비추어 그러한 가능성은 높지 않은 것으로 판단되며, 또한 동 내용은 미국 언론매체에서 전혀 취급하지 않았음.

4. 언론 반응

0 일본이 폐만 작전을 위해 추가지원을 약속하였다는 설명과 함께 1.14 밤 CNN 을 비롯한 주요 TV 뉴스 에 방영된바, 1.14 은 1.15 시한의 전야임에 비추어TV 뉴스 시청율이 특히 높았을것으로 예상됨.

0 1.15. 조간은 W.P 가 JAPAN HINTS AT INCREASE IN ITS DESERT SHIELD AID제하에 4 단 기사로, NYT 가 AVOID WAR, JAPAN TELLS IRAQ 제하에 2 단 기사로보도한바, W.P 는 일본이 폐만에 대한 추가 지원을 약속하였다는것과 함께 WIRTH 상원의원등을 인용, 일본의 지원이 미흡함을 지적하였음.

5. 미국무부 발표문 및 4 항 기사는 연호 및 USW(F)-0164 참조

(대사 박동진-국장)

예고:91.12.31 일반

검토필(1991. 6. 30.)

관리번호	91-91

원 본

외 무 부

종 별 : 초긴급

번 호 : USW-0224 　　일 시 : 91 0116 2037

수 신 : 장관(미북, 대책반, 중근동)사본: 대통령비서실장

발 신 : 주 미 대사

제 목 : 미국의 대이락 작전개시

1. 금 1.16 19:00(당지시간)미국무부 DESAIX ANDERSON 차관보대리(SOLOMON 차관보는 금일 뉴욕 향발)는 본직에 대한 긴급 전화를 통해, BUSH 대통령은 금일저녁 유엔안보리결의안의 이행을 위한 대이락 군사작전을 개시토록 명령을 하달하고, 동 대통령의 뜻에 따라 동 대이락 작전 개시 사실이 노태우 대통령께 즉각 보고되도록 적의 조처를 취해줄것을 요청하였음.

2. ANDERSON 차관보 대리는 당지시간 21:00 에 BUSH 대통령이 전기 작전 개시를 공식 발표할 계획이라고 부언하였음.

3. 이에 본직은 동 BUSH 대통령의 뜻이 즉시 전달되도록 조처하겠다고하고, 이락의 침략을 응징하기위한 BUSH 대통령의 결연한 노력이 신속한 성과를 거둘것을 희구하였는바, ANDERSON 차관보는 아국정부의 적극적 지원에 감사한다고 답변함.

4. 한편, 1.16.19:30 현재 백악관 FITZWATER 대변인은 당지시간 19:00 를 기해 쿠웨이트 해방작전이 개시되어 OPERATION DESERT SHIELD 는 OPERATION DESERT STORM 으로 전환되었다고 발표하였음. 이와관련 당지 매체들은 이락및 쿠웨이트지역 목표물에 대한 공습이 약 18:30 경 개시된것을 관찰된다고 보도하고 있음.

5. 진전사항 추보예정임.

(대사 박동진-장관)

예고:91.12.31 일반

일반문서로 재분류(1991.12.31.)

검 토 필 (1991.6.30.)

미주국	장관	차관	1차보	2차보	중아국	청와대	총리실	안기부

PAGE 1 　　91.01.17 10:58

외신 2과 통제관 BT

0013

원 본

외 무 부

종 별 : 긴 급

번 호 : USW-0231　　　　일 시 : 91 0116 2341

수 신 : 장 관(미북, 대책반, 중근동, 미안)

발 신 : 주 미 대사

제 목 : 미국의 대이락 공격(제 2호, 부쉬 대통령 연설)

부쉬 대통령은 금 1.16 당지시간 저녁 9시 대국민 TV 연설을 통해 2시간전 다국적군 공군이 이락과 쿠웨이트에 대한 군사작전을 개시 (지상군은 미투입)하였다고 공식 발표하였는바, 동요지 아래 보고함.

1. 금번 군사조치는 유엔 결의와 미의회의 동의에 따른것임. 그동안 미국과 유엔의 지속적인 외교적 노력과 아랍국가들의 해결 노력, 베이커 국무장관과 아지즈 이락외상의 제네바 회담, 케야르 유엔사무총장의 중재노력등 모든 합리적인 노력에도 불구하고 평화적인 해결이 이루어지지 않음으로써 어쩔수없이 무력을 사용하게된것인바, 이락의 잠재적 핵무기 시설, 화학무기 공장과 탱크등군사 시설을 공격목표로 하고 있음.

또한 사우디 주둔 현지 사령관 보고에 따르면, 동작전은 계획대로 순조롭게 진행되고 있음.

2. 금번 작전의 목표는 쿠웨이트에 정통정부를 회복하고, 이락이 유엔의 결의를 준수하게함으로써 페르시아만의 안정을 회복하기 위한것인바, 그동안 취해온 대이락 제재조치만으로는 이락의 쿠웨이트 철수라는 목표를 달성할수 없다는 판단에 따른것임.

3. 미국과 유엔은 사태를 평화적으로 해결하기 위해 모든 노력을 다하였으나, 후세인은 이러한 모든 평화적 노력과 미의회의 단호한 결의를 통한사전 경고를 거부하였으므로 다국적군은 무력을 통해서만 평화를 달성할수 있다고 판단, 군사작전을 개시한것임. 전쟁은 조속 종결될것이며, 피해는 최소한도에 그칠것임. 금번 전쟁이 또하나의 베트남이 되지 않을것임을 확언함. 미국의 목표는 이락을 정복하고자하는 것이아니며 쿠웨이트를 해방시키려는 것일뿐임.

(대사 박동진-장관)

미주국	장관	차관	1차보	2차보	미주국	중아국	정문국	청와대
총리실	안기부	대책반						

0014

PAGE 1　　91.01.17 14:02 WG

외신 1과 통제관

길

번호 : USWF-188

수신 : 장관 (중근동, 미북, 미안)

발신 : 주미대사

제목 : 부쉬 대통령 공격 개시 발표

1117

지급

(5매)

.EOF

REMARKS BY PRESIDENT GEORGE BUSH REGARDING THE LAUNCH OF ATTACK ON IRAQ
THE OVAL OFFICE/ 9:00 P.M., EST
ZZ-3-1 page# 1 WEDNESDAY, JANUARY 16, 1991
dest=swh,mwh,pergulf,mme,mideast,iraq,armfor,kuwait,arab,un
data

PRESIDENT BUSH: Just two hours ago, allied air forces began an attack on military targets in Iraq and Kuwait. These attacks continue as I speak. Ground forces are not engaged. This conflict started August 2nd when the dictator of Iraq invaded a small and helpless neighbor. Kuwait, a member of the Arab League and a member of the United Nations was crushed, its people brutalized.

Five months ago, Saddam Hussein started this cruel war against Kuwait; tonight the battle has been joined. This military action, taken in accord with United Nations resolutions and with the consent of the United States Congress, follows months of constant and virtually endless diplomatic activity on the part of the United Nations, the United States and many, many other countries. Arab leaders sought what became known as an Arab solution, only to conclude that Saddam Hussein was unwilling to leave Kuwait. Others travelled to Baghdad in a variety of efforts to restore peace and justice. Our Secretary of State James Baker held an historic meeting in Geneva only to be totally rebuffed. This past weekend, in a last ditch effort, the Secretary General of the United Nations went to the Middle East with peace in his heart -- his second such mission and he came back from Baghdad

CONTINUED

배부처	장관실	차관실	一차보	二차보	기획실	의전장	아주국	미주국	구주국	중아국	국기국	경제국	통상국	정문국	영교국	총무과	감사관	공보관	외연원	청와대	총리실	안기부	공보처
	/	/	/	/				2		②				/						/	/	/	

1201
2분

188 - 1

0015

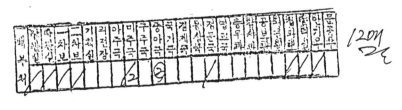

REMARKS BY PRESIDENT GEORGE BUSH REGARDING THE LAUNCH OF ATTACK ON IRAQ
THE OVAL OFFICE/ 9:00 P.M., EST
ZZ-3-2 page# 1 WEDNESDAY, JANUARY 16, 1991
dest=swh,mwh,pergulf,mme,mideast,iraq,armfor,kuwait,arab,un,fns20611
dest+=nucweapon,
data

with no progress at all in getting Saddam Hussein to withdraw from Kuwait. Now, the 28 countries with forces in the Gulf area have exhausted all reasonable efforts to reach a peaceful resolution, have no choice but to drive Saddam from Kuwait by force. We will not fail.

As I report to you, air attacks are underway against military targets in Iraq. We are determined to knock out Saddam Hussein's nuclear bomb potential. We will also destroy his chemical weapons facilities. Much of Saddam's artillery and tanks will be destroyed. Our operations are designed to best protect the lives of all the coalition forces by targeting Saddam's vast military arsenal. Initial reports from General Schwarzkopf are that our operations are proceeding according to plan.

Our objectives are clear. Saddam Hussein's forces will leave Kuwait. The legitimate government of Kuwait will be restored to its rightful place and Kuwait will once again be free.

Iraq will eventually comply with all relevant United Nations resolutions and then when peace is restored, it is our hope that Iraq will live as a peaceful and cooperative member of the family of nations, thus enhancing the security and stability of the Gulf.

Some may ask, "Why act now? Why not wait?" The answer is clear. The world could wait no longer.

CONTINUED

188- 2

0016

REMARKS BY PRESIDENT GEORGE BUSH REGARDING THE LAUNCH OF ATTACK ON IRAQ
THE OVAL OFFICE/ 9:00 P.M., EST
ZZ-3-3-E page# 1 WEDNESDAY, JANUARY 16, 1991

dest=swh,mwh,perqulf,mme,mideast,iraq,armfor,kuwait,arab,un,fns20611
dest+=ecsanct,terr,chemwar,nucweapon,thdwd,easteur,europe,asia,africa
dest+=gas,oil
data

Sanctions, though having some effect, showed no signs of accomplishing their objective. Sanctions were tried for well over five months and we and our allies concluded that sanctions alone would not force Saddam from Kuwait.

While the world waited Saddam Hussein systematically raped, pillaged and plundered a tiny nation -- no threat to his own. He subjected the people of Kuwait to unspeakable atrocities, and among those maimed and murdered -- innocent children. While the world waited Saddam sought to add to the **chemical weapons** arsenal he now possesses an infinitely more dangerous weapon of mass destruction, a nuclear weapon.

And while the world waited, while the world talked peace and withdrawal Saddam Hussein dug in and moved massive forces into Kuwait. While the world waited, while Saddam stalled, more damage was being done to the fragile economies of the **Third World**, the emerging democracies of **Eastern Europe**, to the entire world, including to our own economy.

The United States, together with the United Nations, exhausted every means at our disposal to bring this crisis to a peaceful end. However, Saddam clearly felt that by stalling and threatening and defying the United Nations he could weaken the forces arrayed against him.

While the world waited Saddam Hussein met every overture of peace with open contempt. While the world prayed for peace Saddam prepared for war.

I had hoped that when the United States Congress, in historic debate, took its resolute action Saddam would realize he could not prevail and would move out of Kuwait in accord with the United Nations resolutions. He did not do that.

Instead, he remained intransigent, certain that time was on his side. Saddam was warned over and over again to comply with the will of the United Nations -- leave Kuwait or be driven out. Saddam has arrogantly rejected all warnings. Instead, he tried to make this a dispute between Iraq and the United States of America. Well, he failed. Tonight, 28 nations, countries from five continents -- **Europe** and **Asia**, **Africa** and the Arab League have forces in the Gulf area standing shoulder-to-shoulder against Saddam Hussein. These countries had hoped the use of force could be avoided. Regrettably, we now believe that only force will make him leave.

Prior to ordering our forces into battle, I instructed our

1AA - 3

0017

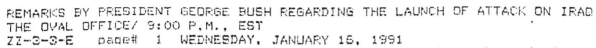

REMARKS BY PRESIDENT GEORGE BUSH REGARDING THE LAUNCH OF ATTACK ON IRAQ
THE OVAL OFFICE/ 9:00 P.M., EST
ZZ-3-3-E page# 2 WEDNESDAY, JANUARY 16, 1991

military commanders to take every necessary step to prevail as quickly as possible and with the greatest degree of protection possible for American and allied servicemen and women. I've told the American people before that this will not be another Vietnam. And I repeat this here tonight. Our troops will have the best possible support in the entire world. And they will not be asked to fight with one hand tied behind their back.

I'm hopeful that this fighting will not go on for long and that casualties will be held to an absolute minimum. This is an historic moment. We have in this past year made great progress in ending the long era of conflict and Cold War. We have before us the opportunity to forge for ourselves and for future generations a new world order, a world where the rule of law, not the law of the jungle, governs the conduct of nations. When we are successful, and we will be, we have a real chance at this new world order, an order in which a credible United Nations can use its peacekeeping role to fulfill the promise and vision of the UN's founders.

We have no argument with the people of Iraq. Indeed, for the innocents caught in this conflict, I pray for their safety. Our goal is not the conquest of Iraq. It is the liberation of Kuwait. It is my hope that somehow the Iraqi people can even now convince their dictator that he must lay down his arms, leave Kuwait and let Iraq itself rejoin the family of peace-loving nations.

Thomas Paine wrote many years ago: "These are the times that try men's souls." Those well-known words are so very true today. But even as planes of the multinational forces attack Iraq, I prefer to think of peace not war. I am convinced not only that we will prevail, but that out of the horror of combat will come the recognition that no nation can stand against a world united, no nation will be permitted to brutally assault its neighbor.

No president can easily commit our sons and daughters to war. They are the nation's finest. Ours is an all-volunteer force, magnificently trained, highly motivated.
The troops know why they're there. And listen to what they say, for they've said it better than any president or prime minister ever could. Listen to Hollywood Huddleston (sp), Marine Lance Corporal. He says, "Let's free these people so we can go home and be free again." And he's right. The terrible crimes and tortures committed by Saddam's henchmen against the innocent people of Kuwait are an affront to mankind and a challenge to the freedom of all.

Listen to one of our great officers out there, Marine Lieutenant General Walter Boomer (sp). He said, "There are things worth fighting for. A world in which brutality and lawlessness are allowed to go unchecked isn't the kind of world we're going to want to live in."

Listen to Master Sargeant J.K. Kendall (sp) of the 82nd Airborne. "We're here for more than just the price of a gallon of gas. What we're doing is going to chart the future of the world for

1AA-4

0018

REMARKS BY PRESIDENT GEORGE BUSH REGARDING THE LAUNCH OF ATTACK ON IRAQ
THE OVAL OFFICE/ 9:00 P.M., EST
ZZ-3-3-E page# 3 WEDNESDAY, JANUARY 16, 1991

the next 100 years. It's better to deal with this guy now than five years from now."

And finally, we should all sit up and listen to Jackie Jones (sp), an Army lieutenant, when she says, "If we let him get away with this, who knows what's going to be next?"

I've called upon Hollywood and Walter and J.P. and Jackie and all their courageous comrades in arms to do what must be done. Tonight America and the world are deeply grateful to them and to their families.

And let me say to everyone listening or watching tonight: When the troops we've sent in finish their work, I'm determined to bring them home as soon as possible. Tonight, as our forces fight, they and their families are in our prayers.

May God bless each and every one of them and the coalition forces at our side in the Gulf, and may He continue to bless our nation, the United States of America.

END

1AA - 5

0019

부시 미통령 대국민 담화요지

- 1.17(목) 11:00-11:12(서울시간) -

o 2시간전 페르시아만 배치 연합군이 쿠웨이트와 이라크내 이라크 군사시설에 대한 공격을 개시하였음. 지상군의 공격은 아직이루어 지지 않고 있음.

o 이라크의 쿠웨이트 침공후 수개월에 걸친 평화적 해결을 위한 지속적인 외교적 노력에도 불구. 이라크의 평화해결안 거부로 전쟁을 선택할 수 밖에 없었음.

o 현재 공군에 의한 공격은 이라크의 핵시설, 화학무기 그리고 기타 군사시설을 목표로 하고 있으며, 이는 28개국의 다국적군측의 공격 계획대로 진행되고 있는 것임.

o 이라크군의 쿠웨이트로부터 축출과 쿠웨이트 합법정부 회복 그리고 중동지역 안정이 확보될 것을 확인함.

o 오늘저녁 전쟁을 개시하게된 이유는 사담 후세인이 평화해결을 거부하면서 화학무기등 대량 살상무기를 비축하므로써 경제 제재 조치만으로는 소기 목적달성이 불가능하다고 판단되었기 때문이며, 다국적국측은 무력사용만이 유일한 해결 방안임을 확신하게 되었음. 또한 무력사용에 의한 해결을 계속 지연시킬 경우, 전세계 경제에 심각한 타격을 줄 우려가 있기 때문.

o 미군은 전세계의 지지를 받고 있으며 미국은 이 전쟁이 매우 짧은 시간에 연합군측의 승리로 끝날 것으로 확신하고 사상자를 최소화하기 위해 최대한의 노력을 기울이고 있음.

o 우리는 무고한 이라크 국민이 인명피해를 입지 않기를 바라며 사담 후세인의 압제로부터 자유로워 지기를 바랄뿐임.

0020

o 미국은 금번 전쟁에서 반드시 승리할 것이며, 어떤 나라도 단결된 세계를 상대로하여 싸워서 이길수 없음을 증명할 것임. 오늘은 역사적인 날로써 우리는 미래를 향한 새로운 국제질서 구축을 위해 진정한 기회를 맞이하고 있음.

o 현재 군사작전은 인명 피해를 극소화하면서 최대한 신속하게 이루어질 것이므로 제2의 베트남전과 같이되지는 않을 것임.

o 페르시아만 지역에 파견된 미군은 모두 지원병으로써 자신들이 왜 거기에 와있는지를 잘 알고 있으며, 모든 인류의 자유를 위해 신속히 전쟁을 끝내고 돌아올 것임.

o 오늘저녁 모든 미국민들은 미국 군인들에게 감사하며, 가능한 빠른시일내에 파병된 미군을 귀환시키기 위해 최선을 다할 것임.

0021

원 본

외 무 부

종 별 : 긴 급

번 호 : USW-0232 일 시 : 91 0116 2341

수 신 : 장 관(미북,대책반,중근동,미안)

발 신 : 주 미 대사

제 목 : 미국의 대이락 공격 (제 3호,국방장관 및 합참의장 기자회견)

연: USW-0231

1. 연호 부쉬 대통령 연설에 이어, CHENEY 장관 및 POWELL 합참의장은 1.16밤 국방부에서 기자회견을 가졌는바, 동기자회견 전문을 USW(F)-0189로 FAX 송부함.

2. CHENEY 국방장관은 부쉬 대통령의 지시에 따라 작일 오후 작전 명령서에 서명하였다하며, 미국외에 영국, 사우디, 쿠웨이트의 전폭기가 금일작전에 참여한 가운데 공격목표는 이락과 쿠웨이트 양국내의 이락군 군사시설에 집중되었다함.

(대사 박동진- 장관)

미주국 장관 차관 1차보 2차보 미주국 중아국 정문국
청와대 총리실 안기부 대책반

PAGE 1 91.01.17 14:03 WG 0022

외신 1과 통제관

번호 : JAN-16-'91 20:44 KOREAN EMBASSY WASHINGTON DC 01[redacted] P.001

수신 : 장 관 (미북, [redacted]안, 중근동. 미안) 발신 : 주미대사 | [redacted] | 장

제목 : 미국의 대 이락공격 (국방장관 및 합참의장 기자회견) (7 매)

SPECIAL DEFENSE DEPARTMENT BRIEFING WITH SECRETARY OF DEFENSE DICK CHENEY
AND CHAIRMAN OF THE JOINT CHIEFS GENERAL COLIN POWELL
THE PENTAGON, WASHINGTON, DC/ 9:20 PM, EST
WEDNESDAY, JANUARY 16, 1991

SEC. CHENEY: Thank you very much, Pete.

Ladies and gentlemen, I know you all heard the speech a short time ago by the President. And while there is not a great deal we can add now we did want to be as forthcoming as we can with you. (120)

At 7:00 tonight, as you all know by now, Eastern Time, 3:00 Thursday morning in the Gulf, the armed forces of the United States began an operation at the direction of the President to force Saddam Hussein to withdraw his troops from Kuwait and to end his occupation of that country.

At the direction of the President, I signed the execute order yesterday afternoon to undertake this operation subject to certain conditions. It was to begin only after we'd met the terms of the resolution passed last Saturday by the Congress. Those conditions have been complied with and proper notice has been given as required. And the operation was not to take place if there had been any last minute diplomatic breakthroughs.

The operation underway tonight, taking place in the pre-dawn darkness of the Persian Gulf, involves allied Air Forces of four nations: the United States, the United Kingdom, Saudi Arabia, and Kuwait. As they undertake their missions they do so after months of careful planning.

At the direction of the President great care has been taken to focus on military targets, to minimize US casualties, and to do everything possible to avoid injury to civilians in Iraq and Kuwait. The targets being struck tonight are located throughout Iraq and Kuwait. Our focus is on the destruction of Saddam Hussein's offensive military capabilities, the very capabilities that he used

to seize control of Kuwait and that make him a continuing threat to the nations of the Middle East. These are the same capabilities that now threaten American and allied forces in the Gulf.

Our goal, the same one we have maintained throughout Operation Desert Shield, is to liberate Kuwait and enforce the resolutions of the UN Security Council. This portion of the campaign directed against Saddam Hussein's offensive military force is an enormously complex undertaking. It involves all of the services of the United States military and hundreds of US and allied aircraft.

It is an on-going operation and we must therefore limit the kind and the amount of information that we provide in these early stages. This obviously is different from what happened in Panama in December of 1989, where most of the operation was over by the morning of the first day.

0189 -1

0023

We understand your need for information about what will happen next and we are well aware of our obligation to keep the American people informed. But you must also understand that we cannot talk about future operations without putting at risk the safety of those who will have to carry them out.

I believe I can speak for all of us at the Pentagon tonight when I say that we had hoped to settle this matter peacefully. This has clearly been an agonizing decision for the President and the Congress of the United States. And we've reached the point of committing our forces to battle very reluctantly only after the most careful consideration.

But no one should doubt our ability and our resolve to carry out our mission and to achieve our objective. I have great confidence in the professionalism and

the dedication and the determination of the men and women of our armed forces. They are, without question, the finest young sailors, soldiers, airmen and marines this nation has ever sent in harm's way. I want to assure all Americans that we will do our very best to carry out the President's orders as quickly and efficiently as possible and at the lowest cost possible.

We'd be happy to respond to a few questions.

Q General Powell, can you describe the Iraqi's air force's resistance, if any, their losses so far and to what extent do you think that you've already achieved air superiority there?

GEN. POWELL: The operation's only 3-1/2 hours old, so I'm not quite prepared to take on your second question. So far there has been no air resistance.

Q Have there been any casualties so far?

SEC. CHENEY: We will at the appropriate time be releasing information on casualties. We're not prepared to release any specifics now. I will simply say that at preliminary reports, we have received in terms of the success of the operation -- and that includes the possibility of casualties -- have been very, very encouraging. The operation appears to have gone very well.

Q Has there been any Iraqi response of any kind?

Q What can you tell us about the SCUD missiles that have been reportedly launched by Iraq?

SEC. CHENEY: There have been a number of reports of SCUD missiles, but insofar as I am aware, they basically are false reports. General Powell may want to say --

GEN. POWELL: -- nothing to add.

Q General, could you give us rundown on the types of aircrafts and numbers that were involved in the raids?

0189 -2

0024

GEN. POWELL: I really can't at this time, because it is an ongoing operation. Let me just say that it involved the Air Force, as mentioned by Secretary Cheney, and sorties in the hundreds.

Q Were there cruise missiles involved with that?

GEN. POWELL: I beg your pardon.

Q Were there cruise missiles involved with that?

GEN. POWELL: I won't comment on specific weaponry. It's an ongoing operation.

Q What targets were we bombing near Baghdad? And are we -- have we bombed any facilities where we think Saddam Hussein might be?

GEN. POWELL: We have not been targeting Mr. Saddam Hussein. The purpose of our bombing facilities in the area of Baghdad is essentially to go after the command and control system of the Iraqi armed forces. And we're looking at principally military targets, command and control installations, air defense sites that could put our planes at risk. But they are militarily oriented targets.

Q Is there any Iraqi response of any kind?

SEC. CHENEY: The response of the Iraqi forces at this point has been limited, I think would be the best way to characterize it. But again, let me emphasize, as General Powell did, we're in the very early stages of this operation. It is likely to run for a long period of time. I realize you've all got legitimate questions about it, but there simply are things we do not know yet, because it is an ongoing operation, because pilots are just now returning and there'll be a lot of work required to assess the success of the -- the initial efforts. And there'll be a lot of follow-up work required, as well.

Q Could you tell us, please, whether or not there have been any indications whatsoever that the Iraqi troops, the 540,000 Iraqi troops in the Kuwaiti theater, have been cut off from their command and control headquarters in Baghdad?

SEC. CHENEY: I wouldn't want to speculate on that at this point.

Q The President said this was strictly an air operation for the time being. When does the US decide to send in the ground forces?

SEC. CHENEY: It is strictly an air operation for the time being and I wouldn't want to speculate on the point at which additional forces might be engaged.

0188 -3

0025

Q Tonight -- (inaudible) -- said on the McNeil-Lehrer Newshour this evening that we are, quote, "now prisoners of our own country, in our own country." Now that we've defended ourselves from naked aggression in the Middle East, how do we

defend ourselves here at home from terrorist attacks?

SEC. CHENEY: I'm confident that we can deal with the terrorist threat.

Q Mr. Secretary --

Q Do any of --

Q Have targets thus far included tanks and artillery?

GEN. POWELL: I don't want to get into specific target sets yet. As the information comes in and builds over time and we can give it to you historically we will give it out. But I'm not prepared to go into specific target sets and what have -- what targets have been hit and have not because it really is just too early to give you that kind of bomb damage assessment.

Q General Powell, if Saddam Hussein says tomorrow, "I give up. I'm sorry. I will withdraw from Kuwait" will you pause in your -- have a pause in your air campaign, or will you continue with it until you knock out all the priority targets?

GEN. POWELL: I will -- I will do whatever the President of the United States directs us to do through the Secretary of Defense.

Q Mr. Secretary?

Q General?

Q Secretary Cheney, from a military perspective, what went into your thinking in deciding to launch the attack at this point this evening? What were the factors?

SEC. CHENEY: Well, I think the -- there were several factors. Of course the President made the basic decision to commit the force. It was affected by, among other things, the expiration of the United Nations deadline that had been set on November 30th when the Security Council voted for the use of any means necessary to get him out. I think it was affected in part as a result of consultation with our allies. But it also was based upon the advice of our senior military commanders in terms of picking a time when conditions appeared to be most favorable for undertaking the operation.

Let me emphasize, though, the the procedure we went through was to plan for execution of the operation at a point after the expiration of the United Nations deadline, but I had no authority to execute the plan until the President instructed me yesterday afternoon to do so, and it was at that point that we signed out the execute order, with the qualifiers I mentioned in my opening statement.

Q Those favorable factors -- can you tell us what some of those were?

0189 -4

0026

SEC. CHENEY: I think I'd just leave it -- leave it --

(Mixed voices.)

Q (Inaudible) -- you surprised that there was no response, sir, a very small response from the Iraqi forces at this point?

SEC. CHENEY: Again, I'm reluctant to characterize the response beyond what we've already said about it. We've not had an opportunity to debrief our pilots yet. Some of them are still flying missions and I think it would be inappropriate at this point to -- to convey the notion that somehow we've got a final fix on it. But I think it would be fair to say, and General Powell may well want to comment on this, that the initial reaction from the Iraqis is such that I'm generally of the opinion that we achieved a fairly high degree of tactical surprise.

(Mixed voices.)

Q Has there been any -- (inaudible) -- Israel or Turkey on the part of Iraq?

SEC. CHENEY: None to -- to my knowledge.

Q Mr. Secretary, could you tell us the President mentioned -- (inaudible) -- that one of the objectives was to take out chemical and nuclear sites. Can you tell us in a general way if that mission was accomplished?

SEC. CHENEY: I can say that we have, in fact, gone after those targets. I do not yet have information on the effectiveness of those efforts.

Q Mr. Secretary, what about word of casualties at Baghdad? You indicated you wanted to spare civilians there. Do you have any sense about how that may or may not have occurred in the city? There was a lot of bombing obviously in Baghdad.

SEC. CHENEY: The best reporting that I've seen on what transpired in Baghdad was on CNN -- (laughter) -- and it

would appear based upon the comments that were coming in from the CNN crew in the hotel in Baghdad that the operation was successful in striking targets with a high degree of precision, at least that's the reporting according to CNN.

Q Was there an Iraqi attempt -- was there an Iraqi attempt to launch a missile, sir?

GEN. POWELL: We've had reports of missile launches but none of them have been confirmed.

Q What about the -- what about the SCUDs in Western Iraq at those air bases on the border? Have you not any reading on that? Those are fairly high priority targets.

GEN. POWELL: Yes, they are a fairly high priority [illegible].

0189-5

0027

(Laughter.)

Q And how did you do?

SEC. CHENEY: I'm not prepared how we did or what we've done --

Q A follow up, a follow up on this. At the end of this operation, this phase of the operation when you get a little better picture could you come back or have one of your staff come back and give us a briefing on it?

GEN. POWELL: You'll be getting regular briefings and we'll be -- as the Secretary said, we're going to be as forthcoming as we possibly can while at the same time preserving operational security.

Q Mr. Secretary, are you confident that your -- that your targetting of command and control sites has left Saddam Hussein the ability to, number one, know what's happening to his forces? And number two, to communicate to you that he wants to quit if he does decide so?

SEC. CHENEY: Again Melissa (sp) I don't have any information at this point on the overall effectiveness of the operation. What I said was the preliminary reports are very positive but we are in the very earliest stages of this and therefore, there is not a lot of detailed information we can give you on what the effect of the bombing campaign has been on specific strategic categories of targets.

Q Is there a military commander to surrender if he decides -

SEC. CHENEY: Pardon?

Q Is there a military commander like Saddam Hussein still alive to surrender if there is such a decision?

SEC. CHENEY: I really don't have anything I can give you on that.

Q How did the coordination with the Saudis go? Did they --

GEN. POWELL: It's gone very well.

Q Did you know where Saddam was when the attacks began and was that a target even though he was not the target?

GEN. POWELL: We have not been tracking Mr. Saddam Hussein for the purpose of targeting him.

Q General, can you characterize in any general way how long the current beginning phase of this operation will continue -- that is the air operation? Will it be the rest of, I guess, tonight and tomorrow morning or throughout tomorrow? Can you give people any kind of general idea how long this first phase will --

GEN. POWELL: The air part of the campaign will continue until the whole campaign is completed. It doesn't end

0189 - 6

0028

[redacted] [redacted]

Q   Do you believe the threat of a missile attack by the Iraqis has been eliminated at this point?

GEN. POWELL: I cannot answer that at this time until we get some assessments in.

Q   Was there any damage to any oil facilities at all?

GEN. POWELL: I don't have bomb damage assessment yet. I can't answer that question.

Q   General, how massive is this first wave? Are we talking 500 missions, a 1,000 missions tonight?

GEN. POWELL: I think tomorrow we'll be in a better position to try to give you a handle on that, but this early in the operation I'm reluctant to give those numbers out until I've had a chance to talk to General Schwarzkopf in greater detail.

Q   General, Navy and --

GEN. POWELL: All US services were involved in this part of the campaign.

Q   And Britain?

GEN. POWELL: Yes.

Q   When you say, General Powell, that there were hundreds of sorties, does that mean that there were not more than 1,000?

GEN. POWELL: I think I'll leave it at that -- between a bread box or something else -- hundreds of sorties.

Thank you all very much.

END

0189 -7

0023

1022시에 보고함.

원 본

외 무 부

종 별 : 긴 급

번 호 : USW-0233 일 시 : 91 0116 2341

수 신 : 장 관(미북,대책반, 중근동,미안)

발 신 : 주 미 대사

제 목 : 미국의 대이락 공격(제 4호, 대이스라엘 공격용 미사일 기지파괴)

대: WUS-0179

1. 당지 CNN 방송의 22:00 뉴스에 따르면 미공군은 개전 초기 이락 서부에 배치되어 있는 대이스라엘 공격용 SCUD 미사일 기자를 파괴하여 이락의대 이스라엘 공격 능력을 감소시킴으로써 이스라엘의 직접 개입 가능성이 다소 줄어 들었다고 전함.

2. 한편 NETANYAHU 이스라엘 외무차관은 22:40 CNN 방송과의 인터뷰를 통해 이스라엘이 침공받을 경우 즉각 반격할 태세를 갖추고 있으나 그럴 필요가 없게되기를 희망한다고 언급 했음.

(대사 박동진-국장)

미주국	장관	차관	1차보	2차보	미주국	중아국	정문국	청와대
총리실	안기부	대책반						

0030

PAGE 1

91.01.17 14:05 WG

외신 1과 통제관

a0007ALL r
b i BC-GULF-NATO-URGENT 01-17 0091
BC-GULF-NATO URGENT
NATO CALLS EMERGENCY MEETING AS GULF WAR ERUPTS

BRUSSELS, Jan 17, Reuter - NATO called an emergency meeting of ambassadors from the 16 allied nations on Thursday after the U.S.-led multinational coalition began attacking Iraqi forces to oust them from Kuwait.

A NATO spokesman would say only that the ambassadors would meet at 0330 AM (0230 GMT).

NATO sources said Secretary-General Manfred Woerner was already at alliance headquarters. The United States and Britain are expected to brief their allies at the meeting on military action taken so far.

MORE NHD PFS WS
Reut01:22 01-17

Airport sources in Bahrain said a squadron of Tornado GR1 fighters took off from the Muharak air base there shortly after 2300 GMT, according to reports received here.

A Press Association correspondent in the region said there were also reports that two Victor in-flight refuelling tankers had also taken off, indicating that the Tornados were heading for strikes deep inside Iraqi territory.

The Tornado has a combat flight radius of about 480 miles (864 kilometers)

Britain has 35,000 men in the Gulf, about 4,000 of them aviators. They man five and a half squadrons of Tornado and Jaguar fighter-bombers or about 72 planes.

cb/bm

AFP 170123 GMT JAN 91

AFP 170124 GMT JAN 91

a0031ALL r
b i BC-GULF-NATO 01-17 0097
BC-GULF-NATO =2 BRUSSELS

It was not immediately clear whether Turkey, the only alliance member bordering Iraq, had been involved in the fighting so far.

The United States has fighters and bombers based in southeastern Turkey.

NATO is not directly involved in the Gulf conflict since the region is outside its traditional theatre of operations. But this would change if Turkey was attacked.

If not, NATO will be a key forum for consultations among the allies. Of NATO allies, only Britain and France have sent ground forces to the Gulf in support of the U.S.-led military buildup.

REUTER NHD PFS WS
Reut01:28 01-17

0031

개9

외 무 부

종 별 : 초긴급

번 호 : USW-0235 일 시 : 91 0117 0054

수 신 : 장 관(대책반, 중근동,미북,미안,기정)

발 신 : 주 미 대사

제 목 : 서울 시간 1.17 13:30 현재 폐만 전황(제 6 신)

당지 CNN 방송이 보도한 서울 시간 1.17 13:30 (당지 시간 1.16 23:30)현재의전황을 하기 요지보고함.

1.금번 공습을 통해 약 100 여군데의 이락내 공군기지가 거의 모두 파괴되고 (약 700-800 대의 이락공군기 파괴), 이락 공군기들은 별다른 대응조치도 취하지 못했다함.

2.이락군의 화학무기 및 핵무기 시설도 거의다 파괴되고, 대 이스라엘 공격시 사용될 것으로 알려진 SCUD 미사일 기지도 거의 다 파괴되었다함. (금번 공습시 SCUD 미사일 역시 발사조차도 되지 못했다함)

3.이처럼 이락 공군력 및 대공 방공망이 거의궤멸됨으로서 미측이 제공권을 장악하게되었을뿐 아니라, 지상군중 최정예 부대인 REPUBLICAN GUARD 의 전력도 상당히무력화되었다함.(계엄사 발표)

4.현재는 다국적군측이 공격을 중지한 가운데 소강 상태가 유지되고 있으나, 인공위성에 의한 이락군 전력의 파괴 상태에 대한 정찰이 종료되는 대로 향후 24시간 이내 에 2,3 차례의 공중공격이 더 있을 것으로 예상됨.

5.한편, 미군 전폭기는 단 한대의 손실도 없이 무사히 귀환하였다하는바, 전기와 같은 금번 작전의 완벽에 가까운 성공은 미 공군사에 기록될만한 것으로 당지 전문가들은 평가하고 있다함. 여사한 성공은, 미측이 최신예 장비를 바탕으로 목표물에 대한 정확한 공격 능력과 전부 참여 부대단위간의 원활한 통신 능력을 보유함으로서 소위 BATTLE MANAGEMENT 를 자신의 사전 계획대로 운영할수 있었던데에 기인하는바, 당지 일각에서는 조속한 시일내에 금번 전쟁이 종료될 것으로 예상하는 낙관론이 대두하고 있기도함.

6.또한 금번 공습을 통해 후세인 궁도 파괴된것으로 알려지고 있으며, 이락의

대책반	장관	차관	1차보	2차보	미주국	미주국	중아국	정문국
청와대	총리실	안기부						

PAGE 1 91.01.17 15:24 WG

외신 1과 통제관 하

0032

대이스라엘 공격 위협은사실상 사라진 것으로 보여진다함.

한편, 터키도 대이락 선전 포고와 미측에 대한 공군기지 사용 허가를 통해 제 2의 대이락 전선을 구축할 가능성이 클것으로 알려짐.

(대사 박동진-장관)

0033

외 무 부

종 별 : 초긴급

번 호 : USW-0236 일 시 : 91 0117 0054

수 신 : 장 관(대책반,중근동,미북,기정)

발 신 : 주 미 대사

제 목 : 이락측 반응(제 7신)

당지 언론 보도에 따르면, 이락측은 바그다드 시간 1.17.08:00 뉴스를 통해 후세인 대통령이 전쟁이 시작되었음을 이락 국민에게 알리면서, 미국에 대해 절대로 굴복하지 않을것이라고 발언했다함.

(대사 박동진-국장)

대책반 장관 차관 1차보 2차보 미주국 중아국 정문국 청와대
총리실 안기부

PAGE 1 91.01.17 15:15 WG

외신 1과 통제관

0034

외 무 부

종 별 : 초긴급

번 호 : USW-0237 일 시 : 91 0117 0054

수 신 : 장 관(대책반,미북,중근동,기정)

발 신 : 주 미 대사

제 목 : 미 의회 반응(제 8신)

금 1.17 미 의회는 본회의를 소집, 미국 주도의 다국 적군 군사 작전을 지지하는 결의안을 채택할 예정인 것으로 알려짐.

(대사 박동진-국장)

대책반 장관 차관 1차보 2차보 미주국 중아국 정문국 청와대
총리실 안기부

PAGE 1

91.01.17 15:16 WG

외신 1과 통제관

0035

외 무 부

종 별 : 초긴급

번 호 : USW-0238 일 시 : 91 0117 0056

수 신 : 장 관(대책반,기협,통일,중근동,미북,기정)

발 신 : 주 미 대사

제 목 : 미 석유 전략 비축분 방출 결정(제 9신)

1.금번 대 이락 공격 개신 관련,부쉬 대통령은 석유 전략 비축분 (6천억 배럴)을 1일 100만배럴씩 방출 조치토록 관련 부서에 지시하였다함.

2.한편, 당지 방소 보도에 따르면 북해산 BRENT유는 배럴당 2불이 하락, 27불에 거래가 형성되고있다함.

(대사 박동진-국장)

대책반 장관 차관 1차보 2차보 미주국 중아국 경제국 통상국
청와대 총리실 안기부 동자부

PAGE 1

91.01.17 15:17 WG

외신 1과 통제관

0036

외 무 부

종 별 : 초긴급

번 호 : USW-0239 일 시 : 91 0117 0325

수 신 : 장관(대책반,중근동,미북,미안,기정)

발 신 : 주미대사

제 목 : 서울 시간 1.17 16:30 현재 페만 전황(제 10신)

연: USW-0235

1. 당지 CNN 방송의 보도에 따르면, 서울시간 1.17 16:30(당지 시간 1.17 02:30)현재 바그다드주변에서 폭음이 들리고 검은 연기가 솟는것이보이기는 하나,이것이 미국의 제 2차 공습 징후인지 여부는 상금 불분명 하다함.

2.다만, 바그다드 시간 1.17 오전 10:30 현재 미국이 주간 공습을 감행하고 있다면, 이는 곧 미국이 이락의 대공 방공망을 무력화시킴으로서 제공권을 장악한것으로 판단할수 있는 명백한 증거인바,향후 각종 군사 시설등 특정 목표물에대한 미국의공중 공격이 보다 더 정확하고 효과적으로 이루어질것으로 전망된다함.

3.한편, 이처럼 미국의 대이락 공습이 성공적으로 진행되고 있는 이상,당분간 미지상군투입은 이루어 지지 않을것으로 예상된다하며,향후 지상군이 투입되는 경우에도 작전 수행이 훨씬 용이할것으로 예상된다함.

(대사 박동진-장관)

대책반	1차보	미주국	미주국	중아국	정문국	안기부

장관, 차관, 2차보. 청와대. 총리실

PAGE 1

91.01.17 17:39 DP

외신 1과 통제관

0037

7a

원 본

외 무 부

종 별 : 긴 급

번 호 : USW-0242　　　　일 시 : 91 0117 1020

수 신 : 장 관(미북, 중근동, 대책반)

발 신 : 주미대사

제 목 : 걸프 작전 (제13신, 미국내 반응)

걸프 작전에 대한 미국 국내 반응을 하기 보고함

1.1.17. NYT 사설

O WHAT THE BOMBS SAID 제하,

O 금번 군사적전은 정당한 목적을 위한 불가피한 무력행사이며,

O HUSSEIN 의 각성을 촉구함.

2.1.17. WP 사설

O THE WAR BEGINS 제하

O BUSH 대통령의 걸프 작전은 UN 과미 의회의 충분한 검토를 통해 이루어진것이며, HUSSEIN 이 자초한 것임.

3.1.17. WSJ 사설

O Q THE BUSH COAILITION 제하

O BUSH 대통령이 과거 대통령과는 달리 국제적 합의를 매우 능란하게 이끌어 냈을뿐 아니라 미국 국민과 결국은 의회의 지지를 확보함으로써, 목표 달성의 기초를 마련 하였으며, 미국이 계속적인 리더쉽을 발휘하도록 희망하는 국제적 기대를 충족 하였음.

4.걸프 작전 개시 직후 실시된 갤럽 POLL 에따르면 응답자의 81 퍼센트가 동 작전을 지지하고, 12 퍼센트가 반대한다는 반응을 보였다 함.

5. USW(F)-0190 참조

(대사 박동진- 국장)

미주국	장관	차관	1차보	2차보	중아국	중아국	정문국	청와대
총리실	안기부	대책반						

PAGE 1　　　　91.01.18 00:41 CG

외신 1과 통제관

0038

원 본

외 무 부

종 별 : 긴 급

번 호 : USW-0243 일 시 : 91 0117 1020

수 신 : 장관(미북,중근동,대책본부)

발 신 : 주 미 대사

제 목 : 페만 사태 상황보고 (제14신)

1. 1.17 (목) 당지 언론 보도에 의하면 BRENT NORTH SEACRUDE 원유가는 계속 하락하며 7불 이상 하락 하였으며 현재 배럴당 21불 60TF에 거래되고 있다함.

2. 유가가 계속하락하고 있는것은 당초 예상과는 달리 중동지역 유전 시설이 파괴되지 않았고, 전쟁이 단기간에 종료될 것으로 전망하기 때문이라고함.

(대사 박동진-국장)

미주국 장관 차관 1차보 2차보 중아국 중아국 정문국 청와대
총리실 안기부 대책반

PAGE 1

91.01.18 00:43 CG

외신 1과 통제관

0039

관리 번호	91/2048

	분류번호	보존기간

발 신 전 보

번 호 : WUS-0179 910117 1105 FK 종별 : 초긴급

수 신 : 주 수신처 참조 대사. ~~총영사~~

발 신 : 장 관 (중근동)

제 목 :

WJA -0228 WUK -0113
WGE -0079 WFR -0087
WCA -0056 WJO -0081
WSB -0116 WTU -0027

귀지에서 파악할수 있는 페르샤만의 전황을 수시로 긴급 보고 바라며, 이스라엘의 참전 여부가 금후 사태 발전의 큰 변수가 될것인바, 이에 관한 정보도 적극 수집 보고 바람. 끝.

(장 관) ~~(미 상 목)~~

수신처 : 주 미, 일, 영, 독, 불, 카이로, 요르단, 사우디, 터키 대사

예 고 : 91.6.30. 일반

보 안 통 제	7L

앙 고 재	91년 1월 17일	중근동과	기안자 성 명		과 장		국 장		차 관	장 관
			전호석		7L					(서명)

외신과통제

0040

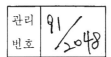

원 본

외 무 부

종 별 : 지 급

번 호 : USW-0245 일 시 : 91 0117 1113

수 신 : 장관(미북,중근동,대책반)

발 신 : 주미대사

제 목 : 걸프 작전(제15신, 미 국방장관 기자회견)

CHENEY 미 국방장관 및 POWELL 합참 의장은 금 1.17. 아침 9:00 미 국방성에서기자회견을 가진바, 동 내용 하기 보고함.

1.지나친 기대감에 대한 경계

0 걸프 작전은 인명 손실과 경우에 따라서는 장기간의 작전이 될수도 있으므로 지나친 낙관을 갖는 것은 곤란함.

2.현재까지의 전황

0 작전 개시후 1,000 회 이상의 출격, THOMAHAWK 크루즈 미사일등으로 이라크 및 쿠웨이트에 대한 공격을 가한바, 주 공격 목표는 (1) 지휘 체제, (2) 방공망, (3)SCUD 미사일 기지, (4) 비행장등을 주로 하였고약 80 퍼센트의 성공율을 보였다고평가됨.

0 자세한 평가는 진행중에 있음.

0 (지상작전이 개시 되었냐는 질문에 대해) 신인도 부인도 할 단계가 아님.

4.연합군의 인명 피해

0 미군기 (F-18 HORNET) 1대 및 영국기 (TORONADO) 1 대가 손실되었으며 미군1명 (조종사) 이 사망함.

0 (이라크 방송은 미군기 14대를 격추하였다고 주장한바 있음)

4.이라크의 저항 능력

0 상기 2항 목표에 대한 공격이 성공적으로 이루어졌으나 (1) 지휘체제는 아직 유지되고 있고, (2) 지하 벙커에 들어 있는 공군기에 대해서는 아직 공격이 이루어 지지 못하였음.

5. 기사회견 전문 팩스 송부함(USW(F)- 0192)

(대사 박동진- 국장)

미주국	장관	차관	1차보	2차보	중아국	중아국	정문국	청와대
총리실	안기부	대책반						

PAGE 1 91.01.18 01:43 CG

외신 1과 통제관

0041

: USW(F) - 0192

: 장 관 (미북, 중동국, 대책반) 발신 : 주미대사

: Cheney 장관, 합참의장 회견) (USW- 첨부물)

보안	
통제	

(10 매)

BRIEFING BY SECRETARY CHENEY AND GENERAL COLIN POWELL FROM THE PENTAGON ON THE STATUS OF FARLANE. DESERT STORM/ THURSDAY, JANUARY 17, 1991

PETE WILLIAMS: Okay, good morning, ladies and gentlemen. In just a moment, the Secretary will have a short opening statement for you. He'll have to leave shortly -- he has been summoned across the river -- and General Powell will remain. May I ask you a favor, if when we get into the question and answer portion, if you would raise your hands and General Powell will point to you to acknowledge your questions.

Mr. Secretary.

SEC. CHENEY: Thank you, Pete. As Pete mentioned, I have to leave after a few minutes. General Powell and I will take a couple of questions, and then I'm going to sneak off and turn you over to my compatriot.

To date, the operation is going very well. I want, though, at the outset of my remarks this morning to emphasize the importance of being cautious in our comments. I don't mean to be critical of our friends in the press corps, but I think it's very, very important for people to remember a number of key things: that this is very serious business, that we are in the very early stages of an operation that may run for a considerable period of time, that there have been casualties and there are likely to be more casualties.

So while we feel very good about the progress to date, it is important, I think, for everyone to be careful about claiming victory or making assumptions about the ultimate cost of this operation in terms of casualties. So far so good, but I would urge all of you to be cautious in your reporting just as we're trying very hard to be very cautious and very precise in terms of what we say about the status of the operation to date.

We've now flown over 1,000 air sorties in the first 14 hours of the operation. There have been over 100 TLAMs, Tomahawk cruise missiles, launched as well. So far, as of 0900 this morning, Washington time, there has been a single American aircraft lost and one British aircraft lost as well.

At present we are in the process of using our intelligence assets to assess the damage that has been achieved. As that process is completed decisions will be made about going back to restrike those targets that require additional attention, while we at the same time continue to pursue and carry out the original plan for mission.

0192 -1

0042

The original [redacted] specifically allowed fo[redacted]is kind of retargeting of targets that need to be hit for a second time. That's a normal part of the operation.

And as I mentioned last night, the operation will continue until we achieve our objectives of forcing Saddam Hussein out of Kuwait and implementing the United Nations Security Council resolutions.

We'd be happy to take your questions.

Q Could you please describe the plane that went down on the American side, the type of plane and number of casualties?

SEC. CHENEY: It involves a single casualty. I don't know that we want to identify the aircrafts, do we?

GEN. POWELL: It was an F-18.

Q Was that a wound or a death?

SEC. CHENEY: A death.

Q What other information do you have about that casualty?

SEC. CHENEY: All I can give you at this time is that the total US losses are
one aircraft and one individual.

Q Did you -- (inaudible) -- any SCUD missiles?

SEC. CHENEY: Insofar as I'm aware there have been no SCUD launches.

Q Secretary Cheney, how would you describe the tactics by Saddam Hussein? Would you say that he could be intentionally laying low as some type of strategy and counterattack or anything?

SEC. CHENEY: That may well be the case, but I think I'm going to yield to my chief military advisor to address that issue.

GEN. POWELL: I'll do it after you leave, sir.

SEC. CHENEY: Okay. Any more questions? Yeah?

Q Can you tell us that the operation is still a total air operation? We have reports of some movement of ground troops near the border. Is there a preparation phase going on for ground forces?

SEC. CHENEY: Again, we never get into the business of speculation about future operations in order to safeguard the security of those operations. The activities that are now underway are obviously primarily the air portion of the campaign. That does not mean that we will not at some point engage ground forces as well. But we don't have anything to announce at this point.

Q Do you expect it to continue for hours or days or weeks? What is your --

0192-2 0043

SEC. CHENEY: As I said earlier, I think the best way to think about it is, is it is the early stages of the air portion of the campaign that we are now embarked upon, and it could run for some period of time. The -- we are prepared to continue the operation just as long as we need to in order to achieve our objectives; our objectives being getting Saddam out of Kuwait and implementing the UN Security Council resolutions. That could be a significant period of time or it could be a relatively short period of time. That will depend upon the success of the campaign and upon how he reacts to it.

Q Mr. Secretary, do you have any reports of damage to aircraft? The French said that four of their aircraft were pretty heavily damaged but they only had one slight injury. How about our aircraft, how are they holding up?

SEC. CHENEY: Again, I'll yield to General Powell on that. My general impression is that they're performing very well, that any damage to aircraft has been minimal except for, of course, that one loss of an aircraft.

Q Mr. Secretary?

Q Mr. Secretary?

SEC. CHENEY: One more question. Bob?

Q Did any Iraqi aircraft take off to engage the attacking force?

SEC. CHENEY: I'm going to leave that to General Powell.

Q Mr. Secretary, could I ask you one more question, sir? Is there any possibility that there will at some point during the air war be some kind of a pause to give Saddam Hussein the opportunity to rethink his commitment to staying in Kuwait, or is this a non-stop operation as far as the coalition is concerned?

SEC. CHENEY: As far as the coalition is concerned, and as far as my orders from the President are concerned, we've been instructed to execute the plan, to carry on these operations until we have achieved our objective. Our objective is to get Saddam Hussein out of Kuwait.

GEN. POWELL: To follow up on a couple of questions, I only have a report of one other US aircraft damaged. There may be others, but those reports have not come into me yet.

Q Do you have any evidence, General, of any counter-offensive at all by the Iraqis, either on the ground or otherwise?

GEN. POWELL: No. The only Iraqi action I'm aware of was the artillery strike across the border into Ra's al Khafji, which you've seen on television, which hit one oil petroleum storage facility. But that's not been followed up, and we have silenced that --

Q How do you account for that? Does it surprise you?

0192-3 0044

GEN. POWELL: [redacted]'ll have to ask them. [redacted]ather pleased that we appear to have achieved tactical surprise. We should not however rule out the possibility of Iraqi action either in the air or on the ground, and I can assure you that we are on the lookout for it.

Q Any damage -- any assessment, sir, of Iraqi aircraft, airfields? Can you give us any rough sense of what you have hit successfully?

GEN. POWELL: Of all of the air sorties that went in, we are rating 80 percent of them as having been effective, meaning the aircraft got to its target, delivered its ordinance, and returned. For those that are in the 20 percent, that includes those that had mechanical problems, weather problems, or because of the very tight control we had over the aircraft, they did not make the kind of positive identification of the target that we required before going in and launching under the rules of engagement to minimize collateral civilian damage.

So, we're very satisfied with that level of performance on the part of our aircraft. We are pleased with the initial results. We have damaged the command and control capability of the Iraqi government and the Iraqi armed forces. We believe we have done reasonably well as best we know right now with the preliminary bomb damage assessment in attacking airfields, in attacking fixed SCUD facilities around the countryside. But I once again caution you that this is very preliminary, only 12 hours into the operation.

David.

Q General Powell, can you give us some idea of the targets that were struck and the priority given to those targets, and the weapons used?

GEN. POWELL: The targets that were struck initially dealt with air defense systems, command and control installations, and the Iraqi air force and their ability to interfere with our air operations. B-52s were used, F-117s, F-15s, F-16s, A-10s, F-111s, F-A18s, A-6s, A-7s, Apache helicopters, Tornadoes from the United Kingdom, Tornadoes from Saudi Arabia, Jaguars from the French, and the Kuwaiti air force will -- is also involved. Specific ordnance loads are those ordnance loads commonly associated with these aircraft. I don't have any specific -- any more specific information on it, David.

Q The cruise missiles -- the Secretary said more than 100 cruise missiles -- what were they used for?

GEN. POWELL: They were used against a variety of targets where their precision was required for the target, or because of the air defense system around those targets, we felt that an unmanned weapon was the best system to use.

It was a very -- I've got to say, it was an extremely detailed, well-thought-out plan. The credit has to go to General Schwarzkopf, and especially to General Horner, the commander of Central Command air forces, for the integration of this plan; enormously complex, and it was a single plan, encompassing all US forces and all allied forces participating in the operation, all responding to the direction of a single commander with a single air tasking order.

Q General, is --

0193-6 0045

GEN. POWELL: [redacted]se me. Mike?

Q General Powell, in laying out your initial list of targets, you dind't mention the Iraqi Republic Guards or ground forces. Where were they in the sequence of the priority of targets and --

GEN. POWELL: I really don't want to -- I'm deliberately trying not to give prioritization or sequencing because it is a plan that is unfolding and there is a concept behind it; and if I say too much about it, then I'm giving away the total concept and I'm not prepared to do that.

Yes, sir?

Q General, do you think --

Q General, can you say if they were -- if they were struck and if you did signifcant damage to them?

GEN. POWELL: They were on the target list and I'm not prepared to give bomb damage assessment on the Republican Guard at this time.

Q General, you singled out the SCUD missile launchers in fixed sites as having been among the first targets that were reached. What about those in the mobile launchers?

GEN. POWELL: It was not to suggest we aren't equally concerned about mobile launchers, but they're much more difficult to target and find. So, they are a high-priority target if we can locate them on the battlefield, so to speak. But because they are mobile they -- you can't predict where they are liable to be. But all of our systems are tuned up and queued, trying to locate mobile SCUD launchers, of course.

Q General, do you feel that in a general sense the attack was effective enough to give the United States control of Iraqi airspace? And if -- if some fall somewhat short of that, perhaps you could just generally tell us how effective you think it's been.

GEN. POWELL: I'm comfortable that we are able to achieve control of Iraqi air space.
That is not to say that the Iraqi air force has been totally destroyed at this time. Since I spoke to you last evening, I've had further reports that suggest they did come up. There were some air-to-air engagements. I'm not prepared to give you the results of the air-to-air engagements except to say we have lost no aircraft as a result of those engagements. So, the Iraqi air force is still out there, and we're going to work on them and their airfields.

Q General Powell, were you sort of surprised that the Iraqi air defenses weren't more effective?

GEN. POWELL: Was I what?

Q Were you surprised that the Iraqi air defenses weren't more effective?

0172-5 0046

GEN. POWELL: I'm very pleased that they weren't more effective. I will not get into the details of why we believe they were not effective because obviously I don't know wish them to know why I believe they were not effective.

Q General, was all of --

Q Were there other Iraqi troop divisions that we targeted and do we have any estimate how many Iraqi soldiers might have been killed in the bombings?

GEN. POWELL: No, I'm not able to answer that at this time. It is a comprehensive campaign with, as I've said many times, air, land and sea components. And we have thought it out. It will unfold over a period of time. But I can't answer your question directly, except to underscore what the Secretary has said and dampen down some of the euphoria. We have just begun a campaign. It'll run for some time.

Q Along those lines, with all of the optimism about the initial stages of this war, what right now is your gravest concern?

GEN. POWELL: I don't know that I have any grave concerns. I'm always concerned about the welfare of our GIs who are participating in the operation, but after 12 and a little -- almost 1/2 hours of this campaign, I am very pleased that our initial objectives have been achieved. I am satisfied with the way the campaign is unfolding.

Q But strategically, what are your concerns right now?

GEN. POWELL: I don't know that I have any particular strategic concerns. My principal concern is to accomplish the mission. We have to remember the mission isn't to bomb a while and pause and see if something happens, the mission is to eject the Iraqi army out of Kuwait and to assist in the restoration of the legitimate government of Kuwait, and our entire campaign plan is focused on those two objectives.

Q What was the extent of the damage to the -- specifically to the chemical and to the nuclear?

GEN. POWELL: They -- we are pleased with the performance of our systems against those facilities. I am not prepared to tell you right now because we don't know yet what the extent of the damage is. We are going to that analysis now. Yes, sir.

Q Could you tell us, General, anything about the reports of heavy air attacks in the Basra area and to what extent have we attacked the fortified positions in Kuwait, the dug-in positions in Kuwait?

GEN. POWELL: Basra, of course, is a center of gravity for Iraqi forces within the Kuwaiti theater of operations and is very much on our target list and in our area of interest, but I don't have specific information and I am not prepared to comment on what we might be doing against dug-in ground forces at this time. It is still unfolding.

01ρ2-6 0047

Q Any repo[illegible] yet of collateral damage [illegible]pecially in Baghdad, and was there any attempt to go after the anti-aircraft units that are within the Iraqi ground forces in southern Iraq and Kuwait?

GEN. POWELL: Certainly we are interested in the anti-aircraft units within the Iraqi ground forces in due course and we want to get the air defense system taken care of to give us absolute freedom of movement through the air.

We have been very sensitive to collateral damage in the Baghdad area and I think the best source of how careful we have been is listening to the CNN reporters who were watching it unfold. We -- that was a -- we were very concerned about the collateral damage, making sure that no innocent civilians were killed or injured, and we were very sensitive to cultural and religious sites within the area.

Q General, can you tell us -- you talked briefly about the sortie rate and 80 percent sorties were effective. Can you comment generally about cruise missiles? How effective were the Tomahawk cruise missiles?

GEN. POWELL: I'm extremely pleased with -- extremely pleased with the effectiveness of the cruise missiles.

Q General, how were Navy aircraft?

GEN. POWELL: Navy aircraft were totally integrated into the single air plan and, frankly, they were all indistinguishable. Obviously where they're located had something to do with where they were targeted to go, but it was one single plan and Navy aircrafts came out of both the Persian Gulf and the Red Sea.

Q From just two carriers, or all six carriers?

GEN. POWELL: I don't want to get into specifically which carriers launched at what time and which aircraft, but it is a single integrated attack plan.

Q General?

Q General Powell, you said last night, General Powell, that you all were not in fact tracking Saddam Hussein or where he was. If one of the primary goals was to knock out Iraq's military leadership why weren't you tracking him?

GEN. POWELL: We were not targeting him per se; we were not, because frankly I have learned from previous experience how difficult it can be to track -- (laughter) -- a head of state in whom you might be interested. And I think we spent a good part of the morning of the 20th of December 1989 in this room discussing that subject. So we simply weren't.

What we were going after was the command and control of Iraqi armed forces, and how their national command authority controls those forces. And that's what we were interested in, rather than chasing somebody around the countryside.

Q General?

0192-7 0048

GEN. POWELL: [redacted], sir. [redacted]

Q Anything on Iraqi troop defections?

GEN. POWELL: No, I don't have anything on Iraqi troop defections.

Q On the command --

Q Defectors, sir --

Q On the command and control, can you give us some assessment, without being overly optimistic, are --

GEN. POWELL: Who's overly optimistic?

Q I'm not saying whether you are or aren't. I'm just saying, can you give us an assessment as to whether the Iraqi troops are in -- they have a chain of command, or whether there is some --

GEN. POWELL: I think we -- I think we have damaged their command and control system. I don't think it's collapsed yet.

Q All right, do you have many defectors, sir?

GEN. POWELL: I do not have any reports on defectors.

Q General Powell, are you concerned about any border activity? Possibly any -- someone else coming in to aid Iraq, possibly an Iran or any type of last-minute coalitions?

GEN. POWELL: I don't expect that. It seems to me the coalition is holding together rather well. I am very pleased with that, and a lot of the soothsaying that went on about how we wouldn't be able to command and control this whole thing -- "the whole thing will collapse and you guys won't be able to manage it" -- I think our experience so far for the last 12 or so hours, we've done that very well.

Q General, you described a pause, you said to see what happened. What does that mean?

GEN. POWELL: I'm sorry?

Q You decsribed -- you talked "a pause" a few minutes ago --

GEN. POWELL: No --

Q -- and you said "to see what happens."

GEN. POWELL: I dismissed that, I think. What I'm saying is we have been given a direction to eject the Iraqi army from Kuwait and to assist in the restoration of the legitimate government of Kuwait and that's what our military campaign is designed to do.

Q General, have you --

Q General --

0192-8 0049

Q General, does your plan --

GEN. POWELL: I'm sorry. You had one, if I may.

Q General, were Iraqi TV and radio transmitters targeted? And are you surprised that they're still on the air?

GEN. POWELL: We were targeting the means by which the leadership of Iraq talks to its soldiers and communicates and maintains control, and I think we have done some considerable damage to that ability; at least according to what Bernie Shaw tells me. (Laughter.) And we will continue to review the bidding on that.

Q Would you --

Q General, we were told that there's a small movement of ground troops. Could you tell us please the extent --

GEN. POWELL: Ours or theirs?

Q Allied troops.

GEN. POWELL: Allied?

Q Could you tell us the extent, please, and where that is taking place?

GEN. POWELL: I'm not confirming that there was such movement. And let me just say that you shouldn't be surprised if you hear reports of such movement. It is one campaign; the air campaign which has gone very well, and I can't tell you how proud I am of all of our airmen and what they've done in the last 14 hours. But it is just one part of the total campaign. The air campaign began last night and will continue to the end.

Now ground campaign does not necessarily mean we're going to cross the border right away; just the positioning of troops in various places I consider part of the ground campaign, the overall campaign. The movement of amphibious forces in the Persian Gulf I consider part of the overall campaign.

And I would hope that the Iraqi leadership, the Iraqi military who may be trying to follow all these events should get greatly concerned about our ability not just to use one tool, but to use all the tools in the toolbox that we brought to this effort.

(Cross talk.)

Q General, what can you tell us about reports that Iraq has this --

GEN. POWELL: Two more. You're first. I'm sorry.

Q Could you just -- could you tell us about reports that Iraq has stuck some of its air defenses in bunkers, be it planes or additional missiles, and if they are prepared then to launch those at some point in the future against us?

0050

0192-9

GEN. POWELL: We[redacted] if they leave their airp[redacted]s in bunkers, then those airplanes are not up giving us difficulty. And we know where the bunkers are, and in due course, we will take care of it.

Q They do exist?

GEN. POWELL: Bunkers, oh yeah. They have hardened bunkers, quite sophisticated hardened bunkers.

Q General, is there any common trend to what caused the losses, such as anti-aircrafts or missiles or what kind of --

GEN. POWELL: Well, there is not a trend. I mean, there's only been two confirmed losses, and I -- and I don't want to get into what those losses were caused by.

Q You couldn't say what their strongest response has been -- (off mike) --

GEN. POWELL: There was a great deal of surface-to-air missile fire, and there was a great deal of anti-aircraft gunfire. But that's as far as I want to get into.

Q General, besides the various installations that we have talked about that we're bombing, are we dropping bombs on Iraqi infantry brigades or other troops?

GEN. POWELL: Allow me to duck that for the time being. The campaign will grow and spread and you will see other parts of it merge in due course, and you will understand the very comprehensive nature in this campaign -- of this campaign. But allow me to dodge that for the moment.

Thank you very much.

Q Can you stop this campaign if there are any diplomatic demarches from --

GEN. POWELL: We will do whatever the President asks us to do.

END

0182-10 0051

호 : USW(F) - 0200

신 : 장 관 (미북. 대책반. 중근동) 발신 : 주미대사

목 : 페만 공격 (호주 정부 지지 성명)

보안 통제

(3 매)

STATEMENT ON THE GULF CRISIS BY AUSTRALIAN PRIME MINISTER, MR. ROBERT HAWKE, THURSDAY, JANUARY 17, 1991

Following is a statement by the Prime Minister, Mr. Robert Hawke, delivered on 17 January, 1991.

PRIME MINISTER HAWKE: Ladies and gentlemen, fellow Australians:

You will recall that on 4 December last, I told Parliament that Australia was prepared to make our naval task force available to serve with allied forces in operations authorized by Resolution 678 of the United Nations Security Council, should that become necessary.

You will also recall that Resolution 678 authorized member states of the United Nations, from 15 January, 1991, to use all necessary means, including force, to uphold and implement the Security Council's previous resolutions -- in essence, the unconditional withdrawal by Iraq from Kuwait.

With profound regret, I must now inform you that the necessity which I foreshadowed in the Parliament five weeks ago has come about.

As a consequence, therefore, the Australian naval task force in the Gulf is now with other members of the United Nations co-operating in armed action to fulfil the United Nations resolutions to enforce the withdrawal of Iraq from Kuwait.

It has been my intention that Parliament, having endorsed the position I put on 4 December, should be given the earliest opportunity to receive a report from me should action be taken in line with that position.

Accordingly, I have decided to recall the Parliament on Monday, 21 January for two days so that I can make, and allow debate upon, such report.

Fellow Australians, I must emphasize from the outset -- and it cannot be repeated too often or stressed too strongly -- that this tragic necessity has one cause, and one cause only. And that is the invasion and occupation of the nation of Kuwait, a member state of the United Nations, by Iraq on 2 August last year -- more than five months ago.

That was the act of war -- and since that time we have sought by means of peace to reverse that act of war.

Since that time, the world community, working through the United Nations, with a unanimity, a strength and unity of purpose without precedent in history, has demanded that the Government of Iraq withdraw unconditionally its armed forces from Kuwait.

0200 - 1

0052

Twelve separate resolutions of the United Nations have been aimed at achieving that result.

Since August, governments of the member-states of the United Nations have worked unremittingly to persuade Saddam Hussein to comply with the will of the world community and to end the crisis he alone provoked.

Literally at the eleventh hour, with the positive support of the allied nations and in particular the President of the United States, the Secretary-General of the United Nations went to Baghdad to make a last appeal for compliance, a last plea for peace.

Like every other initiative undertaken within the framework of the United Nations' resolutions, it was rejected with contempt, and met the same uncompromising refusal to do the one thing that the world community agrees he must do -- give up the nation he has seized and crushed.

That is why Resolution 678 of the United Nations Security Council has come into effect.

And that is why I have directed the Australian naval task force to participate in the operations by that Resolution.

Ladies and gentlemen, fellow Australians, so momentous a decision must be placed -- as it has indeed been taken -- in the broad context of the future -- not only the future of Kuwait, not only the future of the Middle East, but in the context of our future vision of a world striving for peace and freedom.

And our decision is based on five grave considerations.

First, there is the fundamental principle, without which there can be neither peace nor freedom -- the right of every independent nation not to be invaded, not to be the victim of aggression, not to be destroyed.

Second, we act with the commanding moral authority of the United Nations worked so effectively and unitedly to fulfill its charter and the principles of peace and security it embodies.

Third, we have reached this decision only at the end of a process without precedent in history. There is no parallel for the restraint, the patience and the caution with which the world alliance against Saddam Hussein has sought by peaceful means to resolve this conflict.

Fourth, the decision has a clear and achievable goal -- to end this aggression, as a necessary step towards establishing the conditions for peace and stability in the Middle East.

And finally, there is a wider purpose behind our decision. It

0200-2

0053

is a purpose implicit in everything that has been done by the United Nations since last August.

That purpose is to further the great quest for a new world order of peace, security and freedom -- to fulfill the hopes and opportunities springing from the end of the confrontation between the United States and the Soviet Union. Indeed, I believe that, at the bar of history, there will be no greater condemnation of Saddam Hussein than that his aggression has plunged the world into a terrible and needless crisis which threatens the world stability on which those splendid hopes depend.

My fellow Australians, I know that the overwhelming majority of Australians will share my regret -- indeed much deeper than regret -- at the need for this decision. We all of us wish for peace. But we cannot have peace just by wishing for it or just by talking about it. We have to work for it, and sometimes, tragically, we have to fight for it. The great lesson of this century is that peace is bought at too high a price, if that price is the appeasement of aggression.

I know that you all with me will feel that our first thoughts today go to the 884 of our fellow Australian serving men and women most directly affected by this decision.

We have three ships of the Royal Australian Navy serving in the Gulf: HMAS Sydney, Brisbane and Success.

Our thoughts go to these ships' crews, to the medical teams serving on the hospital ships, to the logistic support team in the region, and to the Australians serving on exchange with other allied forces in the Gulf.

War is full of terrible uncertainty. We cannot foretell what will be demanded of our serving men and women. But we can foretell how they will meet those demands.

We are confident of their skills. We are grateful for their devotion. We know they will serve bravely and well, and we hoe, above all, that they will return safely home.

END

0200-3

0054

원 본

외 무 부

종 별 : 지 급

번 호 : USW-0246 일 시 : 91 0117 1113

수 신 : 장관(미북, 중근동, 대책반)

발 신 : 주미대사

제 목 : 걸프 작전 (제16신, 미 의회 반응)

1. BUSH 대통령은 걸프 작전에 대한 의회의 지지를 구하기 위해 금 1.17. 아침의회 지도자들을 백악관에 초치함.

2. 당지 언론은 상원은 금일중, 그리고 하원은 내일중 걸프작전 지지 결의안을 채택할 것으로 전망하고 있음.

(대사 박동진- 국장)

미주국	장관	차관	1차보	2차보	중아국	중아국	정문국	청와대
총리실	안기부	대책반						

PAGE 1

91.01.18 01:43 CG

외신 1과 통제관

0055

원 본

외 무 부

종 별 : 지 급

번 호 : USW-0247 일 시 : 91 0117 1113

수 신 : 장관(미북, 중근동, 대책반)

발 신 : 주미대사

제 목 : 걸프 작전(제 17신, 이락군 부항)

당지 언론은 사우디 주둔 이집트군을 인용 약 50대의 이락 탱크가 연합군측에 부항해 왔다고 보도한바, 사우디군 대변인은 숫자를 박히지 않은채 이락군의 부항이 있었음을 확인 하였음.

(대사 박동진- 국장)

미주국 장관 차관 1차보 2차보 중아국 중아국 정문국 청와대
종리실 안기부 대책반

PAGE 1

91.01.18 01:46 CG

외신 1과 통제관

0056

원 본

외 무 부

종 별 :

번 호 : USW-0251 일 시 : 91 0117 1504

수 신 : 장관(미북,중근동,대책반)

발 신 : 주 미 대사

제 목 : 걸프작전 (제 18신, 언론봉제)

이락 정부는 금 1.17. 10:59 (서울시간 22:59) 바그다드에서 활동중이던 CNN 방송송신을 중단시켰음.

(대사 박동진-국장)

미주국	장관	차관	1차보	2차보	중아국	중아국	정문국	청와대
총리실	안기부	대책반						

0057

PAGE 1

91.01.18 06:49 CG

외신 1과 통제관

원 본

외 무 부

종 별 : 지 급

번 호 : USW-0252 일 시 : 91 0117 1504

수 신 : 장관 (미북,중근동,대책반)

발 신 : 주 미 대사

제 목 : 걸프작전 (제19신, 상황 종합)

금 1.17. 13:35 (서울시간 1.18.03:35) 현재 상황을 종합, 하기 보고함.

1.주사우디 CNN 특파원에 의하면 F-15 기와 TORNADO 기의 출격이 계속되고 있어이락에대한 폭격이 계속되고 있는 것으로 추정된다고함.

2. 지상 작전이 개시 되었다는 조짐은 아직 없는 것으로 보도됨.

3. 터키 외잘 수상은 금조 CNN 과의 인터뷰를 통해 터키 의회가 연합군의 이락 공격을 위한 터키내 기지 사용을 허가 하기로 결의하였다고 말함.

4.한편, 뉴델리 AMERICAN AIRLINE 사무소에서 폭발사건이 발생한바, 인도정부는이락계 테러리스트에 의한 소행일 것으로 보고 있다고 보도됨.

(대사 박동진- 국장)

미주국	장관	차관	1차보	2차보	중아국	중아국	정문국	청와대
총리실	안기부	대책반						

PAGE 1 91.01.18 05:38 CG

외신 1과 통제관

0058

7u

원 본

외 무 부

종 별 : 긴 급

번 호 : USW-0253 일 시 : 91 0117 1504

수 신 : 장관(미북, 대책반, 중근동)

발 신 : 주 미 대사

제 목 : 걸프작전 (제 20신: 부쉬 대통령앞 친서 보도)

연: USW-0241

1. 1.17자 W.P 지는 U.S. ALLIES VOICE SUPPORT OF MOVE 제하의 기사에서 스페인, 일본, 호주, 뉴질랜드 및 한국 정부로 부터 미국의 공격작전을 지지하는 멧세지가 있었다고 전하면서, 특히 미국이 취한 결연한 군사적 조치를 전폭적으로 지지한다는 노 대통령의 서한 내용을 인용 보도했음.

2. 동기사 별첨 FAX 송부함.(USW(F)-0193)

(대사 박동진-국장)

미주국	장관	차관	1차보	2차보	중아국	중아국	정문국	청와대
총리실	안기부	대책반						

PAGE 1

91.01.18 05:15 CG

외신 1과 통제관

0053

번 호 : USW(F) - 0193
수 신 : 장 관 (미북, 대책반, 중근동) 발 신 : 주미대사
제 목 : 걸프 작전(부시 대통령앞 친서 보도) (1 매)

U.S. Allies Voice Support of Move; Castro Demurs

By Richard Homan
Washington Post Foreign Service

Initial international reaction to the U.S.-led attack on Iraq was largely limited to strong expressions of support from traditional American allies, while most other countries—many apparently taken by surprise—said nothing or simply reported the bombing raids without substantive comment.

Swift declarations of support for the multinational use of force to drive Iraq from Kuwait came from Spain and four U.S. allies in Asia: Japan, Australia, New Zealand and South Korea.

As of late last night, the only strong condemnation came from Cuban President Fidel Castro, who learned of the raids as he gave a news conference to Western reporters in Havana. "My feeling is one of sorrow, of deep bitterness," he said. "The responsibility for the war falls on those who fired the first shot . . . essentially, the United States."

The Arab world, which has been split between participation in the anti-Iraq alliance and support of Iraqi President Saddam Hussein was slow to react, and in the Soviet Union, Tass, the official news agency, reported that the United States had begun hostilities but made no comment of its own.

Neighboring Iran, long hostile to the United States and only recently on good terms with Iraq after an eight-year war, reported the bombing raid on its Tehran Radio but noted pointedly that "at present the only source of news from Iraq is American correspondents in Baghdad."

Jordan, which has both backed Saddam politically and expressed adherence to the U.N.-imposed sanctions, delayed reporting the opening of the war until nearly three hours after most of the world learned of it, the Los Angeles Times reported from Amman. There was no immediate statement from King Hussein's government.

The Los Angeles Times quoted a ranking aide to President Hosni Mubarak as saying that the Egyptian president, who is a key Arab participant in the multinational force, first learned of the attack on U.S. cable television.

Palestine Liberation Organization official Basam Abu Sharif told the Associated Press in Tunis, "It is unfortunate that [President] Bush decided to kill to protect the Israeli occupation" of the West Bank and Gaza Strip.

At the United Nations, Secretary General Javier Perez de Cuellar, who made an unsuccessful last-minute appeal to Saddam this week to leave Kuwait in conformance with a dozen U.N. Security Council resolutions, expressed "sorrow," Reuter reported. "I can only be saddened by the beginning of hostilities," he told reporters.

Japan, the sole member of the Group of 7 major industrialized nations that has sent no troops to the gulf, expressed "resolute support for the use of military force . . . as a final measure to retore peace and drive out the invader." Prime Minister Toshiki Kaifu, after an emergency cabinet meeting early today, pledged that "we will provide as much support as we possibly can for the action of the concerned nations and as much assistance as we can for the refugees."

Australian Prime Minister Bob Hawke, who yesterday ordered warships of his country into action in the gulf, condemned Saddam's "aggression," which he said "has plunged the world into a terrible and needless crisis." New Zealand Prime Minister Jim Bolger said everyone hoped and prayed that Saddam would "at last see reason" with the onset of war, the AP reported.

South Korean President Roh Tae Woo, in a message to Bush, said: "I, along with the people of the Republic of Korea, fully support the resolute military actions" the U.S.-led force had begun.

In Madrid, a spokesman for the Foreign Ministry said Spain supported the attack.

One of the few negative reactions in Europe came from Georges Marchais, leader of the French Communist Party. He said those who had allowed the war with its "cortege of killings and indescribable misfortunates" have "a heavy responsibility to the human race." Marchais said these included "Saddam Hussein who provided the excuse, George Bush who wanted it and decided to carry it out and the leaders of the countries who engaged in it, among them, alas, France."

In Falls Church, as Kerry Cadden watched news of the invasion on television about 10 p.m., her telephone rang. It was a man named John Carter, calling from Wales, who had dialed America at random after watching the same events at 3 a.m. his time. He had just wanted to "extend his thanks and that of all of his friends to all Americans for all we're doing in the Mideast for Kuwait and democracy," Cadden said.

"You're always there when we need you and you always do the right thing," she quoted him as saying.

한국관련

Jan. 17, 1991
WP

0060

'9

원 본

외 무 부

종 별 : 긴 급

번 호 : USW-0254 일 시 : 91 0117 1504

수 신 : 장관(미북, 대책반, 중근동)

발 신 : 주 미 대사

제 목 : 걸프작전 (제 21신: 쿠웨이트 조종사 탈출)

AL SABAH 주 쿠웨이트 대사는 1.17 14:00 기자회견을 통해 쿠웨이트 공군기 1대(HORNET) 가 귀환하지 못했으며, 동 전부기 조종사는 이락- 사우디 국경에서 탈출하여 현재 구출작전이 진행중이라고 밝혔음.

(대사 박동진-국장)

미주국 장관 차관 1차보 2차보 중아국 중아국 정문국 청와대
총리실 안기부 대책반

PAGE 1

91.01.18 05:14 CG

외신 1과 통제관

0061

외 무 부

종 별 :

번 호 : USW-0258 일 시 : 91 0117 1613

수 신 : 장관(통일,중근동,미북,해운항만청)

발 신 : 주 미 대사

제 목 : 페만 항행선박에 대한 특별 주의

연: USW-0205

페만전쟁발발, 금일 미 국무부 발표 페만 항행선박에 대한 추가 특별 주의보 및해사청의 동 지역항행 미상선대에 대한 별도 권고문을 별첨 보고함.

첨부: USW(F)-0198

(대사 박동진-국장)

통상국	장관	차관	1차보	2차보	미주국	중아국	중아국	정문국
청와대	총리실	안기부	해항청					

0062

PAGE 1

91.01.18 06:44 CG

외신 1과 통제관

USW(F) - 0198

수 신 : 장관 (통일, 중근동, 미북, 해운항만청) 발신 : 주미대사

제 목 : USW-0258 첨부물 (총3매)

SPECIAL WARNING NUMBER 85.
PERSIAN GULF-ARABIAN SEA-RED SEA.
1. ALL MERCHANT SHIPS ARE ADVISED THAT IRAQ HAS FAILED TO COMPLY WITH UNITED NATIONS SECURITY COUNCIL RESOLUTION 678 AND ARMED HOSTILITIES HAVE COMMENCED IN THE WATERS BORDERING THE NATIONS OF IRAQ AND KUWAIT AND THE ARABIAN PENINSULA INCLUDING THE PERSIAN GULF, NORTH ARABIAN SEA, AND RED SEA. AS HOSTILITIES HAVE COMMENCED, DANGER TO SHIPPING HAS INCREASED. MARINERS ARE ADVISED TO EXERCISE EXTREME CAUTION AND TO MAINTAIN ALERT VISUAL WATCH TO HAZARDOUS CONDITIONS.
2. ALL PROCEDURES OF THE MULTINATIONAL INTERCEPTION FORCE, DESCRIBED IN SPECIAL WARNING NO. 80, REMAIN IN EFFECT.
3. FAILURE OF A SHIP TO PROCEED AS DIRECTED BY THE INTERCEPTING SHIP WILL RESULT IN THE USE OF THE MINIMUM LEVEL OF FORCE NECESSARY TO INSURE COMPLIANCE.
4. ALL SHIPS, INCLUDING WATERBORNE CRAFT AND ARMED MERCHANT SHIPS OR

PAGE 02 RUCKSGG2758 UNCLAS
AIRCRAFT, WHICH THREATEN OR INTERFERE WITH THE MULTINATIONAL INTERCEPTION FORCE WILL BE CONSIDERED HOSTILE AND COULD BE FIRED UPON.
5. CANCEL SPECIAL WARNING 84.
BT
#3758 NNNN

0063

MARAD ADVISORY NO. 91-3 (151945Z JAN 91)

SUBJECT: NAVAL CONTROL OF SHIPPING (NCS) FOR U.S.-FLAG AND EFFECTIVE U.S. CONTROLLED SHIPPING IN EVENT OF HOSTILITIES WITH IRAQ.

TO: MASTERS AND OPERATORS, ALL U.S.-FLAG, AND U.S.-OWNED FOREIGN FLAG MERCHANT VESSELS.

1. THE FOLLOWING MESSAGE WAS ISSUED THIS DATE FROM THE OFFICE OF THE CHIEF OF NAVAL OPERATIONS:

QUOTE.
1. FOLLOWING POLICY APPLIES TO ALL U.S. FLAG AND EFFECTIVE U.S. CONTROLLED SHIPPING NOT UNDER OPERATIONAL CONTROL (OPCON) OF MILITARY SEALIFT COMMAND.

2. U.S. NAVAL AUTHORITIES HAVE NOT YET IMPLEMENTED FORMAL NAVAL CONTROL OF SHIPPING IN THE PERSIAN GULF. THERE IS SUFFICIENT U.S. NAVAL PRESENCE IN THE GULF AREA TO ENSURE THE SAFETY OF ALL U.S. AND ALLIED SHIPPING. THE SITUATION CONTINUES TO BE KEPT UNDER CLOSE REVIEW. SHOULD HOSTILITIES BREAK OUT, SHIPPING IN THE NORTHERN GULF SHOULD PROCEED TO THE SOUTHERN PORTION OF THE GULF, AND ALL SHIPPING NOT YET IN THE GULF WILL BE ADVISED BY NAVAL AUTHORITIES TO REMAIN OUTSIDE UNTIL THE SITUATION STABILIZES. SHIPS CALLING AT PORTS IN THE SOUTHERN GULF WILL PROCEED AS NORMAL BUT MAINTAIN A COMMUNICATIONS WATCH. THIS GUIDANCE WILL BE AMPLIFIED AS EVENTS DEVELOP.

3. SUGGEST ALL MASTERS REVIEW DMA PUB 117 CHAPTER 8 WHICH DISCUSSES NAVAL CONTROL OF SHIPPING.

4. SHIPPING UNDER MSC OPCON WILL CONTINUE TO RECEIVE DIRECTION FROM MSC.
UNQUOTE.

2. THE FOLLOWING PROCEDURES ARE ALSO RECOMMENDED:

A. THE COMMUNICATIONS SYSTEM PROCEDURES UNDER NAVAL CONTROL OF SHIPPING (NCS), TITLED MERCOMMS AND LOCATED IN CHAPTER 8 OF DEFENSE MAPPING AGENCY (DMA) PUBLICATION 117, RADIO AIDS TO NAVIGATION, SHOULD ALSO BE REVIEWED WITH THE VESSEL'S RADIO OFFICER. MARINERS ARE FURTHER ADVISED TO REVIEW THE EMERGENCY COMMUNICATIONS CALL UP PROCEDURES IN CHAPTER 4 NOTING PARTICULAR U.S. NAVAL AND COAST GUARD COMMUNICATIONS STATIONS AND FREQUENCIES.

B. FOR COMMUNICATIONS WITH PATROL SHIP/HELO, ESTABLISH VHF CHANNEL 16 OR 13 CONTACT USING THE FOLLOWING CALL-UP: "US NAVAL WARSHIP, THIS IS (NAME OF VESSEL)." DO NOT USE CALL SIGNS OR REFER TO US NAVAL UNITS AS ANYTHING BUT US NAVAL

0198 -2

0064

WARSHIP/HELO.

C. THE COMMANDER, MILITARY SEALIFT COMMAND SOUTH WEST ASIA (COMSCSWA) IN BAHRAIN IS THE POINT OF CONTACT FOR NCS AND MAY BE CONTACTED BY: TELEPHONE (973 COUNTRY CODE) 713-172 EXT. 272 OR 255; INMARSAT TERMINAL PRIMARY (MSCO BAHRAIN) 1505370, SECONDARY (MSCO AL JUBAIL) 1505367 AND (MSCO AD DAMMAM) 1505372 FOR VOICE AND TELEX; COMMERCIAL TELEX 04907237 (ASU BN); FACSIMILE 728-244. THE MARITIME ADMINISTRATION REPRESENTATIVE IN BAHRAIN (WITH COMSCSWA) MAY BE CONTACTED BY TELEPHONE 713-172 X243, FACSIMILE 712-198.

D. ANY SIGHTING OF A MINE SHOULD BE REPORTED TO COMMANDER MIDDLE EAST FORCE ON VHF CHANNEL 16 OR 13. NOTE POSITION, SET AND DRIFT, AND GENERAL APPEARANCE. ADDITIONALLY, WATCH ALL WATERCRAFT FOR SUSPICIOUS ACTIVITY.

E. MARINERS ARE ADVISED TO MONITOR CLOSELY ALL NAVIGATIONAL WARNING BROADCASTS FOR SPECIAL WARNINGS, MARAD ADVISORIES, MINING HAZARDS, HOSTILE ACTIVITIES, AND NAVIGATIONAL INFORMATION.

F. MASTERS SHOULD NOTE THE FOLLOWING CHECKPOINTS WHICH WERE PREVIOUSLY ESTABLISHED, THAT MAY BE USED AS REFERENCE POINTS: NLO (NAVAL LIAISON OFFICER) RENDEZVOUS 23-35.5N, 058-36E; CHECK POINT ALFA 25-35N, 056-45E; CHECK POINT BRAVO 26-00N, 055-37E; CHECK POINT CHARLIE 25-32N, 054-45E.

3. MARAD IS TRANSMITTING THIS ADVISORY VIA A MULTITUDE OF MEANS TO VESSELS, HOWEVER OPERATORS ARE REQUESTED TO ENSURE THE RECEIPT OF THIS MESSAGE BY THEIR VESSELS.

4. FOR FURTHER INFORMATION REGARDING THE ISSUANCE OF THIS ADVISORY, CONTACT MR. K. TOKARSKI, MARITIME ADMINISTRATION, OFFICE OF SHIP OPERATIONS, CODE MAR-745, ROOM 2123, 400 SEVENTH STREET S.W., WASHINGTON, DC 20590, TELEPHONE (202) 366-5735, FACSIMILE (202) 366-3954, TLX II 710-822-9426 (MARAD DOT WSH). NOTE THAT AFTER NORMAL WORKING HOURS, MESSAGES MAY BE LEFT AT (202) 366-5915, MARAD'S EMERGENCY OPERATIONS CENTER.

M. Delpercio

M. DELPERCIO, JR.
DIRECTOR
OFFICE OF SHIP OPERATIONS

0198-3

0065

외 무 부

종 별 :

번 호 : USW-0266 일 시 : 91 0117 1817

수 신 : 장 관(중근동,기협,경일,미북)

발 신 : 주 미 대사

제 목 : 미국의 전략 비축석유 방출

1. 부쉬대통령은 폐만 전쟁 개시와관련, 1.16(수) 저녁 미국정부가 보유하고 있는 전략비축석유(SPR)의 방출을 지지하였는 바, 동지시에 따라 미에너지부는 향후 30일간 총 33.75 백만 배럴, 1일 1.125 백만 배럴의 SPR을 방출키로 결정하였음.

2. 동 방출 결정과 관련 WATKINS 에너지 장관은 페만전쟁 발생시 OECD국 보유 SPR을 1일 2.5 백만 배럴씩 방출키로한 1.11 국제에너지기구의 결정에 따라 미 국외 독일.일본등 13개국도 자국보유 SPR을 방출할 예정이라고 하면서 폐만전쟁에따라 즉각적인 원유공급 WWPAL사태가 발생할 것으로는 기대하지 않는다고 발언하였음.

3. 미국은 현재 총 585 백만 배럴의 원유를 SPR 로 보유하고 있는바, 1일 3.5백단 배럴까지방출이 가능하다고함.

4. 미에너지부의 상기 SPR 방출관련 보도자료별첨 송부함.

첨부: USW(F)-0201 (2 매)

(대사 박동진-국장)

중아국 2차보 미주국 경제국 경제국 동자부

PAGE 1 91.01.18 09:17 ER

외신 1과 통제관

0066

[redacted]SW(F)-0201
수신: 장관(중근동, 기협, 경일 미북)
발신: 주미대사
제목: USW-0266 첨부(2매)

DOE NEWS

NEWS MEDIA CONTACT:
Mary Joy Jameson, 202/586-5806

FOR IMMEDIATE RELEASE
January 16, 1991

PRESIDENT DIRECTS DRAWDOWN OF STRATEGIC RESERVE

President Bush tonight authorized the Secretary Of Energy to drawdown the Strategic Petroleum Reserve (SPR).

President Bush's authorization tonight to begin releasing government-owned oil stocks is part of an international effort to minimize world oil market disruptions caused by Middle East hostilities. In response to the President's finding, Secretary Watkins immediately ordered the Department to implement a drawdown of 33.75 million barrels of oil, equivalent to a drawdown of 1.125 million barrels per day.

In announcing plans for using the SPR, Secretary Watkins emphasized that he does not anticipate immediate oil shortages due to the current situation.

"By drawing on our strategic stocks, the U.S. is working in close cooperation with its partners in the International Energy Agency (IEA). Our purpose is to take precautionary action early and in doing so, counter any possible disruption of supplies from the Persian Gulf," Watkins said.

Watkins said the U.S. action will be joined by similar stock drawdowns from 13 other nations, including Germany and Japan.

"Acting collectively, the U.S. and its allies intend to reassure the world market," Watkins said. "Consumers should not have any concerns about the availability of petroleum and petroleum products. The SPR was envisioned for exactly the situation we have today. Now is the time to begin taking advantage of the investment we have made in it."

The Department of Energy will issue a "notice of sale" tomorrow specifying the types and location of crude oil it will offer for sale from the government's oil stockpile. The SPR, located along the Texas and Louisiana coastline, holds more than 585 million barrels of crude oil. The Reserve was established in 1975 to protect the U.S. against interruptions in petroleum supplies.

(MORE)

R-91-09

0067

-2-

Concurrently with the authorization to use the SPR, the President directed the Secretary of the Treasury to waive provisions of the Jones Act that require the use of U.S.-flag vessels to transport crude oil from the Reserve. The general, or "blanket," waiver will ensure that the widest range of transportation opportunities is made available for moving SPR oil into all parts of the U.S. market.

"We anticipate releasing 33.75 million barrels of crude oil from the SPR which is equivalent to a drawdown of 1.125 million barrels per day over a 30-day period. This rate is about a third of the Reserve's maximum oil distribution capability of 3.5 million barrels per day that could be called upon should the situation warrant in the future," Watkins said.

Under the international coordinated effort, the 1.125 million barrels per day is the U.S. share of 2.5 million barrels per day to be made available by OECD nations, as agreed to on January 11 by the IEA's governing board.

The IEA will meet again in 10 days to reassess the world oil supply situation and determine whether additional measures are necessary.

Last October and November, the Energy Department ran a test of the Reserve's oil sales and distribution process. Although today's announced action will withdraw more than six times the amount of crude oil sold in last year's test, Watkins said that the exercise gave both industry and the Department increased confidence that oil could be moved into the market efficiently and quickly.

Watkins said that the release of government-controlled oil inventories should send a clear signal to oil markets that supplies will be adequate. This should minimize price increases and inventory buildups.

"If I had a message to markets right now," said Watkins, "it would be to base their decisions on _facts_ such as we are announcing today, rather than on unsubstantiated rumors and fears."

The first oil from the reserve could enter the U.S. market within sixteen days. Due to normal industry and pipeline and vessel scheduling requirements, the bulk of the oil will likely be delivered late in February or in March. Earlier deliveries could occur depending on purchasers' ability to schedule transport.

-DOE-

R-91-09

-2. End

0068

'ㄴ

원 본

외 무 부

종 별 : 긴 급

번 호 : USW-0270 일 시 : 91 0117 1847

수 신 : 장 관 (미북,중근동,대책반)

발 신 : 주 미 대사

제 목 : : 걸프 작전 (제22신:전황 종합)

당지 언론 보도를 중심으로, 1.17. 17:00 (서울시간 1.18. 07:00)현재 전황을 하기 종합 보고함.

1.작일 작전 개시이래, 지금까지의 다국적 공군기출격 회수는 총 약 1,300 회에달하며, 상금 완전히 파괴되지 않은 SCUD 미사일 기지 (특히 이동식 SCUD 미사일 기지), 화학무기 및 핵무기 시설등에 대한 공습이 현재도 진행되고 있다함.

2.다국적군 발표에 따르면 현재까지 3대의 전폭기 (미 공군 소속 F-18, 영국 공군 소속 TORNADO, 쿠웨이트 공군 소속 HORNET) 가 격추된 것으로 알려지고 있으나, 이락측은 55대를 격추시킨 것으로 주장하고 있다함.,

3.한편 미 공군의 B-52 폭격기는 쿠웨이트 북서부와 이락 남부의 REPUBLICANGUARD 주둔 지역에 대해 집중적인 폭격을 실시하고 있다 하며, 미 해군의 전함 위스컨 신호와 미주리호로 부터도 100여기 이상의 TOMAHAWK 크루주 미사일이 발사된 것으로 알려짐.

또한 지상 주둔 다국적 병력도 쿠웨이트 국경지역으로 이동 중인것으로 알려지고 있으나, 공군력사용이 상당 기간 지속된 후에나 (당지 일각에서는 다음주까지도대이락 공습이 계속될것으로 추측)실제 지상전투가 개시될 것으로 저망되고 있음.

4.기본적으로 작전 개시일 (D-DAY) 의 전투 성과가 만족스럽운 것으로 미측은 평갛고 있으며, 부쉬대통령도 이락측이 UN 안보리 결의안을 준수, 쿠웨이트로 부터철수할것읍 강력 촉구하는 한편, 금번 작전이 현재까지 특히 커다란 인명 손실없이 진행될것을 성공적이라 평가하고 있음.

5.요약컨데, 지상 병력 투입수 사상자 수가 증자될 것으로 예상되기는 하나, 현재의 당지 분위기는 승이에 대한 조용한 자신감 (QUIET CONFIDENCE) 으로 충만되어 있는 것으로 감지도며, 여사한 미국내 분위기가 국제 원유가 하락 추세와 주요 증권시장의 주가 상승 경향에도 여실히 반영되고 있는 것으로 관찰됨.끝

미주국 장관 차관 1차보 2차보 중아국 정문국 청와대 총리실
안기부 대책반

PAGE 1

91.01.18 09:08 WG
외신 1과 통제관

0063

원 본

외 무 부

종 별 :

번 호 : USW-0273

일 시 : 91 0117 1921

수 신 : 장 관(미북,동구일, 중근동)

발 신 : 주 미 대사

제 목 : 페만 공격 (제23신 소련 반응)

1. FITZWATER 백악관 대변인은 금 1.17. 정례브리핑을 통해, 소련 정부는 금번 사태가 결국 무력충돌화 하였음에 유감을 표시 한다는 요지의 멧세지를 미국 정부에 보내왔음을 밝혔음.

2.한편, 고르바쵸프 대통령은 1.17. 아래 내용의 성명을 발표 했음 (별첨 팩스 내용 참조 USW(F)-0209)

0 금번 사태는 이락측이 쿠웨이트로 부터의 무조건 철수 요구를 거부했기 때문에 발생했음.

0 소련은 무력 충돌 방지를 위해 마직 순간까지 최선을 다했으나 실패 했으며, 전쟁이 조속 정결될수 있도록 가능한 모든 조치를 취할것임.

(대사 박동진- 국장)

미주국	장관	차관	1차보	2차보	구주국	중아국	중아국	정문국
청와대	총리실	안기부						

PAGE 1

91.01.18 09:22 WG

외신 1과 통제관

0070

번호 : USW(F) - 020[redacted]

수신 : 장 관 (미북. 대[redacted]. 중근동) 발신 : 주미대사

제목 : 페만 공격 (고르바쵸프 대통령 멧세지) (/ 매)

[redacted] 장

TAPED MESSAGE BY SOVIET PRESIDENT MIKHAIL GORBACHEV CONCERNING THE ALLIED ATTACK ON IRAQ, THURSDAY, JANUARY 17, 1991

PRESIDENT GORBACHEV: (Beginning translated by FNS until audio of interpreter begins.) American armed forces along with military units from **Great Britain, Saudi Arabia,** and other governments conducted strikes -- (audio of interpreter begins) -- on military and some industrial objects in **Iraq** on the locations of Iraqi forces. Such a tragic turn was provoked by Iraqi leadership's refusal to follow the demands of the world community and withdraw its forces from Iraq -- from **Kuwait.**

In the beginning of Iraqi aggression, the Soviet Union did all it could to solve an acute international conflict by peaceful means. To the very last minute, we took energetic efforts in order to prevent the war by political means to get independence back to Kuwait.

Having gotten about an hour in advance from Mr. Baker the report on the decision they made, I put the proposal before President Bush to take additional measures through direct contact with Saddam Hussein to get an unpostponable announcement of Iraqi withdrawal from Kuwait.

At the same time, I ordered our Ambassador in Baghdad to get in touch with the President of Iraq and let him know about my talk with George Bush and let him know that, in the interest of Iraqi people and the interest of peace in the region, let him announce that he is ready to withdraw from Kuwait. That would let -- avert war and save Iraq great losses and devastation. I expressed hope that, being judged by the high interests by the people, Saddam Hussein would follow that only saving step.

That same night we also appealed to the leaders of many influential countries -- including **France, China,** Great Britain, **Germany, India, Italy,** to the heads of most Arabic states -- to take combined efforts to localize the conflict and prevent it from spreading. Realizing what consequences for the Arabic people, for American people, for the whole international situation, what losses it can bring, we expressed our deep sorrow that military confrontation could not be averted.

So I'm ready to emphasize one more time we did everything possible to avert the conflict. I want to inform you that, among the Soviet people who are still in Iraq, there's been no casualties. The Soviet people can be sure that the Soviet leadership will take all measures to stop war as soon as possible, and it'll go on cooperating with other countries and the United Nations.

END

0071

원 본

외 무 부

종 별 : 초긴급

번 호 : USW-0275 일 시 : 91 0117 2015

수 신 : 장 관(미북,중근동,대책반)

발 신 : 주 미 대사

제 목 : '' 페'' 만 작전(제24신,이락의 대이스라엘 공격)

1.당지시간 금 1.17. 19:30 언론 보도에 따르면 이스라엘 시간으로 1.18. 02:10 경 이락측이 이스라엘에 대해 총8기의 SCUD 미사일 공격을 가한것으로 알려짐.

CNN 방송에 따르면 최소 2기의 SCUD 미사일이 각각 텔아비브 남부 및 동남교외의 인구 밀집지역을 공격 했다 하며, 이스라엘측 피해 정도와 동 미사일의 화학 무기 탄두 장착 여부는 상금확인되지 않고 있음.

2.전기 SCUD 미사일은 다국적군의 공습으로부터 살아 남은 이동식 SCUD 미사일 발사대로 부터 발사된것으로 추정되고 있는바, 관련 사항 추보예정임

(대사 박동진-장관)

미주국	장관	차관	1차보	2차보	중아국	정문국	청와대	총리실
안기부	대책반							

0072

PAGE 1 91.01.18 10:22 WG

외신 1과 통제관

'4

원 본

외 무 부

종 별 : 초긴급

번 호 : USW-0276 일 시 : 91 0117 2207

수 신 : 장 관(미북, 중근동, 대책반)

발 신 : 주 미 대사

제 목 : ''페'' 만 작전(제25신 이락의 대이스라엘 공격)

1.당지시간 1.17. 21:25 언론 보도 (텔아비브 특파원) 에 의하면, 이스라엘 군당국은 이스라엘을 공격한 스커드 미사일 (텔아비브 2발, 하이파 2발, 인구 비거주지역 3발, 미확인 지역 1발등) 로 인해 7명의 경상자가 발생 하였으며 더 이상 개스마스크를 착용할 필요가 없음을 알렸음.

2.당지시간 1.17. 21:45 언론 보도 (텔아비브 특파원) 에 의하면 이스라엘 군당국은 스커드 미사일에 화학무기가 장착 되었다는 징후가 없으며, 다수의 소규모 재래식 폭약이 장착된 것으로 판단하고 있다함.

(대사 박동진- 국장)

미주국 장관 차관 1차보 2차보 중아국 정문국 청와대 총리실
안기부 대책반

0073

PAGE 1

91.01.18 12:48 WG

외신 1과 통제관

원 본

외 무 부

종 별 :

번 호 : USW-0278 일 시 : 91 0117 2249

수 신 : 장 관(미북, 대책반, 중근동)

발 신 : 주 미 대사

제 목 : ''페''만 작전 (제26신 대이스라엘 공격)

이락의 대이스라엘 공격과 관련, 하기 진전사항 보고함.

1.이스라엘 내각이 대책을 협의하고 있는 것으로 알려지는 가운데, BUSH 국무부장관은 주 UN 이스라엘 대사에게 보복 공격을 자제할 것을 요청한 것으로 보됨.

2. BUSH 대통령은 대 이스라엘 공격에 대한 분노와 비난이 성명을 발표하였고, 이락에 대한 대규모 공습이 계속되고 있다고 함.

3. 이스라엘 에 대한 공격과 함께 다란 공군기지를 중심으로 사우디에도 미사일 공격이 이루어 졌으며 이에 대해 연합군측이 PATRIOT 대사일 미사일로 대응하여 피해는 없었다고 함.

4.이스라엘에 대한 공격 의도에 대해서는 (1)절망에서 나오는 행동이라는 설과, (2) 후세인이 이스라엘 을 공격함으로써 아랍세계의 관심을 끌려는 MACHISOM 적 의도라는 분석등이 언론을 통해 나오고 있음.

(대사 박동진- 국장)

미주국	장관	차관	1차보	2차보	중아국	정문국	청와대	총리실
안기부	대책반							

0074

PAGE 1 91.01.18 12:52 WG

외신 1과 통제관

원 본

외 무 부

종 별 : 지 급

번 호 : USW-0279 일 시 : 91 0118 0542

수 신 : 장 관 (미북,중근동,대책반)

발 신 : 주 미 대사

제 목 : '페'만 작전(제 27신, 전황종합)

1. 18. 05:00 (서울시간 19:00)현재 전황, 하기 보고함.

1. 이스라엘이 이락에 대해 보복 공격을 가할지에 대한 관심이 집중되고 있는 가운데, 미 언론에서는 금번 공격에 대해서는 이스라엘이 보복을 않을 것이라는 관측이 나오고 있음. 연합군은 MOBIL SCUD MISSILE 에 대한 폭격을 집중적으로 하고 있는것으로 보도됨.

2. 지상작전이 개시되었는지도 아직 불분명함.

3. 미 국방부가 07:00 그리고 SCHWARZKOPF 현지 사령관이 07:00-08:00 경 기자회견을 실시할 예정임.

4. 미측 손실은 해군기 A-6, 공군기 F-15 이 각각 1대씩 추가로 실종되어 인명손실 5, 비행기 3대 실종으로 보도되고 있음.

(대사 박동진- 국장)

미주국	장관	차관	1차보	2차보	중아국	정문국	청와대
총리실	안기부	대책반					

0075

PAGE 1

91.01.18 20:24 FC

외신 1과 통제관

원 본

외 무 부

종 별 : 긴 급

번 호 : USW-0280 일 시 : 91 0118 0810

수 신 : 장 관 (미북,중근동,대책반)

발 신 : 주 미 대사

제 목 : 페만 작전(제 28신)

1. SCHWARZKOPS 사령관은 18 07:00(서울 시각 21:00)에 미 공군 HORNER중장과 합동 기자회견을 가진바, 동 내용 하기 보고함.

1. 전황

- 작전 개시이후 36 시간 동안 2,000 회의 출격이 이루어진바, 적중율도 약 80프로에 달함.

- MOBILE SCUD MISSILE 을 확인, 폭격하는 것은 매우 힘든 일이나, 11개의 LAUNCHER 를 확인, 공격중임.

- 이락의 대공망이 소홀했다는 지적도 있으나, 실제로 출격에 참가했던 조종사들의 보고로는 일부 소홀한 지역도 있으나 반면 매우 완고한 대공망을 구축한 지역이많았음.

-해상에서는 상륙선의 집결이 이루어 지고 있고, 지상에서도 추후 작전에 대비한이동이 이루어지고 있음.

2. 연합군 피해

-미군기 3대, 영국기 2대, 이태리기 1 대, 쿠웨이트기 1대손실

3. 지나친 낙관에 대한 경계

-부쉬, 체니, POWELL 이 지적했듯이 이락은 파나마가 아니며 지나친 낙관은 금물임.

- 연합군의 공격은 군사목표로 제한하고 민간인 피해를 가능한 줄이기 위해 최대한의 노력을 기울이고 있음. 회교사원에 대해서도 특별히 고려

4. 폭격장면 공개(HORNER 중장, 전부기가 찍은필름 공개)

- 이번 작전에는 고도의 군사장비를 이용, 매우 정확한 폭격이 가능했음.

- 활주로, SCUD 저장소, 이락 공군사령부등 공습장면 방영

미주국	장관	차관	1차보	2차보	중아국	정문국	청와대
종리실	안기부	대책반					

0076

PAGE 1 91.01.18 22:50 FC

외신 1과 통제관

- AWACS 이용, 연합군간의 긴밀한 협력등이 효과적인 공격에 기여함.
(대사 박동진-국장)

원 본

외 무 부

종 별 : 긴 급

번 호 : USW-0281 일 시 : 91 0118 1028

수 신 : 장 관 (미북,중근동,대책반)

발 신 : 주 미 대사

제 목 : 페만 작전(제 29신, 소련, 이락의 대 이스라엘공격 비난)

1. 18 09:00 당지 언론 보도에 따르면 고르바쵸프 소련대통령은 아랍 각국 지도자에게 보낸 멧세지를 통해 이락의 대 이스라엘 공격은 금번 사태를 아랍-이스라엘간대결로 유도하기 위한 이락측의 술책이라고 비난하고, 페만전쟁이 확대되지 않도록각국이 자제하여 줄것을 촉구했다 함.

(대사 박동진-국장)

미주국 장관 차관 1차보 2차보 중아국 정문국 청와대
총리실 안기부 대책반

0078

PAGE 1

91.01.19 01:12 FC

외신 1과 통제관

원 본

외 무 부

종 별 : 지 급

번 호 : USW-0301 일 시 : 91 0118 1754

수 신 : 장 관 (미북,중근동,대책반)

발 신 : 주미대사

제 목 : 페만작전 (국방부 브리핑)

국방부는 금 1.18 1700 (서울 시각 1.19 0700)미 합참 KELLY 중장(OPERATIONS) 및MCCONNELL 소장(INTELLIGENCE)의 기자 회견을실시한바 동 내용 하기 보고함.

1.전황

0 총 2,107 회의 출격이 있었고, 미사일 196기를발사함.

0 (제공권 을 완전 장악 하였냐는 질문에대함) 아직은 그 단계는 아님.

0 (후세인의 지휘,통제 기능에 대한 질문에 대해)아직은 유효한 지위,통제가 이루어지고 있다고 봄.

0 (REPUBLICAN GUARD 에 대한 공격 여부 질문)공격이 이루어지고 있으며, 계속될것임.

2.피해 상황

0 미군기 A-6 가 1대 추가 실종되어 총 손실은전부기 4대, 조종사 7명으로 늘어남(실종된 조종사가이락의 포로가 되었는지 여부를 질문한데 대해확인은 거부함)

3.지상 작전

0(공군력만으로 전쟁 수행이 가능할것인가질문에) 현재로서는 말할수 있는 단계가 아니나,지상 작전을 수행하기 위한 준비는 하고 있어.

4.당지 시간으로 1.19 0700 사우디 리야드현지사령부에서, 그리고 1530 에 미 국방부에서브리핑이 실시될 예정임.

(대사 박동진-국장)

미주국	장관	차관	1차보	2차보	중아국	청와대	총리실	안기부
대책반								

0079

PAGE 1

91.01.19 08:54 AQ

외신 1과 통제관

관리 번호 H-P8

원 본

외 무 부

종 별 : 지 급

번 호 : USW-0302 일 시 : 91 0118 1810

수 신 : 장관(미북,대책반,중근동)

발 신 : 주 미 대사

제 목 : 페만 사태 국무성 브리핑

주재국 국무부는 1.18 당지 주재 외교단을 국무부로 초치, 중근동 담당 JOHN KELLY 차관보로 부터 대 이락 무력사용 경위에 대한 브리핑이 있었는바, 동 요지 다음 보고함.(당관에서는 유명환 참사관이 참석)

1. 평화적 해결을 위한 외교적 노력

- 미국은 페만 사태의 평화적 해결을 위하여 모든 외교적 수단을 강구하였으나 이락측의 거부로 아무런 성과가 없었음.

- 1.10. BAKER-AZIZ 회담에서도 이락은 전혀 타협의 자세를 보이지 않은바,미국은 이락이 유엔 결의를 준수할 경우 이락을 공격하지 않을 것이며 이락의 주변국에 대한 위협이 감소될 경우 미국은 대규모 군사력을 동지역에 유지하지 않을 것이라고 제의한바 있음.

- 1.13. 유엔 사무총장의 최후의 노력도 이락은 거절하였음.

2. 경제 제재조치의 효과

- 지난 5 개월간 대이락 경제 제제조치는 거의 모든국가가 참여하여 잘 지켜졌으며 그결과로 이락 국민의 생활은 곤란을 겪고 있으나 이락의 전력을 대폭 감소시키지는 못하였음.

-이락은 전력유지를 위해 국민 생활을 희생시키고 있어 앞으로 6 개월 또는1 년 이상 경제조치를 지속시켰다고해도 군사적 보급에 큰 지장을 줄지는 확실치 않음.

3. 무력 사용 목적

- 미국은 유엔 결의안에 명시된것과 같이 이락의 쿠웨이트 점령을 종식시키기 위한것이며 결코 이락을 점령하기 위한것은 아님.

-미국은 이락이 전쟁 종료후 평화국이 되기를 희망하며 군사작전도 민간의 피해를 줄이기 위해 최대한 노력하고 있으며, 종교적, 문화적으로 중요한 지역은목표물에서

미주국 대책반	장관	차관	1차보	2차보	중아국	청와대	총리실	안기부

PAGE 1

91.01.19 08:56

외신 2과 통제관 FE

0080

제외하고 있음.

4. 이스라엘 공격 규탄

-이락의 이스라엘 공격은 무차별로 민간지역을 목표로하였으며 또하나의 침략행위임.

-이락의 대이스라엘 공격 행위는 쿠웨이트 점령 사실로 부터 세계의 관심을돌리려는 냉소적이고 절망적인 행위임.

- 미국은 이스라엘에 대하여 자제하도록 요청하고 있으나 이스라엘은 유엔헌장에 명시된바와같이 자위권을 보유하고 있음.

5. 앞으로의 전망

- 현재 진행중인 전쟁은 오래 지속되지 않을 것이며 이락이 철수하지 않을 경우 계속 참화를 감수해야할것임.

-(대 이락 무력행위를 잠정 중지하는 방안을 질문한데 대해)

무력 사용중지는 이락으로하여금 전력을 회복하는 시간을 제공함으로써 연합군의 피해만 증대시킬 것임으로 의미 없는 일임.

(대사 박동진-국장)

예고:91.6.30 까지

예고문에의거일반문서로 재분류19 91 6 30 서명

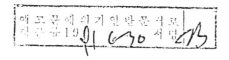

원 본

외 무 부

종 별 :

번 호 : USW-0303 일 시 : 91 0118 1810

수 신 : 장 관(미북,대책반,중근동,동구일)

발 신 : 주 미 대사

제 목 : 페만 작전 관련 부쉬 대통령 기자 회견

금 1.18 12:00 백악관에서 있었던 부쉬 대통령기자 회견시 모두 발언 요지를 하기 보고함.(기자 회견전문은 USW(F)-229 FAX 송부)

1.사막 폭풍 작전은 지금까지 만족스럽게 전개되어 왔음.미측으로서는 특히 다국적군 인명 손실과 민간이에 대한 피해를 최소화하기 위해 노력하고 있는바 단숨에(OVERNIGHT) 승리를 거둘것으로 기대할수 없음. 지나친 낙관론 (EUPHORIA) 은 금물임.

2.이락측의 대 이스라엘 공격 관련, 이스라엘측이 자제를 보이고 있는데 대해사의를 표함. 미-이스라엘간의 긴밀한 협의는 계속되고 있으며, 금일 아침 고르바쵸프 대통령과도 전화 통화를 통해 페만정세를 검토하는 한편 BALTIC 사태에 대한 우려를 전달한바 있음

(대사 박동진-국장)

미주국	장관	차관	1차보	2차보	구주국	중아국	정문국	청와대
총리실	안기부	대책반						

0082

PAGE 1

91.01.19 09:19 WG

외신 1과 통제관

To: 이기주 대변인님
(공보·아프리카 주장)

페르샤灣 戰爭(OP. Desert Storm)狀況

1.19 09:00 現在

1. 戰爭目標

ㅇ쿠웨이트內 이라크軍 逐出

※" 후세인의 降伏이 아니라 쿠웨이트에서 몰아내는 것"

- 聯合司 司令官 報告 -

※일부 『쿠웨이트 回復 및 이라크軍 武裝解除』 擧論中

2. 最初 作戰計劃

1段階 : 制空權 確保, 反擊能力制壓, 戰略目標 破壞(6-7日)

2段階 : 航空爆擊으로 地上軍 및 戰術目標 破壞(2-3日)

3段階 : 地上軍 作戰開始, 戰爭早期 終結(10日 內外)

- 聯合司 司令官 報告 -

3. 作戰概況

ㅇ戰況은 한세대 앞선 技術水準과 壓倒的 航空戰力을 보유한 多國籍軍의 一方的 優勢下에 展開中

ㅇ報道와는 달리 雙方의 被害는 比較的 制限될 可能性

※多國籍軍의 被害는 戰鬪機 10여대에 불과하고 이라크軍도 戰鬪機 및 防空基地 미사일 基地 및 化學戰施設 등이 決定的 打擊을 입었다고 報道되고 있으나 氣象(구름)과 裝備保護 施設로 인해 空軍機의 被害가 생각보다 적으며 SCUD 미사일도 總 66基(彈頭 700發)中 一部(12기)破壞에 不過

- 韓國時間 19일 05:00 美空軍司 브리핑 -

" 化學攻擊威脅은 弱化되었으나 制空權을 完全하게 確保했다고는 말할 수 없다" - 韓國時間 19日 06:30 美國防部 브리핑 -

0083

o 多國籍軍은 海.空軍 爲主 作戰을 遂行中이며 地上軍은 攻擊을 위해 展開中에 있으나 犧牲을 우려, 이라크軍이 충분히 괴멸된 후에 攻擊을 開始할 豫定이나 現在 일부 2段階 作戰이 早期에 竝行中이며 3段階 作戰도 앞당겨질 可能性

※" 地上軍은 적어도 精銳 共和國 守備隊(5-7個 師團)의 戰力이 50% 以下로 弱化된 후 攻擊開始 豫定" (聯合司 司令官 報告)

o 후세인은 이스라엘 參戰을 誘導하여 戰爭樣相의 變化를 試圖하면서 決死抗戰을 强調하고 있으나 投降 및 도망자가 發生하는 등 이라크軍의 士氣는 全般的으로 低下되고 있음

4. 展望

o 地上作戰이 바그다드 地域으로 擴戰될 可能性은 적으나 이라크軍의 主力이 集中된 쿠웨이트 全面의 防禦態勢가 强力할 경우 相對的으로 脆弱한 本土地域 直衝路를 選擇할 可能性도 있음

o 이스라엘 參戰(美國이 抑制中) 可能性, 이라크의 殘餘 化學戰能力, 親이라크 테러集團의 攻擊이 새로운 威脅으로 등장하고 있고,

o 이라크軍의 抗戰意志와 多國籍軍의 地上作戰 早期遂行意志가 變數이며

o 長期戰 可能性도 排除할 수는 없으나 現在로서는 軍事作戰이 最初 計劃(2-3週)보다 早期終結될 可能性

5. 其他 關聯事項

o 旣存計劃('92年까지 7,000名 撤收)外 駐韓美軍 戰力의 撤收 및 轉換可能性 없음

o 北韓은 警戒態勢의 强化外 特異動向 없음

o " 프랑스軍이 最初 空襲時 不參하고 多國籍軍中 相對的으로 被害 (12대중 4대 被擊)가 컸던 것은 프랑스의 재규어 戰鬪機가 舊形이고 夜間攻擊 能力이 未洽했기 때문" - 駐韓 프랑스 武官 報告 -

o 多國籍軍側은 參戰國數가 增加되고 있으며 프랑스, 이태리軍外 카나다軍이 防空作戰에 參與하고 싱가폴은 醫療支援團을 派遣

0084

SUBJECT: PERSIAN G[redacted] CRISIS -- AN UPDATED CH[redacted]LOGY

2. TEXT OF UPDATED CHRONOLOGY FOLLOWS:

JANUARY 3

-- PRESIDENT BUSH, MAKING "ONE LAST ATTEMPT TO GO THE EXTRA MILE FOR PEACE" IN THE GULF PROPOSES THAT SECRETARY BAKER MEET WITH IRAQI FOREIGN MINISTER AZIZ AT GENEVA DURING THE PERIOD JANUARY 7-9.

-- BAKER, IN A TELEVISION INTERVIEW, SAYS HE IS "NOT AS OPTIMISTIC" ABOUT PEACE AS HE WAS BEFORE CHRISTMAS AND NOW BELIEVES FORCE "IN ALL PROBABILITY" WILL BE REQUIRED TO OUST IRAQ FROM KUWAIT.

-- FOLLOWING A TRILATERAL MEETING AT ISLAMABAD, THE FOREIGN MINISTERS OF PAKISTAN, IRAN AND TURKEY ISSUE A STATEMENT CALLING FOR THE TOTAL WITHDRAWAL OF IRAQI FORCES FROM KUWAIT, RESTORATION OF KUWAIT'S INDEPENDENCE AND SOVEREIGNTY, AND FULL IMPLEMENTATION OF ALL RELEVANT UNSC RESOLUTIONS.

JANUARY 4

-- IRAQ'S RULING REVOLUTIONARY COMMAND COUNCIL ANNOUNCES THAT FOREIGN MINISTER AZIZ WILL MEET WITH SECRETARY BAKER JANUARY 9 AT GENEVA.

-- FOREIGN MINISTERS OF THE 12-NATION EUROPEAN COMMUNITY, MEETING IN LUXEMBOURG, ISSUE A PUBLIC STATEMENT: "(THE) MINISTERS REITERATE THEIR FIRM COMMITMENT IN FAVOR OF THE FULL AND UNCONDITIONAL IMPLEMENTATION OF THE RELEVANT RESOLUTIONS OF THE UN SECURITY COUNCIL ... THE ENTIRE RESPONSIBILITY FOR WAR OR PEACE RESTS WITH THE IRAQI GOVERNMENT ALONE..."

JANUARY 6

-- IN AN ARMY DAY ADDRESS, SADDAM HUSSEIN SAYS "KUWAIT IS THE 19TH PROVINCE OF IRAQ'S MAP AND IN IRAQ'S POLITICAL STRUCTURE, AT PRESENT AND IN THE FUTURE."

JANUARY 7

-- UPON HIS ARRIVAL IN LONDON ENROUTE TO GENEVA, SECRETARY BAKER SAYS, "SADDAM HUSSEIN HAS IT WITHIN HIS POWER TO DETERMINE WHETHER THERE IS PEACE OR WHETHER THERE IS NOT PEACE. THE CHOICE IS HIS. WE HOPE HE MAKES THE RIGHT CHOICE."

JANUARY 9

-- SECRETARY BAKER AND FOREIGN MINISTER AZIZ FAIL TO BREAK THE GULF STALEMATE IN MORE THAN SIX HOURS OF TALKS AT GENEVA. AFTERWARD, BAKER EXPRESSES DISAPPOINTMENT: "REGRETTABLY, I HEARD NOTHING THAT SUGGESTED TO ME ANY IRAQI FLEXIBILITY WHATSOEVER ... THE IRAQI LEADERSHIP MUST HAVE NO DOUBT THAT THE 28 NATIONS WHICH HAVE DEPLOYED FORCES TO THE GULF IN SUPPORT OF THE UNITED

0085

NATIONS HAVE BOTH THE POWER AND THE WILL TO EVICT IRAQ FROM KUWAIT."

-- FOLLOWING THE BAKER-AZIZ MEETING, PRESIDENT BUSH REACTS WITH PESSIMISM: "I AM DISCOURAGED," HE SAYS DESCRIBING THE IRAQI ATTITUDE AS "A TOTAL STIFF-ARM. THIS IS A TOTAL REBUFF," ADDING, "I HAVE NOT GIVEN UP ON A PEACEFUL OUTCOME. IT'S NOT TOO LATE."

-- IN A GENEVA NEWS CONFERENCE, AZIZ SAYS BAKER "WAS INTERESTED IN ONE QUESTION ONLY" -- IRAQI WITHDRAWAL FROM KUWAIT. AZIZ ALSO REFUSES TO ACCEPT A LETTER TO SADDAM FROM PRESIDENT BUSH AND THREATENS AN ATTACK AGAINST ISRAEL IN THE EVENT OF WAR.

-- UN SECRETARY GENERAL JAVIER PEREZ DE CUELLAR

ANNOUNCES THAT HE WILL TRAVEL TO BAGHDAD IN SEARCH OF PEACE: "NOW I FEEL IT IS MY MORAL DUTY AS SECRETARY GENERAL OF ... AN ORGANIZATION DEVOTED TO PEACE TO DO EVERYTHING POSSIBLE TO AVOID THE WORST."

JANUARY 12

-- THE U.S. CONGRESS VOTES TO GIVE PRESIDENT BUSH AUTHORITY TO USE MILITARY FORCE TO EXPEL IRAQ FROM KUWAIT. BUSH SAYS, "THIS CLEAR EXPRESSION OF THE CONGRESS REPRESENTS THE LAST, BEST CHANCE FOR PEACE."

-- THE WHITE HOUSE RELEASES THE TEXT OF THE JANUARY 5 LETTER THAT PRESIDENT BUSH WROTE TO SADDAM AND THAT AZIZ REFUSED TO ACCEPT FROM SECRETARY BAKER. AN EXCERPT FOLLOWS: "WE STAND TODAY AT THE BRINK OF WAR BETWEEN IRAQ AND THE WORLD ... A WAR THAT CAN BE AVOIDED ONLY BY IRAQ'S FULL AND UNCONDITIONAL COMPLIANCE WITH UN SECURITY COUNCIL RESOLUTION 678 ... (THE RESOLUTION) ESTABLISHES A 'PAUSE OF GOOD WILL' SO THAT THIS CRISIS MAY END WITHOUT FURTHER VIOLENCE. WHETHER THIS PAUSE IS USED AS INTENDED, OR MERELY AS A PRELUDE TO FURTHER VIOLENCE IS IN YOUR HANDS AND YOURS ALONE."

-- UN SECRETARY GENERAL PEREZ DE CUELLAR ARRIVES IN BAGHDAD FOR TALKS WITH SADDAM AND AZIZ.

-- FIVE AMERICAN DIPLOMATS, INCLUDING CHARGE JOSEPH WILSON IV, DEPART THE U.S. EMBASSY IN BAGHDAD.

-- THE STATE DEPARTMENT ORDERS THE EXPULSION OF ALL BUT FOUR OF THE DIPLOMATS ASSIGNED TO THE IRAQI EMBASSY IN WASHINGTON "TO REDUCE IRAQ'S ABILITY TO ORCHESTRATE TERRORISM."

JANUARY 13

-- PEREZ DE CUELLAR DEPARTS BAGHDAD, SAYING "ONLY GOD KNOWS" IF THERE WILL BE WAR IN THE MIDDLE EAST.

-- SADDAM, REJECTING A PLEA TO LEAVE KUWAIT FROM SYRIAN LEADER HAFEZ ASSAD, DECLARES: "OUR 19TH PROVINCE (KUWAIT) HAS BECOME A BATTLEFIELD FOR THE SHOWDOWN IN WHICH (THE ARAB PEOPLE) WILL BE TRIUMPHANT." HE URGES

0086

-- SPEAKER OF THE HO[redacted] THOMAS FOLEY (D. - WASHI[redacted]N), WHO OPPOSED THE CONGR[redacted]ONAL USE OF FORCE RESOLU[redacted]N SAYS THE NATION FACES A "VERY REAL PROSPECT" OF WAR AND VOWS THAT CONGRESS WILL PROVIDE ALL NECESSARY FINANCIAL AND POLITICAL BACKING TO PRESIDENT BUSH AND THE ARMED FORCES.

JANUARY 14

-- PEREZ DE CUELLAR RETURNS TO NEW YORK SAYING IT'S A "LITTLE BIT LATE" FOR PEACE INITIATIVES AND ADDING, "I HAVE NOT BEEN OFFERED ANYTHING FROM THE IRAQI AUTHORITIES WHICH I CAN CONSIDER A STEP TOWARD PEACE."

-- WHITE HOUSE PRESS SECRETARY MARLIN FITZWATER SAYS MILITARY ACTION "COULD OCCUR AT ANY POINT" AFTER THE UN DEADLINE (12:00 MIDNIGHT EST TUESDAY, JANUARY 15) AND COMMENTS, "ANY MOMENT AFTER THE 15TH IS BORROWED TIME."

-- IRAQ'S RUBBER-STAMP NATIONAL ASSEMBLY GIVES SADDAM A FREE HAND TO CONDUCT A "HOLY WAR" AGAINST "THE FORCES OF AGGRESSION LED BY THE UNITED STATES."

JANUARY 15

-- UNITED NATIONS DEADLINE FOR IRAQI WITHDRAWAL FROM KUWAIT.

-- A LAST-MINUTE FRENCH PEACE INITIATIVE FAILS WHEN IRAQ DECLINES TO RESPOND AND THE U.S. AND OTHER SECURITY COUNCIL MEMBERS EXPRESS SERIOUS RESERVATIONS. THE PROPOSAL IMPLIED LINKAGE OF THE SOLUTION TO THE GULF CRISIS WITH THE ARAB-ISRAELI DISPUTE.

-- PEREZ DE CUELLAR MAKES A FINAL, PERSONAL APPEAL FOR PEACE TO SADDAM HUSSEIN, NOTING THAT "THE WORLD STANDS POISED BETWEEN PEACE AND WAR" AND URGING SADDAM "TO TURN THE COURSE OF EVENTS AWAY FROM CATASTROPHE AND TOWARD A NEW ERA OF JUSTICE AND HARMONY BASED ON THE PRINCIPLES OF THE UNITED NATIONS CHARTER."

JANUARY 16

-- U.S. AND COALITION FORCES LAUNCH OPERATION "DESERT STORM," BOMBING MILITARY TARGETS IN IRAQ AND KUWAIT. BUSH SAYS, "THE UNITED STATES TOGETHER WITH THE UNITED NATIONS, EXHAUSTED EVERY MEANS AT OUR DISPOSAL TO BRING THIS CRISIS TO A PEACEFUL END . . SADDAM HUSSEIN MET EVERY OVERTURE OF PEACE WITH OPEN CONTEMPT."

JANUARY 17

-- IN AN INFORMAL EARLY MORNING MEETING OF THE UN SECURITY COUNCIL, THE U.S., UK AND FRANCE BRIEF COUNCIL MEMBERS ON MILITARY ACTIONS TAKEN PURSUANT TO UNSC RESOLUTION 678. SECRETARY GENERAL PEREZ DE CUELLAR SAYS HE IS "SADDENED" BUT STATED FIRMLY THAT THE ACTIONS WERE TAKEN WITHIN THE FRAMEWORK OF RESOLUTION 678. BAKER 0087
BT

원 본

외 무 부

종 별 : 지 급

번 호 : USW-0312 일 시 : 91 0119 0716

수 신 : 장관(미북,중근동,대책반)

발 신 : 주 미대사

제 목 : 걸프전 관련 상황 종합 보고

당지 시간 1.19 05:00 현재 걸프전 관련 상황을 하기 종합 보고함.

1.언론 보도에 따르면, 이락군 통신 시설및 SCUD 미사일 기지등을 주 목표로 하는 다국적군 공군의 집중 공습이 현재 24시간 내내 쉬지 않고 계속되고 있다함.

(바그다드 시내의 전기, 수도, 전화 시설등도 많은 피해를 입었다 함)

2.또한 이스라엘 시간으로 1.19 오전 이락측이 수기의 SCUD 미사일 (재래식 탄두 장착)을 텔아비브 내주거 지역등에 대해 발사 하였으나 약 10 명의 부상자만 발생한것으로 알려짐.

(구체적 피격 지점등에 대해서 는 이스라엘측이 보도 통제)

.이스라엘측은 이와 관련 대 이락 보복 의사를 공식 천명 하였으나, 보복의 시기와 방법등에 대해서는 구체적 언급을 회피한 것으로 알려짐.

3.한편, 쿠웨이트 접경 지역의 이락군 야포 진지에 대해 미군의 공격용 헬리콥터등에 의한 공격이 있었으며 이로 인해 이락군 40 여명이 사망한 것으로 알려지고있으나, 구체 사항은 상금 확인되지 않고있음.

4.이락측은 바그다드 주재 외국 언론 특파원(총 38명)에 대해 3-5 일내에 출국할것을 명령하였다 하며, 주 다란 미국 총영사관은 다란 공항에 취항하던 민간 여객노선의 운영이 중단된점등을 감안, 다란 일원에 거주하는 미국인 취업자 등이 자발적ㅋ출국(VOLUNTARY DEPARTURE) 을 원하는 경우 미군용 수송기편을 제공할 것이라고 발표하였다 함.

(대사 박동진-국장)

미주국 대책반	장관	차관	1차보	중아국	정문국	청와대	총리실	안기부

2차보 상황실

PAGE 1 91.01.19 22:06 DA

외신 1과 통제관

0088

원 본

외 무 부

종 별 :

번 호 : USW-0313 일 시 : 91 0119 0950

수 신 : 장관(미북,미안,중근동,대책반)

발 신 : 주 미대사

제 목 : 부쉬 대통령 동정

주재국 부쉬 대통령은 킹목사 탄신일 (1.21) 을 포함 (,주말 연휴 기간을 CAMPDDAVID 별장에서 보낼 예정이며 1.21(화) 저녁경 워싱톤으로 귀경 할것 이라함.

(대사 박동진- 국장)

미주국 장관 차관 1차보 2차보 미주국 중아국 정문국 청와대
총리실 안기부 대책반

상황실

PAGE 1

91.01.19 23:57 DA

외신 1과 통제관

0089

관리 번호	91/254

외 무 부

종 별 : 지 급

번 호 : USW-0314 일 시 : 91 0119 0950

수 신 : 장관(미북,중근동,미안, 대책반)

발 신 : 주 미 대사

제 목 : 걸프전 전망

1. 당지 언론 보도 및 당관이 접촉한 각계 군사문제 전문가의 견해에 따르면, 현재 진행중인 집중 공습 위주의 대 이락 공격 방식은 2 월 까지도 계속될 가능성이 크며, 특히 이락측이 대이스라엘 공격시 사용한 SCUD 미사일 기지를 완전 분쇄키 위해서라도 여사한 공군력 위주의 대이락 공격이 상당기간 지속될것이라 함(현재 이락측이 사용가능한 SCUD 미사일의 정확한 숫자는 알려지지 않고 있으나 수십기(약 30) 에 이를것으로 추측된다함)

2. 한편 , 주재국 주요 방송 매체들은 걸프전 개전 이래 긴급 방송 체제를 갖추고 전황을 시시각각으로 보도하는등 비상태세를 유지해 왔으나, 작 1.18. 오후부터는 정규 편성 프로그램 내용을 방송하고 광고 방송도 재개하고 있으며, 군사작전의 단편적 보도 보다는 걸프전의 향후 전개 양상 및 전망을 위한 문제들을 중심으로 보도 초점을 바꾸고 있음.

(대사 박동진- 국장)

19 예고:91.6.30.까지 에 의거 일반문서로 재 분류됨.

검토필(1991. 6. 30.)

미주국	장관	차관	1차보	2차보	미주국	중아국	정문국	청와대
안기부								

PAGE 1

91.01.20 00:40

외신 2과 통제관 CW

0090

관리 번호 91-1928

원 본

외 무 부

종 별 : 긴 급

번 호 : USW-0317 일 시 : 90 119 1858

수 신 : 장관(반기문 미주국장)

발 신 : 주 미 대사(유명환 참사관)

제 목 : 걸프전

대호, 걸프전의 배경 및 상금까지의 전황 과 전망 에 대한 당관 관찰을 다음 보고함.

(1)미국의 목표

- 8.2. 이락의 쿠웨이트 침공이래, 동 사태와 관련 미국이 공개적으로 천명해온 4 대 목표는 그간 기보고한바 와 같음.

-동 4 대 목표외에 BUSH 대통령, BAKER 장관등 미 고위층의 발언 및 의회 토론등을 통해 이해되고 있는 미국의 정치, 전략적 목표에는 다음 요소들이 포함됨.

가. POST- COLD WAR 시대에 있어 새로운 세계 질서 확립(미국의 계속적인 지도적 역할 확보, 지역분쟁의 방지 및 지역세력간 헤게모니 쟁탈전 특히 약육강식적 침략 억제)나. 세계 원유 시장과 공급의 안정화

다. 중근동 지역의 미국의 핵심우방에 대한 안전보장(사우디, 이스라엘, 터키등)

라. 지역 균형 및 안정 체제 구축

-금번 대이락 군사작전의 목표는 일단, 쿠웨이트의 해방(이락군의 추방)으로 표방되고 있으며, 미국의 군사작전은 이락의 파괴나 점령이 아니라는점이 수차 공개적으로 천명되고 있음. (이락내로의 지상전 확대의 경우 올수 있는 장기전에 대한 미국민의 거부감, 이락에 대한 지나친 보복시 정치적 부작용, 아랍측 연합군 일부의 군사목표 확대 반대등의 요인을 감안할때, 금번 작전은 쿠웨이트의 해방과 쿠웨이트 구정부의 회복에 국한될 것으로 전망)

(2)걸프전의 배경

-금번 전쟁의 배경에 대한 다각도의 분석은 그간 보고한 미국의 각계 시각을 참고 바람.

다만, 현재 미국 조야에는 금번 전쟁이 HUSSEIN 의 잔인한(RUTHLESS) 사고방식과

미주국

PAGE 1

91.01.20 11:35

외신 2과 통제관 BA

0091

오판으로 인하여 어차피 불가피하지 않았느냐는 공감이 형성되어 있었음.

-HUSSEIN 의 쿠웨이트 점령, 합병의 동기는 쿠웨이트 원유등 자산획득, 항만 확보, 중동에서의 패권장악, 개인적 야심의 충족등을 들수 있으나 , 유엔 안보리 결의를 이행치 않고 미국과의 일전을 선택한 데에는 배타심과 자존심이 강한 아랍 문화의 특성을 감안할때 미국에 대한 굴복으로 정치지도자로서의 지위 또는 권력을 상실하기 보다는"제국주의 초강국" 과의 대항을 통해 오히려 정치적이득을 취할수 있다는 무리한 계산도 작용한 것으로 보임.

-미국측으로서의 대이락 공격은 쿠웨이트의 해방 이라는 목표 실현을 위해 불가피하기 때문에 취해진 것이나, 미국으로서도 국내 정치적 부담 및 경제, 외교적 제약으로 인해 반드시 군사작전을 선호했던것은 아닌것으로 관찰됨 (NATO 동맹국 및 유럽제국 외에 소련등 과거 적대국과 아랍권을 총망라, 국제적 연합 세력 형성과 유엔 안보리 결의를 통한 압력에 우선 주력)

(3) 전황

-종합 전황은 기 수시 보고한 내용 참조

(4) 전망

가. 군사 작전상 전망

-당지의 일반적 평가는 D-DAY 의 공습이 이예상외의 큰 성과를 올렸으며, D3 까지 공습(AIR-POWER) 을 통한 작전은 상당히 성공적인 것으로써, 일단 장기화의 가능성은 크게 줄어들고 있다고 보고 있음.

-그러나 이락이 대이스라엘 미사일 공격을 통한 이스라엘의 참전과 아랍 연합 와해 기도 , 사우디 유전지대에 대한 공격, 주요 국제도시에서의 테러 자행등의 제반 OPTION 외에도 쿠웨이트 에서의 농성 또는 지상군의 선제 공격등의 전술을 구사할 가능성등을 감안할때, 전쟁이 양상이 여하히 전개될것인지는 속단하기어려움(이락군이 필사적인 선제공세로 나올 경우 급격한 확전이 될 가능성도 있음)

-다만, 미국은 성공적인 외교(이스라엘 에 대한 계속적 자제 당부, 소련을 통한 대이랍 멧세지 전명) 및 계속적인 이락의 스쿠드 미사일 파괴, PATRIOT 미사일 방공망 및 운용 UNIT 제공등 이스라엘에 대한 군사적 지원을 통해, 상금 이스라엘의 보복과 이에 따른 대중동전의 혼란을 방지하고 있음(1.19. 상호 BUSH 대통령은 SHAMIR 수상에게 전화, 협조를 요청한바 있으며, 이스라엘 각의는 대이락 보복을 자제하기로 하였다고 보도됨)

PAGE 2

0092

-또한 사우디 유전에 대한 이락측의 공격능력도 현재로서는 회의적으로 평가되는바, 1.18. 유가의 하락은 여사한 군사 전망을 반영하고 있음.

-따라서 D4 이후에는 여하히 쿠웨이트 주둔 이락군을 몰아내느냐는데 군사작전의 초점이 주어질것으로 보이는바, 연호 보고와 같이 최소한 D7 까지는 물론경우에 따라서는 2 월 중에도 공습이 계속되어야 한다는 것이 당지 군사 전문가들의 일반적 관찰임.

-당지 일부 전문가들은 미국이 피아간 대규모 사상자를 내게될 전면 지상공격에 돌입하기 보다는 이락-쿠에이트간 보급로에 대한 공습, 북부 쿠에이트에 대한 상륙등 경제적 작전을 통해 쿠웨이트 주둔군을 고립, 자멸을 유도 하는것이 바람직하다는 견해를 표시하고 있음.여사한 제안은 미국측으로서 바람직한 대안이긴 하나, 지상작전은 이락군의 움직임, 의도, 능력을 감안, 전쟁 종결수단으로 최후에 전개될 전망임.

나. 전략, 외교적 전망

-그간 미국내에는 금번 사태의 종결과 관련, 다음과 같은 전략적 고려가 있어야 한다는 의견이 대두되어 왔음.

(1) 이락의 공격 능력 파괴 또는 제약, 특히 핵, 생.화학 , 미사일 능력 박탈

(2) 지역 안정을 위한 안보 체제 형성(일정수준 미군사력의 "PRESENCE")

(3) 전후 지역 세력 균형 유지를 위해 이락군의 완전 파괴 자제

(이락의 대 시리아, 대 이란 견제 역할 보존)

(4) 이스라엘의 요르단 서안 점령 문제 해결등 포괄적 중동 평화 방안 대처

-상금 , 당관 실무 접촉을 통해 , 미측의 검토 방향을 탐문한바, 미측 관계관들은 군사적 양상의 전개에 대한 판단이 어려운 시점에서 종전후 외교전략의 추진 방향이 본격 검토되고 있지 못하고 있다는 반응을 보이고 있음.

그러나 미국으로서는 제반 상황을 감안할때, 다음 방향으로 종전후 지역 정책을 추진할것으로 예상됨.

(1) 이락의 공격적 군사력(핵, 생화학 무기등 포함)의 재획득을 방지 하기위한 제한적 경제 제재 조치 계속 추진

(공격무기 확산금지를 위한 국제적 협력 방안 검토 포함)

(2) 이락 정권의 성격 변화 유도

(3)현재의 COALITION 을 바탕으로 한 지역 안보 체제 유도

PAGE 3

0093

(4)중동 평화를 위한 아랍 및 소련측 제안에 대한 전향적 대응 및 소련의 건설적 역할 환영(쿠웨이트 정권 회복후, 적당한 시점에서 중동국제회의 및 이스라엘 PLO 간 직접 협상 유도)

(5) 온건 아랍 정권 유지의 기반 강화를 위한 아랍내 점진적 민주화 가능성모색

다. 기타

-전쟁의 성공적 수행을 위해서는 BUSH 대통령의 정책에 대한 국내, 국제적 지지가 긴요 하다는것이 미국 조야, 여야 를 막론한 공통된 인식 이므로 BUSH 행정부는 이러한 지지의 계속적 확보를 위해 국내외적으로 보다 적극적인 자세를 취할것임.

-따라서 전쟁이 초기의 긴장상태를 벗어나서, 예측 가능한 패턴으로 전개되어 나가는 시점에서 , 미 행정부는 미 의회등 국내의 지지확보를 위해 각국의 기여가 확대 되어야 한다는 견지에서, 독일, 일본, 아국등에 대해 추가 기여를 구체적으로 요청해올것으로 예상됨.

91.12.31. 일반

일반문서로 재분류(1991.12.31.)

검 토 필(1991.6.30.)

PAGE 4

0094

관리 번호	91-103

원 본

외 무 부

종 별 :

번 호 : USW-0318 일 시 : 91 0119 1903

수 신 : 장관(미북, 중근동,대책반,기정)

발 신 : 주 미 대사

제 목 : 걸프전 진행동향(BUSH대통령 동정)

1. 금 1.19. BUSH 대통령은 CAMP DAVID 에서 SHAMIR 이스라엘 수상과 통화를 통해 이락에 대한 이스라엘 공격 자제를 평가하고 , 이스라엘 에 대한 최신예PATRIOT 방공망과 운용 UNIT 파견 제공을 통보한 것으로 알려짐

2. 금번 미국의 대 이스라엘 지원(특히 병력 파견) 결정은 그간 미군의 직접 지원을 받은바 없는 이스라엘 방위 역사상 새로운 선례를 남긴다는 데서 아랍제국의 비상한 관심을 끌고 있는것으로 보이나, 미국으로서는 현재 이스라엘의대이락 공격 방지에 최우선 순위를 두고 있기 때문에 불가피하게 취한 조치로 판단됨.

3. 금일 BUSH 대통령은 부통령, 국무장관, 국방장관, 합참의장, 비서실장, 안보 보좌관, 부보좌관 과 함께 연두 교서와 미국의 에너지 정책에 관해 논의하였음.

4. BUSH 대통령은 명일 FOLEY 하원의장 내외를 CAMP DAVID 로 초치 걸프전 현황 등에 관해 협의할 예정임.

(대사 박동진- 국장)

91.12.31. 까지

일반문서로 재분류(1991.12.31.)

검 토 필(1991.6.30.)

미주국 장관 차관 1차보 2차보 중아국 청와대 안기부

PAGE 1

91.01.20 10:36

외신 2과 통제관 FE

0095

원 본

외 무 부

종 별 :

번 호 : USW-0319 일 시 : 91 0119 2323

수 신 : 장 관(미북,중근동,미안,대책반 ,기정)

발 신 : 주 미 대사

제 목 : 전쟁포로 대우

미 국무부는 금 1.19. 오후 주미 이라크 대사관 관계관을 초치, 금번 걸프 전쟁에서 발생한 포로에 대한 대우와 관련 '' 1949 전쟁포로에 관한 제네바 협약'' 서명당사국으로서 동 협약을 준수할것을 환기하는 내용의 외교 공한을 수교한 것으로 알려짐.

(대사 박동진- 국장)

미주국 장관 차관 1차보 2차보 미주국 중아국 정문국 청와대
총리실 안기부

PAGE 1

91.01.20 13:31 WG
외신 1과 통제관
0096

원 본

외 무 부

종 별 :

번 호 : USW-0320 일 시 : 91 0119 2324

수 신 : 장 관(미북,중근동, 대책반,기정)

발 신 : 주 미 대사

제 목 : 걸프 전쟁(미국 여론 조사)

금 1.19. 미국 각지에서 반전 데모가 발생한 가운데 금일 당지 CNN 방송이 실시한 여론조사 결과에 따르면 대부분의 미국인이 부쉬 대통령의 공격개시 결정을 지지하는 것으로 밝혀 졌는바, 동 여론 조사 주요 내용 아래 보고함.

1.부쉬 대통령의 전쟁 결정

찬성 82 퍼센트

반대 14 퍼센트

2.미국 정부의 페만 사태 처리 방법

찬성 86 퍼센트

반대 9 퍼센트

3.걸프 전쟁의 최종 승리자

연합국측 73 퍼센트

승자도 패자도 없을 것임 20 퍼센트

(대사 박동진- 국장)

미주국 장관 차관 1차보 2차보 중아국 정문국 청와대 총리실 안기부

PAGE 1 91.01.20 13:32 WG

외신 1과 통제관

0097

원 본

외 무 부

종 별 : 지 급

번 호 : USW-0321 일 시 : 91 0120 1200

수 신 : 장관(미북,중근동,대책반)

발 신 : 주미대사

제 목 : 걸프 전쟁(SCHWARZKOPF 회견)

SCHWARZKOPF 사령관은 금 1.20 10:30 NBC TV,11:30 CBS 와 회견을 가진바,주요 내용을 하기보고함.

1.전황

.(SCUD 미사일) 30기의 정착식 발사대는 거의 파괴된것을 추정되며, 20기 이상의 NIBUKE 발사대중 16 대가 파괴된것으로 추정됨.

.(핵시설) 3기의 핵 발전소가 모두 파괴됨.

.(지휘,통제) 지휘,통제 체제에도 상당한 타격이 가해진것으로 봄.

.(방공망및 공군력) 유효한 저항을 하지 못하고 있으며, 앞으로도 이러한 상황이변하지 않을것으로 봄.

. 23 명의 이락군 포로를 생포하고, 전선 전체에 걸쳐 소규모의 투항이 시작되고있음.

2. 전망

.(지상군 투입 필요성 여부) 현재로서는 전망이 불투명함.

.(프랑스 SCHMIDT 장군이 이번 전쟁이 2-3개월 더 계속될것이라고 말한데 대해서) 현재로서는 예측하기에 너무 이름.

.(이락의 화학무기 사용 가능성에 대하여) 여태까지는 사용이 없었으나 앞으로사용할 가능성도 있다고 봄.

(대사-국장)

미주국	장관	차관	1차보	2차보	중아국	정문국	청와대	총리실
안기부	대책반							

0098

PAGE 1 91.01.21 04:00 DQ

외신 1과 통제관

외 무 부

종 별 :

번 호 : USW-0325 일 시 : 91 0121 1204

수 신 : 장관(미북)

발 신 : 주미대사

제 목 : 걸프전에 대한 미국 조야 견해

1. 1.20-21 간 미 언론 및 매체를 통해 제기되고 있는 걸프전에 관한 견해와 관련,점차 전쟁의 수행 방법으로 부터 전쟁의 종결 및 전후 처리방안에 대한 제안이 대두되고 있음.

2. 이와관련, NYT 의 THOMAS FRIEDMAN 은1.20 분석기사를 통해 미국이 추구하는 승리의 MALK표를 분석하는 가운데 향후 ①미국이 추진코자하는 지역안정의 방안,②미 지상군을 아랍 연합군 또는 유엔군으로 교체,③다자지역 안보체 구상 또는 다양한 양자 안보관계 구성)을 제시하고,④미국경제 회복(연방채무부담 감소등)에 필요한 유가의 유지 노력,⑤향후 신질서 수립에 필요한 아랍반국의 경제개발 방안의 추진과 아랍부국 및 섭아국의 적극 참여가 필요하다는 점을 소개하고있음.

동인은 미국이 비록 신질서의 수립과 고통의 해소를 주창하고 있으나 많은 과거의 유산이 그대로남아 있을 가능성을 문제점으로 지적하고 있음.

3. 한편, HIGH-TECH 무기의 효용이 미국 행정부,의회 및 일반국민에게 강한 인상을 주고 있는가운데 TV 대담프로들은 의회의 진보파들이 향후 미국 무기체계의공급과 관련, 여하히 국방예산 편성 논의에 대처할것인지 문제와,그간 PEACE-DIVIDEND 의 확대와 관련한 논의가 변질될것인지 여부에 관한 문제를 조심스럽게 제기하고있음.

4. 금 1.21. W.P. ROWLAND EVANS 와 ROBERT NOVAK 칼럼은 미국 행정부가 그간전쟁수행 전략 추진에만 몰두, 전후문제 처리에는 별다른 VISION 을 갖고 있지 않았다고 지적하고,최근에야 ROBERT GATES NSC 부보좌관을 중심으로 전후 전략이 수립되고 있다고 하면서, 중동에서의 반미 감정의 확산 방지가 가장 중요한 선결 문제라는 견해를 표시하였음.

5. NYT 지 JAMES RESTON 은 금일 미국이 지상전을 피할 방안이 있다고 하면서 (보급로 차단등),대규모 지상전 돌입에 반대하는 주장을 기고 하였음.

(대사 박동진 - 국장)

미주국	장관	차관	1차보	2차보	중아국	정문국	상황실	청와대
총리실	안기부							

PAGE 1 91.01.22 02:38 DP

외신 1과 통제관

0099

74

원 본

외 무 부

종 별 :

번 호 : USW-0326 일 시 : 91 0121 1501

수 신 : 장관(미북,중근동,대책반)

발 신 : 주미대사

제 목 : 걸프 전쟁 관련 기자 회견

걸프 전쟁 관련 부쉬 대통령, 이글버거 국무부 장관 , BURTON MOORE 걸프전쟁작 전담당 소장이 금1.21 (월) 기자 회견을 실시 하였는바, 요지를 하기보고하며 전문은 팩스 송부함.

1.부쉬 대통령

가.계기:폴리 하원 의장과 캠프 데이비드 에서 돌아와 백악관 잔듸에서

나.주요 내용

0 사담 후세이의 미국인 전쟁포로에 대한 가혹행위는 미국은 물론 세계를 분노케하고 있음.

0 전쟁 포로에 대한 가혹행위로 세계의 지지를얻을수 있을것이라고 생각한다면 이는 완전한 오판이며 미국의 전쟁 수행에도 영향을 미치지 않을 것인바, 전재포로에대하여 국제법에 따른 정당대우를 하여 주도록 경고함.

2.이글버거 부장관

가.계기: 미국의 PATRIOT 요격 미사일의 이스라엘배치 점검차 텔아비브를 방문하여

나.주요 내용

0이스라엘이 이락의 SCUD 미사일 공격에 대한 반격을 자제하고 있는 것을 평가함. 그러나 반격자제의 대가로 미국이 이스라엘에 PATRIOT 미사일을 제공하는것은아니며 어느나라든 자위권을 가지고있음을 인정함.

3. MOORE 소장

가.계기: 사우디 리야드의 미 총사령부 일일 정세브리핑시

나.주요 내용

0 연합군의 이락.쿠웨이트내 목표에 대한 공습이 계속되고 있는바, 지금까지 이락군 비행기 17기를 격추하였으며, 아측의 피해는 미국기 9기, 기타 연합국측

미주국	장관 ✓	차관	1차보	2차보	중아국 ✓	정문국	상황실 ✓	청와대
총리실	안기부							

PAGE 1 91.01.22 05:27 DN

외신 1과 통제관

0100

비행기 5 기의 총 14기임

첨부: USW(F)-250

(대사 박동진- 국장)

PAGE 2

0101

번호 : USW(F) - 02

수신 : 장 관 (미북, 중근동, 대리청사) 발신 : 주미대사

제목 : 걸프 전쟁 관련 기자회견 (부시 대통령) (12 매) USW-0326 첨부물

REMARKS OF PRESIDENT BUSH AND HOUSE SPEAKER TOM FOLEY UPON RETURNING FROM CAMP DAVID/ THE WHITE HOUSE LAWN/ MONDAY, JANUARY 21, 1991

PRESIDENT BUSH: Let me just say a quick word about the brutal parading of these allied pilots. I was talking to Speaker Foley about this coming down, and it is very clear that this is a direct violation of the -- every convention that protects prisoners. The International Red Cross, I understand, certified to that today.

In the first place, this is not going to make a difference in the prosecution of the war against Saddam. It's not going to make a difference. I've said that before. I said that when he brutally held hostages that numbered up into the thousands, and it's not going to make a difference. But I would make the strongest appeal that these people be treated properly, that they be given the treatment that is accorded to them under the international conventions, and they are not being. And America is angry about this, and I think the rest of the world is, because this morning I talked to more of our coalition partners.

And so it is backfiring. If he thought this brutal treatment of pilots is a way to muster world support, he is dead wrong. And I think everybody is upset about it.

Speaker, I won't put words in your mouth, but...

SPEAKER FOLEY: Well, I concur absolutely, what the President said, it's a clear violation of the Geneva provisions for the protection of prisoners of war, and it will have very, very strong repercussions not only throughout the United States, but throughout the world if these violations continue.

Q Mr. President!

Q Mr. President!

PRESIDENT BUSH: No, I can't do a press conference. I do want to say something though about the Baltic states.

I am increasingly concerned -- we had a statement on that yesterday. I would again appeal to the Soviet Union leaders to resist using force. And we've heard the European countries speaking out on this now, and the world is very much concerned about that, as well.

So thank you all very much.

Q Mr. President!

Q Will he be held accountable, Mr. President? Will he be held accountable?

PRESIDENT BUSH: You can count on it.

END

250-1

0102

번호 : USW(F) -

수신 : 장 관　　　　발신 : 주미대사

[redacted]안 통제	68

제목 : 걸프전쟁 관련 기자회견 (이글버거 부장관) (1 매)

LAURENCE EAGLEBURGER, DEPUTY SECRETARY OF STATE/ EXCERPT OF NEWS CONFERENCE IN TEL AVIV_AS BROADCAST ON CNN MONDAY, JANUARY 21, 1991

RICHARD ROTH (CNN NEWS): Now taking a look this afternoon at the Patriot missiles here in Israeli is Deputy Secretary of State Laurence Eagleburger. He termed the damage done by the Iraqi Scud attacks earlier in the week as "awful," but he did hear some cheers from residents who said American ws doing a good thing in fighting Iraq.

Later, Eagleburger held a news conference. He said he admired Israel's restraint in not responding militarily to the Iraqi missile attack. And then with a healthy dose of sarcasm, Eagleburger responded to reports he was here in Israel to seal a deal -- Patriot missiles for a "no retaliation" policy.

MR. EAGLEBURGER: (Audio begins in progress) -- are not here to do. We are not here, if I may quote, "to be on hand to prevent unilateral action should Iraq attack again," unquote. I was not aware that I had been made a member of the Israeli cabinet. That is a decision for the Israeli government to make.

We are not -- and again, I quote -- "to see to it that under almost any circumstances there will be no Israeli reaction," unquote. I have explained in the statement, and I will not go beyond it, that we recognize the sovereign right of any government to defend itself.

I have also said that we in the United States admire the fact that the government of Israel so far has shown restraint.

END

240-2

0103

번호 : USW(F) -

수신 : 장 관

발신 : 주미대사

제목 : 걸프전쟁 관련 기자회견 (Moore 소장)

(10 매)

DEFENSE DEPARTMENT CENTCOM BRIEFING/ BRIEFER: MAJOR GENERAL BURTON MOORE, DIRECTOR OF OPERATIONS, US CENTRAL COMMAND
10:00 A.M., EST/ RIYADH, SAUDI ARABIA/ MONDAY, JANUARY 21, 1991

STAFF: Welcome, ladies and gentlemen, to the United States Central Command's daily news briefing. Today we will hear from Major General Burton R. Moore, Director of Operations for United States Central Command. General Moore will give us an update on events in Operation Desert Storm. Following his presentation we will have a question and answer session.

Ladies and gentlemen, General Moore.

GEN. MOORE: Thank you. Good afternoon, ladies and gentlemen. We are now well into the fifth day of Operation Desert Storm. Air operations by US Air Force, US Navy, US Marine Corps, as well as allied air forces, continue to concentrate on targets in Iraq and Kuwait. We have now flown more than 8,100 sorties in support of our campaign objectives. We have focused on key elements of Iraq's war-fighting capability.

In the past 24 hours, we downed two more Iraqi aircraft, bringing the total to 17. We lost one US aircraft to hostile fire in the past 24 hours -- a US Navy F-14 Tomcat. Since Desert Storm began, we have lost nine US and five allied aircraft to hostile ground fire. An Army Apache AH-64 and a UK Tornado were also lost in the last 24 hours due to non-combat related accidents.

Our ground forces of the US Army, Marine Corps, and allies continue to defend in Saudi Arabia. While there has still been no direct hostile contact between our forces and those of Iraq, we have received some sporadic Iraqi artillery fire.

US naval forces continue to conduct operations in the Arabia Gulf, the Gulf of Oman and the Red Sea. Maritime intercept operations continue with almost 7,000 intercepts to date.

As you are all well aware, last night Patriot batteries in Riyadh and Dhahran engaged Iraqi SCUD missiles aimed at Saudi Arabia. Our reports indicate that the batteries in Dhahran successfully engaged two SCUD missiles in that area while a third SCUD impacted in waters off the coast of Saudi Arabi. In Riyadh, our reports indicate the six SCUD missiles were fired. Our Patriot battery successfully engaged all six.

During the engagements at Riyadh there was some collateral damage to a building near Riyadh air base.

However, we have no reports beyond that although preliminary reports

270 -3

0104

DEFENSE DEPARTMENT [redacted] BRIEFING/ BRIEFER: MA___ENERAL BURTON
MOORE, DIRECTOR OF OPERATIONS, US CENTRAL COMMAND
10:00 A.M., EST/ RIYADH, SAUDI ARABIA/ MONDAY, JANUARY 21, 1991
DC-1-1 page 2

suggest that it was debris from an intercepted SCUD or possibly a Patriot missile had malfunctioned, and we'll get more to you on that as it becomes available. We have no reports of casualties. We are working with Saudi officials and they will provide you additional information as it becomes available.

In summary, we are continuing to execute our campaign plan in accordance with our overall campaign objectives. That completes my remarks and I'll try to take your questions.

Q Is the total now 12 SCUDs fired last night, then? It was 10 with four in Riyadh.

GEN. MOORE: The reports that we have is that there were a total of 10 SCUDs fired last night -- excuse me, total, six in Riyadh, two in Dhahran, one off the coast and then one several days ago.

Q General, you may have seen, as some of us, pictures of American pilots captured by the Iraqis, held as prisoners of war. I wonder whether you would care to comment, as an Air Force General, on that event? And secondly, to give us some sense of how you feel that treatment is affecting your operations and the emotions of your own pilots?

GEN. MOORE: I did not see the pictures. I heard some of the tapes. I would comment not only as an Air Force Major General but as an American citizen, and that is to say that while we are happy that our airmen survived the intercepts and the hostile fire, we hold Iraq accountable to treat them in accordance with the Geneva Convention. Yes?

Q Sir, what is -- (source audio break) -- to why Iraq is targeting Riyadh? Do you think it's to actually hit targets or to frighten the population, or to -- what is your best guess?

GEN. MOORE: Well, I think to know what Iraq is trying to do, of course you would obviously have to try to get into their mind, I would only say that whatever their reason, I think the results of their efforts have been very feeble. Yes?

Q What is your assessment of what a lot of people are calling Saddam's "rope-a-dope" strategy, now he is giving us just a taste of what he has and he's got a lot more to come with chemical warfare in store too?

GEN. MOORE: That is always a possibility. We plan to

CONTINUED

2fo -2

0105

DEFENSE DEPARTMENT CE [redacted]M BRIEFING/ BRIEFER: MA[redacted]ENERAL BURTON MOORE, DIRECTOR OF OP IONS, US CENTRAL COMMANI[redacted]
10:00 A.M., EST/ RIYADH, SAUDI ARABIA/ MONDAY, JANUARY 21, 1991
DC-1-2 page 1

dest=sdd,dd,dod,defense,saudiar,armfor,iraq,kuwait,pergulf
dest+=airc,uk,missile,weapons,fns32003,fns11976,israel,pow,polpris
dest+=intel,terr,pol,iran
data

continue to execute our campaign in accordance with our objectives on our time schedule. We plan for the worst; we hope for the best. We have good people, good equipment, and I think the results to date would suggest that we are well on our way to our objectives.

Q The problem of -- do you have -- can you make an assessment of what he has in his own arsenal, what he has left, and what he can deliver?

GEN. MOORE: Well, I can't give you an exact answer as to what he has.

Q (Off mike.)

GEN. MOORE: No. I would rather not speculate.

Yes?

Q Only a few days ago, the military was making much of the fact that there was, what was being described as a trend in Iraq's missile firings: eight, I believe on Friday, three on Saturday. Now we find ourselves back up to 10. Does that change your assessment of the effectiveness of your attempts to track down the Scud launchers?

GEN. MOORE: Well, as I said, we continue to aggressively pursue his fixed and mobile Scud capability. It is too early to say that we have those objectives obtained, but we continue to try to take them out as fast -- we are pursuing that objective as aggressively as is reasonably possibly. And again, I would say that the results of his efforts to launch Scuds -- both here and in Israel have been very ineffective.

Yes?

Q The British officer has said that the effect of seeing POWs on television is likely to at least irritate airmen -- British airmen. Would you say that goes -- that that's the same for American pilots, when they see their colleagues exhibited like this?

GEN. MOORE: We expect that our colleagues -- both US and allied will be treated humanely and in accordance with the US-Geneva Convention.

Yes?

Q General, how many of the 8,100 sorties are actual combat

250-5

0106

sorties, as opposed to logistical flights behind the lines?

GEN. MOORE: They all are combat sorties, although some fall in the category of combat support.

Q Well, how many -- how many are actually those directed against Iraqi military positions?

GEN. MOORE: I would rather not give you that number.

Q General, can you tell us, from your intelligence assessments of the Scud launchings last night, how many launchers were involved in these ten launchings? Where were they? Did you mount any attacks against them? And do you know if you've taken any of them out?

GEN. MOORE: For operational security reasons, I would not want to tell you, nor would I tell you, exactly how many launchers or where they are. I would tell you that in accordance with our campaign plan, we will continue, and have aggressively pursued launchers when we find them, and when we fix them and when we can attack them. And we'll continue to do that.

Q Can you tell us if you've taken any of them out?

GEN. MOORE: I think we have taken some of them out. We are nowhere near completing our campaign objectives. Do not draw anything else from that statement, please.

Q General, the bombing of the Iraqi positions that are dug in in the -- at the Kuwaiti border -- is that around -- when you're saying "around the clock," do you mean it's continuously, or do you mean four hours on, a few hours off -- how does it work? Can you just give us an idea of what --

GEN. MOORE: We are not on a four-hour on, four-hour off schedule. We are conducting around the clock operations, as you said.

Q (Off mike) -- these bombs falling on the troops that are dug in?

GEN. MOORE: We are always pursuing Iraqi troops, both in Iraq and Kuwait, yes.

Q General?

GEN. MOORE: Yes.

Q A couple of days ago, two Patriots had been fired unintentionally, as we were told. I know there's a possibility that the damage happened here is because of one of the Patriots. How safe is this operation?

250-6

0107

DEFENSE DEPARTMENT CE[redacted]M BRIEFING/ BRIEFER: MAJ[redacted]ENERAL BURTON MOORE, DIRECTOR OF OPERATIONS, US CENTRAL COMMAND
10:00 A.M., EST/ RIYADH, SAUDI ARABIA/ MONDAY, JANUARY 21, 1991
DC-1-2 page 3

GEN. MOORE: I think I would say that the investigation on those two Patriots is ongoing, and I would rather couch it in the context of, again, every Scud missile that has been launched at Riyadh or Dhahran has been successfully engaged by Patriot missile.

Yes?

Q There's been some comment previously from officers suggesting that all of the fixed launchers have been taken out, and I believe General Schwarzkopf said 16 of an estimated 20 mobile launchers. You said you continue to aggressively pursue fixed and mobile launchers. Does that mean there are still fixed launchers in operation?

GEN. MOORE: We have not achieved 100 percent of our objectives against the fixed sites, the mobile sites and his Scud missile capability.

Yes?

Q General, a few days ago, General Schwarzkopf showed some very impressive films to us demonstrating the pinpoint accuracy of bombing missions over Bagdhad. Have we used that skill in pinpoint bombing to go after any targets, any terrorist targets in Bagdhad, the headquarters of Abu Abbas or Abu Nidal?

GEN. MOORE: We have used our technology, our pinpoint accuracy, as you describe it and that is correct and the highly qualified crews to attack selected targets that we feel are part of Iraq's war-fighting capability and we will continue to do that. Yes?

Q A follow-up. Would you consider those to be part of Iraq's war capability, those terrorist targets?

GEN. MOORE: I think it would be inappropriate for me to identify specific targets at this time.

Q Would you please give us some detailed information about how much you have destroyed Saddam Hussein's capability to talk to his ground troops in Kuwait, to communicate with them? I don't want you to give away operational secrets, but give us some assessment of how badly that communication line with the ground troops has been affected so far?

GEN. MOORE: We have indications that we are effectively degrading a good portion of his ability to communicate with his troops, although we have not eliminated that capability completely and we will continue to pursue that.

Q Give us an example.

GEN. MOORE: Just his command and control structure to his

240-57

0108

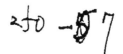

integrated air defense.

Q General, there have been allegations by the Iraqis and also by the Iranians that you are attacking residential areas, civilian targets. How do you react to those allegations?

GEN. MOORE: That's not correct. I think you have seen the films. Our technology and our ability has allowed us to really pinpoint the targets that we need to hit and it is not nor will it be our policy to attack innocent civilians. Our argument is not with the people of Iraq, it is with Saddam Hussein and his military.

CONTINUED

250 -8

0109

DEFENSE DEPARTMENT C[redacted]M BRIEFING/ BRIEFER: MA[redacted] GENERAL BURTON MOORE, DIRECTOR OF O[redacted]IONS, US CENTRAL COMMAN
10:00 A.M., EST/ RIYADH, SAUDI ARABIA/ MONDAY, JANUARY 21, 1991
DC-1-3-E page 1

dest=sdd,dd,dod,defense,saudiar,armfor,iraq,kuwait,pergulf
dest+=fns32003,fns11976,intel,france,missile,weapons
dest+=ussr,iran,jordan,arab,pow,polpris,nuclear,nucweapon
dest+=chem,chemwar
data

** PLEASE NOTE THIS IS A RESEND OF "DC-1-3-E" THE FIRST SEND HAD AN INCORRECT HEADER. THANK YOU **

Q General?

GEN. MOORE: Yes?

Q What kind of intelligence coordination do you have with the allied forces, because you speak about three Scuds on the eastern province and six in Riyadh, and the French army speak of six on the eastern province and four on Riyadh? So, is there really intelligence coordination between you?

GEN. MOORE: I -- (laughs) -- (press laughter) -- uh, yes, there is. And I would remind you of what you all familiar with and that is the fog of war. And those of you who have seen this event from last night know that if you were standing in a certain spot you reacted and saw a certain thing happen and somebody else down the street might have described it quite differetly. The coordination is ongoing. I will say, you know, we are still early in nailing down exactly what happened. But as I said, our reports are as I stated them to you.

Yes?

Q General, I have two questions, one quick one, one a little bit more difficult. Are B-52s being used on Baghdad, or targets anywhere near Baghdad?

GEN. MOORE: For operational reasons, I would not like to tell you what is being used exactly used exactly where. However, our B-52s are being used to meet our campaign objectives and they have been participating from D-Day.

Q A couple of days ago the weather was supposed to be a factor in battle damage assessment. Has the weather improved, and do we have a better sense now as to what has been accomplished in the raids?

GEN. MOORE: While we have seen some improvements off and on in the weather, the weather patterns continue as they have for the past few days and it has continued to impact our ability to get battle damage assessment, although there are other ways of knowing how successful we are. And again, we use that in our planning.

GEN. MOORE: Yes, please?

260 -9

0110

Q Sir, yesterday, I believe, 14 out of a certain number of mines were identified as being of Iraqi origin. Have any mines been identified as being of other origin, positively?

GEN. MOORE: There are no mines that I'm aware of of being other than an Iraqi origin.

Q General

GEN. MOORE: Yes?

Q There have been a number of varied estimates on the number of SCUD launchers that the Iraqis possess. Did in fact the Russians sell them all their SCUD launchers, and if so, why can't we find out from the Russians precisely how many systems they provided for the Iraqis?

GEN. MOORE: In response to your first question, I don't know if the Russians all of their SCUD launchers and that makes it impossible for me yo addres the second question.

Yes?

Q General, just to go back to the weather for just a second. I mean, it makes it difficult for damage assessment, but cold you also tell me what or what not bad weather -- what you can or cannot do because of the cloud cover?

GEN. MOORE: Well, what we can and cannot do is not the issue. We have systems that are able to make compensation, it is a factor in our planning, and will contiue to be a factor in our planning. Would we like the waather to be better? Yes.

Q Could you tell us how many of the coalition aircraft losses occurred over Iraq, how many over Kuwait and whether the anti-aircraft weapons that the Iraqis have appear to be more effective in one place than the other?

GEN. MOORE: For reasons of both operational security and the safety of the crews which may be evading in the areas in which they were shot down, I would request that I not answer that question.

Q Can you confirm reports that some Iraqi planes have been taking refuge in Iran?

GEN. MOORE: I'm sorry, can you say the -- please --

Q Can you confirm reports that some Iraqi planes have been taking refuge in -- through the north into Iraq?

GEN. MOORE: I am not aware of any such reports.

Q General, I think that the mesage yesterday wants to

250-18

0111

encourage you to start the ground attack. Do you think that you will go to this battle earlier than you had decided?

GEN. MOORE: We will execute our campaign plan on our schedule when we are ready and when it's appropriate, and I would not predict or speculate beyond that.

Q General?

GEN. MOORE: Yes, there was a voice here in the middle.

Yes?

Q It's been suggested by those leaving Baghdad that they're far from dividing the people of Iraq against their leader. The pinpoint accuracy bombing has united them. They feel that they are able to unite and the morale is quite high. Have you anything on that?

GEN. MOORE: I have no comment on that. We will continue to try to use our technology to the best of our ability to minimize civilian casualties.

Q Sir, is there any indication that Jordan or any other Arab country is likely to join these hostilities on the side of Iraq?

GEN. MOORE: I have nothing to suggest that.

Q General, you have stated the policy repeatedly on the -- about bombing only military targets and avoiding civilian areas. We understand that fully. But do you have any way of assessing whether there are civilian casualties, collateral damage of that kind? And if so do you have any kind of a reading on it that you can give us as to what -- how much of this there might have been apart from what the Iraqis say about it?

GEN. MOORE: I do not and I haven't even seen any news reports or heard of any news reports where the Iraqis may be suggesting that. I really can't just answer. I know nothing about that.

Q General, you say you heard the statements from the downed fliers, the POWs. Is it your estimation that these statements were made under coercion, and if so, based on your experience in survival school, can you describe what kind of atmosphere they were made in?

GEN. MOORE: Well, that would really be speculative and I would not want to do that, nor would I want to say any more about those individuals that are reportedly held hostage because of their safety if nothing else.

Q (Name inaudible) -- from Kuwait Television. What would be your advice for the people of Kuwait for the near future?.

GEN. MOORE: The people of Kuwait living in exile or in Kuwait?

250-11

0112

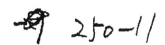

Q In Kuwait.

GEN. MOORE: Keep the faith.

Q General, how many Patriot missiles were fired last night?

GEN. MOORE: I would -- for operational reasons I will not answer that question, thank you.

Q General, can you elaborate a little on the general statements we've already heard that Iraq's nuclear facilities -- General Schwarzkopf referred to four of them, and I think a Saudi spokesman has referred to the chemical facilities -- have been largely destroyed? Can you tell us -- can you confirm it, and can you elaborate on what exactly that means?

GEN. MOORE: I would agree with what General Schwarzkopf said yesterday, that we have set back his nuclear capability for some time, and we continue to make strides against his chemical capability. And I would not like to be any more specific, again, for operational reasons.

Q General?

STAFF: One more question, please.

Q General?

GEN. MOORE: Yes.

Q Do you know where is the Iraqi air force?

GEN. MOORE: The Iraqi air force is one of two places; they are in large Iraqi spare parts areas across Iraq or they are hiding in bunkers. They have not come up very much, as you know. And when they have come up to engage US and allied air forces they have been shot down.

Q Thank you.

GEN. MOORE: Thank you very much.

Q Thank you, General.

END

~~10~~
250-12 (END)

0113

SITUATION IN THE GULF

January 21, 1991

INTRODUCTION

THE U S. HAD HOPED THAT THE GULF CRISIS COULD HAVE BEEN RESOLVED PEACEFULLY.

THE U.S. AND ITS ALLIES IN THE COALITION INITIATED COMBAT OPERATIONS ONLY AFTER IT HAD BECOME CLEAR THAT ALL DIPLOMATIC AND PEACEFUL OPTIONS HAD BEEN EXHAUSTED.

THE GOVERNMENT OF IRAQ WAS GIVEN EVERY OPPORTUNITY TO RESOLVE THIS ISSUE BY PEACEFUL MEANS BY COMPLYING WITH UN SECURITY COUNCIL RESOLUTION 660 AND SUBSEQUENT RESOLUTIONS. IT CHOSE TO SPURN THE CHANCE FOR PEACE.

DIPLOMATIC EFFORTS

EXTENSIVE DIPLOMATIC EFFORTS HAVE BEEN UNDERWAY FOR THE PAST FIVE AND A HALF MONTHS TO PERSUADE IRAQ TO COMPLY WITH THE WILL OF THE INTERNATIONAL COMMUNITY

-- THE ARAB LEAGUE, THE EUROPEAN COMMUNITY THE U.N. SECRETARY GENERAL AND A NUMBER OF INDIVIDUAL ARAB AND EUROPEAN STATES TRIED TO FIND A DIPLOMATIC SOLUTION TO THE CRISIS. ALL EFFORTS WERE REBUFFED BY IRAQ.

-- IN HIS JANUARY 9 MEETING WITH SECRETARY BAKER IN GENEVA, IRAQI FOREIGN MINISTER TARIQ AZIZ DEMONSTRATED NO FLEXIBILITY AND NO WILLINGNESS TO COMPLY WITH UN SECURITY COUNCIL RESOLUTIONS.

-- IN OUR MEETING WITH TARIQ AZIZ, WE REITERATED THAT THE US WOULD NOT ATTACK IRAQ OR ITS MILITARY FORCES IF IRAQ COMPLIED FULLY WITH THE SECURITY COUNCIL RESOLUTIONS AND MADE NO FURTHER PROVOCATION

-- WE TOLD AZIZ THAT ONCE IRAQ WITHDRAWS FROM KUWAIT AND IRAQ'S THREAT TO ITS NEIGHBORS RECEDES, WE HAVE NO INTENTION OF MAINTAINING LARGE U.S. FORCE LEVELS IN THE GULF.

-- WE TOLD AZIZ THAT THE U.S. SUPPORTED THE CALL IN SECURITY COUNCIL RESOLUTION 660 FOR IRAQ AND KUWAIT TO SETTLE THEIR DIFFERENCES PEACEFULLY AFTER IRAQI WITHDRAWAL.

0114

-- WE STRESSED THAT IRAQ COULD AVOID A CONFRONTATION AND MILITARY ACTION BUT THE CHOICE WAS IRAQ'S TO MAKE.

ON JANUARY 13, THE U.N. SECRETARY GENERAL WAS REBUFFED BY IRAQ FOR A SECOND TIME, IN THIS CASE IN A DIRECT ATTEMPT TO PERSUADE SADDAM HUSSEIN TO WITHDRAW FROM IRAQ PEACEFULLY.

THROUGHOUT THE SEVEN WEEK "PAUSE OF GOODWILL" ESTABLISHED BY UN SECURITY COUNCIL 678 BETWEEN NOV. 30 AND JAN. 15, IRAQ MADE CLEAR THAT IT CONSIDERED SECURITY COUNCIL RESOLUTIONS TO BE INVALID AND THAT IT HAD NO INTENTION OF COMPLYING WITH THEM.

-

SANCTIONS

ECONOMIC SANCTIONS HAVE HAD A SIGNIFICANT IMPACT. IRAQI IMPORTS AND EXPORTS HAVE BEEN CUT SUBSTANTIALLY AND SECTORS OF THE IRAQI ECONOMY ARE EXPERIENCING SUBSTANTIAL DIFFICULTIES.

BUT AFTER MORE THAN FIVE MONTHS OF OPERATION, IT HAD BECOME CLEAR THAT SANCTIONS ALONE WOULD NOT INDUCE IRAQ TO COMPLY WITH UNSC RESOLUTIONS AND WITHDRAW FROM KUWAIT.

THE MAIN EFFECT OF SANCTIONS HAS BEEN TO LOWER THE STANDARD OF LIVING OF THE IRAQI PEOPLE . SADDAM HUSSEIN HAS MADE IT CLEAR THAT HE IS NOT CONCERNED ABOUT THE HARDSHIPS BORNE BY THE IRAQI POPULACE .

-- HE ASO HAS MADE CLEAR HIS READINESS TO TRANSFER RESOURCES FROM THE CIVILIAN SECTOR TO THE ARMED FORCES IN ORDER TO PRESERVE HIS MILITARY CAPABILITIES.

BY JANUARY, WE HAD DETERMINED THAT IRAQ WOULD BE ABLE TO MAINTAIN LARGE AND POWERFUL LAND AND AIR FORCES, AS WELL AS A SUBSTANTIAL CAPABILITY TO REPLACE AMMUNITION AND MATERIEL, EVEN IF SANCTIONS WERE GIVEN ANOTHER SIX TO TWELVE MONTHS TO OPERATE.

-- IN SHORT, ECONOMIC SANCTIONS WOULD NOT HAVE PRODUCED IRAQI COMPLIANCE WITH U.N. SECURITY COUNCIL RESOLUTIONS EVEN IF THE INTERNATIONAL COMMUNITY HAD BEEN ABLE TO MAINTAIN A HIGH DEGREE OF COMPLIANCE WITH THE SANCTIONS REGIME.

0115

WAR AIMS

IN THE FIRST DAYS AFTER THE IRAQI INVASION OF KUWAIT PRESIDENT BUSH ANNOUNCED FOUR OBJECTIVES THAT WOULD GUIDE U.S. POLICY. THESE GOALS ARE:

-- AN IMMEDIATE, COMPLETE UNCONDITIONAL IRAQI WITHDRAWAL FROM KUWAIT.

-- RESTORATION OF THE LEGITIMATE GOVERNMENT OF KUWAIT.

-- PROTECTION OF U .S. CITIZENS ABROAD .

-- SECURITY AND STABILITY IN THE PERSIAN GULF.

THESE FOUR PRINCIPLES CONTINUE TO GUIDE US.

-

AS PRESIDENT BUSH STATED IN HIS ADDRESS TO THE AMERICAN PEOPLE ON JANUARY 16 "OUR OBJECTIVES ARE CLEAR. SADDAM HUSSEIN'S FORCES WILL LEAVE KUWAIT, THE LEGITIMATE GOVERNMENT OF KUWAIT WILL BE RESTORED TO ITS RIGHTFUL PLACE, AND KUWAIT WILL ONCE AGAIN BE FREE."

EVEN THOUGH U.S. AND ALLIED FORCES ARE STRIKING MILITARY TARGETS IN IRAQ, OUR GOAL IS NOT THE DESTRUCTION, OCCUPATION, OR DISMEMBERMENT OF IRAQ.

-- AS PRESIDENT BUSH SAID LAST TUESDAY NIGHT, "IRAQ WILL EVENTUALLY COMPLY WITH ALL RELEVANT UNITED NATIONS RESOLUTIONS AND THEN, WHEN PEACE IS RESTORED, IT IS OUR HOPE THAT IRAQ WILL LIVE AS A PEACEFUL AND COOPERATIVE MEMBER OF THE FAMILY OF NATIONS, THUS ENHANCING THE SECURITY AND STABILITY OF THE GULF."

CONDUCT OF WAR

THE U S. AND ITS ALLIES IN THE COALITION ARE CONDUCTING MILITARY OPERATIONS IN FULL COMPLIANCE WITH APPLICABLE INTERNATIONAL CONVENTIONS ON THE LAWS OF ARMED CONFLICT.

-- WE HAVE DELIBERATELY PLANNED OPERATIONS SO AS TO MINIMIZE DAMAGE TO CIVILIANS.

-- WE ALSO ARE ATTEMPTING TO AVOID DAMAGING RELIGIOUS OR CULTURAL SITES IN IRAQ AND KUWAIT.

WE HAVE WARNED IRAQ TO AVOID THE USE OF WEAPONS OF MASS DESTRUCTION AND TO RESPECT ITS OBLIGATIONS UNDER THE LAW OF ARMED CONFLICT AND THE GENEVA PROTOCOL OF 1924 BANNING THE FIRST USE OF CHEMICAL WEAPONS.

0116

WE ALSO HAVE MADE IT CLEAR THAT WE WILL HOLD THE IRAQI LEADERSHIP RESPONSIBLE FOR ANY ACTS OF TERRORISM CARRIED OUT AGAINST US OR OUR ALLIES.

WE INTEND TO CONTINUE MILITARY OPERATIONS UNTIL IRAQ COMPLIES WITH ALL RELEVANT U.N. SECURITY COUNCIL RESOLUTIONS WE SEE NO NEED FOR A 'PAUSE' IN HOSTILITIES TO ALLOW SADDAM HUSSEIN TO REGROUP HIS FORCES.

-- AS PRESIDENT BUSH SAID YESTERDAY, IRAQ MUST WITHDRAW FROM KUWAIT "WITH NO CONCESSIONS AND NO CONDITIONS."

WE HOPE TO BRING HOSTILITIES TO A CONCLUSION AS SOON AS POSSIBLE, CONSISTENT WITH FULL IMPLEMENTATION OF ALL RELEVANT U.N. SECURITY COUNCIL RESOLUTIONS.

ISRAEL

THROUGHOUT THE GULF CRISIS, SADDAM HUSSEIN HAS TRIED TO TURN WORLD ATTENTION AWAY FROM HIS AGGRESSION AGAINST KUWAIT AND TOWARDS ISRAEL.

THIS IS NOTHING MORE THAN POLITICAL CYNICISM AND HYPOCRISY. IRAQ DID NOT CARRY OUT ITS AGGRESSION AGAINST KUWAIT TO RESOLVE THE STATUS OF THE OCCUPIED TERRITORIES. HE DID NOT FIRE MISSILES AGAINST ISRAEL LAST NIGHT IN ORDER TO HELP THE PALESTINIAN PEOPLE.

I WOULD NOTE THAT LAST NIGHT'S ATTACK WAS UNPROVOKED IT WAS NOT DIRECTED AT MILITARY OBJECTIVES. SADDAM RATHER TARGETED HIS MISSILES AGAINST CITIES, WITH THE OBJECTIVE OF INFLICTING MAXIMUM DAMAGE AGAINST CIVILIANS.

THIS ATTACK WAS UNDERTAKEN BECAUSE SADDAM HUSSEIN BELIEVES IT WOULD SOW DISSENSION WITHIN THE INTERNATIONAL COALITION ARRAYED AGAINST HIM. WE BELIEVE IT IMPERATIVE THAT ALL STATES RECOGNIZE THE IRAQI ATTACK ON ISRAEL FOR WHAT IT WAS -- A DESPERATE AND CYNICAL ATTEMPT TO DIVERT WORLD ATTENTION FROM THE NECESSITY OF OVERCOMING IRAQI AGGRESSION.

CONCLUSION

WE ALL HOPE THAT THE CURRENT FIGHTING WILL NOT GO ON FOR LONG AND THAT CASUALTIES WILL BE HELD TO AN ABSOLUTE MINIMUM

BUT THE CHOICE BETWEEN WAR AND PEACE LIES IN THE HANDS OF SADDAM HUSSEIN. HE WILL EITHER COMPLY WITH THE WILL OF THE INTERNATIONAL COMMUNITY AS EMBODIED IN TWELVE U.N. SECURITY COUNCIL RESOLUTIONS BY WITHDRAWING FROM KUWAIT OR HE WILL FACE THE CONTINUED DEVASTATION OF WAR.

0117

관리 번호	91/659

외 무 부

종 별 : 지 급

번 호 : USW-0359 일 시 : 91 0122 1825

수 신 : 장관(미북,중근동,대책반)

발 신 : 주 미 대사

제 목 : 걸프 전쟁

당관 임성준 참사관은 금 1.22 오후 미 상원 군사위 JUDITH FREEDMAN 전문위원과 상원 외무위 동아태 소위 RICHARD KESSLER 전문위원을 각각 방문, 걸프만전쟁과 관련한 의회 동향을 탐문한바 요지 아래 보고함.

1. 임 참사관은 작 1.21 의료 지원단 사우디 파견 동의안이 우리 국회에서 여야 합의에 의한 압도적 지지로 통과됨에 따라, 동 지원단 전원이 1.25 까지 사우디에 배치될 예정임을 통보하였던바, 동 전문위원들은 그와같은 신속한 조치를환영한다고 말하고 한국정부가 지난해말 분담금 기여에 이어 의료 인력을 제공한 사실은 동맹국들의 역할 분담(BURDEN-SHARING)에 관심 있는 의원들로 부터도 환영열 받을것으로 본다고 말함.

2. 전쟁 수행과 관련한 의회의 역할을 문의한데 대해 상원 군사위 소속 의원들은 매일 오후 3 시 국방성으로부터 전황 보고를 청취하고 있으나, 의회로서는 이미 전쟁이 개시된 만큼 전쟁의 수행에 필요한 예산 조치, 주둔군의 사기 진작책(세금 감면등)전쟁 지원 역할을 수행하며, 지상군 투입 시기등 전술 전략적인 사항에 대하여는 군사 당국의 판단에 간섭할수 있는 입장이 아니라고 말함.

3. 공중 폭격의 효과, 장기전 돌입 가능성등의 질문에 대하여, 전문위원들은 초기 단계에서 미군을 포함한 연합군측의 주도권 장악을 거론하면서 전재의 조기 매듭 가능성에 낙관적인 견해를 표명함(KESSLER 전문위원은 2 월까지는 지상군 투입등으로 전쟁을 매듭지을수 있을것이라고 전망)

4. 전쟁의 결과가 미국내 정치에 미칠 영향에 대하여, FREEDMAN 전문위원은전쟁이 종결되는 시점에서 어느정도의 사상자가 발생할것인지 여부가 부쉬 대통령의 정치 생명에 결정적인 영향을 미칠것인바, 현재까지의 추세로 보아 초기 단계이기는 하나 미 국민들은 부쉬 대통령의 판단이 옳았던것으로 평가(여론 조사시 지지율 80

미주국	장관	차관	1차보	2차보	중아국	청와대	총리실	안기부

PAGE 1 91.01.23 09:14

외신 2과 통제관 BW

0118

프로)하고 있으며, 민주당은 국민들의 여론을 잘못 판단하는 오류를 범한것으로 볼수 있어 이것은 1992 년 대통령 선거시 결정적인 약점으로 작용할수 있을것이라는 의견을 보임.

(대사 박동진-국장)

91.12.31 까지

검토필(1991. 6.30.)

PAGE 2

0119

원 본

외 무 부

종 별 :

번 호 : USW-0364 일 시 : 91 0122 1905

수 신 : 장 관(미북,중근동,미안,대책반)

발 신 : 주미 대사

제 목 : 전황 보고

1. 당지 시간 1.22. 10:00 실시된 리야드 주둔 현지미군 GESK부의 전황 브리핑 내용에 따르면 현재까지 약 10,000 회 이상의 공습 출격이 있었으며 아직 본격적인 지상 전투는 벌어지지 않고 있으나 이락측이 미지상 병력에 대해 간헐적인 야포공격을 가 하고 있다함.(브리핑 내용중 관련 부분은 USW(F)-0267 로 팩시편 송부)

2. 한편 사우디 시간으로 1.22 오전 재래식 탄두를 장착한 이락측 SCUD 미사일 6발이 사우디를 향해 발사되었으나, 일부는 미측 PATRIOT 미사일에 의해 요격되고 또 일부는 사막등에 떨어져다함.

(대사 박동진-국장)

미주국	장관	차관	1차보	2차보	미주국	중아국	정문국	청와대
총리실	안기부	대책반						

PAGE 1 91.01.23 10:31 WG

외신 1과 통제관

0120

원 본

외 무 부

종 별 :

번 호 : USW-0375 일 시 : 91 0123 1741

수 신 : 장 관(미북, 중근동, 대책반)

발 신 : 주 미 대사

제 목 : CHENEY 및 POWELL 기자회견

걸프 전쟁이 개시된지 1주일이 경과된 금 1.23. CHENEY 국방장관 및 POWELL 합참의장은 미국방부에서 그간 전쟁경과를 종합하는 기자회견을 가진바, 동 내용을 FAX (USW(F)-0278)송부함.

(대사 박동진-국장)

미주국 장관 차관 1차보 2차보 중아국 정문국 청와대 총리실 안기부 대책반

PAGE 1

91.01.24 10:14 WG

외신 1과 통제관

0121

번호 : USW(F) - 8

수신 : 장 관 (미북, 중근동, 대책반) 발신 : 주미대사

제목 : Cheney, Powell 기자회견 (첨부물) (13 매)

보안 통제	

DEFENSE DEPARTMENT/SPECIAL BRIEFING WITH: SECRETARY OF DEFENSE DICK CHENEY; GENERAL COLIN POWELL, CHAIRMAN, JOINT CHIEFS OF STAFF; PETE WILLIAMS, 2:00 P.M. EST/WEDNESDAY, JANUARY 23, 1991

MR. WILLIAMS: Okay, good afternoon, ladies and gentlemen. Secretary Cheney and General Powell are here to answer your questions. The Secretary will have a short statement.

I'm going to have to get out that way. I think there's no escape on this side.

And then General Powell will walk you through. We'll have some charts here. And after the briefings are over the charts will remain here so that you can photograph them. And we will try this afternoon to provide you smaller handouts of those.

So let me at this point turn it over to the Secretary.

Excuse me, sir.

SEC. CHENEY: Well thank you very much, Pete.

Operation Desert Storm has now been underway for approximately one week as of this evening. We believe that it's gone very well and we wanted to take this opportunity to try to put things in perspective and then try to respond to some of your questions.

Let me begin by expressing the pride that we all feel in the men and women of our armed forces who are carrying out these operations. It is an extremely complex and often dangerous undertaking and they have our admiration and our gratitude. I also want to say to the families of those held prisoner or missing in action that they are in the prayers of all Americans in these very difficult days.

I want to repeat what I told all of you last week at the beginning of this conflict. I urged caution in describing the events in the Persian Gulf, especially in claiming victory too soon. The next day the President expressed his concern about what he called the initial euphoria in some of the early reactions and stories about the operation. I also said that this operation was likely to run for a long period of time.

Yesterday, with Operation Desert Storm in its sixth day, I noticed a newspaper headline which said, quote, "War Drags On." (Light laughter.) Finally, this morning I noticed that the Style section of the Washington Post had three separate stories about the press covering the war in the Gulf. As an old Washington hand, I know that having the press reporting on the press reporting on a story is usually

0178 -1

0122

a sign that they've run out of things to say about the story. (Laughter.) So, Colin and I decided to spend a little time with you this afternoon to see if we could give you some new information.

Some important qualifiers to keep in mind as we go through the briefing this afternoon -- and many of these may be obvious, but I think need to be restated -- the Iraqis, Saddam Hussein, have a very large military force. Depending upon what criteria you use, certainly one of the largest in the world; some have said the fourth largest in the world. In the last decade, he spent over $50 billion on armaments. The force possesses thousands of tanks, hundreds of aircraft, over a million men in uniform, missiles, et cetera.

In the Kuwaiti theatre of operations in Kuwait and southern Iraq, there are over a 120 brigades, some 30-plus divisions, dug in in that area. I don't think anyone here expected that we would get rid of all that capability within the first week of the operation.

Over 10,000 separate sorties have been flown on combat and support missions in just the past seven days. Our goal remains the same, to liberate Kuwait by forcing Saddam Hussein out. And to do that, we have to weaken his military force and to go after his offensive military capability.

In pursuit of that objective, we began by concentrating on a carefully planned set of military targets that we will continue to hit over the course of the next several days and weeks. We've started with command and control, with his communications facilities, his air defense units and radars, his airfields, his Scud missile launchers. We've gone after the factories where Iraq has produced chemical and biological weapons and, until recently, continued working on nuclear weapons. We've also gone after the mainstay of Saddam's land forces, the Republican Guard units located near the Iraqi-Kuwaiti border. All of these targets we chose in advance. The pilots of the allied air forces have operated in accordance with clear instructions to launch weapons only when they are certain they've selected the right targets under correct conditions.

Iraq, on the other hand, has chosen to launch a highly inaccurate weapon, the Scud missile, at major population centers with no certainty about where the Scuds will land. In contrast, we have carefully chosen our targets and we bombed them with precision. Based on the reports we're getting from our pilots and the evidence of gun camera recordings, many of which you've seen, the bombing missions are going well. The missions are based on the target list drawn up before the operation started. At the same time, we've been eager to know about the kind of damage which we've been able to cause. That's why we do bomb damage assessment. And these assessments are now coming in and will be used to make judgments about the success of our efforts to date and to guide the planning of future operations.

I want to caution you again that a military operation of this intensity and complexity cannot be scored every evening like a college track meet or a basketball tournament. I know how hard it is for you to cover this kind of an operation when you cannot see what's going on inside Iraq or occupied Kuwait. Some of you have been critical of us for not putting information out more quickly.

0172-2

0123

I understand you[illegible]int, but we want to be [illegible]ain that we don't rush down here with premature words of success. We are deliberately waiting until we have some confidence in the results of specific categories of targets. That may well not fit the 24-hour cycle that you're held to, but we want to have confidence in what we are saying before we say it.

Two final points. There may well be surprises ahead for us. No one should assume that Saddam Hussein does not have significant remaining military capability. We have to anticipate that he will try to use that against us and our allies. We have to assume that he may seek to launch air strikes and more Scuds or hit oil fields or generate terrorist attacks. He is a man who will use any means at his disposal to break up the coalition and to avoid defeat. But he cannot change the basic course of the conflict. He will be defeated.

Our first obligation here in the Pentagon is to carry out the President's orders and to win the war. We must also do everything possible to do it in a manner that holds American and allied casualties to an absolute minimum.

We recognize that we also have an obligation to provide as much information as possible about the progress of our efforts to the press. We will do that. But you, the members of the press, have to understand that, first and foremost, we must safeguard the security of future operations to protect the lives of those who will be asked to carry them out.

With that, I'd like to turn the briefing over to my colleague, Colin Powell, the Chairman of the Joint Chiefs, with a general overview of the status of the operation today.

Colin?

GEN. POWELL: Thank you, Mr. Secretary.

Let me also express my pride, and I expect it's the pride of all Americans, at the professionalism with which the men and women of the armed forces have carried out this operation so far. And, of course, I share the Secretary's concern about our missing in action, and our prayers are with the families of those who have lost loved ones, and especially with the families of those who do have missing

in action who may well be prisoners of war.

This is the end of the first week of operations, and what I'd like to do is for a few moments take stock with you in an attempt to dampen out the oscillations between euphoria and distress that sometimes catches us up every hour on the hour. And I'd like to do that by first reminding you of the military operational objective that we set out to accomplish, and that is simply to eject the Iraqi army from Kuwait. All of our activities must ultimately support this fundamental military objective, and of course, when we achieve that objective, we then will be in a position to restore the legitimate government of Kuwait and provide for the security of the region.

0218-3

0124

Let me also remind you once again, as we have said here previously, this is an air-land-sea campaign, not just an air campaign which at some point will end and then something else starts. It is a single, coherent, integrated air-land-sea campaign. The campaign plan has executed so far pretty much as we have expected, with a few exceptions. The weather turned more severe after 2-1/2 days of operations than we had expected.

We knew we were going to have two and a half days, and we thought we'd lose a day or two to weather conditions, but those weather conditions were more severe than we expected when they finally hit -- when the front came in -- and lasted a little bit longer than we expected. As a result, a number of our planned missions had to be aborted. The BDA process has been behind schedule because of cloud cover and other weather problems, and we have had to cancel some target coverage. All this means is that we have to make that up over time, but we are still essentially on our original game plan.

The other point I might make is that we devoted more effort than we initially thought we might have to to go after the Scud targets that you have reported on so -- so much in the last several days. Mobile Scuds were the problem that we had anticipated they would be, and now that we are into it -- and I'll say more about Scuds later -- we are finding that it's taken more of an effort on our part to go after those Scuds than we had anticipated. But notwithstanding these sorts of problems, we're pleased with week one, and we are satisfied that the contribution that the strategic air campaign is making to our overall objective is a good contribution and is about what we expected.

What I'd like to do is discuss certain parts of the air phase of the campaign and the results we've achieved in an effort to answer your questions with respect to how are we doing, how effective has the operation been so far. Let me first talk -- start talking about the air-to-air part of the campaign, how it's been going with respect to US air forces engaged in aerial combat with Iraqi air forces.

Iraqi air-to-air interception to date has been for the most part totally ineffective. In air-to-air engagements the results are 19 Iraqi interceptors destroyed in aerial combat, and we believe the most we might have lost is one. We were carrying it as zero until earlier today when we did some more analysis, talked to some pilots, and one of our planes may have been hit in air-to-air engagements. So at best, 19 to zero; at worst at the moment, 19 to one. Their losses in the interceptor category have all been F-1s and MiG-29s, their first-line interceptor aircraft. Other losses that they have sustained raise their total combat aircraft losses to something in the neighborhood of 41.

But the real measure of effectiveness, the real way to look at this and make an assessment of how we are doing is not by the number of aircraft downed, or how many sorties we've flown, or how many bunkers we have hit and how many bombs we've dropped. The real measure of effectiveness is what has the Iraqi air force been able to do to interfere with Operation Desert Storm. And the fact of the

027A-4

0125

matter is that one week period of time, no Iraqi airplane has conducted a single ground attack against any coalition target. And with the one exception of perhaps one airplane that may have been downed, the Iraqi air force has not been able to interfere with our air operations.

When you consider that the Iraqi air force has had a massive amount of money and resources invested into it over the years and have some 800 fighter bombers and interceptors, I think it's fair to say that this has not been, so far, a very good return on the investment that Saddam Hussein has put into the air force.

Nevertheless, it is a large air force. It has a latent capability. It has the ability to conduct defensive operations and offensive operations if they can ever get their act together. But as you will see in the course of the briefing, their sortie rate is down and their ability to operate has pretty much been constrained.

Can we turn this one over, please? (Referring to map.)

By way of illustration, this may -- for those of you who wish to count the little dots, there are 66 little dots -- and they reflect -- somebody will count, I'm sure of that. They reflect

main operating bases in red, dispersal airfields in blue. And then the general Scud launch areas from the west out to Israel and from the east down south into Riyadh are shown by the black hatchet marks.

This is a very extensive airfield system. Hardened bunkers -- you've seen pictures of them -- underground command and control installations, hardened fuel facilities, hardened ammo facilities. But the fact of the matter is that after one week of operation we are not being challenged by this air force and, in fact, within the last 24 hours we have only seen activity at the air bases that you see being pointed out to you with the little yellow dot in the middle of the red.

(To staff) Would you go over them again very quickly?

These are the only ones that have shown any active work in the last 24 hours.

Now, if I can turn to this chart just to give you another illustration. This summarizes what I said earlier; 411 interceptors, 398 fighter-bombers -- 809 total -- killed 19 in aerial combat, another 22 confirmed kills on the ground for a total of 41 in this category. They have a lot of other kinds of aircraft that could run this total up to roughly 1,400 if you add in transports and helicopters and things of that nature. But for the combat category, the thing that we worry about, this is the number.

Now I'm not really concerned about this number at the moment. They are, for the most part, on the ground in hardened shelters trying to hide and survive. In due course they may wish to come out and challenge us, or they just may try to ride it out for as long as possible. These numbers will rise over time as we continue the campaign to go after shelters, go after bunkers, and essentially rip up the air force in its entirety.

0278-5

0126

Let me turn now to another part of the air battle, and that has to do with ground to surface air defense systems, the SAMs and anti-aircraft guns.

This chart reflects at -- a high level of aggregation, because I don't want to give away too much information -- but the main air defense fanbelts are the red circles, and then the circles going all around the country reflect their early warning capability at the beginning of the operation; [it is] an extremely large sophisticated air-defense system, principally with Soviet equipment -- Soviet missile equipment, some French, some US -- that was captured, as well as a very comprehensive system of trying to integrate all of those missile systems and gun systems in hardened command and control centers around the country.

The fact of the matter is that we were able to attack this air defense envelope with great success over the last week by first taking out their early warning capability -- blinding them -- and then going after the operating centers -- the various sector operating centers that they used -- to wire this all together, and for the most part we have not been seriously affected by this very large air defense system.

We have had a total of ten aircraft lost, as you know. As we go through the analysis of how we lost those aircraft, at the moment it appears we lost two by SAM fire -- surface-to-air missile fire -- and three more by ground fire, and the other five we're still taking a look at. But when you take a look at our total losses of only ten US aircraft -- and I'll show you a chart here, I think -- here it is -- show you a chart there that, well, this says SAM-one [lost plane], AAA [ground fire]-three. I had it the other way around.

But it's something close to that, and I apologize for the difference in numbers. But when you take a look at the total of 16 aircraft losses for the coalition in it's entirety, and you consider the number of combat sorties that have been flown and the numbers of single aircraft that are involved in this operation, somewhere between 1,000 and 2,000 aircraft, this is a very low loss rate for an operation of this type.

Putting all that together, we can conclude that allied air forces have achieved air superiority over not only the Kuwaiti theater of operations, but throughout the entire theater to include Iraq. We can debate whether it's air superiority as defined by an American doctrine or air supremacy, as some of my British colleagues have alluded, or local air superiority, as some of my friends in Riyadh say. I used to teach the subject. I own the JCS publication that has the definition in it, which I helped write when I was a captain, and I can assure you that this qualifies for the definition of air superiority. When you can operate in an unhindered way, as we have been operating, over an area like this against an air force that size and with an air defense system that sophisticated, we have achieved air superiority.

That is not to say that a young pilot who is taking off will say, "Powell says we have air superiority. I've got nothing to worry about." Not at all. We're dealing with an enemy that is resourceful, an enemy that knows how to work

0278-6

0127

around problems, [illegible] enemy that is ingenious. [illegible]u can be sure that while we're here today, they're in Baghdad trying to figure out workarounds, trying to determine where their weaknesses are and see if they have capability to fix those weaknesses. And every pilot that goes against this environment still has to be concerned that he is going against an environment
that has the potential of taking down his airplanes. So we are not getting complacent. We are not writing this off. But in terms of

how it looks at General Schwarzkopf's level and my level, we have air superiority, and with that air superiority, we can now begin to use our air forces to simply maintain this superiority and start to concentrate down closer to the Kuwaiti theater of operations, remembering once again our military objective is the Iraqi army in Kuwait. With a free run of the area as much as possible, there will still be losses, and I don't want to understate that, but in general, air superiority.

Any pilot will tell you, though, that the real danger is guns, and as we get closer in to the Kuwaiti theater of operations and our op tempo picks up, we will focus a great deal of our attention on knocking down the anti-aircraft gun threat to our pilots so that they can get even lower and make their strikes more effective as we go after discrete units on the ground in due course.

Before turning to the Iraqi army, let me be totally joint and say a word about the Iraqi navy, a navy of almost no capability, a limited number of patrol boats. We have destroyed several of those patrol boats, we have taken out a Silkworm site that they were manning, and we have also sunk -- or severely damaged -- it isn't sunk, and in fact, it is floating -- but severely damaged a ship they had been using to lay mines. And also within the last week, we have destroyed a number of the mines -- I think the count is 24 -- of the mines that have been floating free in the Persian Gulf.

So I think we have dealt with the mine threat for the moment, and in due course, if the Kuwaiti navy in --
if the Iraqi navy in some way decides to come out any more and challenge us with these minor and insignificant patrol boats, it is indeed a manageable threat.

Let me turn now to the Iraqi army in the Kuwait theater of operations. As the Secretary pointed out, this is a large combined arms army. It has tanks, it has personnel carriers, it has air defense guns, it has very redundant resiliant -- resiliant communications between the different operating eschelons of the army. It has stockages of food, ammunition, and parts with the army in-theater, and they have a very elaborate supply system comign down from the interior of the country to sustain that army.

Our strategy to go after this army is very, very simple. First, we're going to cut it off, and then we're going to kill it. To cut it off, that began last week when we started to go after the nerve center, the brains of the operation, the command and control of the operation, and the lines of communication that come out of Baghdad and other places in the country, flowing down the Tigris and Euphrates valleys, down these lines of communications, to try to support somewhere in the neighborhood of a half a million men down here in the Kuwaiti theater of operations. So all we have been

0278-7

0128

doing to be in c[illegible]ol over here and begin s[illegible]ring this and try to deaden the nerve endings up here, all goes back to our original military objective to get rid of the army that is in Kuwait.

Now that that has started we will intensify this cutting off process, go after the line of -- lines of communications as they enter the vicinity of Basra, and as the come out of Basra going down to the army -- going after the command and control means, the means by which they exercise command and control over that force in the theater, going after mobility, trucks that move supplies forward, anything that allows that army to function we will now go after. And as we get into the process of cutting it off we will also step up the process of killing it by going after his stockpiles, ammunition, food; stripping away their gun air defense, using air attacks. And, if it becomes necessary, we are assembling a fairly sizeable ground force that can finish off the job should that be necessary.

I also want to emphasize that we have quite a capability at sea with naval gunfire, with naval aviation, as well as quite a formidable amphibious capability with our Marine forces. And, as some of you know, our two Marine expeditionary brigades are conducting practice operations today.

I'm not telegraphing anything. I just want everybody to know that we have a toolbox that's full of lots of tools, and I brought them all to the party. General Schwarzkopf has them all at the party.

So, how are we doing with respect to that major operational objective, the Iraqi army in Kuwait? We are really just starting in earnest. And I've got to make a point to you that assessing the damage on a deployed army in the field is quite a different proposition from assessing the damage on a building that you've just hit. You've seen some great film footage of a laser-guided bomb going down the vent shaft of a building; boom, it blows up, it burns down; there you have it. It doesn't work that way when you have a deployed armored brigade in the field.

They're spread out. They're dug in. They're hiding. They're not standing out there like a building. They're avoiding air attack. They are going to put out dummies to try to deceive you as to their exact locations. They are going to put in primary positions and alternate positions and supplementary positions. They are going to dig in their lines of communication. They are going to put in overhead cover. Those tanks are designed not to be easily destroyed. And so going after that kind of unit is a much more
[illegible]
But they are vulnerable, there's no question about it. And we are now turning our attention and selecting munitions and selecting target packages to go after that army, which in effect is sitting out there not doing anything. It has not moved since the operation began. There has been no major -- in fact, there have been no minor shifts of units around. It is, for the most part, sitting there, dug in, waiting to be attacked, and attacked it will be. But it is also sitting there without air support, without anything to keep the attack from being prosecuted against them, and with each passing day, with a reduced ability to bring in logistics down the lines of communication.

02-7-8

0129

There is no question that this large force will become weaker every day. That's absolutely mathematical. We are going to do everything we can to make sure that army cannot be reinforced with new troops, and over time they will have increasing difficulty to resupply it.

Yet that army has good soldiers. The units are of varying quality. The Republican Guard, as we've said many times, is quite good. Other parts of the force are not quite so good. We have anecdotal evidence of some low morale and anecdotal evidence of some defections, but it is not a trend yet. We have started to get some bomb damage assessment on the Republican Guard units that we've been striking. In some cases, the analysts who look at these photos, and I look at them as well, tell me that, "You see that unit out there? It's taken about 40 percent damage." I can't tell that. You've got to be an expert. But there is damage taking place. Other units that we have hit, we've looked at the photographs and said, "We didn't get a good hit on that. They're just too dispersed, we've got to go back and do it again." Very low, or light damage against that unit.

So, you are not going to get, and we will be unable to give you the kind of rapidly moving and adjusting scorecard on how we're doing against that army for some time. You really don't know how you're doing against an army until that army tries to perform its function. If it's just sitting there taking the punishment, we know we're hurting it. We really don't know how badly we've hurt it until it starts to move, or until it comes up on the radios so we can hear it talking to other units, until we can see defections come out of it, or if it's necessary to go in and fight it. So we are seeing some anecdotal evidence, but the BDA is still out on that, and we really have only begun to do the job on it.

I'd like to close by saying a few words about some of the strategic campaign targets we had up here. First, I want to -- let me just make one point on this slide I forgot earlier. As a measure of effectiveness of how we're doing in the air campaign, I just pulled these two things out. I've laundered them so you can't really tell what I'm talking about, because I don't want the Iraqis to know what I'm talking about. But trust me. Trust me. (Laughter.)

This reflects, in order of magnitude, of electronic emissions out of the Iraqi radar system. And it shows that early in December and through December, they were operating about over here with SAM/AAA radars and with early warning radars. On the 17th of January, as you would expect, it peaked up to here. And over the last week, it has come down to here. This represents well over a 95 percent reduction.

Now, it's a combination of damage we have done, as well as, I suspect, clever operational security techniques on their part, to keep us from knowing exactly what's going on or how badly they have been damaged. I am also sure they are trying to work around and reconstitute capability so they can get back up. And so I don't want to overstate it, just to give you a measure of effectiveness and to let you know, this is how we try to measure what's going on out there.

0272-9

0130

And this also is, by another measure of effectivenes -- and I'm sorry for this being so small, we just finished it -- shows you their daily sortie rate, and this was before the action began on the 30th of December. They were running about 235 sorties a day during that period. If weather was bad earlier in December, a little lower. But just as a benchmark, 235 sorties. The day of the war, they ran 116 sorties,
and for the last couple of days they've been running 31 to 40 sorties. Once again, the kind of measure of effectiveness that is more useful to us than is how many sorties we flew or how many bombs we dropped, et cetera, et cetera.

A couple of things about specific campaign targets that really go to the issue of how to make sure that when this is all over the kind of threat that has existed in the region is quite different than the threat that existed before it began.

First, with respect to nuclear weapons, we have targeted that nuclear facility they have very carefully. I have looked at the bomb damage assessment myself with trained analysts and I think I can confirm for you that the two operating reactors they had are both gone. They're down; they're finished. And the one that the Israelis took care of some years ago remains down.

With respect to chemical facilities, the focus of our effort for the first week has been on their production capability and their ability to field munitions. There are hundreds of bunkers out there, and it would have been a waste of our effort to keep chasing every single bunker which may or may not have chemical weapons

stored in them because they have dispersed a lot of that chemical weapon capability that they have out to operating units. So we concentrated on production facilities and the facilities that they use to put the material into actual weapons to be delivered. And we have had quite a bit of success. And without getting into specifics, I think I can say that we have done considerable damage to their ability to continue producing chemical weapons.

But they still have a chemical weapons capability. Their artillery can fire chemical weapons; their multiple-launch rocket systems, their free rocket over ground systems, and their air force does have that capability. So it's a still a threat to allied forces in the region.

With respect to their biological warfare facilities, we have gone after those and created quite a problem for them, I think. We have seriously damaged those facilities. There was a story earlier today about the infant formula factory. It is not an infant formula factory no more than the Rabta
chemical plant in Libya made aspirin. It was a biological weapons facility, of that we are sure, and we have taken it out. And we will continue to seek out any other facilities that we believe are involved in the production of biological weapons.

With respect to their national command authority and their command and control systems, they are very good at this. They have redundant systems, resiliant systems, they have work-arounds, they have alternatives, and they are still able to command their forces. They have not lost command and control of their forces or of the country. But they are doing it without benefit of their Ministry of

0278-10

0131

Defense, their Defense Intelligence Center, their main communications nodes, and they're doing it for the most part on generator power because we have taken care of the central power system within the city. He still does retain the ability to command and control.

We are also now turning our attention increasingly -- attention increasingly to military production facilities: how he makes bombs, how he makes weapons, how he makes repair parts. This is a target category at our leisure over time. We're in no hurry. We don't want to waste sorties on things that are further down the priority list if we can get to them further down the priority list.

The most significant problem we have right now are the Scuds. There is no doubt about it. When you think of what Saddam Hussein has done for the past week, he has not thrown a single military punch back at us. What he has done is use this weapon of terror, the Scuds, as was mentioned earlier by the Secretary, to go after populations, to go after cities. Why? As a weapon of terror, to try to expand the conflict, to try to draw in the Israelies. And I must say I'm extremely pleased with the restraint that the Israeli government has shown so far. But it is a vexing problem.

They are mobile systems, and some of them are very

sophisticated Soviet mobile systems. Others are nothing more than a flat-bed truck with a rail on it that they've locally fabricated. We only have estimates of how many of these weapons they have, but we have made it a high priority to locate these weapons and to go after them, and a significant part of our capability is directed toward that Scud facilities -- those Scud facility and mobile Scuds.

Now, I know there's been a great deal of interest in bomb damage assessment. I wish I could show you the photographs that we have access to, but because of sources and methods, and because we are in an ongoing operation, and because we do not want an enemy to have knowledge of what our real capabilities are, we cannot show you those photographs. What I have done instead is I have made some line drawings -- had some line drawings made. They are rather crude. They are kind of cartoonish. But I just want to give you a sense of what our analysts look at, and I will assure you that what I'm about to show you comes directly from the actual imagery, but we have obviously done it in a way that it does not give away any of our capability.

This was a large production facility, part of his military infrastructure. It was struck by precision weapons in the first couple of days of the operation. And this is a very accurate reflection of what the thing looks like, total destruction.

And the point I want to make is our analysts can see this to this level of detail and give us high assurance that this place has been destroyed.

Okay?

Q Can you say what was produced there at all?

GEN. POWELL: It was an unconventional production facility.

02/P-11

0132

Here is an example of a bunker complex. And it's a case where we went after selected buildings. These two were revetted. They had barriers around them. We went after them with precision weapons -- went after these with precision weapons. I think this one was done over a period of a couple of days. You go strike it. You get an assessment back of the amount of damage you have inflicted on a facility. You go back and strike it again. This has received enough damage that I would suspect that the targeteers over in CENTAF are not going to waste a sortie at this time going back and taking care of this last remaining building. These were the key ones. These three fed into what was happening at these two facilities. And so we have essentially destroyed this, even though there might still be a building standing. And I'm just using it as illustrative to the process

through which our bomb damage assessment people go through. This next one is a case where initially we went in, destroyed -- here's the bunker complex -- destroyed this bunker. This one was hit once and we had to go back and do it again to get the level of damage that we needed.

This one was also struck, and as the analyst looks at it, part of it is still intact, the top. This part, the lower part, has been blown through, but since the analyst can't see what happened under the part that still has a roof over it, he will not declare this destroyed. They tend to err on the conservative side. This one has completely been damaged because there was no need to waste a sortie or risk a pilot going against that one. We knew what we were looking for in this complex, so we are satisfied with this target even if somebody were to come along and say, aha, you only got 75 percent or 80 percent because this one is still there. We didn't need to hit that one, it has no relevance to the rest of the facility.

(Aside) I don't know what else we got back there, Mike. And this is -- this is an example which I like to put up for my British colleagues. One of the things we did early on to deal with the airfields and to keep the air force on the ground was to essentially interdict the airfields so they couldn't be used. And you can do that very quickly by trying to crater the runways.

In this particular case, this shows a British weapons system -- which I think was briefed earlier out of Riyadh, I believe by a British officer -- but it's a JP-233 which goes across the runway and is very effective at cutting concrete. And it will cut up the concrete -- break it up -- so that the airfield cannot be used for some period of hours -- and I don't want to get into how long that might be. It depends on the airfield, it depends on the kind of concrete, it depends on the kind of cut that's made -- and we'd use this weapon system and other weapon systems that we have to try to cut this airfield in a number of places to keep in from being used for a while. And then we can come back to it at our leisure and take care of what is on that airfield.

In this case, the pilot elected to cut these taxiways here so that the aircraft in these hardened aircaft shelters could not get out to the actual runway to take off. And that's that.

0218-12

0133

Let me conclude there by saying, as the Secretary said, I am satisfied with the campaign.
We have been trying to tell everybody in the beginning that we would do it in time and do it as smartly as we can. We are in no hurry. We are not looking to have large numbers of casualties. But it is

an integrated campaign, each part of the campaign bearing some relationship to the ultimate objective of ejecting the Iraqi army from Kuwait.

0278-13

0134

14

원 본

외 무 부

종 별 : 긴 급

번 호 : USW-0384 일 시 : 91 0123 1848

수 신 : 장 관 (미북,대책반,중근동)

발 신 : 주 미 대사

제 목 : 걸프 전(언론 동향)

걸프전 관련 당지 언론 동향을 아래 보고함.

1. 1.23자 W.P 지는 '' SADDAM'S WAITING GAME''제한의 기사에서 현 전황과 관련, 이락측은 연합군의 초기 공습으로부터 상당 부분의 군사력을 온전한 상태로 유지, 기습 공격을 위한 준비를 진행 시키고 있으며, 후세인의 전략은 전쟁을 최대한 지연 시키면서 지상전을 유도, 미군의 인명패히를 극대화시킴으로서 월남전에서 처럼 미국내 여론을 이용민군을 철수케 하는것이라고 경고 했음 (별첨FAX USW(F)-275 참조)

당지 전문가들도 실제 이락측의 전쟁 수행 능력이 연합국측에서 예상한것보다 강력한상태이며, 따라서 공중 폭격은 앞으로 3-4주 이상 동안 지속될것으로 예상하고있음.

2.1.23 자 NYT 및 WP 사설은 걸프 전쟁에 대한 정부의 정보 통제로 국내 여론을 오도할 위험성이 있음을 경고 했는바, 요지 아래와같음.

(별첨 FAX USW(F)-269 참조)

0 NYT 지

- ''BACK UP THE BOMBING BOASTS'' 제하의 사설에서 미 정부가 걸프전에 대한 정보를 지나치게 통제함으로서 국민들이 정확한 전황을 알수 없을뿐 만 아니라 점차 대정부 불신감이 발생하고 있다고 주장함.

- 동 사설은 연합군의 초기 공습으로 대부분의 목표물 및 군사 시설이 파괴되었다는 미국 정부의 발표와는 달리 현재 이락의 공군및 스커드 미사일이 건재하고 있음을 지적하면서 정부의 정보 통제에 따른 여론 오도는 월남전에서와 같은 결과를 낳을 소지가 있다고 우려함.

0 WP 지

- ''THE NINTENDO ISSUE'' 제한의 사설에서 금번 전쟁은 고도 정밀 무기의

미주국	장관	차관	1차보	2차보	중아국	정문국	청와대	종리실
안기부	공보처	대책반						

PAGE 1

91.01.24 09:26 WG

외신 1과 통제관

0135

성능만이 부각됨으로서 마치 일반 국민들에게는 전자 게임과 같은 착각을 불러 일으실수 있음을 지적하면서 수많은 군인들의 참전 사실및 현대 무기의 대량 살상, 파괴성, 전쟁의 참혹상등이 정확히 묘사, 올바른 여론을유도해야 한다고 주장했음.

3.한편 1.22자 CSM 은 '' THE WORLD FROM TOKYO ((제하의 기사 (USW(F)-0273) 에서, 전 세계가걸프 전쟁에 몰두해 있는 가운데 일본은 오히려 소련과의 관계 개선에 최대 역점을 두고 있으며 금년 4월로 예정된 고르바쵸프 대통령의 일본방문시 북방 영토 문제, 평화 조약 서명 문제등 양국간의 주요 현안이 타결되어 일본 외교의 새방향을 제시할 것으로 보도 했음.

동 기사는 현재 페만 사태와 관련 미국 각계에서 일본의 미온적 태도에 불만, 추가 지원을 강하게 요구하고 있으며, 또한 통상 마찰로 인해 미일 관계가 계속 악화되어 왔음을 지적하고, 일본이 소련및 아시아 국가들과의 관계 개선을 통해 외교의 다원화를 추구하게된것도 이러한 배경에서 난온 것으로 분석함.

(대사 박동진-국장)

PAGE 2

0136

국가안보관계검토 76

관리 번호	91-156

원 본

외 무 부

종 별 : 긴 급

번 호 : USW-0386 일 시 : 91 0123 1928

수 신 : 장관(미북,대책반,기정)

발 신 : 주 미 대사

제 목 : 걸프 사태 관련 국무부 브리핑

미 국무부는 1.23(수) 당지 주재 NATO 국가 대사 및 한국, 일본, 호주 대사를 초치하여 KIMMIT 정무차관이 걸프 사태 관련 미국의 입장및 연합군의 결속 필요성등에 대해 브리핑을 실시한바, 요지 다음 보고함(당관에서는 본직및 유명환 참사관이 참석함)

1. 우방국의 협조에 대한 사의 표명

-걸프 사태 관련 미국은 그간 우방국간의 긴밀한 협조를 통해 공동의 목표 달성을 위한 결속을 강화하여온데 대해 감사하며 이러한 노력을 앞으로도 계속 지속될것으로 기대함.

-이락은 금번 전쟁을 이락대 미국의 전쟁으로 이끌어 갈려고 시도하고 있는바, NATO 국가및 기타 동맹국으로 부터의 병력, 군사 지원은 이러한 이락의 기도를 저지하는데 긴요함. 특히 터키는 이락과 국경을 같이 하고 있기 때문에 전술적으로 중요한 역할을 제공하고 있음.

2. 전쟁의 목표및 성과

-미국및 연합군은 유엔 안보리 결의에 따라 쿠웨이트로부터의 이락의 완전 철수, 쿠웨이트 합법 정부의 회복 및 지역의 평화와 안전 확보라는 목표를 달성하기 위해 무력을 사용하고 있는바, 유엔 결의는 이를 위한 무력 사용의 국제법적인 근거를 마련하여 주고 있음.

-현재까지의 군사 작전은 사전에 계획된대로 진행되고 있으며, 그 성과에 대해서는 다소 상이한 판단을 할수 있겠으나 공중 폭격은 하나의 일관된 작전으로서 계속되고 있음.

-지금까지 12,000 회 출격하였으며 그중 절반은 COMBAT SORTIE 였음.

3. 걸프 사태 관련 외교적 노력

미주국 장관 차관 1차보 2차보 중아국 정문국 청와대 총리실
안기부

PAGE 1 91.01.24 11:03
외신 2과 통제관 BW
0137

-안보리 일부 회원국은 잠정 휴전을 하고 외교적 노력을 통해 사태 해결을 하는 방안을 이야기 하고 있으나 이러한 생각은 전혀 의미가 없는 것으로 봄.

-이미 미국은 이락측에 대해 지난 11.30 부터 1.15 까지 45 일간의 기간을 두고 모든 외교적 수단을 사용하였으나 전혀 타협의 소지를 보이지 않았음.

-미국은 어떠한 양보도 하지 않을것이며 유엔 결의에 명시된 목표를 완전히달성할때까지 무력 사용을 계속할것임.

4. 이스라엘의 대이락 보복

-국무부 이글버거 부장관이 이스라엘 정부와 긴밀한 협의를 한바 있으나 이스라엘 정부는 공개적으로 또한 더욱 명확한 어조로 보복할것이라고 경고 하고 있음.

-지금까지 이스라엘은 훌륭한 자제력을 발휘하여온바 있으나 스커드 미사일이 발사되고 있는 서부 이락지역에 배치되어 있는 이락군에 대한 보복도 하나의 방안으로 고려되고 있는것으로 보임.

5. 연합군에 대한 추가 지원

-미국은 우방국들의 연합군에 대한 군사적, 재정적 지원에 감사하며 추가적인 지원을 기대하고 있음.

-1.30 예정된 재정 공여국 회의는 일부 국가의 편의를 고려, 2.5 워싱턴 에서 개최하는것으로 재조정하고 있음.

6. 대 테러 대책 강화

-미국은 우방국 각국과 양자 협력을 통해 테러 정보 교환및 대처 능력을 강화하기를 희망하는바, 이락의 대항 능력이 아직 상존하고 있기때문에 경계를 늦추어서는 안될것으로 생각함.

-이락은 테러 수단을 전부 계획(BATTLE PLAN)과도 연계하여 사용할것으로 보이는바, 이들은 모두 위장된 신분으로 이동하고 있는것으로 판단하고 있음.

-미국은 예상되는 이락및 동조 세력들에 의한 테러를 사전에 방지하기 위한노력에 매우 높은 우선 순위를 두고 있음.

-미국은 걸프 사태 발발 이후 3 분야의 대책반(TASK FORCE)를 구성한바, KUWAIT TASK FORCE, CONSULAR TASK FORCE 및 TERRORISM TASK FORCE 로서, 테러 대책반은 인질에 대한 대책및 테러 위험을 사전에 탐지하여 제거하는것임.

-미국인에 대한 테러 위험을 줄이기 위해 중동 인근 지역의 미국 기관 주재인원은 필요 요원을 제외하고는 철수시킬 예정임.

PAGE 2

0138

7. 질의 응답 요지

-(이스라엘이 각의에서 대이락 보복을 하기로 결정한데 대한 견해를 문의한데 대해) 이스라엘이 원칙의 문제로서 보복하기로 결정했다는것은 처음 듣는 이야기는 아닌바, 그러한 보복이 임박한것인지는 모르고 있음.

이스라엘이 보복을 결정하는것은 군사적인 결정이라기 보다는 정치적 결정이라고 생각함.

-(아미티지 특사의 요르단 방문 목적을 문의한데 대해) 요르단은 지역적, 군사적으로 중요한 나라로서 대 이락 경제 제재 조치에 협조적인 자세를 견지하여 왔음. 더우기 이락이 요르단의 영공을 통해 이스라엘을 공격하고 이스라엘 비행기도 필요시 요르단 영공을 통해서 이락에 보복 공격을 해야 하기 때문에 요르단의 태도가 중요함. 요르단으로 하여금 연합군의 쪽에서 협조하도록 유도하는것이 필요하다고 봄.

-(유엔을 중심으로 휴전을 통해 연합군의 목적을 달성하는 방안을 문의한데대해)연합군의 무력 사용 목표는 명확하며 일관성있게 계속 이러한 노력을 경주할것이나, 그렇다고 후세인이 평화적으로 철수할수 있는 기회를 박탈하는것은 아님.유엔의 역할은 연합군의 목적이 달성되는 단계에서 감시군을 파견한다든지 또는 장기적 평화 유지 방법을 강구하는데 있어 필요할것으로 봄.현재로서는 어떠한 평화적 방안이라 할찌라도 후세인으로 하여금 다시 전투 준비를 위해 무장할수 있는 기회를 줄뿐인바 후세인이 노리는것은 지상전을 통해 많은 사상자가 발생하도록 하여 연합군의 결속을 무너트리고 반전 분위기를 고취시키는것임.

-(이스라엘이 보복할 경우 아랍 연합군에 미치는 영향을 문의한데 대해) 이스라엘이 보복한다 하더라도 그 대상이 SURGICAL STRIKE 에 국한될 경우는 아랍 연합군도 이해를 할것으로 봄.이집트 및 시리아는 이락의 이스라엘 공격을 비난하고 있으며 이스라엘의 입장을 어느정도 이해하고 있음. 이스라엘 자신도 상황이 통제할수 없는 사태로 발전하는것을 우려하고 있으며 후세인이 펼쳐논 계략에말려들지 않아야 된다는점을 잘알고 있음.

-(이락이 쿠웨이트 유전지대에 대한 방화를 자행한것인지 문의한데 대해) 동 상황이 이락측에 의해 조직적이고 광범위한 유전 지대를 대상으로 고의적으로이루어진것인지 아직 모르나, 이락이 스스로 방화할 정도로 절망적인 상태는 아직 도달하지 않았다고 생각함. 이락의 그러한 기도에 대해 미국은 이미 경고를한바 있으며 이락은 그것이 무엇을 의미하는지 알고 있을것으로 봄.

-(연합군의 공습 작전 결과와 관련 예상하지 못한 요소가 있었는지를 문의한데 대해) 이락이 스커드 미사일을 계속 발사하고 있는 상황과 관련 좀더 세밀한 검토가 필요하다고 생각하며, 당초 전투 지휘 본부에 대한 폭격을 통해 지휘망이 마비될것으로 기대하였으나, 계속 이스라엘 및 사우디에 대한 간헐적 미사일 공격을 하는등, 이락군의 작전 지휘가 계속 유지되는점에서 볼때 지하 통신망이 있는것으로 보임.

이락은 가급적 전쟁을 장기화 시켜 자신의 정치적 목표를 달성하려고 하고 있으나 연합군의 작전은 계속될것임.

-(연합군이 유아 밀크 공장을 폭격하였다는 보도와 관련한 질문에 대해) 이락은 정보 조작을 통한 심리전을 전개하고 있는바, 동 공장은 외형적으로 볼때 철조망이 쳐지고 방공포가 배치된곳임.미국은 이락이 심리전에 사용하지 못하도록 종교적 성지는 목표물에서 제외하고 있음. 이락은 병력을 학교나 회교 사원으로이동 시킴으로서 이를 악용하고 있음.

-(걸프 전쟁에 대한 중공 및 소련의 입장을 문의한데 대해) 중공및 소련은 안보리 이사국으로서 유엔 결의안 내용을 이제와서 반대할수는 없는 입장이라고 생각함. 미국은 중.소 뿐만 아니라 여타 안보리 회원들과 협의를 계속하고 있는바, 좋은 반응을 받고 있음.

예멘 및 쿠바등은 안보리 비공식 회의를 통해 자신들이 생각하는 평화안을 검토하도록 제안할것으로 알고 있는바, 전혀 현실성이 없는것이라고 봄.

(대사 박동진-국장)

91.12.31 일반

일반문서로 재분류(1991.12.31)

검 토 필 (1991.6.30.)

PAGE 4

0140

원 본

외 무 부

종 별 : 지 급

번 호 : USW-0388 일 시 : 91 0124 1212

수 신 : 장관(미북, 동구일,경일)

발 신 : 주미대사

제 목 : 소련 국내 정세에 대한 미 언론 관찰

1. 금 1.24. W.S.J. 지는 현재 세계의 관심이 걸프전에 집중되고 있으나, 이러한 위기를 틈타 더욱 중요한 변화가 일어나고 있음에 유의해야 한다는 전망을 하면서, 소련의 반동적 회귀와 중국의 억압 정책의 계속에 대한 비판 사설을 개재함

(1956 년 스웨즈 운하 위기시, 소련의 항가리 침공,1988년 미국의 정치 지도자 암살과 소련의 체코 침공등)

2.금 1.24 NYT 지는 사설을 통해 소련의 고가 어음 회수를 통한 통화 흡수 정책을 비판하고, 소련의 경제 회복은 여사한 미봉책으로 해결 불가능 하다고 지적함. 동 사설은 소련의 경제, 사회적 병리가 내부로 폭발해 가고 있으며, 고르바쵸프는 어쩔줄 모르고 허둥대고 있다고 비유함.

(대사 박동진- 구장)

미주국 구주국 경제국 1차보 안기부 중아국

PAGE 1

91.01.25 04:59 DQ

외신 1과 통제관

0141

깁

원 본

외 무 부

종 별 :

번 호 : USW-0390 일 시 : 91 0124 1533

수 신 : 장 관(미북,중근동,대책반)

발 신 : 주 미 대사

제 목 : 걸프전쟁(주요 논조)

금 1.24. 주재국 주요 일간지의 논조를 하기 보고함.

1. NYT. MURAVCHIK (AEI 연구원)기고 AT LAST, PAXAMERICANA

0 걸프전쟁은 장기적으로 3가지 중요한 여파를 미칠것임.

0 국내정치적으로 적극적 외교정책에 반대해온 민주당의 체질 개선을 가져올 것임.

0 중동 정치에 있어서는 서방 및 이스라엘에 대한 저항을 유일한 정치적 자산으로 활용해온 아랍지도자들의 퇴조를 불러올 것임.

0 국제 정치적으로는 탈냉전 국제 정치질서 수립과정에 있어 미국의 위상을 더욱 높임으로써 진정한 의미에 있어서의 PAX AMERICANA 가 구현될것임.

2. W.P SINIORA (팔레스타인 일간지 편집장) 기고 A PALESTINIAN'S PLEA

0 걸프전쟁은 서방과 이슬람의 알력을 더욱 악화시킬것임.

0 이슬람은 미국을 비롯한 서방이 쿠웨이트 침공에 대해서는 극히 민감한 반응을 보이면서도, 팔레스타인 문제에 대해서는 냉담한것을 이해할수없음.

3. W.P. MCGRORY (고정 칼럼니스트)기고 IF NOTNOW, WHEN

워싱턴에서 1.26(토) 에 대규모 반전 시위가 있을 예정임.

0 (1) 아직 지상전이 시작되지 않아 미국 사상자가별로 발생하지 않았고,

(2) 이스라엘에 대한 SCUD 미사일 공격이 이락에 대한 반감을 야기하였으므로 이번 반전시위는 큰호응을 못얻을 것으로 보이나, 참가자들의 열의는 매우 진지함.

4. W.S.J. PAUL KENNEDY (YALE 대교수, DECLINIST)A DECLINING EMPIRE GOES TO WAR

0 현재 미국이 걸프전에 개입하고 있는데에는 1630년대의 스페인과같이, 기울고 있는 국력에 대한 성가를 만회한다는 정치적 기대감이 작용하고 있음. 그러나, 미국이 성가 (REPUTATION) 을 진정으로 회복하기 위해서는 도시 재개발, 교육진흥등 국내문

미주국 장관 차관 1차보 2차보 중아국 정문국 청와대 총리실
안기부 대책반

PAGE 1 91.01.25 10:11 WG

외신 1과 통제관

0142

제부터 해결해야 함.

O KENNEDY 교수는 동기고를 통해 자신이 THERISE AND FALL OF GREAT POWERS을 통해 주장한 주요논거를 재인용하면서, 능력에 넘치는 의무를 부담하는 것은 제국주의적 과도 팽창 (IMPERIALOVERSTRETCH)의 결과를 가져올수 있다고 경고함.

(대사 박동진-국장)

원 본

외 무 부

종 별 : 지 급

번 호 : USW-0391 일 시 : 91 0124 1533

수 신 : 장관(~~미북,중근동~~,미안, 대책반)

발 신 : 주미대사

제 목 : 걸프전 전황 관련 보고

연: USW-0375

당지 주요 언론의 걸프전 전황 평가 및 분석기조를 하기 요지 보고함.

(대체로 연호 기자회견 내용을 토대로 보도)

1. 이락측이 가까운 장래에 굴복할 가능성은 별무한것으로 보이는바, 후쎄인 대통령은 예비통신 체제(BACKUP COMMUNICATION SYSTEM) 를 이용, 이락군에지휘 계통을 계속 장악하고 있는것으로 보임.

특히 이락측이 계속 SCUD 미사일을 발사하고있고, 폭격으로 인한 활주로 피해드KDKV 어느정도는지속적으로 복구하고 있는점등을 감안할때 전황을 낙관적으로 판단하기에는 어려운 측면이 있음.

2. 또한 쿠웨이트등에 주둔하고 있는 이락 지상군의경우 참호속에 은닉, 산개되어있기 때문에현재오 같은 공중 폭격으로 전력을 완전 궤멸시키기는 어려울 뿐만 아니라, 이들 지상 전력에 대한피행 상황을 공중 정찰을 통해 정확히 평가 하기도 어려움.

3. 한편, 현재 이락측은 각종 전부기드KDKV 철저히요새화된 격납고에 숨겨 놓음으로써 다국적군의공습에도 불구, 자국 공군력을 계속 보존하고 있는것으로 보이는바,해,공군력의 측면에서 자국군이다국적군의 상대가 안된다는 점을 잘인식학H선은 ''죽은체 하는 (PLAYING POSSUM)'' 시늉을하고 있는것으로 보임.

4. 여하튼 ,미측으로서는 지상전 발발시의 다국적군피해를 최소화 하기 위해 현재의 공습 위주 공격방식을 당분간 계속 유지할것으로 보이는바, 앞으로도 향후 최소 2주 이상은 지상병력이 투입되지 않을것으로 보는것이 당지의 지배적 견해이며, 또 EK지일각에서는 금번 걸프전이 최소 3개월 이상 계속될것으로 보고 있기도 함.

5. 한편, NSC 등을 중시믕로 부쉬 행정부의 걸프사태 관련 대중동 정책 검토는 계속

미주국	장관	차관	1차보	2차보	미주국	중아국	정문국	청와대
총리실	안기부	대책반						

PAGE 1 91.01.25 08:03 AQ

외신 1과 통제관

0144

되고 있는것으로 보이는바, 이락 군사력을 완전히 궤멸시키는 경우 초래될 힘의 진공상태를 이란, 실리아등이 악용할 가능성 및 중동 지역의 전전 세력 균형상태를계속 유지해야 할 필요성드KDKV 감안, 대이락무력사용의 정도와 범위를 여사한 정치적 고려 사항과 어떻게 조화 시키느냐는 상반된 고민 (CLAUSEWITZIAN DILEMMA) 이 현재 미 행정부의 주요정책검토 사항인것으로 보임.

(대사 박동진- 국장)

PAGE 2

0145

원 본

외 무 부

종 별 :

번 호 : USW-0404 일 시 : 91 0124 1824

수 신 : 장 관(중근동, 미북, 기협, 경일)

발 신 : 주 미 대사

제 목 : 유가 및 주식 동향

1.24(목) 유가 및 주식동향을 아래 보고함

1. 원유 및 석유제품 가격9뉴욕상품시장,3월 인도가격)

가. 원유: 배럴당 21.71(전일대비 0.33 불 하락)

나. 휘발유: 갤런당 63.05 센트 (전일대비 0.5센트 하락)

다. 난방유: 갤런당 69.85 센트 (전일대비 0.3 센트하락)

2. 주식 (DOW JONES INDUSTRIAL INDEX): 2,643.07 (전일대비 24.01 상승)

(대사 박동진-국장)

중아국 2차보 미주국 경제국 정문국 안기부 동자부

PAGE 1

91.01.25 10:36 WG

외신 1과 통제관

0146

원 본

외 무 부

종 별 : 지 급

번 호 : USW-0419 일 시 : 91 0125 1553

수 신 : 장 관(미북,중근동,미안,대책반)

발 신 : 주 미 대사

제 목 : 걸프전 전황 보고

금 1.25 당지 주요 언론의 걸프전 전황평가 및 분석을 전반적으로 종합한 요지를 하기 보고함.

1. 다국적군의 대이락 공격이 공습 위주로 진행됨에 따라, 이락및 쿠웨이트 상공의 기상 조건이 공습결과 판단등 다국적군 작전 수행에 큰 영향을 미치고 있음.

또한 이락측도 구름등으로 인해 공중 관찰이 용이치 않은 지역에서 SCUD 미사일을 발사 함으로서 이락측 이동식 SCUD 미사일에 대한 다국적군의 집중 파괴 노력을 어느정도는 무력화 시키고있는 것으로 보임.

2. 부쉬 행정부는 최근 기자 회견등을 통한 대언론 접촉시, 걸프 전쟁이 수개월이상 걸릴것이라는 점등을 강조함으로서 금번 전쟁이 신속히 종료될것이라는 일반 국민들의 기대감을 억제시키기위해 노력하고 있음.

특히 당초 예상했던 병력 수준(약 43만명)을 훨씬 상회하는 약 50만 이상의 미군병력이 걸프 지역에 파병될것으로 전망되는 바, 동 병력수송 작전이 종료될때까지본격적인 의미의 지상전은 시작되지 않을것으로 보임.

3. 걸프전 관련 전비는 현재 1일 평균 약 5억불이상이 소요되는바, 여사한 대규모 전비 조달을 위해서는 증세나 차관 도입등의 방법중 택일하여야함. 그러나 현재 미 경제가 불황에 빠져 80년대레이건 행정부의 군비 확장 정책을 통해TOMAHAWK 크루즈 미사일등 각종 소모성 무기의 재고가 충분한 뿐만 아니라 금번 걸프 사태의 기본성격이 임시적인점등을 감안, 증세를 통한재원 조달은 현명치 못한 방안일것으로봄.

오히려 자국 경제가 튼튼한 가운데, 중동산 원유에 대한 의존도가 크면서도 걸프 지역에 병력을 파견치 않고 있는 일본과 독일이 많은 재정부담을 져야할것임.

(대사 박동진-국장)

중아국 대책반	차관	1차보	2차보	미주국	미주국	정문국	청와대	총리실
	장관							

PAGE 1

91.01.26 07:32

외신 1과 통제관

0147

외 무 부

종 별 : 지 급

번 호 : USW-0420 일 시 : 91 0125 1553

수 신 : 장 관(미북,중근동,대책반)

발 신 : 주 미 대사

제 목 : 걸프 전쟁(언론 논조)

금 1.25 자 주재국 주요 일간지의 논조를 하기보고함.

1. NYT 사설 '' ALL THE WAY ON THE GULF ?''

0 미국이 당초의 전쟁 목표를 확대하여 후세인의 몰락,이락 군사력의 완전 붕괴등을 시도할 경우의 위험성을 경고함.

0 목표 확대시 대규모 지상전 및 인명 피해 불가피

0 이락의 완전 붕괴는 이락,시리아,터키등 인근아랍국가의 야심 자극

0 중동 지역의 세력 균형 유지를 위해 제한적인전쟁 목표 수행이 바람직

2. W.P 지(EVANS AND NOVAK 기고문) ''INTIMATIONSOF A LONG WAR''

0 부쉬 행정부내에서 장기전에 대한 우려가 고조되고있음.

0 만약 전쟁이 장기화될 경우, 연합군으니 결속악화,아랍 제국의 반감 고조,의회및 여론의 지지상실 예상

3. CSM 지 MARVIN FEUERWERGER(전 국방부 부차관보)기고문 '' A FRAMEWORKFOR WINNIG THE PEACE''

0 걸프전 종결에 시급히 대비, 추진해야할 과제로서지역의 군사적 균형 유지를 위한 구조 형성을 제시함.

- 이란-이락간 군사 균형 및 시리아 견제
- 지역 전체의 군사비 지출 제한
- 지역 군비 통제 장치 마련
- 위기시 개입을 위한 국제적 매카니즘 마련(미지상군의 장기 주둔은 부정적 효과)
- 아랍-이스라엘 분쟁등 지역분쟁 해결 촉진(미.소가 중심이된 지역 회의와 당사자간 직접 협상)

4. WSJ,NBC 합동 여론 조사 결과(WSJ 지보도)

중아국 대책반	차관	1차보	2차보	미주국	정문국	청와대	총리실	안기부

PAGE 1 91.01.26 07:42

외신 1과 통제관

0148

0 미국인의 압도적 다수가 유엔이 위임한 쿠웨이트해방이라는 목표 달성외에도이락의 군사력 파괴또는 사담 후세인의 제거등 확대된 목표에 대해서도 지지 표시

- 쿠웨이트 해방: 91 프로 찬성
- HUSSEIN 제거: 73 프로 찬성

(대사 박동진-국장) ER

PAGE 2

0149

원 본

외 무 부

종 별 :

번 호 : USW-0428 일 시 : 91 0125 1744

수 신 : 장관(중근동,미북,기협,경일)

발 신 : 주미대사

제 목 : 유가및 주식동향

1.25(금) 유가 및 주식동향을 아래 보고함.

1. 원유 및 석유제품가격(뉴욕상품시장,3월 인도 가격)

가. 원유: 배럴당 21.35 불 (전일대비 0.36 불하락)

나. 휘발유: 갤런당 63.05 센트(전일과 동일)

다. 난방유: 갤런당 69.35 센트 (전일대비 0.5센트 하락)

2. 주식 (DOW JONES INDUSTRIAL INDEX): 2,659.41 (전일대비 16.34 상승)

(대사 박동진-국장)

중아국 1차보 2차보 미주국 경제국 경제국 정문국 안기부

PAGE 1

91.01.26 08:54 ER

외신 1과 통제관

0150

홍/김

원 본

외 무 부

종 별 :

번 호 : USW-0432 일 시 : 91 0125 1758

수 신 : 장관(미북, 중근동, 영사,기정)

발 신 : 주미대사

제 목 : 걸프 사태 관련 테러 동향

1. 금 1.25. 국무부 정례 브리핑시 표제 동향 관련 TUTWILER 대변인 발표 내용을 USW(F)-0324 로 FAX 편 송부함.

동 대변인은 세계 각지의 테러 발생 및 테러현황을 일별하는 가운데 주한미대사관도 테러공격의 가능성(POTENTIAL)을 고려, 일과후 미국인들이 자주 모이는 곳에 대한 출입을 삼가토록자국인들에 대해 권고하고 있다고 설명하였음.

(대사 박동진-국장)

미주국 차관 1차보 2차보 중아국 정문국 영교국 안기부 대책반

장관

PAGE 1

91.01.26 08:52 ER

외신 1과 통제관

0151

미중(서불) 원본 김.

외 무 부

종 별 : 지 급

번 호 : USW-0447 일 시 : 91 0126 1436

수 신 : 장 관(미북,중근동,미안,대책반)

발 신 : 주 미 대사

제 목 : 걸프전 관계기사 (우방국 역할 분담)

금 1.26 W.P 1 면에 ALLIES PLEDGE MORE MONEY TO SHARE COSTS OF BATTLE 제하의 기사가 게재된바 동주요 내용 하기 보고함.(기사 원본은 USW(F)-327기송부)

0 최근 우방국들이 폐만전쟁 비용에 대한 기여금증액을 발표한데 따라, 우방국 기여금 총액은 총 300억불에 달하게됨.

0 최근 일본은 90억불,쿠웨이트는 135억불,독일은10억불을 추가 분담하겠다고 발표한바, 이는 원유의 안정적 공급으로부터 가장큰 혜택을 받는우방국이 걸프전의 비용 분담에 있어서는 형평에 어긋나게 분담을 적게하고 있다는 미국내 여론 및 미의회의 분위기를 완화하기 위한 조치임.

0 미하원 예산위 LEON PANETTA 위원장(민주-캘리포니아)은 금번 전쟁에 있어서미국이 95푸로의 군사적 부담과 희생을 지게되면, 향후 신국제 질서라는 개념은 환상에 불과한것이될것이라고 지적하면서 걸프전쟁의 비용은 우방국간에 공평히 분배되어야 하고, 우방국의 분담규모는 해당국의 경제력과 이락의 원유공급통제를 방지함으로써 얻는 반사적 이익을 감안해야한다고 언급함.

0 최근 이와관련, 우방국의 분담 규모를산출하는 방안으로 총전비를 450억불로 상정하고 이중 20 푸로는 미국, 20 푸로는 일본,나머지 60 푸로는 사우디, 쿠웨이트및 기타 걸프지역 국가가 부담한다는 원칙을 부쉬 행정부가 검토하고 있다는 소문이 있었음.

0 부시 행정부측은 작 1.25. 우방국 분담 총액목표를 밝히기를 거부하였지만, TUTWILER 국무부 대변인은 행정부가 우방국에 대한 분담규모를 주먹구구식으로 산정하고 있지 않으며, 구체적액수를 제시할것이라 밝혔음.

0 누가 전비를 부담하느냐는 문제는 이미 연 3000억불 이상의 재정.무역적자로 허덕이고 있는 미국으로서는 국가 재정에 심각한 영향을 미치는문제로 인식되고 있음.

미주국	차관	1차보	2차보	미주국	중아국	정문국	청와대	총리실
안기부	대책반	장관						

PAGE 1 91.01.27 09:20 ER

외신 1과 통제관

0152

0 쿠웨이트는 현재까지 최대의 재정지원을 공약하였으며, 가장 신속히 공약을 이행하고 있음.

사우디 아라비아는 1.17 760백만불의 현금을 미국에 지원한바 있고, 주로 (전쟁물자, 항공유, 탱크트럭 및 사우디 주둔군 지원)의 지원에 주력하고있음. 일본은 추가로 공약한 90억불은 의회의승인을 얻는 대로 모두 현금으로 지원할 예정이고, 독일은 최근 추가공약 10억불을 합쳐 총 36억불을 공약하였으며, 콜 수상은 이와는 별도로 수십 억불에 달하는 대미국 직접 지원을 언급한바 있음.

0 의회내 일각에서는 1.2일 현재 우방국들이 이행한 현금 분담금액이 45.6억불에 불과한것을 예로들며 우방국들의 분담약속 이행 태도를비난하고 있음.

0 TIMOTHY WIRTH (민주-콜로라도) 상원의원은금번 사태로 인해 예기치 않은 이익을 보고 있는산유국들의 역할 분담이 미흡함을 지적하고, 일본의 90억불 추가지원도 9일간의 전비에 불과한대수롭지 않은 것으로 평가하고 있으나, 부시 대통령은 일본의 90억불 추가지원조치에 대해 대단히만족한다고 발언한바 있음.

(대사 박동진-국 장)

PAGE 2

0153

원 본

외 무 부

종 별 :

번 호 : USW-0448 일 시 : 91 0126 1500

수 신 : 장 관(미북, 중근동, 미안, 대책반)

발 신 : 주 미 대사

제 목 : 걸프전 전황보고

금 1.26 당지 주요 언론의 걸프전 전황보도및 동관련 각계 견해를 종합한 요지를 하기 보고함.

1. 전황보도

1) 미국정부는 이라크군이 쿠웨이트 연안에 전대미문의 엄청난 양의 기름을 방출시켜 해양을오염시키고 있다고 발표함.

한편 이락측은 다국적군의 이락 유조선 공격으로 기름이 누출되고 있다고 유엔에제소함. 이락측의 기름방출 의도에 대해서는 조만간 예상되고있는 상륙작전등 다국적군의 군사작전 지연 방해, 환경테러 (ACT OFENVIRONMENTAL TERRORISM)또는 다국적군의 분열획책 기도등 다각도로 분석되고 있으나 미측은 동 기름 누출이 전쟁시작 이전에 예측되었던 가능성의 하나로 군사작전에는 별 영향이 없다고하고 있음.

또한 미국방부는 시가지 전투등 경우에따라 이락군에 대해 최류탄가스 또는 구토제와같은 전투력만 상실시키는 비살상용 가스(NONLETHAL GAS)의 사용을 허가했으며, 일부 군사전문가는 동허가가 이락측의 화학무기 사용에 대한좋은 구실을 제공할수 있다고 우려하고 있음.

2) 한편 다국적군의 대규모 지상공격을 앞두고 이락 및 쿠웨이트내 군사목표물에 대한 공습이 계속되고 있으나 기상조건으로 인해 일부 목표물에 대한 공습이 지연되고 있음.

미확인된 쿠웨이트내 소식통에 의하면 대규모 공습으로 쿠웨이트 점령 이락군 사상자가 많이 발생했으며 식량부족등 군수지원 부족으로 사기가 크게 저하된 상태라고 하고 있음.

다국적군 지휘관및 군사전문가들은 지상전의 성공적 수행을 위해서는 이락 전력의

미주국 대책반	장관	차관	1차보	2차보	미주국	중아국	총리실	안기부

PAGE 1 91.01.27 10:08 FG

외신 1과 통제관

0154

사전 무력화가 필요하며 이를 위한 공습이 최소한 2주내지 4주정도 계속되어야 할것으로보고 있음. 일부 미군 지휘관들은 특히 새로 도착한 기갑부대의 장비 및 부품의전선이동이 지연되고 있어 대규모 지상전까지 수주가 더 소요될것으로 보고 있어 조만간 대규모 지상전이 있을것으로는 예상되지 않음.

2. 각계 견해

1) W.P 지 (EDWIN M. YODER.JR. 기고문)UNCONDITIONAL SURRENDER-AN EXTRARAGANT DEMAND

0 이락에 대한 무조건 항복요구와같이 전쟁목적을 확대할 경우의 위험성 및 COST 경고.

- 2차대전 당시 무조건 항복 요구로 적의 전의를 부추켜 전쟁종결 지연.

- 한국전 당시 북진통일 정책 추구로 중국의개입 초래 및 그후 대중관계 악화.

2) W.P 지 (CARL T. ROWAN 기고문) A WARNO ONE WILL WIN.

0 전쟁 확대시의 문제점 경고 및 조기 종전주장.

- 이락내 군사시설 공격 및 사담 후세인 제거만으로 중동 평화가 이루어지지않음.

- 설사 사담 후세인을 제거하더라도 원유의 안정적공급을 위해서는 이지역에미군주둔이 불가피할지모르며, 이는 결국 미국 납세자의 부담이 될것임.

- 중동평화 및 안보를 위해 쿠웨이트 문제뿐만 아니라 팔레스타인 문제를 포함한 포괄적인 국제회의 필요.

3) 최근 각언론은 후세인의 제거 또는 전범재판 회부등을 포함. 전쟁의 목표 확대(UNCONDITIONAL SURRENDER)를 주장하는 견해들을 다수게재한바 있음.

(대사 박동진-국장)

길

원 본

외 무 부

종 별 : 지 급

번 호 : USW-0449 일 시 : 91 0126 1530

수 신 : 장 관(미북,중근동)

발 신 : 주 미 대사

제 목 : BUSH 대통령 기자회견

1. 작 1.25 부시 대통령은 공화당 전국위원회위원장 취임을 위해 사임한 YEUTTER농무장관의 후임으로 MADIG'AN 하원의원(농업위간사) 지명을 발표하는 기자회견 기회에 (동 의원회견 대동), 별전 (FAX)요지의 질의응답을가졌음.

2. BUSH 대통령은 최근 사담후세인의 잔인성에 대한 응징(전범처벌 또는 제거)여론이 높아지고 있는 가운데, 동인의 제거도 전쟁의 목적이냐는 질문에, 미국의 목표는 쿠웨이트의 해방이며, 개인이 목표물은 아니라는 기본 입장을 재차반복하면서도이락의 붕괴(DESTABILISATION)을 원하지는 않으나, 이락의 현재와같은 잔인한짓 (포 로의 고문,이용,해상오염,이스라엘 거주지에 대한 무차별 공격등)을 계속하는것은허 용치않겠다고 답변함.

3. 한편 동 대통령은 SUPER BOWL이 중지되어야되지 않느냐는 질문에 전쟁은 심각한 것이지만 일상생활은 계속 되어야하고 (LIFE GOES ON), 걸프만의 장병들의 사기를 위해서도 SUPERBOWL은 진행되어야한다고 자신감을 표명함.

미주국 1차보 중아국 대책반 그차보 차관 장관 청와대 총리실

안기부

PAGE 1

91.01.27 10:21 DP

외신 1과 통제관

0156

길

외 무 부

종 별 : 지 급

번 호 : USW-0453 일 시 : 91 0127 1755

수 신 : 장 관(미북,중근동,미안,대책반)

발 신 : 주 미 대사

제 목 : 걸프전 전황 보고

금 1.27 당지 주요 언론의 걸프전 전황 관련 주요 보도 요지를 하기 종합 보고함.

1. 이락측이 계속 방출하고 있는 원유는 걸프지역의 기상조건 (북서풍)으로 인해 빠른 속도로 남하하고 있는바, 명일쯤 사우디의 주바일항 인근에 도착할것으로 보임. 현재로서는 이락측의 여사한 환경테러 작전에 대응할 뚜렷한 대책이 없는것으로 보이며, 주바일 지역에 위치한 해수처리시설 (염분제거를 통해 해수를 담수화하는 시설로서, 리야드를 포함하는 사우디 동부지방 주민및 다국적군에 대한 식수공급원)의 가동에 도 영향이 미칠것으로 전망됨.

2. 관련 기관의 정보 판단에 따르면, 공군력에만 의존해서는 이락군의 쿠웨이트 철수를 유도하는것이 어려울 것으로 보인다 함. 즉, 이락군은 각종통신망, 활주로 및 미사일 발사대등에 대한 공습 피해를 비교적 신속하게 복구하고 있는바, 여사한 이락측의 대응능력을 감안, 미 군부내에서는 대이락 공중공격의 정책적 관심사항을 +공군력에만 의존한 대이락 승리가능여부+ 에서 + 공군력에 의한 이락군 전력 약화 가능정도+ 로 전환하였다 함. 또한 이에 따라, 실제 주요 공습 대상도 미사일 발사대 및 활주로등 전략적 목표물로부터 지상전의 승패에 관건이 되는 도로, 교량등 보급망, 일단 파괴되면 복구가 불가능한 탄약등 군수물자 저장소 및 REPUBLICANGUARD 를 포함하는 지상군 밀집배치 지역으로 전환 (SHIFT FROMSTRATEGIC INTERDICTION TO BATTLEFIELD PREPARATION) 하고있다 함.

한편, 당지 일각에서는 이락측 지상전력 (병력, 탄약재고, 통신망)의 약 30-50푸로가 파괴된후에나 다국적군 지상병력의 투입이 본격화될 것으로보고 있다하며, 따라서 금번 걸프 전쟁이 장기전화할 것으로도 예측하고 있다 함.(전술한바와 같이 이락측이 공습 피해를 신속히 복구할 수 있는 이유는 각종 케이블등 관련 물자를 충분히 비축하고 있고, 약 5만명에 이르는 전투공병단이

미주국	장관	차관	1차보	2차보	미주국	중아국	정문국	청와대
총리실	안기부	대책반						

91.01.28 08:59 WG

외신 1과 통제관

DE 0157

이란-이락전등을 통해 많은 경험과 기술을 축적했기 때문에 가능한 것으로 보인다
함.)
(대사 박동진-국장)

PAGE 2

0158

길

원 본

외 무 부

종 별 : 지 급

번 호 : USW-0454 일 시 : 91 0127 1755

수 신 : 장 관(미북, 중근동, 아일, 미안, 대책반)

발 신 : 주 미 대사

제 목 : 걸프전쟁 관련 언론 논조

금 1.27 자 주요 일간지 논조를 하기 요지 보고함.

1. NYT : JAPAN COUNTS THE COSTS OF GULF ACTION- OR INACTION+

0. 일본은 걸프사태 관련 재정지원 문제등에 대한 일반국민의 부정적 시각과 자국의 보호자(PATRON)격인 미국의 눈총사이에서 균형을 유지하기 위해 노력하고 있음.

0. 그러나 대부분의 일본인들은 금번 사태를 +강건너 불+ 정도로 인식하고 있으며, 일본정부가 재정지원 문제등관련 어떤 결정을 내리던지, 결국은 외부의 압력때문에 그러한 결정을 내린다는 인상을 주고 있음.

(NO MATTER HOW HARD THEY TRY, THE JAPANESE SEEM TO END UP LOOKING AS IF THEY ARE ACTINGIN RESPONSE TO PRESURE.)

0. 예컨데 재정 지원관련, 일본정부는 동 지원금액이 군사작전과 연관된 목적을위해 쓰여져서는 안된다는 단서를 달고 있으며, 걸프사태관련 일본정부가 보다 더적극적 역할을 담당해야한다고 주장하는 사람들도 일본이 국제적 비난을 피하기 위해서는 무언가를 해야만 한다는 소극적 입장에서 여사한 주장을 전개하고 있을 뿐임.

2. NYT 지 SADDAM AND HIS STRATEGY OF DESPOERATION+

0. 후세인은 미국과의 전쟁에서 군사적 승리를 거둘수 없다는 점을 잘알고 있는바, 다음과같은 수단을 통해 자신과 현 이락정권의 생존을확보함으로서 일종의 정치적 승리를 거두는것이 현재의 목적임.

- 전쟁의 장기화를 통한 다국적 연합군와해(아랍권에서는 모로코, 이집트, 터어키, 구라파에서는 불란서, 독일, 소련이 각각 현재의 대 이락 봉쇄전선에서 이탈할 가능성이 있음).

미주국	장관	차관	1차보	2차보	아주국	미주국	중아국	청와대
총리실	안기부	대책반						

91.01.28 09:01 FG

외신 1과 통제관

0159

- 자신을 대미 성전의 승리자로, 또 동시에 아랍권내지 제 3세계의 순교자로부각시킴으로써 선전전의 승리추구.

- 지상전 개전을 통한 다국적군의 대규모 인명손실 초래.

- 이스라엘의 개입 유도를 통한 전쟁의 확대.

0. 지금까지는 이스라엘이 대이락 보복 자제를 통해 국제적 동정을 유발하고 이락측의 전쟁포로 심문내용 방송이 오히려 국제적으로 반이락 분위기를 조성하는등 훗세인의 상기 전략이 소기의 목적을 달성치 못하고 있음.

0. 훗세인은 이락의 능력을 과대 평가하는 경향이 강한바, 자구의 전력이 궤멸하는 극한의 순간까지도 이를 인식하지 못하는 문자 그대로의 극한정책을 추구할 가능성도 있음.

(대사 박동진-국장)

김

원 본

외 무 부

종 별 :

번 호 : USW-0458 일 시 : 91 0128 1157

수 신 : 장관(미북,중근동,대책반)

미중 사본

발 신 : 주 미대사

제 목 : 걸프 전쟁 (주요 논조)

1.28 당지 주요 언론의 논조를 하기 보고함.

1. W.P 사설 POLITICS AND THE GULF

0 YEUTTER RNC 의장 및 GRAMM 상원의원은 걸프전쟁을 공화당대 민주당의 이슈로 부각시키고자 하는바, 전쟁수행을 위해 초당적 노력이 필요한 상황에서 값싼 정치적 이익을 얻으려는것은 현명치 못함.

2. W.P. WILLIAM RASPBERRY (고정 기고가) 기고 THEPSYCHIC TOLL OF A GROUNDWAR

0 미국인들은 오랜전쟁을 거부하는것이 아니라, 불분명한 목적을 위해 희생하는것을 거부하는것임.

0 전쟁이 장기화되고, 지상전이 개시되어 인명피해가 늘어나면 반전 데모가 격화될것이며, 아랍의 결속도 와해될것임.

0 BUSH 는 몇주간의 폭격후 전쟁을 일단종식시키고 경제제재로 복귀해야함.

3. NYT. MICHAEL HOWARD(YALE 대 교수) 기고 CLAUSEWITZ: MAN OF THE YEAR ?

0 CLAUSEWITZ 가 이야기 했듯이 전쟁을 이기는 3요소는 (1) 정부, (2) 군대, (3) 국민의 지지임.

0 정부와 군대가 아무리 유효하게 대처한다 하더라도 국민의 지지가 없이는 전쟁을 성공적으로 이기지 못한다는 것은 걸프 전쟁에도 그대로 적용되는 원칙임.

4. NYT. WILLIAM SAFIRE (고정 기고가) 기고 REMEMBERTHE KURDS

0 터키가 연합군에 대해 협조적 자세를 보이고 있는것은 (1) 걸프 전쟁후 전후처리과정에서 기름, 또는 영토의 배당을 받고 (2) EC 와의 관계를 강화하기 위한 것임.

0 KURD 족도 바그다드에 대해 깊은 원한을 갖고 있으므로 미국으로서는 이락에 대한 지상전을 전개함에 있어 터키와 KURD 족을 활용해야 함.

5. 관련 기사 팩시 송부함. (USW(F)-0342) .끝

미주국	장관	차관	1차보	2차보	미주국	중아국	청와대	종리실
안기부	대책반							

PAGE 1

91.01.29 06:45 DA

외신 1과 통제관

0161

길

관리 번호	91-177

원 본

외 무 부

종 별 : 지 급

번 호 : USW-0472 일 시 : 91 0128 1830

수 신 : 장관(미북,중근동,미안,대책반)

발 신 : 주 미 대사

제 목 : 걸프전 관련 부쉬 대통령 연설

1. 금 1.28 부쉬 대통령은 전국 종교 방송인 협회 회의(NATIONAL RELIGIOUSBROADCASTERS MEETING)석상에서 행한 연설을 통해, 금번 걸프 전쟁이 다음과같은 이유를 고려 도덕적으로 정당한 전쟁(JUST WAR)이라는점을 중점 강조함(연설문 전문은 USW(F)-0351 FAX 송부)

가. 대이락 공격의 목적(이락군 철수등)이 정당함.

나. 참전 목적이 달성되는 즉시, 걸프 지역 주둔 미군은 철수할것이며, 미국은 이락의 붕괴(DESTRUCTION)를 추구치 않음.

다. 금번 전쟁은 유엔등으로 부터도 국제적인 지지를 받고 있음.

라. 개전 이전, 걸프 사태를 평화적으로 해결하기 위해 모든 외교적 수단이다 동원되었음.

마. 미국은 민간인 사상자를 최소화하기 위해 노력하고 있으며, 승리에 대한 확신이 있었기에 무력 사용을 개시 했음 (결과적으로 승리치 못하는 전쟁은 JUST WAR 가 아님)

2. 금번 연설은 최근 미 국내의 각종 반전 집회및 논의를 의식, 여사한 반전론의 주요 원천이라 할 종교계 인사들을 나름대로 설득하기 위한 의도에서 행해진것으로 보이며, 금번전쟁으로 인한 이락의 지나친 불안정을 원치는 않는다고언급한점이 특히 주목됨.

(대사 박동진-국장)

91.12.31 일반

일반문서로 재분류(1991.12.31.)

검 토 필 (1991.6.30.)

미주국 대책반	장관	차관	1차보	2차보	미주국	중아국	청와대	안기부

PAGE 1

91.01.29 09:01

외신 2과 통제관 BT

0162

김

원 본

외 무 부

종 별 :

번 호 : USW-0476 일 시 : 91 0129 1455

수 신 : 장 관(미북, 중근동, 대책반)

발 신 : 주 미 대사

제 목 : 걸프전 (주요 논조)

금 1.29. 당지 주요 언론 논조를 하기 보고함.

1. W.P. JIM HOAGLAND (고정 기고가) GERMANY: TIMIDITY IN A TIME OF CRISIS

0 일부 NATO 국, 특히 도고일은 걸프전에 비협조 적임.

0 걸프전에 대한 미국의 입장은 전후 세계 질서의시 금석이라는 것인바, 독일은 NATO 는 동.서관계에만 한정되는것이고 중동과는 무관하다는 입장임.

0 이러한 독일의 태도는 구주 주둔 미군의 완전한 철수, NATO 체제의 와해로 연결될수 있음.

2. W.P. JEAN KIRKPATRICK (전주 UN 대사) AFTER THE WAR

0 중동 정치는 폭력의 저농으로 얼룩져 왔으며, 걸프전은 이러한 폭력적 전통의 산물임.

0 걸프전 이후에 중동에 평화가 정착되기 위해서는 사담 후세인, PLO 등 폭력을 옹호하는 아랍지도 세력이 철저히 분쇄 되어야 함.

0 전후 중동의 세력 균형을 위해 이락의 현 정치체제가 유지되어야 한다는 이야기는 중동의 현실을 모르는 발상임.

3. NYT, 사설 WAR'S SHARED PRICE-AND COSTS

0 우방국의 지원 약속으로 전비 부담 문제는 일단 진정된것으로 보임.

0 그러나 전쟁이 확대 될수록 우방이 직면하는 문제와 미국 국민의 반대가 확산될수 있으므로 BUSH 대통령은 전쟁의 목적이 구체적으로 무엇인가를 분명히 해야함.

4. USW(F)- 0367 참조

(대사 박동진- 국장)

미주국	장관	차관	1차보	2차보	중아국	정문국	정와대	총리실
안기부	대책반							

PAGE 1

91.01.30 09:22 WG

외신 1과 통제관

0163

길

원 본

외 무 부

종 별 : 지 급

번 호 : USW-0478 일 시 : 91 0129 1639

수 신 : 장 관(미북, 중근동, 미안, 대책반)

발 신 : 주 미 대사

제 목 : 걸프전 전황 관련 언론보도

금 1.29 당지 주요 일간지의 걸프전 전황 관련보도 요지를 하기 보고함.

1. 약 60 대의 전투기 및 폭격기를 포함하는 이락공군기 80여대가 이란으로 이동한것으로 알려짐.

현재 이란은, 금번 걸프전쟁 관련 중립을 지킨다는 기본 입장에 따라, 전기 이락공군기들도 압류할 것이라고 공식 발표하고 있으나, 이란-이락양국간에 어떤 묵계가있었을 가능성도 배제키 어려움.

2. 한편, 이락측의 원유 해상 방출 관련, 쿠웨이트내 송유 시설에 대한 미 공군기의 국부 공격(SURGICAL STRIKE)이 성공함으로써 동 원유방출은 일단 종료되었다 함.

3. 또한 작일 바그다드 주재 CNN 특파원과 훗세인 대통령간의 기자 회견 내용에 따르면, 훗세인 대통령은 전세가 막바지에 이르는경우 화학무기를 사용할수도 있다는 점을 암시했다함.

(대사 박동진-국장)

미주국	장관	차관	1차보	2차보	미주국	중아국	정와대	총리실
안기부	대책반							

PAGE 1 91.01.30 08:07 FG

외신 1과 통제관

0164

관리 번호	91-709

외 무 부

종 별 : 지 급

번 호 : USW-0525　　　　일 시 : 91 0130 2006

수 신 : 장관(미북,동구일,중근동,대책반)

발 신 : 주 미 대사

제 목 : 미소 외무장관 공동 기자 회견(걸프전)

연 USW-0323,0471

1. 소련 베스메르트닉 외무장관의 1.26-29 간 워싱턴 방문 기간중 양측간 합의 내용을 1.29 저녁 공동 기자 회견 형식으로 발표한 것과관련 , 당지 언론은대체로 다음 네가지 요인에 주목하는 견해를 보였음(USW(F)-0379,0384 참조)

-이락의 쿠웨이트로 부터의 철수 및 적대 행위 종식을 위한 최초의 구체적 방안의 제시(이락측의 분명한 철수 용의 표명 및 구체적 실천)

-이락 자체의 파괴가 목표가 아니라는 그간 미 행정부의 공약 확인

-지역 분쟁 해결 및 여타 세계적 관심사 해결을 위한 미소간의 협력 관계 유지 확인

-중동 평화 추진을 위한 미소 협력, 특히 아랍-이스라엘 분쟁 해결의 필요성 인식

2. 금번 양국 외무 장관간의 공동 발표는 최근 미국내에서 걸프전의 목표의확대(이락 정권및 군사 능력의 파괴 또는 점령)를 주장하는 여론이 점증되어 왔고, 부쉬 대통령도 수차 이락의 즉각 철군과 유엔 안보리 결의의 완전한 준수가 있기까지는 전투의 중단이 있을수 없다고 한점에 비추어 미 행정부 입장의 변화로 받아 들여지고 있음.

3. 그러나, 일부 전문가에 의하면, 소련측의 계속 확고한 협조를 필요로 하는 미 행정부측이 원칙을 타협하지 않는 선에서 유연한 입장을 보인것은, 아랍 및 유럽국가들의 일부 우려(미국이 지나치게 강경하다는 지적)를 불식하고, 연합국측의 입장을 강화하려는 전술적 차원에서 합의 되었다고 하는 관찰도 있음.

4. 그간 미 행정부는 금번 사태에 있어서 소련의 협조를 성공적 사태 해결에 필요한 중요한 요소로 간주하여 왔으며, 중동 국제 회의등 이락측의 주장에 대해 공개적으로 반대하는 입장을 표시하여 왔으나, 수차에 걸친 미소 고위 협의시에는

미주국　장관　구주국　중아국　청와대　안기부　대책반

PAGE 1　　　　91.01.31　10:52

외신 2과　통제관 FE

0165

중동 평화가 포괄적으로 다루어져야 한다는 소련측 입장에는 유연한 반응을 보여 왔음.

5. 동 미소 외무장관간 회담 상세 내용은 추보 예정임.

(대사 박동진-국장)

91.12.31 일반

검토필(1991.6.30.)

PAGE 2

0166

관리 번호	91 -144

외 무 부

종 별 : 지 급

번 호 : USW-0538　　　　일 시 : 91 0131 1842

수 신 : 장관(미북,미안,중근동,동구일,대책반)

발 신 : 주 미 대사

제 목 : 미소 외무장관 회담 II (걸프전)

연 USW-0525,0537

1. 연호 미측 브리핑(SEITZ 구주 차관보)요지는 다음과같음.

가. 개괄적 평가

-미측은 금번 미소 외무장관 회담을 통해 미국의 정책 입장에 대한 소련의 지속적 협력을 확보할수 있었다는점을 성과로 평가하고 있음.

-금번 공동 성명을 통해, 미국으로서는 기존의 입장을 변경한바 없으며, 오히려 소련이 계속 유엔 안보리 결의를 준수하고, 다국적군 연합 세력에 남아 있을것이라는점을 분명히 했다는 측면이 중요하다고 믿음.

나. 소련측 입장 개진

-소측은 걸프 사태 해결을 위한소 협력 관계를 수차 강조하고, 유엔 안보리결의의 준수를 지지하는 소측 기본 입장을 분명히 하였음(별도의 다른 내면의 의도가 없음을 강조)

-소측은 쿠웨이트 해방이라는 연합국측 목표를 지지하며, 연합국측 노력을 어렵게하는 입장을 취하지 않을것임을 약속함.

-소측은 다만, 전쟁의 질적, 공간적 확대(ESCALATION)와 이락의 파괴(DEMOLITION)는 원치 않고 있다고 하고 아직도 정치적 해결이 불가능하지 만은 않다는견해를 표시함.

다. 공동 성명 합의

-미측은 걸프만 사태 해결을 위한 양 강대국간 공동 보조를 강조하기 위해 공동 성명의 채택을 추진한바, 미측으로서는 대이락 입장 및 아랍-이스라엘 분쟁과 관련 여하한 입장의 변경도 의도하지 않았음.

-다만,-적대 행위의 종식-부분은 소측 요청에 따라 검토한바, 표현은 양측 합의에

미주국	장관	차관	1차보	2차보	미주국	구주국	중아국	청와대
안기부	대책반							

PAGE 1　　　　91.02.01 11:28

외신 2과 통제관 FE

0167

따른것임.

-미측으로서는 공동 성명을 통해 새로운 제안을 시사할 의도가 전혀 없었음.금번 성명은 기본적으로 헬싱키 공동 성명의 연장임.

2. 동 브리핑후, 금번 공동 성명 내용중 특히,-적대 행위 종식-에 관한 부분이 일반 대중과 일부 언론에 대해 과거 입장의 변경이 아닌가 하는 혼란을 주고 있다는 일부 참석자들의 질문에 대해 SEITZ 차관보는 쿠웨이트로부터의 즉각 철군과 유엔 결의의 완전한 준수를 촉구하는 미국의 기본 입장에는 전혀 변화가 없다고 수차 강조하고, 다만 이락측이 일단 철군 공약을 하고, 이를 위한 구체적조치를 즉가 취하는경우, 동 조치가 적대 행위의 일단 정지를 위한 필요 조건이된다는 의미이지 단순한 -공약-만이 어떠한 협상을 하기 위한 충분 조건이 되는것은 아니라고 설명함.

3. 또한 동 차관보는 많은 사람들이 전쟁의 수행(CONDUCT OF WAR)에만 관심을 쏟는 나머지, 외교의 고유한 기능은 계속 된다는점을 간과하고 하면서 교전 당사자간 전부 종식을 위한 조건을 제시하는것은 당연한 일이며, 연합국들의 오해가 없기를 바란다고 수차 강조함.

4. 관찰

-그간 당관의 보고와같이 미측은 금번 신임 -베- 외상 방미 를 통해 걸프 사태와 관련한 소련측의 협력을 계속 확보하는데 중점을 두었던것으로 보이는바,소측은 미.소 협력 관계의 지속, 동서 관계의 악화 방지를 위해 계속적 협조를다짐한것으로 보임.

-다만, 소측은 걸프전 개전에 따른 고르바쵸프 성명에서 보였듯이, 확전의 반대, 정치적 해결의 모색에 중점을 두어 아랍측의 명분을 보다 배려하는 입장을취했는바, 미측은 기본 입장의 훼손없이 이러한 소측 입장을 수용토록한것으로보이며, 특히 이와관련, SEITZ 차관보는 중동 평화의 정착을 위해 미국은 소련의 건설적, 적극적 역할을 환영한다고 발언함.

-당관의 관찰로는 연호 보고와같이 이락측과의 문제 해결에 있어 구체적 효과를 염두에 두고 공동 성명이 이루어진 것으로는 보이지 않으며, 미국이 외교적노력을 완전히 배제하지 않는다는점을 과시하는데 보다 큰 목적이 있었던것으로보임.

-한편, 당지 언론 일각에서는, 백악관측이 금번 공동 성명 발표 사실을 사전에 충분히 보고 받지 못했으며, 또 부쉬 대통령의 연두 교서 발표에 대한 언론COVER 가 동 공동 성명의 급작스런 발표로 인해 다소 잠식된 점을 SUNUNU 비서실장등이 크게 불평했다고 보도함(관련 상세는 FAX 편 기송부한 NYT 기사등 참조)

PAGE 2

0168

(대사 박동진-국장)

91.12.31 일반

재 분 류(1991.6.30)

PAGE 3

0169

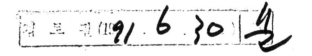

정 리 보 존 문 서 목 록

기록물종류	일반공문서철	등록번호	2012090525	등록일자	2012-09-17
분류번호	772	국가코드	US/XF	보존기간	영구
명 칭	걸프사태 : 미국의 대응, 1990-91. 전6권				
생 산 과	북미과/안보과	생산년도	1990~1991	담당그룹	
권 차 명	V.6 1991.2-3월				
내용목차	* 2.22 Bush 대통령 기자회견, 2.23 정오까지 이라크측의 쿠웨이트로부터 철군 개시 천명 2.23 미군 및 연합군, 걸프 지상전 개시 (저녁부터) 2.27 Bush 대통령 종전 선언				

0001

외 무 부

종 별 :

번 호 : NYW-0159 일 시 : 91 0203 1800

수 신 : 장관(해신,정홍)

발 신 : 주 뉴욕총영사(문)

제 목 : 걸프전쟁 2.3일 논조

1.NYT 는 사설 +PATRIOT 성과만 보고 SDI 성능을 기대할수 없음+ 에서 부시대통령이 년두교서에서 SDI 를 다시 떠올린점을 지적, 아직까지 그렇게 비용이 많이들고 기술적으로도 확실치 않은 우주 무기를 개발할 필요가 없다고 주장함.

2.NYT OPED 면 기고문 +독일과 일본의 마지못한 행동+ (WALTER RUSSEL MEAD 기)은 걸프전쟁에서 독일과 일본의 미국과 이해를 달리하는 입장이 반영되지않은 부시대통령의 +새 세계질서+를 비판하고 냉전이후 새롭고 현실적인 대외정책을 준비해야 한다고 주장함. 또 NYT 일요판 특집중 +부시의 성전 (워싱톤 지국 MAUREENDOWD기)은 대통령이 걸프전의 정당성을 주장하면서 기독교적인 윤리를 들어 도덕성을 강조한 부분이 세계의 다른 불의에 대한 미국의 책임을 무겁게하고 있다고 비판함.

3.NYT OPED 면 FOREIGN AFFAIRS 난 (LESLIE GELB 기)은 사담 후세인이 쿠웨이트 철군 조건으로 휴전을 전격 제의하여 불가피한 군사적 패배를 정치적 승리로 되돌리려고 한다고 분석하고 부시대통령의 대책을 묻고있음.

4.NYT 일요판 특집중 +경제, 아직 걸프전쟁 영향없음 +(PETER PASSELL 기)은현재 불황속에서 치루어지는 전쟁이기는 하지만 사우디가 맡고 있는 석유공급이 원활한점, 지난 20년간 축적된 재래식 무기재고가 충분한점등, 아직까지는 전쟁으로 경제가 타격을 받고있지 않다고 분석함.

한편 NYT 경제면 논평란에서는 의회예산실이 1일 전비를 7천 4백만불, 연간 270억불로 계산하고 있다고 보도함.

5.NYT 일요판 특집중 카이로 특파원 YOUSSEFIBRAHIM 은 걸프전쟁이 중동전역에걸쳐 아랍각국이 안고있는 정치체제 문제등과 맞물려 비록 동맹국 중에도 국민들간의 전쟁 찬반론이 비등하고 있어 전후대책에 관한 CONSENSUS 가 절실하다고

공보처	장관	차관	1차보	2차보	미주국	중아국	정문국	청와대
총리실	안기부	대책반						

PAGE 1 91.02.04 20:51 DA

외신 1과 통제관

0002

보도함.

6.NYT 는 국방부가 이락군 피해 예측을 발표하지 않는다는 기사에서 연합군측 피해를 사망 12명 부상 9명 실종 23명 포로 8명으로 보도함.

(원장-관장)

74

원 본

외 무 부

종 별 :

번 호 : USW-0581 일 시 : 91 0204 1712

수 신 : 장 관(미북, ~~중근동~~,미안)

발 신 : 주 미 대사

제 목 : 기사 보고

1. 금 2.4. NYT 지에 게재된 LIMITED WAR, MAXIMUM ADVATAGE 제하의 브레진스키 박사 기고문은 다국적국의 쿠웨이트 해방이라는 제한적 목표를 달성하는 선에서 금번 전쟁이 종료되어야하며, 전쟁이 장기화 하면 할수록 미국이 저야할 정치적 부담이 증대될것이라는 요지의 주장을 폄.

2.한편 금 2.4. 자 WSJ 지의 ENDING THE WAR: RANGE OF SCENARIOUS TO BRING HOSTILIES TO A CONCLUSION 제한의 기사는 후세인 대통령의 자발적 굴복 가능성과 다국적국에 의한 이락의 완전 궤멸 가능성을 공히 배제한 가운데, 금번 사태는 쿠웨이트내 이락군붕괴, 쿠데타에 의한 이락의 내부적 붕괴, 국제적 중재를 통한 이락측의 자진철군, 미군 철수등의 네가지 씨나리오중 한가지 형태로 종결될 가능성이 크다고 주장함.

(대사 박동진- 국장)

미주국	장관	차관	1차보	2차보	미주국	중아국	중아국	정문국
청와대	총리실	안기부						

PAGE 1

91.02.05 10:06 WG

외신 1과 통제관

0004

報告畢

長 官 報 告 事 項

1991. 2. 8.
中 近 東 課

題 目 : 美國의 戰後 中東 安保 構想

戰後 中東地域 平和定着 關聯 5가지 課題

①걸프지역 安全保障 ②域內 軍縮 ③經濟復舊 및 再建 ④이스라엘, 아랍, 팔레스타인間 和解, 平和 達成 ⑤美國의 對中東 에너지 依存度 減縮

베이커 美國務長官의 2.6. 下院 外務委員會 92년도 國際關係 豫算聽聞會 證言 內容中 美國의 戰後 中東 安保 構想에 대한 言及 要旨를 아래와 같이 報告합니다.

1. 미국의 전후 중동 안보 구상 내용

가. 걸프地域 安全 保障

o 目標와 原則 ①侵略沮止 ②領土 不可侵 ③紛爭의 平和的 解決

o 地域機構 및 國際社會의 役割

① 一次的으로 域內 國家와 GCC등 地域 機構의 主動的 役割

② UN 및 域外 國家들은 이러한 努力을 積極 支援

o 安保體制 構築까지의 軍事的 選擇

① 아랍 地上軍 配置 ② 유엔 平和 維持軍 派遣 ③ 域外國 地上軍 配置 (美國은 地上軍 維持 計劃 없음)

나. 걸프地域內 在來式 武器 및 大量 殺傷武器 擴散 防止

o 이라크의 大量 殺傷武器 生産 및 保有 能力 除去

o 域內 國家間 軍備 競爭 抑制

o 信賴 構築 措置 適用 檢討

0005

다. 經濟 復舊 및 再建

- ㅇ 쿠웨이트, 이라크 戰後 復舊 支援
- ㅇ 長期的으로 걸프地域內 自由貿易 및 投資 擴大 圖謀
- ㅇ 經濟成長 促進을 위한 經濟 政策 樹立 支援 必要
- ㅇ 域內 國家의 水資源 開發에 力點

라. 이스라엘, 아랍, 팔레스타인間의 진정한 和解, 平和 達成

- ㅇ 이스라엘과 팔레스타인 民族間의 對話는 中東地域 平和 定着 과정의 必須的 部分

마. 美國의 對中東 에너지 依存度 減縮

- ㅇ 에너지 保存, 에너지 保有量 增大, 대체 에너지 開發等

2. 분석 및 평가

가. 미군 장기주둔등 미국의 정책구도에 대한 의구심 해소

- ㅇ 전후 중동안보문제는 일차적으로 역내 국가들의 책임이며 역외 국가들은 지원 차원에 머물것임과 미지상군 유지 계획이 없음을 분명히 밝힘으로써 아랍권등 일부의 의구심 해소 노력

나. 전후 중동지역 안보 협력체제 윤곽 시사

- ㅇ 중동평화 안보유지 관련한 GCC등 지역기구의 역할을 강조, 전후 지역안보 체제가 일부 서방권에서 논의되고있는 GCC Plus 구상(GCC 6개국에 이집트등 온건 아랍국 포함)에 가까와질 가능성 시사

다. 이라크의 공격용 군사력 제거방침 공식 확인

- ㅇ 베이커 국무장관이 직접 이라크의 대량 살상무기 생산 및 보유능력 제거 방침을 언급, 주변국에 위협이 되는 이라크의 강대한 군사력 (특히 비재래식 무기)을 제거하는 것이 미국의 전쟁 목표의 하나임을 공식 확인

라. 팔레스타인 문제 해결을 위한 국제적 노력 강화 전망 시사

- ㅇ 이스라엘과 팔레스타인 민족간의 대화가 중동지역 평화 정착 과정의 필수적 부분이며 미국이 이를 위해 계속 노력할 것임을 언급, 전후 팔레스타인 문제 해결을 위한 국제적 노력 강화 전망 시사
- ㅇ 팔레스타인 문제 해결에 있어 이집트, 사우디등 반이라크 아랍국가의 역할 증대 시사(단, 미국의 구체적 복안은 불언급)

0006

마. 중동지역에서의 자본주의 시장 경제 확산 주창

o 전후복구 이후 역내 자유무역 및 투자 확대, 경제성장을 촉진하는 경제정책 수립 지원 필요성을 천명, 중동국가들이 자본주의 시장 경제를 적극 도입토록 간접 촉구 (미국, 수원국의 자본주의 시장 경제 채택을 원조 공여 기준의 하나로 시행중).

바. 아랍권내 반미, 반서방 감정 고조 현상에 대한 대응

o 베이커 국무장관이 이 시점에 생기 대응을 밝힌 것은 걸프전이 계속되면서 다국적군의 공습으로 민간인 희생과 이라크 피해가 늘어감에 따라 아랍권내 반미, 반서방 내지 친이라크 대중운동이 확산되고 회교원리주의자들이 동 운동을 선동하고 있는데 대해 대응 필요성을 느꼈기 때문으로 보임.

o 팔레스타인 문제 해결 노력 강화 및 전후 이라크 복구지원 의사 표명과 기존의 경기 부흥 가능성 부인 등은 이러한 맥락에서 나온 것으로 분석됨. 끝.

0007

報告畢

長 官 報 告 事 項

1991. 2. 9.
中 近 東 課

題 目 : 美國의 戰後 中東 安保 構想

戰後 中東地域 平和定着 5個項 課題

①걸프지역 安全保障 ②域内 軍縮 ③戰後復舊 및 復興 ④이스라엘, 아랍, 팔레스타인間 和解, 平和 達成 ⑤美國의 對中東 에너지 依存度 減縮

베이커 美國務長官의 2.6. 下院 外務委員會 92년도 國際關係 豫算聽聞會 證言 内容中 美國의 戰後 中東 安保 構想에 대한 言及 要旨를 아래와 같이 報告합니다.

1. 美國의 戰後 中東 安保 構想 内容

가. 걸프地域 安全 保障

- 目標와 原則 ①侵略沮止 ②領土 不可侵 ③紛爭의 平和的 解決
- 地域機構 및 國際社會의 役割
  ① 一次的으로 域内 國家와 GCC등 地域 機構의 主動的 役割
  ② UN 및 域外 國家들은 이러한 努力을 積極 支援
- 安保體制 構築까지의 軍事的 選擇
  ① 아랍 地上軍 配置 ② 유엔 平和 維持軍 派遣 ③ 域外國 地上軍 配置 (美國은 地上軍 維持 計劃 없음)

나. 걸프地域内 在來式 武器 및 大量 殺傷武器 擴散 防止

- 이라크의 大量 殺傷武器 生産 및 保有 能力 除去
- 域内 國家間 軍備 競爭 抑制
- 信賴 構築 措置

0008

다. 戰後 復舊 및 復興

o 쿠웨이트, 이라크 戰後 復舊 支援

o 長期的으로 걸프地域內 自由貿易 및 投資 擴大 圖謀

o 經濟成長 促進을 위한 經濟 政策 樹立 支援 必要

o 域內 國家의 水資源 開發에 力點

라. 이스라엘, 아랍, 팔레스타인間의 진정한 和解, 平和 達成

o 이스라엘과 팔레스타인 民族間의 對話는 中東地域 平和 定着 과정의 必須的 部分

마. 美國의 對中東 에너지 依存度 減縮

o 에너지 保存, 에너지 保有量 增大, 대체 에너지 開發等

2. 分析 및 評價

가. 美軍 長期駐屯等 美國의 政策構圖에 대한 ~~依舊~~疑懼心 解消

o 戰後 中東安保問題는 一次的으로 域內 國家들의 責任이며 域外 國家들은 支援 次元에 머물것임과 美地上軍 維持 計劃이 없음을 분명히 밝힘으로써 아랍권등 一部의 ~~依舊~~心 解消 努力

나. 戰後 中東地域 安保 協力體制 輪廓 示唆

o 中東平和 安保維持 關聯한 GCC등 地域機構의 役割을 强調, 戰後 地域安保 體制가 一部 西方圈에서 論議되고있는 GCC Plus 構想(GCC 6個國에 이집트등 온건 아랍국 포함)에 가까와질 可能性 시사

다. 이라크의 攻擊用 軍事力 除去方針 公式 確認

o 베이커 國務長官이 直接 이라크의 大量 殺傷武器 生産 및 保有能力 除去 方針을 言及, 周邊國에 威脅이 되는 이라크의 강대한 軍事力 (특히 非在來式 武器)을 除去하는 것이 美國의 戰爭 目標의 하나임을 公式 確認

라. 팔레스타인 問題 解決을 위한 努力 强化 示唆

o 이스라엘과 팔레스타인 民族間의 對話가 中東地域 平和 定着 過程의 必須的 部分이며 美國이 이를 위해 繼續 努力할 것임을 言及, 戰後 팔레스타인 問題 解決을 위한 努力 强化 示唆

0003

o 팔레스타인 問題 解決에 있어 아랍國家의 役割을 强調한 것은 이집트, 사우디等 穩健아랍國의 役割을 增大시키려는 意圖인 것으로 보임. (단, 美國의 具體的 腹案은 不言及)

o 팔레스타인 問題 解決을 위한 美側의 誠意 表示는 사담후세인의 걸프 事態와 팔레스타인 問題 連繫 主張 및 유엔 決議 不移行 關聯 이스라엘과 이라크를 놓고 二重基準을 適用한다는 이라크側의 非難을 意識한 結果로 分析됨.

마. 中東地域에서의 資本主義 市場經濟 擴散 主唱

o 戰後復舊 以後 域內 自由貿易 및 投資 擴大, 經濟成長을 促進하는 經濟政策 樹立 支援 必要性을 闡明, 中東國家들이 資本主義 市場經濟를 積極 導入토록 間接 促求

바. 아랍권내 反美,反西方 感情 高潮 傾向에 대한 對應

o 베이커 國務長官이 이時點에 상기 內容을 밝힌 것은 걸프전이 繼續되면서 多國籍軍의 空襲으로 民間人 犧牲과 非軍事施設 被害가 늘어감에 따라 아랍권내 反美, 反西方 내지 親이라크 大衆運動이 擴散되고 回教 原理主義者들이 동 運動을 煽動하고 있는데 대해 對應 必要性을 느꼈기 때문으로 보임.

o 베이커 長官의 發言 內容中 팔레스타인 問題 解決 努力 强化 및 戰後 이라크 復舊支援 意思 表明과 美軍의 長期 駐屯 可能性 否認等은 이러한 맥락에서 나온 것으로 分析됨. 끝.

0010

관리 번호	91-1407

외 무 부

종 별 : 긴 급

번 호 : USW-0692 일 시 : 91 0211 1811

수 신 : 장관(미북,아일,중근동)

발 신 : 주 미 대사

제 목 : 부쉬 대통령 방일

연: USW-0433

당관 안호영 서기관은 금 2.11 국무부 일본과 WINTON 부과장과 접촉, 부쉬 대통령 방일 가능성및 기타 일.미 관계 현안에 대해 탐문한바, 동 내용 하기 보고함.(이하 MINTON 부과장 발언 내용)

1. 걸프전의 확전으로 말미암아 4 월 중순으로 예정된 고르바쵸프의 방일 이전에 BUSH 대통령이 방일할 가능성은 거의 없다고 봄.이에 따라 가이후 수상이90.3 PALM SPRINGS 방문에 이어 다시 방미하여 고르바쵸프 방일에 대비한 일.미 협의를 갖는 방안이 논의되고 있음(아직 구체화된 계획이 아니므로 각별한 보안 유지를 요청)

2.(90 년 하반기 유엔 평화 협력 방안 토의시 가이후의 친미 성향에 대한 비판이 제기 되었던바, 가이후 수상이 BUSH 의 답방없이 2 번에 걸쳐 방미하는 것이 이러한 정치적 부담을 악화 시키지 않을지 문의한데 대하여) 가이후 수상의친미 성향에 대한 비난은 주로 사회당등 야권에서 나오는것이고, 자민당 내에서는 미.일 관계의 건전한 유지가 책임있는 정치인의 덕목으로 간주되므로 그러한 문제는 심각한것이 아니라고 생각됨.

3.(일본이 약속한 걸프전 지원 경비 90 억불의 일본 의회 통과 전망을 문의한데 대하여) 공명당의 협조를 얻는것이 중요한바, 공명당은 (1) 일본이 지원하는 경비가 살상용 무기 구입에 사용되어서는 안되고,(2) 동 경비 마련을 위해 급격한 증세가 이루어져서는 안되며,(3) 이번 조치가 자위대 중동 파견으로 이어져서는 안된다는 입장을 견지하고 있음.

4. 그러나 (1)의 문제는 국무부의 해명으로 해결이 되었고(일본의 지원이 비살상 무기 구입에 사용되도록 한다는 TUTWEILER 대변인원 발언), (2) 의 문제는 90 억불의 일부를 기존 예산으로 충당하는 식으로 해결되며,(3)에 대해서도 자민당과 일본

미주국 장관 차관 1차보 2차보 아주국 중아국 청와대 안기부

PAGE 1 91.02.12 09:26

외신 2과 통제관 BW

0011

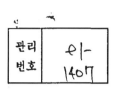

정부가 응분의 배려를 하고 있는것을 알고 있음.(가령 자위대 소속 C-130 중동 파견이 90 억불 의회 통과에 장애가 된다면 수송기 파견 계획을 취소)일본 정부는 현재 야당과의 비공식 협의를 갖고 있는바, 법안 제출은 다음주 중에 있을것으로 예상됨.

5. (90 억불 지원이 일본 정치에 미칠 파장을 문의한데 대하여) 그럴 가능성이 많지는 않으나 90 억불 지원안이 의회 통과에 실패하면 가이후 수상의 정치적 위상에 막대한 손실이 올것이고, 의회 통과가 된다 하더라도 90 억불에 달하는 증세라는것이 국민들로서는 매우 부담 스러운 것이므로 가이후 수상이 당장은아니더라도 금년 하반기로 예정된 자민당 당수 선거시에 가이후에 대해 정치적책임을 묻게될 가능성이 많은것으로 봄(MINTO 부과장은 금번 조치로 인한 정치적 책임을 1960 년 일미 방위 조약 개정시 이를 통과 시킨 기시 수상이 사임한것이 비유)

(대사 박동진-국장)

91.12.31 일반 검 토 필(1991.6.30)

PAGE 2

0012

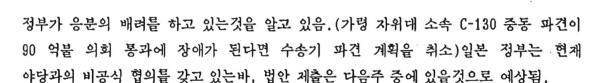

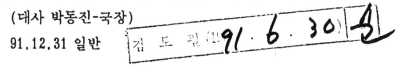

원 본

외 무 부

종 별 :

번 호 : USW-0737 일 시 : 91 0213 1742

수 신 : 장 관(미북,중근동,대책반)

발 신 : 주 미 대사

제 목 : 걸프전 (이락 민간인 대규모 사상)

1. 2.12. 연합군 폭격에 의해 이락 민간인 수백명의 사상자가 발생한것과 관련, 백악관 FITZWATER 대변인은 특별 성명을 발표하고, 국무부 TUTWEILER 대변인도 정오 브리핑을 통해 긴 논평을 행하는등, 주재국은 동사건으로 말미암은 미국에 대한 국제적 비난과 반전무드 확산방지를 위해 최대한의 노력을 경주하고 있는 것으로 관찰됨.

2. FITZWATER 대변인은 (1) 수백명의 사상자가 발생한 시설이 민간인을 위한 방공호가 아니고 이락군의 지휘.통제 본부인데 이락이 의도적으로 민간인을 동군사목표에 밀집시킨 것이며, (2)이락은 다른곳에서도 민간인을 이용한 군사목표 보호를 실시하고 있고, (3) 민간인 살상이 결국 후세인의 쿠웨이트 침공에 기인한것임을 강조하였고, 국무부도 같은 취지의 논평을 행함.

3. 백악관 및 국무부 논평 전문 별첨 송부함.

첨부: USW(F)-0543)

(대사 박동진-국장)

미주국	장관	차관	1차보	2차보	중아국	정문국	청와대	총리실
안기부	대책반							

0013

PAGE 1

91.02.14 10:08 WG

외신 1과 통제관

[illegible] : USW(F) - 05[illegible]

수신 : 장 관 (미북, 중동1, 대책반) 발신 : 주미대사 | 보 안 통 제 | [illegible]

제목 : USW-0737 의 첨부물 (2 매)

STATEMENT BY WHITE HOUSE SPOKESMAN MARLIN FITZWATER, THE WHITE HOUSE
11:45 A.M., EST, WEDNESDAY, FEBRUARY 13, 1991

MR. FITZWATER: Last night coalition forces bombed a military command and control center in Baghdad that, according to press reports, resulted in a number of civilian casualties.

The loss of civilian lives in time of war is a truly tragic consequence. It saddens everyone to know that innocent people may have died in the course of military conflict. America treats human life as our most precious value. That is why even during this military conflict in which the lives of our servicemen and women are at risk we will not target civilian facilities. We will continue to hit only military targets.

The bunker that was attacked last night was a military target, a command and control center that fed instructions directly to the Iraqi war machine, painted and camouflaged to avoid detection, and well documented as a military target. We have been systematically attacking these targets since the war began.

We don't know why civilians were at this location, but we do know that Saddam Hussein does not share our value in the sanctity of life. Indeed, he time and again has shown a willingness to sacrifice civilian lives and property that further his war aims. Civilian hostages were moved in November and December to military sites for use as human shields. POWs reportedly have been placed at military sites. Roving bands of execution squads search out deserters among his own ranks of servicemen. Command and control centers in Iraq have been placed on top of schools and public buildings. Tanks and other artillery have been placed beside private homes in small villages. And only this morning, we have documentation that two MiG-21s have been parked near the front door of a treasured archeological site which dates back to the 27th Century B.C. His environmental terrorism spreads throughout the Persian Gulf, killing wildlife and threatening human water supplies. And finally, Saddam Hussein aims his Scud missiles at innocent civilians in Israel and Saudi Arabia. He kills civilians intentionally and with purpose.

Saddam Hussein created this war. He created the military bunkers, and he can bring the war to an end. We urge him once again to save his people and to comply with the UN resolutions.

Thank you very much.

Q What do you mean "thank you very much"? We'd like to ask you some questions.

543-1 Q Aren't we having a briefing?

Q Marlin?

STAFF: Can I have your attention, please. The briefing will continue in one minute. That will be regular briefing rules.

배부처	장관실	차관실	一차보	二차보	기획실	의전장	아주국	미주국	구주국	중아국	국기국	경제국	통상국	정문국	영교국	총무과	감사관	공보관	외[illegible]

0014

STATE DEPARTMENT REGULAR BRIEFING, BRIEFER: MARGARET TUTWILER
12:17 PM, WEDNESDAY, FEBRUARY 13, 1991

I would tell you from the State Department, to parallel what Marlin himself has already expressed, that we deeply regret any civilian casualties that result from our actions. It is not the policy of the United States government to intentionally target civilians. It is the policy of Saddam Hussein. For our part, we have gone to extreme length, often at the risk to our own pilots, not to target civilians or areas where they live. Indeed, any civilian casualties are a result of a war that Saddam Hussein imposed. Had he complied with the will of the international community, ended his aggression and withdrawn from Kuwait there would be no war.

Unfortunately and tragically, the Iraqi people are paying the price for his aggression. The United States did not invade, annex, or destroy Kuwait; Saddam Hussein did. It is Saddam, not the allied coalition, who continues to put his narrow ambitions above the well-being of his people and the welfare of his country. It is Saddam Hussein, not the allied coalition, who continues to purposely attack civilian targets in Israel and Saudi Arabia. It is Saddam Hussein, not the allied coalition, who abuses prisoners of war and destroys the ecology of the Gulf. It is Saddam Hussein, not the allied coalition, who continues to defy the will of the entire international community. And it is Saddam Hussein who has the ability to stop the violence by immediately withdrawing from Kuwait. But once again, his personal, ruthless ambitions makes him indifferent to the cost to his own people.

END

0543-2

-0015

원 본

외 무 부

긴

종 별 : 긴 급

번 호 : USW-0757 일 시 : 91 0215 0929

수 신 : 장관(미북,중근동,대책반)

발 신 : 주미대사

제 목 : 걸프전(이락의 철군 시사)

1.이락의 쿠웨이트 로 부터의 철군 시사 성명과 관련,

백악관 FITZWATER 대변인은 금 2.15. 08:30 짤막한 성명을 발표,

(1) 이락 성명의 전문을 입수하지는 못하였으나 이락의 철군 제의는 전제조건을단것으로 이해되며 ,

(2) 이락은 말보다 행동으로 철군의지를 보여야 할것이라고 함.

2. BUSH 대통령은 금 2.15. 메사츄세츠주 엔도버에 소재하는 PATRIOT 미사일공장을 방문하고,메인주 KENNEBUNKPORT 에서 주말을 보낼 예정이었는바, BUSH 대통령이 동 계획을 취소할지 여부는 알려지지 않고 있음.

3.당지 방송에 의하면 미 국방성은 이락의 금번 성명에 관계없이 군사작전을 계속 수행할 의지를 표명하였다 하며, 한편 사담 후세인이 금번 성명을 통하여 쿠웨이트로 부터 철군 할 경우

(1) 후세인이 계속 상당한 군사력을 유지하게 하고,

(2) 미국을 비롯한 서방 세계에 대해 아랍의 저력을 보여준 지도자라는 정치적 소득을 누리게 되며,

(3) 금번 성명이 PRIMAKOV 소련 특사의 이락방문등 소련을 중심으로 한 외교적 중재의 소산이라는 인상을 주게 될 경우 금후 중동 정치에 있어 소련의 영향력이 증대 될것이라는 등의 분석이 대두되고 있는바, 금번 성명에 대한 주재국 평가등 추보위계임.

4. FITZWATER 대변인 성명 팩스 (USW(F)-0561)

송부함.끝

(대사 박동진-국장)

미주국 장관 차관 1차보 2차보 √중아국 정문국 √상황실 청와대
총리실 안기부 √대책반

PAGE 1 91.02.16 00:21 DQ

외신 1과 통제관 개

0016

번호 : USW(F) - 0501   0215 0910

수신 : 장 관(미북, 중근동, 대책반) 발신 : 주미대사

제목 : USW - 757 첨부물

보안 통제	

(1 매)

WHITE HOUSE STATEMENT ON ANNOUNCEMENT TODAY BY THE REVOLUTIONARY COMMAND COUNCIL OF IRAQ, WHITE HOUSE BRIEFING ROOM, 8:30 AM (EST)
FRIDAY, FEBRUARY 15, 1991

MARLIN FITZWATER: We have not yet examined a full official text of the Revolutionary Command Council's statement. But it clearly contains conditions for Iraqi withdrawal from Kuwait.

The United Nations Security Council resolutions are clear in their insistence that the withdrawal be complete and unconditional. Promises alone are not sufficient. There must be not only agreement to comply with all United Nations Security Council resolutions, but also immediate and concrete actions on the ground.

Thank you very much.

END

0017

관리 번호	91-420

원 본

외 무 부

김

종 별 : 긴 급

번 호 : USW-0766 일 시 : 91 0215 1548

수 신 : 장관(미북,중근동,대책반)

발 신 : 주 미 대사

제 목 : 이라크 철군 발표에 대한 미측 반응(1)

대 WUS-0600

연 USW-0757

1. 금 2.15 오전(10:00) 부쉬 대통령은 미 과학 진흥협회(AMERICAN ACADEMYFOR ADVANCEMENT OF SCIENCE)회의 석상에서의 연설을 통해 이락측의 금번 철군제안이 "터무니 없는 속임수(CRUEL HOAX)"에 불과할뿐만 아니라, 오히려 새로운 조건을 제시하고 있다고 동 제안을 일축하였는바, 부쉬 대통령 주요 언급 요지 하기 보고함(관련내용 USW(F)-0568 로 FAX 송부)

가. 이라크 군은 쿠웨이트로부터 무조건 철수 하여야하는바, 역내 여타 문제와의 연계는 철수라고할수 없음.

나. 이락군의 대규모 철수가 가시적으로 실현 되지 않는한, 다국적군의 현재 작전은 계속 진행될것임.

다. 이락군부와 이락 국민들이 후세인 축출을 위해 자발적으로 필요한 조치를 취하는것도 걸프 사태를 평화적으로 해결하는 또다른 한 방법일것임.

2. 당관 관찰

가. 전기 연설시, 부쉬 대통령은 자신도 이락측의 철군 소식을 듣고 당초는다행으로 생각하였으나 이락측 발표문을 정밀 분석하고 우방국들과 의견을 긴급히 교환해 본바, 이락측이 속임수를 쓰고 있는것으로 결론이 내렸다고 하고, 이에 따라 현재의 군사 작전을 계속 진행 시켜 나가기로 하였다고 언급하였는바, 심리전적 차원에서 미국 내외의 여론이 이락측 제안에 현혹되지 않도록 주의를환기 시키고 있는것으로 보임.

나. 기본적으로 현재 미 행정부는 금번 이락측 제안을 시간을 벌기 위한 전술적 차원의 태도 변화로 평가하고 있는것으로 관찰되는바, 이락측이 철군하고 있다는

미주국	장관	차관	1차보	2차보	중아국	정문국	청와대	안기부

PAGE 1 91.02.16 07:20

외신 2과 통제관 CW

0018

명시적 증가가 드러나기 전까지는 여사한 부정적 평가를 계속 유지할것으로 전망됨.

다. 또한 공습 위주의 대이락 공격이 성공적으로 진행되고 있는 현 상황하에서, 미측으로서는 군사적인 관점에서 볼때 동 작전을 중단하지 않는것이 바람직 하다고 인식하고 있는것으로 보이며, 금번 걸프 사태가 향후 어떠한 방향으로전개되든(즉, 이락측이 쿠웨이트로부터의 철군을 실행에 옮기든, 아니면 지상전이 개시되든지 간에 상관없이) 미측으로서는 이락측 지상 전력의 50 프로 파괴라는 당초의 군사적 목표를 그대로 추구하는것이 유리하다고 판단하고 있는것으로 보임(이락측 전력의 파괴 정도등에 대해서는 FAX 편 기 송부한 금일자 NYT 기사 참조)

라. 현재까지의 미측 태도로 보아 이락측이 "연계"조건등을 포기하지 않는한 미측의 대이락 공격은 계속 진행될것으로 보이는바, 이와 관련 다국적군에 참여하고 있는 아랍권 국가들의 동향 및 쏘련의 태도가 향후 주요 변수로서 작용할것으로 전망됨. 한편, 금일 연설시 부쉬 대통령도 다국적 우방국간의 협의 과정에서 이락측이 쿠웨이트 철수 의사를 처음으로 인지한 점은 주목을 받았다고(RECOGNIZE)언급 하였는바, 이 행정부로서도 외교적으로 수세에 처하지 않도록 세심한 배려를 하고 있는것으로 보임.

(대사 박동진-국장)

예고:91.12.31 일반

일반문서로 재분류(1991.12.31.)

검 토 필 (1991.6.30.)

PAGE 2

0019

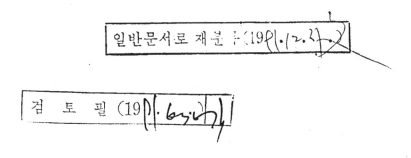

관리번호	91-423

원 본

외 무 부

종 별 : 긴 급

번 호 : USW-0774 일 시 : 91 0215 1727

수 신 : 장관(미북,중근동,대책반)

발 신 : 주 미 대사

제 목 : 이라크 철군 발표에 대한 미측 반응(2)

연 USW-0757(1),0766(2)

1. 금 2.15 오후 부쉬 대통령은 메사추세츠주 엔도버 소재 RAYTHEON MISSILE SYSTEMS PLANT(패트리어트 미사일 제조 공장)를 방문, 미사일 생산 공정에 참여하는 근로자들을 위한 격려 연설에서도 연호(2)와 동일한 내용으로 이락측의 무조건 철군을 재 촉구함(연설문 전문은 USW(F)-0588 로 FAX 송부)

2. 한편[84f2. 한편, 부쉬 대통령은 PRESIDENT'S DAY(2.18)가 포함된 이번 주말 연휴 기간을
연호(1)의 예정대로 KENNEBUNKPORT 별정에서 보낼 예정이라함.

3. 또한 전기 1 항의 연설에 앞선 기자들과의 질의, 응답시도 부쉬 대통령은 대이락 공격을 중단치 않을것이라는 점을 재강조 하고, 금번 이락측 제안이 다국적군 참여국간의 결속에 아무런 영향을 미치지 못하고 있다고 강조함(질의, 응답 전문은 USW(F)-0587 로 FAX 송부)

(대사 박동진-국장)

예고:91.12.31 일반

일반문서로 재분류(1991.12.31.)

검 토 필 (1991.6.30.)

미주국 장관 차관 1차보 2차보 중아국 정문국 청와대 안기부

PAGE 1

91.02.16 07:58

외신 2과 통제관 CW

0020

번호 : USW(F) - 0587

수신 : 장관(미북,중근동,미안보) 발신 : 주미대사

보안 통제

제목 : 패트리어트 미사일 공장 방문시 부쉬대통령 대언론 질의, 응답 (2 매)

QUESTIONS AND ANSWERS WITH PRESIDENT BUSH
DURING A PHOTO OPPORTUNITY AT RAYTHEON MISSILE SYSTEMS PLANT
ANDOVER, MASSACHUSETTS/FRIDAY, FEBRUARY 15, 1991

Q Mr. President, is there any indication that Iraqis are turning around and going home?

WHITE HOUSE STAFF: (To press.) Okay, lights please. Thank you.

PRESIDENT BUSH: What was that?

Q Do you think that it's words only -- this Iraqi statement?

PRESIDENT BUSH: What statement? You mean this morning?

Q Yes.

PRESIDENT BUSH: Oh, there's no evidence of any withdrawal. I mean, as I said down in Washington, it is a -- it's a cruel ploy. What he did was reiterate some conditions and add some new ones, and it's totally unacceptable to everybody.

You know, my heart goes out to the people that -- in Iraq that you saw kind of jumping with joy early on, firing their weapons -- which is, I guess there, a sign of joy -- in the air -- and only to recognize when the fine print came out that it was a step backwards. So there's no sign of any withdrawal. I wish there were -- so does the whole world.

Q No sign of hope at all?

Q (Inaudible) -- the coalition, sir?

Q What do you think the use of the word "withdraw" means? It's the first time we've heard that.

PRESIDENT BUSH: I don't know. It doesn't mean the compliance with the United Nations resolutions. Until that happens, regrettably, there will not be a cessation of hostilities. There will be no pause, be no cease-fire, there will be no reliving experiences in the past that were unhelpful to a peaceful, satisfactory conclusion of the war. And so there's nothing in this thing to offer hope. I wish I thought there was, but no.

Q Any sign, sir, that this affects any members of the coalition?

PRESIDENT BUSH: No, they're all -- the ones we talked to are all solid and got on this thing the minute they saw the -- saw the declaration coming out of Baghdad, pronounced it -- pronounded it -- (with initiative?) -- pronounced it dead on arrival because there wasn't anything new or significant. There was just some more

0587-1

0021

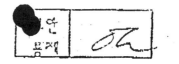

conditions, including asking the American taxpayer to pay for -- pay for damage in Iraq. It's the other way around. The reparation sanctions are called for under the United Nations, reparations where Iraq undoes the damage that it's done to its neighbors. I don't know how you would pay for the loss of human life in Kuwait, the brutality to 15- to 20-year-old Kuwaitis just this last week. You can't make amends for that.

But this was a cruel ploy and the world saw it as such, including the coalition, which is just as solid today as it's ever been.

Now I've got to get on and learn something more about the Patriot. But thank you all very much.

Q Thank you.

END

0587-2 (END)

0022

관리 번호	91-402

원 본

외 무 부

김

종 별 : 지 급

번 호 : USW-0777 일 시 : 91 0215 1754

수 신 : 장관(미북,중근동,대책반)

발 신 : 주 미 대사

제 목 : 이락의 철군 발표에 대한 미측 반응

대: WUS-0600

1. 대호 관련, 당관 유 참사관은 금 2.15 국무부 정무 차관실 KARTMAN 보좌관을 면담하여 미측의 반응을 문의한바, 다국적군 지상군의 투입이 임박함을 감지한 후세인 대통령이 이를 지연시키기 위하여 어중간한 성격의 철수 제안을 내놓은것으로 본다고 말하고, 동 제안 발표직후 바그다드 시민들이 축제 분위기로 들떠 있었다는 사실은 이락측의 이번 전쟁이 국민적 지지를 받지 못하고 있다는점을 여실히 들어내고 있는바, 이러한 분위기가 쿠웨이트등 일선의 이락군들에게도 전달되는 경우는 오히려 군부내의 전투 의지가 크게 저하됨으로서 추후 다국적군의 지상 작전을 보다 용이하게 만들수도 있을것으로 본다고 설명함.

2. 또한 동 보좌관은 지상 전투가 개시되든 아니든 지금까지의 상황을 종합적을 볼때 전쟁이 오래 지속되지 않을것으로 본다는 낙관적인 견해를 표명하면서,최근 소련이 전후 아랍국에 대한 발언권 및 입지 확보를 위해 외교적인 제스쳐를 강화함으로서 미국으로서도 다소 부담이 되고 있다고 말함.

(대사 박동진-국장)

91.12.31 일반

일반문서로 재분류(1991.12.31.)

검 토 필(1991.6.30.)

미주국	장관	차관	1차보	2차보	중아국	정문국	청와대	총리실
안기부								

PAGE 1

91.02.16 09:42

외신 2과 통제관 BW

0023

관리 번호	91-425

7/2

외 무 부

종 별 :

번 호 : FRW-0575 일 시 : 91 0215 1750

수 신 : 장관(중일,구일,미북,정일)

발 신 : 주 불 대사

제 목 : 걸프전(주재국 전망)

연:FRW-0538

대:WFR-0248

당관 박참사관은 2.14. 불 국제관계연구소(IFRI) KODMANI-DARWISH 중동연구부장과의 면담 및 동 2.15. 외무성 SASTOURNE 걸프전 전담과장과 오찬을 갖고,주재국 정부 및 학계의 사태전망을 청취하였는바, 동 주요 요지를 하기 보고함.

1. 전쟁추이

-미국은 막강한 이락의 지상군사력, 기상조건 및 최근 있은 이락 민간인 살상공개등 예기치 않은 상황에 불구, 지상전을 속히 결행하고자 할 가능성이 많아졌음.

-라마단은 전쟁에 크게 우려되는 요소는 아니나, 작전지역의 기상(고온) 및사막지형 적응 미숙 또는 6 월 성지순례 기간까지 전쟁이 장기화 되면 사우디 주둔 명분이 퇴색되고, 아랍권 및 회교권의 반미 감정만 고조시킬 것이므로, 미측은 이를 염두에 두지 않을수 없음.

-이락은, 미측이 핵무기를 사용치 않는한, 현대전에서도 지상군이 가장 중요한 위력을 지닌다고 판단, 가급적 조속한 시일내 지상전 대결을 기다리고 있으나, 선도발은 삼가고 소련을 통한 외교적 노력 및 이락 민간인 살상을 서방 언론에 PLAY UP 시켜, 서방의 감상적인 인권중시 여론에 호소, 미국을 정책적인 혼란에 빠트려, 상황과 국제여론을 자국에 다소 유리하게 전개되도록 심리전을 계속할 것으로 보임.

-이락의 쿠웨이트 철군이 선행되지 않는한 소련을 중심으로한 외교적 중재노력의 성공 가능성은 많지 않음. 또한 그간 일개월여에 걸쳐 있은 서방의 공폭등 맹공으로 인해, 이락측의 저항이 무너지기 시작하였으며, 계속 전쟁을 하려면전력을 재정비키 위한 시간을 벌 필요가 있으므로 이락은 소련등을 통해 종전과는 달리 협상해결의

중아국	장관	차관	1차보	2차보	미주국	구주국	정문국	청와대
안기부								

PAGE 1 91.02.16 07:52

외신 2과 통제관 CW

0024

자세가 있음을 시사하는 것으로 보임.

2. 전후 판도

가. 전쟁이 가열되어 양측 민간 희생자가 속출하면, 이락의 파괴나 분할은 국제사회및 회교권의 반발을 야기시킬 것이므로, 현 이스라엘 리쿠드 정부의 강력한 압력에 불구, 미국이 전쟁을 이락까지 확대시키기는 어려울 것임.

나. 이를 토대로 볼때, 하기와 같은 가정이 가능한바

1)회교권의 반발을 의식, 미국은 일단 사우디 철수, 쿠웨이트에 합법 친미정권 수립, 동국과 양자 안보조약 체결로 쿠웨이트에 잔류

2)재건된 쿠웨이트, SADDAM 이 없어진 이락등을 현 유명무실한 G.C.C. 에 편입, 미국과 G.C.C. 간 집단 안보조약 체결로 GULF 지역의 미 군사력 유지 및

3)전후 주요한 역할이 기대되는 애굽, 시리아 및 G.C.C. 전체를 총망라한 광범위한 집단안보 체제 구축등이 있음.

다. 이를 위한 미국은, 단기적으로는 이란의 친이락 참전 방지, 장기적으로는 이란의 미국 걸프잔류 묵인등을 위해, 대이란 관계개선 및 제반 회유책을 강구할수 있으나, 이란이 전후 미국 중심의 아랍권 집단 안보체제가 구축되는 것은극력반대할 것이므로 미국도 이에대한 별도 대책을 수립해야 할것임.

라. 중동 재편 관련, 이스라엘과 시리아는 요르단 붕괴, 레바논 분할 및 팔레스타인 약화등 일맥 이해가 일치하는 면이 있으므로, 시리아는 조만간 대이스라엘 관계개선 작업(과거에도 비밀교섭이 있었다 함)에 박차를 가할것임.시리아가 기대하는 골란고원의 반환은 이스라엘측이 응하지 않을 것이나, 대미 관계개선에 있어 이스라엘의 도움은 필수적이므로 쏘 지원상실후 다국적군에 합류한 시리아로 볼때는 대이스라엘 관계개선은 필요 불가결한 현실임.

마. 이스라엘은 전후 중동평화 국제회의 수락에 계속 냉담할 것으로 보이는바, 이는

1)이스라엘의 대화 상대는 약화된 PLO 가 아닌, 점령지 팔인이란 기본입장 고수 및

2)BUSH 대통령의 재선에 필요한 미국내 유태인 로비의 제반 지원 필요성등을 감안할때 93 년 이전까지 미국이 이스라엘에게 국제회의 수락을 강력히 권고할 입장이 못됨을 잘알고 있기 때문임.

바. 쏘련은 더이상 중동문제를 방관하면, 미국이 걸프지역에 계속 주둔, 쏘련과 국경을 같이하는 4 국(터키, 시리아, 이락, 이란등)을 조정, 쏘련을 포위, 위협하는

사태가 발생할 것에 대비, 현재 발트와 서방의 경제원조라는 불리한 입장에도 불구, 향후 걸프전 문제에 있어 보다 적극적인 외교적 역할을 모색할 것임. 끝.

(대사 노영찬-국장)

예고:91.12.31. 일반

일반문서로 재분류(1991.12.31.)

검토필(1991.6.30.)

PAGE 3

0026

관리 번호	91-342

원 본

외 무 부

종 별 : 지 급

번 호 : USW-0787 일 시 : 91 0219 1718

수 신 : 장관(미북,중근동,동구일,미안)

발 신 : 주 미 대사

제 목 : 부쉬 대통령의 소련측 중재안 거부

1. 금 2.19 백악관에서의 의회 지도자 면담에 앞서 부쉬 대통령은 금번 소련측 중재안이 전쟁 종결을 위한 요건에 크게 미흡하다고 언급함으로써, 미측으로서는 이를 수락할수 없다는 입장임을 밝힘.

여사한 미측 입장은 소련측에도 이미 전달되었다하며, 소련측 중재안의 구체적 내용은 소련측 요청에 따라 밝혀지지 않았는바, 전기 부쉬 대통령 발언 내용 전문은 USW(F)-0607 로 FAX 편 송부함.

2. 한편 금일자 W.P 지의 THE GORBACHEV PEACE PLAN 제하의 사설은 기본적으로 금번 소련측 중재안을 전후의 걸프지역 국제관계를 재정립해 나가는 과정속에서 소련의 영향력을 확보해 나가기 위한 사전 포석의 성격으로 분석하는등, 대부분의 당지 언론이 비판적인 시각에서 고르바쵸프 대통령의 제안을 보도하고 있는점이 주목됨.

(대사 박동진-국장)

예고:91.12.31 일반

일반문서로 재분류(1991.12.31.)

검토필(1991.6.30.)

미주국	장관	차관	1차보	2차보	미주국	구주국	중아국	정문국
청와대	안기부							

PAGE 1 91.02.20 07:38

외신 2과 통제관 BW

0027

호 : USW(F) - 0607

보안 통제	

수 신 : 장 관(미북,중근동,동구일,미안) 발신 : 주미대사

제 목 : 부쉬 대통령의 소련측 중재안 거부 (/ 매)

QUESTIONS AND ANSWERS WITH PRESIDENT BUSH DURING PHOTO OPPORTUNITY WITH BIPARTISAN CONGRESSIONAL LEADERS FROM THE HOUSE AND SENATE, THE CABINET ROOM, THE WHITE HOUSE, TUESDAY, FEBRUARY 19, 1991

Q Mr. President, is the Soviet proposal acceptable to you?

PRESIDENT BUSH: Well, let me -- let me just make one comment and then I won't take any questions about it. But I do appreciate President Gorbachev's providing me a copy of his proposal -- not the Iraqi proposal -- or his proposal to Iraq, actually -- concerning the Gulf, the conflict there. And we provided last night comments to the Soviet Union.

Let me just reiterate, as far as I'm concerned, there are no negotiations. The goals have been set out; there will be no concessions. We're not going to give. And so on his proposal, President Gorbachev asked that I keep the details of it confidential and I'm going to do that. I will -- will respect that -- that request in the interest of thoroughly exploring the initiative.

But very candidly, it -- and I have been frank with him on this -- while stressing appreciation for his sending it to us, it falls well short of what would be required. And I would leave it right there for now.

Q Does that mean we're going to have a ground war?

PRESIDENT BUSH: That means I'm going to leave it right there for now.

STAFF: (To press) Okay, lights please. Thank you.

END

0028

02/19/91 17:34 ☎202 797 0595 EMBASSY OF KOREA --- WOI 001/001

원 본

외 무 부

종 별 :

번 호 : USW-0827 일 시 : 91 0220 1947

수 신 : 장 관(미북,중근동)

발 신 : 주 미 대사

제 목 : 걸프 사태 관련 국무 장관 발언

금 2.20 베이커 장관은 현재 방미중인 데마크 여왕을 위한 연회석상에서의 건배사를 통해, 이락측이 즉각 쿠웨이트로부터 무조건 전면 철수해야만 한다는점을 재천명하는 한편, 여하한 방식으로든 (ONE WAY OR ANOTHER) 이락 점령군이 금명간 (SOON) 쿠웨이트를 떠날 것이라고 언급함으로서 소련측 제안에 대한 미측 반응에 다소의 융통성이 있을수도 있다는 암시를 표시한것으로 당지 일부 언론에서는 보도하고있는바, 베이커 장관 발언 내용 USW(F)-0619 FAX편 송부함.

(대사 박동진-국장)

미주국	장관	차관	1차보	2차보	중아국	정문국	청와대	총리실
안기부								

0029

PAGE 1

91.02.21 13:17 WG

외신 1과 통제관

(F) - 0619

신 : 장 관 (미북, 중근동) 발신 : 주미대사

보안 통제	

목 : 걸프사태 관련 국무장관 발언 (/ 매)

EXCERPT OF REMARKS BY SECRETARY OF STATE JAMES BAKER DURING A TOAST IN HONOR OF THE QUEEN OF DENMARK AS BROADCAST ON CNN, THE US STATE DEPARTMENT WEDNESDAY, FEBRUARY 20, 1991

REID COLLINS: This just in. Secretary of State Baker toasted the Queen of Denmark visiting the United States today said that the war will end with unconditional acceptance of all the United Nations resolutions pertaining to Iraq and predicted it will end, as he put it, "soon." And this is what the Secretary of State had to say.

SEC. BAKER: The United Nations mandate is crystal clear and there can be no negotiation over its meaning and there should be no confusion over what must be done. Iraq must leave Kuwait immediately, totally and unconditionally. And Iraq must comply fully with the other applicable Security Council resolutions. Anything short of that is unacceptable. Anything short of that contradicts, indeed rejects, the expressed will of the international community.

For over five months the world waited peacefully and waited patiently for Iraq to withdraw from Kuwait and for Saddam Hussein to end the war that he began on August the 2nd. Instead of peace he chose war. It is a war that we did not seek, but it is also a war that we shall not lose.

So now, one way or another, the Iraqi army of occupation will leave Kuwait. And one way or another, the army of occupation of Iraq will leave Kuwait soon.

MR. COLLINS: And he added, and so Kuwait will be liberated, and he said "soon."

END

배부처	장관실	차관실	一차보	二차보	기획실	의전장	아주국	미주국	구주국	중아국	국기국	경제국	통상국	정문국	영교국	총무과	감사관	공보관	외연원	청와대	총리실	안기부	문공부
	/	/	/	/				2		/2				/						/	/	/	

0030

검토

원 본

외 무 부

종 별 : 지 급

번 호 : USW-0847 일 시 : 91 0221 1846

수 신 : 장 관(미북,중동 1,미안)

발 신 : 주 미 대사

제 목 : 후세인 연설에 대한 미측 반응

금일 바그다드 라디오 방송을 통해 발표된 강경일변도의 후세인 연설관련, 백악관 FITZWATER대변인 및 국무부 TUTWILER 대변인은 여사한 이락측 반응에 대해 공히 실망을 표시하면서 다국적군의 대이락 공격은 예정대로 계속 진행될 것이라는 입장을 표시한바, 양인 발언 내용 USW(F)-0632 FAX 편 송부함.

(대사 박동진-국장)

미주국 장관 차관 1차보 2차보 미주국 중아국 정문국 청와대
총리실 안기부

0031

PAGE 1

91.02.22 09:03 WG

외신 1과 통제관

: USW(F) - 0632

: 장　　관(미북, 중동1, 미안)　발신 : 주미대사

보안 통제	

(2 매)

: 후세인 연설에 대한 미측 반응

STATE DEPARTMENT REGULAR BRIEFING
BRIEFER: MARGARET TUTWILER
/THURSDAY, FEBRUARY 21, 1991

Q　No, I'm just asking. Okay. Has the Secretary and his group of advisors heard the speech from Saddam Hussein this morning? And do you have any preliminary reaction?

MS. TUTWILER: Yes. The Secretary didn't personally listen to the speech. He has obviously had experts in the building who did, and Arab translators, bring him what, you know, our translation of the speech was.

The State Department's reaction is obviously very similar to the one that Marlin just gave from the White House, is that we see nothing in Saddam Hussein's speech today which indicates that he understands and accepts the necessity for Iraq to comply fully with United Nations Security Council resolutions related to the Gulf. We and other members of the coalition have made clear that this is the only way for a peaceful resolution of the conflict. We regret that the Iraqi leadership continues to defy the will of the international community in this regard. The coalition's military effort will continue on schedule.

Q　Do you see any degree of difference, the fact that he, for the first time in my recollection, is talking publicly of a withdrawal?

MS. TUTWILER: Well, my memory serves me correct, I believe last Friday, Jim, he put out a statement on Baghdad Radio saying that he would withdraw "if," and then had about nine conditions.

Q　But that was the Revolutionary Council. This was him, personally, as President of the republic of Iraq. Did -- well, a short question. Do you see any nuance, any degree of difference or any -- any handhold anywhere that might indicate that he's looking for a way out?

MS. TUTWILER: I want to be fair, and as you yourself said, in our preliminary look at this speech, and I'm not sure that we have had an opportunity in the 40 minutes I believe it's been since it was given, to have an exact literal word-by-word Arabic translation of it. Having said that, I would say that we do not have or see much room for optimism. We basically found it to be yet another disappointment. We would once again say that, as you all know, that he, Saddam Hussein, can stop the suffering that he is personally in our opinion inflicting on his own country and is showing again a total disregard for the people of Iraq.

0632-1

0032

: USW(F) -

: 장 관

:

발신 : 주미대사

보안 통제	

(매)

STATEMENT BY WHITE HOUSE SPOKESMAN MARLIN FITZWATER PRIOR TO WHITE HOUSE BRIEFING, THE WHITE HOUSE, 11:20 A.M., EST
THURSDAY, FEBRUARY 21, 1991

MR. FITZWATER: Well let me just read a few sentences in response to Saddam Hussein's speech.

The statement by Saddam Hussein this morning is disappointing. He repeats the same invective and disregard for the United Nations mandate that we have heard so often since August 2nd. In vowing to continue the war he once again demonstrates his determination to maintain the aggression against Kuwait and the absence of compassion for his people and his country.

For our part, the coalition forces remain on the course set by the 12 United Nations resolutions. Our forces remain on a steadfast course. The liberation of Kuwait continues.

Q Can we put that out?

MR. FITZWATER: Let's go to questions.

Q Can we put that out?

Q Can we have a brief filing break, Marlin?

Q Yeah, a five-minute filing break?

MR. FITZWATER: Okay, fine. Five minutes.

END

0632-2

0033

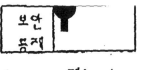

관리 번호	91-498

원 본

외 무 부

종 별 : 긴 급

번 호 : USW-0852 일 시 : 91 02212020

수 신 : 장관(미북,중근동,동구일,미안)

발 신 : 주 미 대사

제 목 : 걸프전 종식을 위한 소-이락간 협의 결과

1. 금 2.21 1900 당지 CNN 방송 보도에 따르면, 고르바쵸프 대통령과 AZIZ 이락 외상이 2 시간반 에 걸친 회담 결과, 아래 8 개항의 걸프전 종전 절차에 합의한것으로 알려짐.

가. 이락군은 쿠웨이트로부터 전면 무조건(FULL AND UNCONDITIONAL)철수

나. 전투 행위 중지(CESSATION OF HOSTILITIES)이후 제 2 일(SECOND DAY)부터 이락군 철수 개시

다. 이락군의 철수는 일정 기한(FIXED TIME)내에 실시

라. 이락군이 2/3 이상 철수한 시점부터 대이락 경제 봉쇄 해제

마. 이락군 철수 종료 이후, 금번 사태 관련 채택된 제반 유엔 안보리 결의안은 무효임(NULL AND VOID)을 선언

바. 휴전(CEASEFIRE)이후 양측 포로 석방

사. 이락군 철수는 유엔 감독하, 금번 사태에 참여하지 않은 국가(UNINVOLVED NATIONS)들이 감시하는 가운데 실시

아. 기타 관련 상세에 대해서는 계속 협의

2. 미측은 현재 백악관을 중심으로 전기 종전안에 대한 미측 입장을 협의중인것으로 알려지고 있는바, 당지 언론 보도등에 나타난 향후 전망등은 다음임.

가. 유엔 안보리 결의안의 무효 선언 문제및 철수 시한 관련 문제등과 관련미측이 전기 제안에 대하 반대 입장을 전개할 가능성도 배제할수 없으나, 일단국제 여론및 미국내 분위기는 동 제안의 원칙적으로 수락하는 방향으로 전개될것으로 전망되는바, 여사한 상황에서 미측이 지상전을 개시하기는 어려울것으로 봄.

나. 다만, 구체적인 휴전 일자가 지정되기 전까지 미측으로서는 당분간 대이락 공중 폭격을 계속 실시함으로서 종전 이전 이락군 전력을 가능한 한 파괴하기 위해

미주국	장관	차관	1차보	2차보	미주국	구주국	중아국	청와대
안기부								

PAGE 1 91.02.22 11:21

외신 2과 통제관 FE

0034

노려고할것으로 봄.

다. 금번 전쟁이 이처럼 소련측의 주도적 노력에 의해 종결된다면, 중동 지역내에서의 소련측의 국제적 위상은 보다 더 고양될 것으로 보이는바, 향후 중동 전후 질서를 구축해 나가는 과정에서 나타날 미소간의 협력 또는 갈등 관계가탈 냉전 시대의 국제 관계의 방향을 가늠해볼수 있는 시금적이 될것으로 보임.

라. 전기 종전안을 통해 이락측 으로서는 우선 국내적으로 후세인 정권의 보존을 도모코자 하는것으로 보이며, 팔레스타인 문제와의 연계등이 명시적으로 포함되지는 않았으나, 동 문제등이 전후 처리 과정에서 자연스럽게 대두될 것이므로 아랍권 내에서도 어느 정도의 정치적 영향력을 유지할수 있을것으로 보임.

마. 또한 미측으로서는 전기 종전안을 수락하는 경우 외형상 걸프 사태 발생 초기 부터 내세워온 4 대 목표를 기본적으로는 달성하는 셈이며, 탈 냉전 시대의 국제 관계에 대한 최초의 도전 사례인 금번 사태를 성공적으로 (특히 지상전 개전으로 인한 막대한 인명 손실을 회피했다는 점에서)처리했다고 자평할수 있을것임.

마. 다만, 유엔 안보리 결의안이 무효임을 수락 한다는것은 미국으로서도 다소 문제점이 있을것으로 보이는바, 미측이 전기 종전안을 아무런 수정없이 받아들이기는 어려울것으로 봄.

3. 미 행정부의 공식 반응은 발표되는대로 보고 예정임.

(대사 박동진-차관)

91.12.31 일반

일반문서로 재분류(1991.12.31.)

검 토 필(1991.6.30.)

PAGE 2

0035

원 본

외 무 부

종 별 : 긴 급

번 호 : USW-0854 일 시 : 91 0221 2246

수 신 : 장 관(미북,미안,중근동,동구일)

발 신 : 주 미 대사

제 목 : 걸프전(소 .이락 종전 조건 제시)

1. 기 보고한바와 같이 소련측에 의한 이락의 쿠웨이트 철수 수락을 포함한 8개항 조 건 발표와 관련 현지 시간 2.21 저녁 8:45 백악관 FITZWATER 대변인은 미측의 일차 반응을 발표하였음.

2.동 대변인은 GORBACHEV 대통령이 금일 저녁 6:47 부쉬 대통령에게 전화, AZIZ 외상과의 협의 내용을 상세히 설명해왔다고 밝히고부쉬 대통령은 다국적 연합국들과 협의할 예정이며, 금일밤 소련측 제안을 상세히 검토할 예정이라고 밝힘.

3.동 대변인은 전쟁은 일단 정해진 계획대로 수행되어 나갈것임을 강조하고, 소련측 제안에 대한 미측 반응에 대해서는 금일밤중 검토가 있을것이며, 명일 오전 발표가 가능할것이라고 답변함.

4.동 대변인은 부쉬 대통령이 소련.이락측제안에 대해 미측이 문제로 느끼고 있는 점과, 분명히 해결되어야할 점등을 지적했다고 하면서, 이락이 관련 유엔 결의안들을 완전 준수하고, 쿠웨이트로부터 철수하는것이 가장 효율적인 문제해결 방식이라는 미국의 기본 입장을 다시 한번 강조 했음. 동 대변인은 미국은 쏘.이락 협상에 참여자가 아니며, 단순히 협상 내용을 통보 받았을뿐이라는 점도 분명히 했음.

5.여사한 백악관측 발표와 관련, 당지 언론은 미국이 상금도 소련.이락측의 제안에 대해 많은 문제점을 느끼고 있고, 특히 미국이 공식적인 목표로 천명하고 있지는 않으나 사담 후세인을 제거하고 이락의 군사력을 현저히 궤멸시켜야 금번 전쟁의 목적이 달성된다는 인식을 하고 있음에 비추어, 부쉬 행정부는 어려운 국면을 맞고 있다는점을 지적하면서도, 금일 FITZWATER 대변인의 발표에서는 최근 미국측이 사용했던 거부 (REJECTION) 또는 미흡 (FULL SHORT OF) 이라는 용어를 사용치 않고 단순히 우려 (CONCERN)가 있다는 표현을 사용한점이 상황의 진전으로 해석도 가능하다는 견해를 제시 하고 있음.

미주국 장관 차관 1차보 2차보 미주국 구주국 중아국 정문국
청와대 총리실 안기부

PAGE 1 91.02.22 13:19 WG

외신 1과 통제관

0036

6.현재 당지언론에서는 미국및 연합국측의 공식반응은 현지시간 명일 오전에나 결정, 발표될것으로 기대하고 있는 가운데, 지상전으로의 동입 여부, 소련의 의도에 대한 분석및 향후 중동에서의 미소 관계, 군사작전이 현 단계에서 중단될 경우 이락측의 지연 전술 행사 가능성, 중동 각국의 입장 분석등에 관한 해석과 전문가간 토론이 활발히 진행되고 있음.

7.동건 진전 사항 추보 예정임.

(대사 박동진-국장)

번 호 : USW(F) - 0[redacted]

수 신 : 장 관 (미북, 미안, 중근동, 동구일) 발신 : 주미대사

제 목 : 이라크전 (소련측 제안에 대한 미 백악관 반응) (3 매) 가

— Fitzwater 백악관 대변인 기자회견 (2.21. 20:45)

MR. FITZWATER: President Gorbachev called President Bush at 6:47 p.m. this evening to discuss his conversation with Iraqi Foreign Minister, Tariq Aziz. President Gorbachev outlined all of the major points of the Soviet initiative developed by himself and the Foreign Minister. President Bush thanked President Gorbachev for his intensive and useful efforts but raised serious concerns about several points in the plan.

President Bush said the United States will consult with its coalition partners on the proposal. We are in the process of examining the Soviet initiative tonight. The United States and its coalition partners continue to prosecute the war.

That is the sum and substance of the situation that we have at this point. I'll try to answer a few questions.

Q Marlin?

MR. FITZWATER: (Jim ?)

Q Did President Gorbachev give any indication that once President Bush gave him these concerns, that he was going to take those back to Aziz, and did he leave any hope that there may be some give on the part of Iraqis on those points the President raised?

MR. FITZWATER: They didn't discuss follow-on procedures. President Bush did say that we would be examining these points tonight and we will be considering, then, how we intend to respond. I would not expect anything -- any response tonight, anything before tomorrow. But in terms of what happens then, that really is contingent upon -- how we view the various points in this plan and what action needs to be taken at that time.

Helen?

Q What are the concerns? What are the chief drawbacks as the administration (would see them ?)

MR. FITZWATER: Well, we don't want to go into the individual points, of course. This plan was just announced by the Soviets very -- a short time ago. The telephone conversation lasted approximately 33 minutes. And although they did get a chance to go through the major points, we obviously have a considerable analysis to do.

But I would emphasize again that as they went through the various points, President Bush did state the concerns that he felt the coalition would have on this matter, both in terms of points that are in the plan that we have problems with, as well as issues that are not included. So there are a number of issues to resolve.

-1-

0038

02/21/91 22:38 ☎202 797 0595 EMBASSY OF KOREA --- WOI ☑001/003

Q But this does hold up the ground war, doesn't it?

MR. FITZWATER: The ground war is a matter that is still under consideration. The war itself continues. We will continue to seek compliance with the UN resolutions. And the President will make decisions concerning the ground war as appropriate. This process that was initiated by the Soviets is continuing at a rather intensive pace, but there is no change at this point in our schedule for prosecution of the war.

Frank?

Q This is during the meeting itself -- was Aziz in communication with the President? Was there any two-way on that?

MR. FITZWATER: No. There was no one else on the phone call and no other communications.

Q Does President Bush see now here a chance for the first time since August 2 to reverse the invasion of Kuwait and actually come about this without launching a ground war?

MR. FITZWATER: Well, there have been innumerable chances since August 2 in the sense that Saddam Hussein could have pulled out at any time. That still is the fastest and most efficient way to end this war. In terms of this initiative, it's just too soon to characterize it. We need to take a look at it, but I would say again that we have had our hopes erased before. After a serious examination, there have been significant problems, and certainly the President has indicated there could well be some difficulties here. But we are taking a look at it.

Q But how could he prosecute a ground war if, indeed, the talks are proceeding in Moscow?

MR. FITZWATER: Well, that's not a issue at the moment. We are proceeding the war -- the air war continues. There's been no decision on the ground war at this time. And we continue to pursue the matter in the Persian Gulf in the most effective and efficient military way possible.

Michael?

Q The President has said all along that the 12 UN resolutions are what Saddam Hussein must live up to. In the points that the President raised that he doesn't like, the possibility sounds like that there may be a negotiation underway to drop one or more of those points. Can the President live with anything less than full acceptance of all 12, as long as Iraq pulls out of Kuwait?

MR. FITZWATER: There is no negotiation underway with the -- regard to the United States. I remind you again that this is a matter between the Soviet Union and Iraq, that we are commenting on

6742-

0039

02/21/91 22:39 ☎202 797 0595 EMBASSY OF KOREA --- WOI 002/003 their proposal, and we are not directly involved in that sense. I would repeat once again as well that compliance -- full compliance with the 12 UN resolutions is the goal we seek, and the -- those are the guideposts that we would use in judging any consideration of withdrawal.

Q Are you willing to go beyond those 12, though, to scale back any of those 12?

MR. FITZWATER: We have said repeatedly that we must have full compliance with the 12 UN resolutions. There's no change in that situation. Rita?

Q Marlin, aside from raising serious considerations here, you said that "We've had our hopes raised before." While -- in the process of reviewing this, do you at least see that there is some hope here, that this peace proposal could work if some of the problems that the President sees are worked out?

MR. FITZWATER: I just don't want to give it any characterization until we've had a chance to give it the full analysis of the United States government. Let's take one more question. Charles?

Q How can you say there are no negotiations going on when Gorbachev tells you his points and you tell him which ones are objectionable, and basically ask him to go back to Tariq Aziz and say about these points. Are those not negotiations? Is he not negotiating on your behalf?

MR. FITZWATER: We haven't asked him to do anything. He's asked our views on these matters. We'll provide them, as we have in the last few days, but I reiterate again that this is a matter between the Soviets and Iraq, and we are appreciative that -- of the communication that has told us of these discussions, but we are not a part of the negotiations.

Thank you very much.

END

6343-

0040

02/21/91 22:39 ☎202 797 0595 EMBASSY OF KOREA --- WOI ▣003/003

報 告 事 項

報告畢

1991. 2. 22.
美 洲 局
北 美 課(8)

題 目 : 이라크-쏘련간 종전안 합의

1. 경 위

o 2.11(월) 프리마코프 소련 대통령 특사 이라크 방문

o 2.18(월) 고르바쵸프 대통령, 방소중인 Tareg Aziz 이라크 외무장관 에게 소련의 평화안 제시

o 2.21(목) 이라크, 소련의 평화안에 조건을 붙여 수락

2. 소.이라크 합의 종전안(소련 이그나텐코 대변인 발표내용)

1) 이라크군의 전면 무조건 철군

2) 휴전 성립 2일후 철군 개시

3) 철군은 추후 합의될 일정에 따라 시행

4) 철군이 2/3이상 달성시 대이라크 경제제재 조치 해제

5) 철군 완료후 대이라크 모든 유엔 안보리 제재결의의 무효화

6) 휴전 발효후 모든 전쟁 포로 석방

0041

7) 철군 과정은 관련 당사자가 아닌 유엔 안보리가 지명하는 제3국에 의해 감시

8) 구체적 사항은 계속 협의중이며, 최종 내용은 2.22. 또는 2.23. 중 유엔 안보리와 협의후 발표 예정

3. 각국 반응

가. 미 국

o 2.21(목) 피츠워터 미 백악관 대변인의 임시 논평

- 워싱턴 시간 2.21(목) 19시부터 약30분간 고르바쵸프-부쉬 대통령간 통화, 종전안을 미측에 설명함.
- 미국은 현재 이 안을 평가(evaluation)중이며, 다국적국 지도자들과 협의중이므로, 공식 반응은 유보함.
- 종전 협상은 소련과 이라크간에 이루어지고 있으며, 미국은 협상에 관여하고 있지 않음.
- 미국의 전쟁 수행 계획은 불변임.

o 미 상원 Dole 공화당 원내총무

- 부쉬 대통령에게 결정에 신중을 기할 것을 촉구(동 종전안에 회의적)

o 미 언론 반응

- 미국의 결정이 매우 어렵게 되었으며, 완전 수락도 완전 반대도 곤란한 것으로 평가
- 쿠웨이트로 부터의 완전 철수 목적 달성도 가능한 상황에서 전쟁을 계속할 필요가 있느냐는 의문이 제기되며 일부 Coalition 국가의 부정적 입장도 우려
- 반면, 동 종전안을 수락시 미국의 종전후 입지 약화와 쏘련의 입지 강화, 동시에 전후 처리에도 주도적 위치 손상된다는 우려

나. 중국, 교황청, 이집트등 몇개국은 긍정적 반응

0042

관리번호	91-481

76 원 본

외 무 부

종 별 : 긴 급

번 호 : USW-0857　　　　일 시 : 91 0222 1449

수 신 : 장관(미북,중동1,동구1,미안)

발 신 : 주 미 대사

제 목 : 부쉬대통령 연설(대이락 철수 시한 제시)

1. 금 2.22. 10:30 부쉬 대통령은 백안관에서 기자회견을 갖고, 작일 소-이락간에 합의된 종전 제안을 수락할수 없다는 점을 밝히는 한편, 명일정오까지 이락측이 쿠웨이트로부터 철군을 개시할것을 천명하였는바, 언급요지 하기 보고함.(발언 내용 전문은 USW(F)-0636 로 FAX 편 송부)

가. 미국과 다국적군 참여국들은 이락군의 쿠웨이트로부터의 무조건 즉각 철수를 요구하는 제반 유엔 결의안을 실천할 결의를 갖고 있음.

나. 작일 발표된 종전 제안이 외견상 합리적으로 보이기는 하나, 사실상 여러가지 조건을 달고 있으므로 다국적군측으로서는 수락할수 없음.

다. 현재 이락측은 쿠웨이트내 각종 원유생산 시설등에 대한 방화, 파괴행위를 자행함으로써 쿠웨이트를 초토화하려하고 있음.

라. 미행정부 내부 협의 및 다국적군 참여국과의 협의를 거친 끝에, 명일정오까지 이락측이 쿠웨이트로 부터 즉각, 무조건 철군을 개시할 것을 요청하며, 동 요청에 대한 훗세인의 수락은 공개적이고 믿을 만한 방식으로 발표되어야만 한다는 점을 강조함.(전기 철군 개시 시한은 당지 시간인것으로 추정됨.)

마. 이락군 철군 절차등에 관한 상세는 추후 별도 발표함.(동 내용은 발표되는대로 FAX 송부 예정)

2. 분석및 관찰

가. 부쉬 대통령이 전기와같이 소-이락측 제안을 수락할수 없다고 밝힌 가장 주요한 이유는, 동제안이 포함하고 있는 대이락 경제 봉쇄의 해제와 유엔 안보리 결의안의 무효화 선언 조건이 미국측으로서는 수락하기 어려웠기 때문인 것이라고함.

나. 당지 일부언론에서는 금일 미측제안을 일종의 최후 통첩으로 간주, 명일 정오까지도 이락측이 철군을 단행하지 않는경우, 지상전이 곧 이어 개전될 것으로

미주국　장관　차관　1차보　2차보　미주국　구주국　중아국　청와대
총리실　안기부

PAGE 1　　　　91.02.23　06:10
외신 2과　통제관 DO
0043

전망하고 있기도하나, 미국으로서는 나름의 정해진 스케쥴에 따라 쿠웨이트 주둔 이락 지상군 전력의 파괴 정도 및 금번 제안에 대한 이락측 반응등을 보아 가면서 지상전 개시 여부 및 일자를 결정지을 것으로 예상됨.

다. 한편 형식적인 차원에서 볼때, 부쉬 대통령이 소-이락측 제안에 대한 수정 제안을 제시하지 않고, 완전히 새로운 형식의 제안을 제시한 점이 주목되는바, 이는 소-이락측 제안을 바탕으로 종전이 이루어지는 경우 중동지역 전후 질서 재편 과정에 대한 소련측의 정치적 영향력이 절대적으로 증가하는 데에 반해, 미국측은 무력 사용에만 집착했다는 인상을 심어줄수도 있고, 또 미국측으로서는 종전 관련 외교적 해결 절차에 관한 주도권도 계속 장악하고자 하는 의도를 갖고 있기 때문인것으로 관찰됨.

라. 기본적으로 금일 미측 제안에 대한 이락측의 방응 여하에 따라 걸프 사태의 종결 방식이 정해질 것으로 보이는바, 이락측이 이를 거부하는 경우 지상전 개전의 가능성은 보다 더 높아질 것임.

(대사 박동진-차관)

예고:91.12.31. 일반

일반문서로 재분류(1991.12.31.)

검 토 필 (1991.6.30.)

PAGE 2

0044

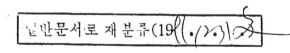

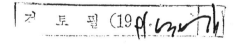

FEB.22 '91 12:15 KOREAN E ||||SHINGTON DC

P.001

: USW(F) - 0636

: 장 관 (미북, 중동1, 통기, 발신 : 주미대사
차북 미안)

:

보안 통제	[redacted]

(1 매)

첨부

REMARKS BY PRESIDENT BUSH THE WHITE HOUSE ROSE GARDEN, 10:40 A.M. (EST)
FRIDAY, FEBRUARY 22, 1991

PRESIDENT BUSH: Good morning. The United States and its coalition allies are committed to enforcing the United Nations resolutions that call for Saddam Hussein to immediately and unconditionally leave Kuwait. In view of the Soviet initiati ve, which very frankly we appreciate, we want to set forth this morning the specific criteria that will ensure Saddam Hussein complies with the United Nations mandate.

Within the last 24 hours alone, we have heard a defiant uncompromising address by Saddam Hussein, followed less than 10 hours later by a statement in Moscow that, on the face of it, appears more reasonable.

I say "on the face of it," because the statement promised unconditional Iraqi withdrawal from Kuwait, only to set forth a number of conditions. And needless to say, any conditions would be unacceptable to the international coalition and would not be in compliance with the United Nations Security Council Resolution 660's demand for immediate and unconditional withdrawal.

More importantly and more urgently, we learned this morning that Saddam has now launched a scorched earth policy against Kuwait, anticipating perhaps that he will now be forced to leave. He is wantonly setting fires to and destroying the oilwells, the oil tanks, the export terminals, and other installations of that small country. Indeed, they are destroying the entire oil production system of Kuwait. And at the same time that that Moscow press conference was going on and Iraq's Foreign Minister was talking peace, Saddam Hussein was launching Scud missiles.

After examining the Moscow statement and discussing it with my senior advisers here late last evening and this morning and after extensive consultation with our coalition partners, I have decided that the time has come to make public with specificity just exactly what is required of Iraq if a ground war is to be avoided.

Most important, the coalition will give Saddam Hussein until noon Saturday to do what he must do,
begin his immediate and unconditional withdrawal from Kuwait. We must hear publicly and authoritatively his acceptance of these terms. The statement to be released, as you will see, does just this, and informs Saddam Hussein that he risks subjecting the Iraqi people to further hardship unless the Iraqi government complies fully with the terms of the statement. We will put that statement out soon. It will be in considerable detail, and that's all I'll have to say about it right now. Thank you very much.

END

059 P01 LENINPROTOCOL '91-02-23 02:10 0045

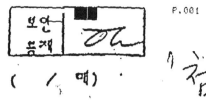

US STATEMENTS ON IRAQI WITHDRAWAL FROM KUWAIT

BEGIN TEXT OF PRESIDENT BUSH'S PRESS CONFERENCE FEBRUARY 22, 10:33 A.M., WHITE HOSE ROSE GARDEN

PRESIDENT BUSH: GOOD MORNING. THE UNITED STATES AND ITS COALITION ALLIES ARE COMMITTED TO ENFORCING THE UNITED NATIONS RESOLUTIONS THAT CALL FOR SADDAM HUSSEIN TO IMMEDIATELY AND UNCONDITIONALLY LEAVE KUWAIT.

IN VIEW OF THE SOVIET INITIATIVE, WHICH VERY FRANKLY WE APPRECIATE, WE WANT TO SET FORTH THIS MORNING THE SPECIFIC CRITERIA THAT WILL ENSURE SADDAM HUSSEIN COMPLIES WITH THE UNITED NATIONS' MANDATE.

WITHIN THE LAST 24 HOURS ALONE, WE HAVE HEARD A DEFIANT, UNCOMPROMISING ADDRESS BY SADDAM HUSSEIN, FOLLOWED LESS THAN 10 HOURS LATER BY A STATEMENT IN MOSCOW THAT ON THE FACE OF IT APPEARS MORE REASONABLE.

I SAY "ON THE FACE OF IT" BECAUSE THE STATEMENT PROMISED UNCONDlTIONAL IRAQI WITHDRAWAL FROM KUWAIT ONLY TO SET FORTH A NUMBER OF CONDITIONS, AND NEEDLESS TO SAY, ANY CONDITIONS WOULD BE UNACCEPTABLE TO THE INTERNATIONAL COALITION AND WOULD NOT BE IN COMPLIANCE WITH THE UNITED NATIONS SECURITY COUNCIL RESOLUTION 660'S DEMAND FOR IMMEDIATE AND UNCONDITIONAL WITHDRAWAL.

MORE IMPORTANTLY AND MORE URGENTLY, WE LEARNED THIS MORNING THAT SADDAM HAS NOW LAUNCHED A SCORCHED EARTH POLICY AGAINST KUWAIT, ANTICIPATING PERHAPS THAT HE WILL NOW BE FORCED TO LEAVE. HE IS WANTONLY SETTING FIRES TO AND DESTROYING THE OIL WELLS, THE OIL TANKS, THE EXPORT TERMINALS AND OTHER INSTALLATIONS OF THAT SMALL COUNTRY. INDEED, THEY ARE DESTROYING THE ENTIRE OIL PRODUCTION SYSTEM OF KUWAIT. AND AT THE SAME TIME THAT THAT MOSCOW PRESS CONFERENCE WAS GOING ON AND IRAQ'S FOREIGN MINISTER WAS TALKING PEACE, SADDAM HUSSEIN WAS LAUNCHING SCUD MISSILES.

AFTER EXAMINING THE MOSCOW STATEMENT AND DISCUSSING IT WITH MY SENIOR ADVISERS HERE LATE LAST EVENING AND THIS MORNING, AND AFTER EXTENSIVE CONSULTATION WITH OUR COALITION PARTNERS, I HAVE DECIDED THAT THE TIME HAS COME TO MAKE PUBLIC WITH SPECIFICITY JUST EXACTLY WHAT IS REQUIRED OF IRAQ IF A GROUND WAR IS TO BE AVOIDED.

MOST IMPORTANT, THE COALITION WILL GIVE SADDAM HUSSEIN UNTIL NOON SATURDAY TO DO WHAT HE MUST DO--BEGIN HIS IMMEDIATE AND UNCONDITIONAL WITHDRAWAL FROM KUWAIT. WE MUST HEAR PUBLICLY AND AUTHORITATIVELY HIS ACCEPTANCE OF THESE TERMS. THE STATEMENT TO BE RELEASED, AS YOU WILL SEE, DOES JUST THIS, AND INFORMS SADDAM HUSSEIN THAT HE RISKS SUBJECTING THE IRAQI PEOPLE TO FURTHER HARDSHIP UNLESS THE IRAQI GOVERNMENT COMPLIES FULLY WITH THE TERMS

0046

OF THE STATEMENT. WE WILL PUT THAT STATEMENT OUT SOON. IT WILL BE IN CONSIDERABLE DETAIL, AND THAT'S ALL I'LL HAVE TO SAY ABOUT IT RIGHT NOW. THANK YOU VERY MUCH.

END BUSH TEXT

BEGIN WRITTEN STATEMENT ON IRAQI WITHDRAWAL (READ TO THE MEDIA BY MARLIN FITZWATER AT 1300 FEBRUARY 22):

THE SOVIET ANNOUNCEMENT YESTERDAY REPRESENTS A SERIOUS AND USEFUL EFFORT WHICH IS APPRECIATED. BUT MAJOR OBSTACLES REMAIN. THE COALITION FOR MANY MONTHS HAS SOUGHT A PEACEFUL RESOLUTION TO THIS CRISIS IN KEEPING WITH THE UN RESOLUTIONS.

AS PRESIDENT BUSH POINTED OUT TO PRESIDENT GORBACHEV, THE STEPS THE IRAQIS ARE CONSIDERING WOULD CONSTITUTE A CONDITIONAL WITHDRAWAL AND WOULD ALSO PREVENT THE FULL IMPLEMENTATION OF RELEVANT UN SECURITY COUNCIL RESOLUTIONS. ALSO, THERE IS NO INDICATION THAT IRAQ IS PREPARED TO WITHDRAW IMMEDIATELY.

FULL COMPLIANCE WITH THE UN SECURITY COUNCIL RESOLUTIONS HAS BEEN A CONSISTENT AND NECESSARY DEMAND OF THE INTERNATIONAL COMMUNITY. THE WORLD MUST MAKE SURE THAT IRAQ HAS, IN FACT, RENOUNCED ITS CLAIM TO KUWAIT AND ACCEFTED ALL RELEVANT UN SECURITY COUNCIL RESOLUTIONS. INDEED, ONLY THE SECURITY COUNCIL CAN AGREE TO LIFT SANCTIONS AGAINST IRAQ, AND THE WORLD NEEDS TO BE ASSURED IN CONCRETE TERMS OF IRAQ'S PEACEFUL INTENTIONS BEFORE SUCH AN ACTION CAN BE TAKEN. IN A SITUATION WHERE SANCTIONS HAVE BEEN LIFTED, SADDAM HUSSEIN COULD SIMPLY REVERT TO USING HIS OIL RESOURCES ONCE AGAIN, NOT TO PROVIDE FOR THE WELL-BEING OF HIS PEOPLE, BUT INSTEAD TO REARM.

SO IN A FINAL EFFORT TO OBTAIN IRAQI COMPLIANCE WITH THE WILL OF THE INTERNATIONAL COMMUNITY, THE UNITED STATES AFTER CONSULTING WITH THE GOVERNMENT OF KUWAIT AND OTHER COALITION PARTERS, DECLARES THAT A GROUND CAMPAIGN WILL NOT BE INITIATED AGAINST IRAQI FORCES IF PRIOR TO NOON NEW YORK (UN) TIME SATURDAY, FEBRUARY 23, IRAQ PUBLICLY ACCEPTS THE FOLLOWING TERMS AND AUTHORITATIVELY COMMUNICATES THAT ACCEPTANCE TO THE UNITED NATIONS. THE TERMS ARE AS FOLLOWS:

-- BEGIN LARGE-SCALE WITHDRAWAL FROM KUWAIT BY NOON, NEW YORK (UN) TIME, SATURDAY, FEBRUARY 23;

-- COMPLETE MILITARY WITHDRAWAL FROM KUWAIT IN ONE WEEK. (GIVEN THE FACT THAT IRAQ INVADED AND OCCUPIED KUWAIT IN A MATTER OF HOURS, ANYTHING LONGER THAN THIS FROM THE INITIATION OF THE WITHDRAWAL WOULD NOT MEET RESOLUTION 660'S REQUIREMENT OF IMMEDIACY.);

0047

-- WITHIN THE FIRST 48 HOURS, REMOVE ALL ITS FORCES FROM KUWAIT CITY (TO ALLOW FOR THE PROMPT RETURN OF THE LEGITIMATE GOVERNMENT OF KUWAIT), FROM ALL PREPARED DEFENSES ALONG THE SAUDI-KUWAIT AND SAUDI-IRAQ BORDERS FROM BUBIYAN AND WARBAH ISLANDS AND FROM KUWAIT'S RUMAYLLAH OIL FIELD;

-- WITHIN THE ONE WEEK SPECIFIED ABOVE, RETURN ALL ITS FORCES TO THEIR POSITIONS OF AUGUST 1, IN ACCORDANCE WITH RESOLUTION 660;

-- IN COOPERATION WITH THE ICRC, RELEASE ALL PRISONERS OF WAR AND THIRD-COUNTRY CIVILIANS BEING HELD AGAINST THEIR WILL, AND RETURN THE REMAINS OF KILLED AND DECEASED SERVICEMEN, THIS ACTION TO COMMENCE IMMEDIATELY WITH THE INITIATION OF THE WITHDRAWAL AND TO BE COMPLETED WITHIN 48 HOURS;

-- REMOVE ALL EXPLOSIVES AND BOOBY-TRAPS, INCLUDING THOSE ON KUWAITI OIL INSTALLATIONS, AND DESIGNATE IRAQI MILITARY LIAISON OFFICER(S) TO WORK WITH KUWAITI AND OTHER COALITION FORCES ON THE OPERATIONAL DETAILS RELATED TO IRAQ'S WITHDRAWAL, TO INCLUDE THE PROVISION OF ALL DATA ON THE LOCATION AND NATURE OF ANY LAND OR SEA MINES;

-- CEASE COMBAT AIRCRAFT FLIGHTS OVER IRAQ AND KUWAIT EXCEPT FOR TRANSPORT AIRCRAFT CARRYING TROOPS OUT OF KUWAIT AND ALLOW COALITION AIRCRAFT EXCLUSIVE CONTROL OVER AND USE OF ALL KUWAITI AIRSPACE; AND

-- CEASE ALL DESTRUCTIVE ACTIONS AGAINST KUWAITI CITIZENS AND PROPERTY AND RELEASE ALL KUWAITI DETAINEES.

THE UNITED STATES AND ITS COALITION PARTNERS REITERATE THAT THEIR FORCES WILL NOT ATTACK RETREATING IRAQI FORCES AND, FURTHER, WILL EXERCISE RESTRAINT SO LONG AS WITHDRAWAL PROCEEDS IN ACCORDANCE WITH THE ABOVE GUIDELINES AND THERE ARE NO ATTACKS BY IRAQ ON OTHER COUNTRIES. ANY BREACH OF THESE TERMS WILL BRING AN INSTANT AND SHARP RESPONSE FROM COALITION FORCES IN ACCORDANCE WITH UNSC RESOLUTION 678.

END STATEMENT.

0048

관리 번호	91-488

7b

원 본

외 무 부

종 별 : 초긴급

번 호 : USW-0858 일 시 : 91 0222 1631

수 신 : 장관(미북,중동1,동구 1,미안)

발 신 : 주 미 대사

제 목 : 미측 종전 제안

연: USW-0857

1. 연호 1. 마. 항 관련, 백악관 FITZWATER 대변인은 금 2.22 정례 기자 회견시, 구체적인 이락군 철군 절차를 아래와같이 제시함(발표 내용 전문및 질의 응답등은 USW(F)-0637 로 FAX 송부)

가. 뉴욕 시간으로 명일 정오까지 이락측은 쿠웨이트로부터 대규모 철군을 개시하되, 동 철군은 1 주 이내에 종료되어야함.

나. 철군 개시후 48 시간 이내에 이락측은 쿠웨이트시(KUWAIT CITY) 로부터 모든 병력을 철수 시키고 쿠웨이트 합법 정권이 복구되도록 하여야함.

다. 또한 철군 개시후 48 시간 이내에 이락측은 모든 전쟁 포로를 석방 하여야함.

라. 이락측은 쿠웨이트 원유 생산 시설등에 설치된 폭발물은 모두 제거하고, 기 매설된 지뢰 및 기뢰의 위치와 성격등에 관한 정보를 제공 하여야 함.

마. 철수 병력 수송시외에는, 이락 항공기의 이락및 쿠웨이트 영공 운항을 불허하며, 쿠웨이트 영공은 다국적군의 배타적 통제하에 놓임.

바. 이락측은 쿠웨이트 국민및 재산에 대한 파괴 행위를 중단하고, 지금까지 억류된 모든 쿠웨이트인을 석방 하여야함.

사. 다국적군은 철수하는 이락군에 대해서는 공격을 가하지 않을것임.

2.FITZWATER 대변인은 전기 발표에 앞서 다음과같이 미측 입장을 추가 언급함.

가. 작일 발표된 소련측 제안이 진지하고 유용한 노력(A SERIOURS AND USEFUL EFFORT)이기는 하나, 주요 장애는 그대로 남아 있음.

나. 이락측이 생각하고 있는것은 일종의 조건부 철군인바, 이와같은 형식으로는 유엔 안보리의 제반 결의안이 충분히 실천될수 없음.

다. 대이락 경제 봉쇄는 오직 유엔 안보리만이 해제할수 있는바, 전기 구체적

미주국 장관 차관 1차보 2차보 미주국 구주국 중아국 청와대
총리실 안기부

91.02.23 07:29
외신 2과 통제관 BW

0049

제안에 대한 이락측 동의가 공개적이고 공식적인 방법을 통해 명일 정오(뉴욕시간)이전까지 유엔에 전달된다면 지상전을 회피할수 있을것임.

3. 분석및 관찰

가.FITZWATER 대변인은, 금일 미측 제안에 대한 소련측 반응을 묻는 기자 질문에 대해, 미소 양국 수뇌부간에 충분한 사전 협의(VERY GOOD AND USEFUL DISCUSSIONS)가 있었다는점만을 주로 강조하였는바, 금일 미측 제안 관련 미소간에어느 정도의 이견이 상존하고 있을 가능성이 큰것으로 보임.

나. 특히, 동 대변인은 미측으로서도 소련의 평화적 해결 노력을 평가한다(APPRECIATE)고 언급한점이 주목되는바, 미측으로서는 가능한한 미소간의 공동 보조를 유지해 나가는 가운데 금번 사태를 해결함으로서 탈 냉전 시대의 근간이라 할 미소 협력 관계를 계속 보존해 나가고자 하는 의도를 시사 하였음.

다. 한편 1530 현재 당지 CNN 방송 보도에 따르면 이락측은 공보부 성명을 통해 전기 미측 제안을 "수치스러운 최후 통첩"(SHAMEFUL ULTIMATUM) 이라고 비난하면서, 동 제안의 수락 여부는 명확인 밝히지 않는 가운데, 중.소 및 다국적군 비참여국으로 유엔 안보리가 중립위원회를 구성, 다국적군 공격으로 인한 이락및 쿠웨이트에 대한 피해 정도등을 조사 하자는 제안을 제시하였는바, 관련 동향등 추보 예정임.

(대사 박동진-국장)

91.12.31 일반

일반문서로 재분류(1991.12.31.)

검 토 필 (1991.6.30.)

PAGE 2

0050

관리 번호	91-149

원 본

외 무 부

종 별 : 지 급

번 호 : USW-0859 일 시 : 91 0222 1642

수 신 : 장관(미북,중동1,동구 1, 미안)

발 신 : 주 미 대사

제 목 : 소-이락측 종전 제안에 대한 미측 입장

예고문에 의거 재분류(1991.12.31.)
직위 성명

연:USW-0857

1. 연호, BUSH 대통령의 소측 평화안에 대한 성명 발표와 관련, 2.22(금) 당관 유명환 참사관은 백악관 및 국무부 관계관과 접촉, 미측의 검토 배경을 문의한바, 요지 다음 보고함.

가. 미측은 금번 소련의 평화안에 대학 과거 어느때 보다도 심각하게 세부적으로 검토한바 금일 새벽까지 최고위층에서 직접 주요 연합군 참여국과도 협의를 거쳐 결정한것임.

나. 걸프전의 진행 방향은 연합군이 결정할 문제이며 후세인이나 소련이 주도하도록 할수는 없음. 특히 소련안은 이락군의 철수 시한이 불분명하며 쿠웨이트의 합법정부 수복 및 배상에 관한 유엔 결의는 이락군의 철수후에도 계속 유효해야 함.

다. 현 사애에서 휴전이되고 이락군의 철수가 중간에 그칠경우 불안정한 휴전상태가 지속됨으로써 연합군의 군사적, 외교적 및 재정적 부담은 더욱 증대될 것이기 때문에 후세인을 제외한 어느누구의 이익도 될수 없음.

라. 걸프전은 신속히 그리고 연합군의 주도하에 종결되어야만 중동평화가 정착될수 있는바, 금번 연합군의 결정에 가급적 많은 우방국의 적극적 지지가 필요하며 이점에서 한국으로부터도 이를 지지하는 성명을 기대함.

2. 상기(라)항은 국무부 관계관이 비공식적으로 언급한 사항이지만 아측이 연합군의 걸프전 종식 노력에 적극 참여하고 있는점을 부각시킬수 있다는 점에서아측이 유엔 안보리 결의에 따라 쿠웨이트로 부터 즉각적이고 무조건적인 이락군의 철수를 요구한 금번 연합군(미국)의 결정을 지지한다는 취지의적절한 논평을 하는 방안을 검토, 회보 바람.

(대사 박동진-국장)

검토필 91. 6. 30 김

미주국 장관 차관 ~~1차보 2차보 미주국 구주국~~ 중아국 청와대
총리실 안기부

PAGE 1

91.02.23 07:32
외신 2과 통제관 BW
0051

예고:91.12.31 일반

PAGE 2

0052

원 본

외 무 부

종 별 : 지 급

번 호 : USW-0861 일 시 : 91 0222 1700

수 신 : 장 관(~~미북, 중근동~~, 대책반)

발 신 : 주 미 대사

제 목 : 걸프전 (소련 휴전안에 대한 논조)

2.21. 발표된 소.이락 휴전안에 대한 당지 언론의 논조를 하기 보고함.

1. W.P. 사설 THE IRAQI-SOVIET PROPOSAL

0 소.이락 휴전안은 (1) 어떤 수단을 동원해서라도 권좌에 머무르려는 후세인의 야욕과, (2) 중동지역에서 소련의 영향력 (PRESTIGE)을 높이려는 고르바쵸프의 이해가 맞아 떨어져 성사된 것임.

0 백악관의 냉정하고 유보적인 반응은 정당한 (JUSTIFIED, HARDLY SURPRISING) 것으로 평가됨.

2. W.P EVANS AND NOVOK (고정기고가)기고 SAME OLDSOVIETS

0 소련은 (1) 중동지역에서 소련의 영향력을 증대시키고, (2)군부를 비롯한 국내 보수 세력에 영합하여 이락에 대한 휴전안을 내놓았음.

0 BUSH 대통령은 냉전후 신 국제질서의 파트너로서 고르바쵸프를 대해 왔으나, 소련은 시종이중적 태도 (DOUBLE GAME ALL ALONG) 를 보여왔음.

0 미국은 1.16. 대 이락전 개시전에 소련에 사전에 이를 알려 주었던바, 소련은 이 정보를 이락에 누설한바도 있음.

3. NYT PETER RODMAN (JOHNS HOPKINS 대 FELLOW)기고 DON'T BACK DOWN: HUMILIATE HUSSEIN

0 소련의 휴전안이 받아들여지면 후세인은 유엔결의안을 무효화한다는 정치적 성공과, 상당한 규모의 군사력을 유지한다는 군사적 성공을 거두게될것임.

0 CHURCHILL 의 교훈대로 승리 +후+ 에 관대할수는 있으나, 승리 +전+에 관대해서는 안됨.

4. NYT A.M. ROSENTHAL (고정 기고가)기고 THE LIFE OF SADDAM HUSSEIN

0 소련은 중동에서의 영향력 회복을 위해 후세인이 권좌에 남기를 간절히 바라고

미주국	장관	차관	1차보	2차보	중아국	정문국	청와대	총리실
안기부	대책반							

PAGE 1

91.02.23 09:16 WG

외신 1과 통제관

0053

있음.

0 미국은 고르바쵸프에 대해 시종 최고의 선의를 가지고 대해 왔으나 고르바쵸프는 미국의 이익과 중동 평화에 반하는 행동을 취하고 있음.

0 미국은 소련의 실체에 대해 다시 한번 생각해야 함.

5. NYT ANTHONY LEWIS (고정 기고가)기고 IT IS AVICTORY

0 소련의 휴전안이 몇가지 중대한 결함을 내포하기는 하나, 지상전을 회피할수 있는 기회를 제공하였다는 점은 평가할 만함.

0 이러한 상황에서 BUSH 대통령이 대규모의 지상전을 감행하는 것은 정치적으로 불가능 (POLITICALLY IMPOSSIBLE) 할 것임.

6. 상기 논설 FAX 송부함.(USW(F)-0638)

(대사 박동진-국장)

PAGE 2

0054

FEB.22 '91 17:05 KOREAN EMBASS WASHINGTON DC P.001

USW(F) - 0638

수신: 장관 (미북, 중동, 대책반) 발신: 주미대사

제목: 걸프전 (言論論說) USW - 첨부물 (5 매)

The Iraqi-Soviet Proposal

A SMILING Soviet spokesman announced in Moscow last night a "positive" result to the latest Soviet-Iraqi consultations. The new position seems a precise blending of two things: 1) Saddam Hussein's hope to use Mikhail Gorbachev's and the Soviet Union's emerging ambitions in order to draw out a negotiating process that will let him stay in power, well armed and available for further adventures, and 2) Mikhail Gorbachev's hope to ensconce the Soviet Union as the broker of a Gulf peace—and perhaps also to revive his own prestige. This new position is remote from the stated goals of the United States and the allied coalition it leads. The White House's cool, reserved reaction was justified and hardly surprising.

Under the Iraqi-Soviet package, Iraq would leave Kuwait, but on an unspecified "fixed term" and apparently with full weaponry. So much for the American demand that Iraq leave on a quick schedule inconsistent with taking out the equipment that would leave it a regional menace. Economic sanctions would be ended automatically after just two-thirds of the forces were out; all remaining U.N. resolutions, including evidently the key one (678) that authorizes the U.N. "to restore international peace and security in the area," would be voided after all the forces were out. So much here for the intent of almost all members of the military coalition to use the U.N. statements to reduce Iraq's armed might and potential and to bring a new stability to the Gulf as a whole. This highly conditioned proposition was being described in Moscow as "unconditional withdrawal."

Iraq and the Soviet Union hope to involve the United Nations as early as today in consultations on these issues. That is bound to complicate any American decision to continue applying and even to increase military pressure in order to win withdrawal terms closer to the international standard. What needs most to be kept in mind, however, is that the allied coalition did not come all this way in order to establish in Iraq, with Saddam Hussein, a potentially revitalized regional threat. It is the coalition that must have the first voice in determining what needs to be done "to restore international peace and security in the area."

Of the Soviet Union it can be said that, using its diplomatic tools, it did what it could to end Iraqi aggression against Kuwait. But the American-led coalition has in addition military tools, and a strong U.N. mandate to employ them, and plenty of good strategic and political reason as well. It is not only Moscow, which is trying to cultivate his favor, that Saddam Hussein must satisfy, but the coalition, which has a broader, more legitimate and less self-interested purpose. The war in the Gulf will properly be over when Iraq meets the United Nations' originally stated, reasonable terms.

Feb. 22, 1991
WP

0638 - 1

0055

070 P01 LENINPROTOCOL '91-02-23 07:00

관 발신 : 주미대사

보안	
통제	

(매)

Rowland Evans and Robert Novak

Same Old Soviets

After two years of painstaking, personal U.S. diplomacy to develop a cozy relationship with the men in the Kremlin, Mikhail Gorbachev's failure to alert George Bush in advance about his Iraqi peace initiative suggests the old world order persists.

"This was a supreme double cross," one national security analyst inside the administration confided to us. President Bush's commitment to President Gorbachev was answered with a Soviet bid to reassert influence in the Middle East by coming to the rescue of Saddam Hussein's regime. It looked very much like the same old Soviets.

Bush, in private even more than in public, showed no inclination to postpone at Gorbachev's request the ground assault against Iraqi legions. Nevertheless, the Soviet gambit must be mortifying for him. In fudging a half-century-old commitment to freedom for the Baltic states, the United States had purchased Soviet compliance with the use of American force in the Gulf but not the much-advertised global partnership with the Kremlin.

The reason for belated Soviet entrance on the Gulf diplomatic stage is viewed by administration officials in narrow terms. "Iraq was the No. 1 Soviet cash customer [for arms] in the '80s," one of them told us, "and there are hopes that it can be so again."

Soviet ambitions in the Gulf transcend the arms merchant's role, though. Collaboration with Iran in seeking to avert a land war raises aspirations for a Moscow-Tehran entente changing the region's power relations. Although Arabs never have liked the Soviets much, that may change now that Gorbachev has tried to put his body between the Americans and the Iraqis.

But the Soviet peace initiative cannot be separated from internal uproar in the Soviet Union. U.S. officials clinging to the Bush-Gorbachev link say that the Soviet president is under intense pressure from his own military high command, which is humiliated by what it perceives as a string of international setbacks culminating in the failure of their arms and their clients in Iraq. What Bush advisers won't concede is the extent to which Gorbachev has cast his lot with the generals in fighting democracy and reform.

Indeed, Gorbachev looks like a willing participant in this reversion to old-style Soviet diplomacy. As early as the Helsinki summit last September, he signaled he would not accept junior status in Bush's new world order.

The Soviets have been playing a double game all along. Bush administration officials have turned away from reports of Soviet war material leaking into Iraq during six months of the boycott. Well-informed U.S. sources say Washington's advance warning to Moscow that the air war would begin Jan. 16 was passed through Soviet military channels to the Iraqis.

The true Soviet attitude was suggested in the nonreaction to the outrageous performance on his visit to Moscow by Syria's minister of defense, Lt. Gen. Mustafa Talas. He assailed the United States for using the crisis as a pretext for getting a military foothold in the Persian Gulf, while the Syrians and Soviets were pure heart of heart in desiring only that Saddam leave Kuwait. Talas was not contradicted by his Soviet hosts, who on the contrary implied that they agreed with him.

The attitude was confirmed this week when Soviet Foreign Minister Alexander Bessmertnykh snapped that Bush had no right to comment on the Soviet peace proposal because it was addressed to Saddam, not to him.

At that day's meeting with congressional leaders, the president gave no indication of being miffed with the Soviets, but in fact the foundation of his foreign policy is under severe attack. Put simply, Gorbachev is determined that Saddam's regime personally survive the war, and Bush is determined that it does not.

That follows a familiar road taken by the Communists who have ruled the Russian empire for over 73 years. But it is a disappointment for an American president who has closed his eyes to domestic thuggery in hopes that the Kremlin will behave in a civilized manner internationally for the first time since the Bolsheviks took over.

Feb. 22, 1991
WP

6638-2

0056

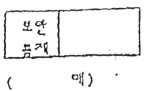

FEB.22 '91 17:06 KOREAN [redacted]SY WASHINGTON DC P.003

: USW(F) -

: 장 관 발신 : 주미대사

보안 통제	

:

(매)

Don't Back Down: Humiliate Hussein

By Peter W. Rodman

WASHINGTON

The Soviet peace proposal and Iraq's apparent qualified acceptance of it starkly raise the question of the advantages and disadvantages of a compromise — one that might save Saddam Hussein's face politically and militarily.

Some experts have argued all along that an outright victory by the allied coalition would be counterproductive: The U.S. would pay a huge price in Middle East for the destruction of an Arab country. Mr. Hussein would "win" politically even if he loses militarily and too conclusive a victory would weaken Iraq too much. Thus a compromise, like the Soviet-Iraqi one, is said to be not simply an acceptable fallback but strategically the best outcome.

These ideas are flawed in their logic and perverse in their implications. They are based on a misreading of the Arab world. True, no one should underestimate the many sources of instability and festering resentments after a victory by the U.S.-led coalition. But when the dust settles, and Iraq's military power and Saddam Hussein's pretensions lie in ruins, it is not self-evident how he and his policies will be vindicated. On the contrary, they will be discredited by their cataclysmic failure.

Moreover, Mr. Hussein's blunders will have brought about two of his worst nightmares — the weakening of OPEC (the inevitable result of the oil glut that will follow the war) and the expansion of U.S. role in the region.

Peter W. Rodman, who was a senior official on National Security Council staff in the Reagan and Bush Administrations, is a fellow at the Johns Hopkins Foreign Policy Institute.

Reality eventually intrudes, even in the Middle East. Just as Nasser was deflated by the 1967 Arab-Israeli war, a fiasco for Egypt, and Qaddafi by the American bombing raids of Libya in 1986, the message will be clear. Mr. Hussein in defeat will look a lot less formidable than he after Aug. 2.

That is precisely why it is essential that the war end unmistakably in his defeat. Any excess of scruple by the allies — a cease-fire in ambiguous circumstances, face-saving diplomatic formulas or an easing up of the conduct of the war — would be wrongheaded and dangerous.

Deny him a political victory.

When the war is over, anything that allows him to claim a shred of victory or to trumpet that he fought the world to a standoff will guarantee the very instabilities that many fear. The Soviet plan, as announced last night, would offer him the political success of abrogating several key U.N. resolutions and the military success of averting destruction of his forces. His strength in the Arab world would be preserved; down the road, he would be able to intimidate his neighbors again. The best insurance against this is an outcome, military or political, that discredits him utterly.

This is not an argument for expanding our war aims; the liberation of Kuwait can continue to be our focus. But the perception of the unambiguous defeat of Saddam Hussein is crucial. We should devoutly wish for his removal from power, but we probably cannot guarantee that. The best we can do may be to create conditions — his expulsion from Kuwait and the humiliation of his army and Republican Guards — that would undermine him. Whether this can be accomplished by diplomacy alone is far from clear. But one thing is clear: his survival as leader is strategically tolerable only if he has been politically shrunken by a clear defeat.

Nor should we fear a vacuum if we win militarily. Iraq is a resilient country, the No. 2 oil power in OPEC after Saudi Arabia. Its economy will eventually recover after the war ends and sanctions are lifted. Syria and Iran are not in a good position to bid for hegemony anyway: Syria has neither the oil wealth nor the Soviet backing it would need for military dominance; Iran lacks the political cohesion and advanced military technology that Iraq has.

If the U.S. remains a security factor in the region, we will be able to restore a rough equilibrium. Therefore, it is absurd to fear victory. It is absurd to use speculative fears of hypothetical future problems with other countries as an excuse not to confront the Iraqi threat.

The epigraph to Churchill's war memoirs included the motto "magnanimous in victory." It never occurred to him to be to be magnanimous *before* victory — letting the dictator come up for air so that he could claim he was not defeated. □

Feb. 22, 1991
NYT

0638-3

0057

070 P03 LENINPROTOCOL '91-02-23 07:02

JSW(F) -

경 관 발신 : 주미대사

보안	
통제	

(매)

ON MY MIND | A. M. Rosenthal

The Life of Saddam Hussein

In its new move to regain political power in the Middle East, the Gorbachev Government has one vital goal: the survival of Saddam Hussein.

Of course, that happens to be precisely the result that would be most dangerous for the United States and the Middle East. It would keep the whole region at arms, and soon enough, again at war.

Washington has not been rude enough to point out the conflict of interests. But as Saddam Hussein maneuvers to win the peace by accepting the Soviet "eight-point peace plan," it is easy to see what the Kremlin has at stake in his life and rule.

If he goes, through assassination or a political coup, which for a Mideast dictator is a temporary halfway house to extinction, Moscow will lose its only remaining ally in the area. Also: its best customer for weapons. Also: the military and political prestige it invested in Saddam Hussein for so long.

But if Saddam Hussein hangs on, the benefits to the Kremlin will be enormous, and continuing. Many Muslims loathe him, which the West tends to forget. But those who do adore him, particularly Palestinians and our recent friend the King of Jordan, would correctly see the Kremlin as Saddam Hussein's savior.

Moscow would rebuild Iraq's armed forces. That would be a nice piece of business for the K.G.B. and Army generals with whom Mr. Gorbachev is allied.

With Saddam Hussein ruling in postwar Baghdad, the Soviet Union would be the only intermediary between him and enemies in Islam or the West. So without contributing a rifle or a ruble during the war, Mr. Gorbachev would influence the entire Middle East after the war.

But for the U.S. — no benefits, just trouble without end. As long as Saddam rules, the U.S. will have to keep large forces in the Middle East. The U.S. armed forces would be his hostage. Under Moscow's plan, Saddam would keep his army, planes, tanks and dictatorship. This is victory?

Every Arab nation that opposes him now would face his terrorism immediately, subversion always, domination eventually.

But his justification for existence would be the conquest and extermination of Israel and the Israelis. Americans like to think the Israeli Army and Air Force can do anything. Maybe. But it took the full military and industrial power of the United States to face down the might of Iraq.

Mistakes in the Soviet 'peace plan.'

Saddam Hussein would live for the day when he would cross Jordan into Israel — by land, air or chemical missile. The Israelis would be fools if they sat and waited for him to come get them. They won't.

Now, for years President Bush and his Secretary of State could not have been sweeter to Mr. Gorbachev. They praised him every hour on the hour, rounded up help for him. As for the Baltics — what Baltics?

But there goes President Gorbachev acting against American interests and any hope of a stable Mideast. The sorrow of it is we are surprised.

The "experts" in government, journalism and academia who made careers pandering to Mr. Gorbachev still talk of the danger of his being overthrown.

But the future is already the past. Mr. Gorbachev gave the Soviet Union an important measure of free expression — not free politics. But when he decided glasnost was endangering rather than promoting his goal of keeping the Soviet system alive, he cut back fast.

He was not pushed into it by "them" — some cabal of hard-nosed civilians and generals. He is them. Mr. Gorbachev has been overthrown already, by Mr. Gorbachev.

So the Soviet President finds it quite natural and appropriate to try to assert power in the Middle East.

The experts, including Mr. Bush and Secretary of State James Baker, never prepared Americans for that. They could not because they refused to see it themselves.

Washington talked itself into believing that Mr. Gorbachev was an essential partner in the new world order, whatever that is. But when Mr. Gorbachev moved, Washington was caught off guard. Then his new Foreign Minister contemptuously said it was not even Mr. Bush's business to reject the "peace plan"; a great partner.

But since the invasion of Kuwait, Mr. Bush has shown that he understands the danger of the killer of Baghdad. Perhaps Washington will look more clearly at the Kremlin now. Perhaps Mr. Bush will decide where American interests conflict with Moscow's — as in the survival of Saddam Hussein — and say so to Americans at home and in the desert. □

Feb. 22, 1991
NYT

-638-4

0058

3.22 '91 17:08 KOREAN EMBASSY WASHING——C P.005

발신 : 주미대사

보안	
통제	

(매)

ABROAD AT HOME | Anthony Lewis

It Is a Victory

BOSTON

The late-night agreement between Moscow and Baghdad poses hard questions for President Bush. But it entitles him to claim a great victory of principle. And that is the way he should frame his reply: as a statement of victory.

Saddam Hussein is going to withdraw from Kuwait. That is the bottom line. Half a day after a hard-line speech in which he said he would not leave, he agreed to do so.

Some of the terms will be hard for President Bush and even some Americans who have disagreed with him about the war to swallow.

One is the requirement that all United Nations resolutions about the gulf crisis be canceled, including the call for payment of reparations by Iraq. Why shouldn't Iraq pay for the horrors it has inflicted on Kuwait? On the other hand, is there any realistic expectation of payment in Iraq's stricken state?

Another difficult provision calls for the lifting of economic sanctions on Iraq when its withdrawal from Kuwait is two-thirds complete. Sanctions could be a useful tool to keep degrees of international control on what Saddam Hussein may do in future.

But against the doubts over those clauses there is the overwhelming human fact of the peace agreement: It would spare the United States and its allies a ground war. That President Bush could insist on a massive ground attack in this circumstance seems politically impossible.

A ground war must be off now, at least until the new situation is clarified. But President Bush could keep the air attacks going on Iraqi forces in the Kuwait area while he goes into what amounts to a negotiating phase.

Mr. Bush can answer the proposal with modifications of his own. But the thought here is that he should frame his answer in affirmative terms, treating this as a victory on the fundamental question of Iraq's aggression in Kuwait.

There will be voices on the American Right urging Mr. Bush to say a flat no. Those conservative voices want the United States to expand the aims of the war from freeing Kuwait to removing Saddam Hussein.

A recent editorial in The Wall Street Journal was an example of such thinking.

Saddam Hussein, it said, must be removed "by death, flight or, preferably, capture." The editorial did not shy from urging that American forces battle on as far as necessary to capture him.

It indeed would be a blessing to have a different president of Iraq at the end of this affair. Saddam Hussein is a vicious tyrant who would make as much trouble as he could if in office, even with his military power largely destroyed.

But to have American armies pursue him across Iraq and capture him would be the surest way to make him a martyr. All his propaganda about the imperialist conspiracy against him would be borne out in the minds of many Arabs and other third world peoples.

And if American forces fought their way to Baghdad, what would they do then? Install a U.S. proconsul to govern Iraq? Choose a new president? Either of those courses would arouse profound hostility among Arabs, who have long since made clear their feelings about the way Britain and France installed rulers over them after World War I.

The coalition wisely formed by President Bush to undo the Iraqi occupation of Kuwait would split over such an expansion of war aims at the very moment peace is a possibility. The United Nations Security Council would not authorize it. Britain might go along, but even that is not a certainty.

Thunderbolt from Moscow.

The political consequence, then, would be to remove the international support that gave the allied cause legitimacy. The divisions provoked by an American decision to go on to Baghdad would end what hope remains of Mr. Bush's "new world order."

The idea of carrying this war on to Baghdad to capture Saddam Hussein rests, in the end, on a fundamental illusion. That is the belief that complicated political problems can be solved by military action — unilateral American military action.

The Middle East is a stew-pot of conflicting religions, races, dreams. Secretary of State Baker was surely right when he said the United States must address the region's problems "with a due sense of modesty." We ought to have learned in Lebanon the danger of trying to impose solutions.

The one great recent success in easing Middle East conflicts was a substitution of politics for force. Anwar Sadat and Menachem Begin made peace, and their work endures amid so much instability and fear. □

Feb. 22, 1991 NYT

0638-5

070 P05 LENINPROTOCOL '91-02-23 07:03

0053

관리 번호 91-498

원 본

외 무 부

종 별 : 긴 급

번 호 : USW-0875 일 시 : 91 0222 1919

수 신 : 장관(미북,중동 1,동구 1,미안)

발 신 : 주 미 대사

제 목 : 걸프전 종식을 위한 소련측 신 제안

1. 금 2.22 1800 현재 당지 CNN 방송 보도에 따르면, AZIZ 이락 외상이 상금 모스크바에 계속 체류 하고 있는 가운데, 소련측이 다음과같은 6 개항의 새로운 제안을 이락측에 제시하였으며, AZIZ 외상은 이를 본국 정부에 보고, 회신을 대기하고 있는 중이라 함.

가. 이락측은 쿠웨이트로부터 무조건 철수함.

나. 동 철수는 정전(CEASEFIRE)후 익일부터 개시함.

다. 철수 기한은 21 일이며, 쿠웨이트시로부터의 철수는 4 일내에 이루어져야함.

라. 철수후 대이락 경제 제재 조치는 해제함.

마. 철수 개시후 72 시간 이내에 전쟁 포로 석방을 개시함.

바. 다국적군 비 참여국으로 구성된 감시단이 유엔 안보리 의 중재로 동 철수를 감시함.

2. 또한 동 방송에 따르면, 소련측은 외무부 대변인의 기자 회견등을 통해 다국적군의 지상전 개전이 여사한 평화적 해결 노력에 장애를 초래할것이라고 언급하는등, 미국측에 대해 지상전 개전을 자제토록 간접 촉구하고 있는바, 기 보고한바와같이 미소간에는 어느정도의 견해차가 상존하고 있는것으로 보임.

3. 한편, 현재 이락은 소련측만을 대화 상대로 인정하면서 사태의 해결방안에 대해서는 별다른 반응을 보이지 않고 있는바, 만약 전기 소련측 제안과 금일 발표된 미측 제안의 중간 정도 선에서 실질적으로 모종의 타협이 이루어진다면, 외형상 소련이 행한 중재자로서의 역할이 더욱 부각될것이며, 그 경우 미국이 중동 지역 전후 질서 재편 과정상 차지할수 있는 외교적 입지는 상당히 좁아질것으로 전망됨.

4. 따라서 현재로서는 여사한 타협의 전망은 희박하며 일단 부분적인 지상전이 불가피한것으로 보이는바 그러한 타협은 사태가 좀더 진전된 이후 연합군측의 상황이

미주국	장관	차관	1차보	2차보	미주국	구주국	중아국	정문국
청와대	총리실	안기부						

PAGE 1

91.02.23 10:12
외신 2과 통제관 BW

0060

악화될 경우에야 모색될것으로 관측됨.

(대사 박동진-국장)

91.12.31 일반

검 토 필 (1991.6.30.)

일반문서로 재분류(1991.12.31.)

PAGE 2

0061

관리 번호 91-380

가 원 본

외 무 부

종 별 : 지 급

번 호 : USW-0876 일 시 : 91 0222 1916

수 신 : 장관(미북,미안,중근동,아일)

발 신 : 주 미 대사

제 목 : 걸프전 관련 세미나

1. 당지 HERITAGE FOUNDATION 주관하에 - AMERICA AND ASIA AFTER THE GULFWAR- 제하의 세미나가 금 2.22 HERITAGE FOUNDATION 강당에서 개최된바, 주요 토의 내용을 하기 보고함.

2.KARL JACKSON(NSC 아시아 담당 보좌관)

0 미국은 금번 사태를 통해 VIETNAM WAR SYNDROME 에서 벗어나 미국의 국제적 지도력에 대해 자신감을 갖게 되었음. 즉 PAUL KENNEDY 등이 제시한 미국 쇠퇴론이 틀렸다는것을 보여준 계기였다고 평가됨.

0 또하나 금번 사태와 관련 특기할것은 일본이 종래의 내부 지향적 자세에서 벗어나 국제사회의 노력에 적극적으로 참여하려는 의지를 보였다는것임.일본의 적극적 참여로 말미암아 국제 관계에 있어 새로운 시대(NEW ERA OF JAPAN'S INVOLVEMENT IN WORLD AFFAIRS)가 열리고 있다고 보며, 미.일 관계는 단순히 양자 문제를 떠나 국제 문제에 대해 협의하고 협력하는 GLOBAL PARTNERSHIP 으로 발전하고 있음.

3. 기무라 주미 일본 공사

0 미국내에서 걸프전에 대한 일본의 대응이 너무 늦고, 너무 소극적이라는 인상이 있으나 이것은 사실과 다른것임.

0 일본은 금번 사태를 통해 미국만이 진정한 의미에서의 초강대국이며, 국제사회가 위기에 직면했을때 이를 해결할 지도력을 가진 국가라는 사실을 다시한번 확인하였으며, 아울러 일본은 미국과 함께 걸프전에 참여하고 있는것을 자랑스럽게 생각함.

0 일본은 경제력에 있어서는 SUPERPOWER 이나, 정치, 군사력에 있어서는 그렇지 못하므로 특히 미.일간의 협력이 중요하다고 봄.

0 한편 일본내에서는 일본이 걸프전에 큰 기여를 하고 있음에도 정책 결정 과정에

미주국	장관	차관	1차보	2차보	아주국	미주국	중아국	정문국
청와대	안기부							

PAGE 1

91.02.23 10:10

외신 2과 통제관 BW

0062

참여하지 못하고 일본의 기여에 대해 정당한 평가를 받지 못하고 있다는 불만이 있음.

4.HERITAGE FOUNDATION 은 걸프전 개막 이후 미국 조야의 관심이 걸프전 해결을 위한 미.NATO , 미.소, 미.아랍 관계에만 경사되고 아시아에 대한 정당한 평가가 부족하다는 취지에서 금번 세미나를 개최한것으로 평가되나 2.21 소.이락휴전안이 발표됨에 따라 언론등의 큰관심을 끌지 못한것으로 판단됨.

(대사 박동진-국장)

91.12.31 까지

일반문서로 재분류(1991.12.31.)

검 토 필 (1991.6.30.)

PAGE 2

0063

관리번호	91-146

원 본

외 무 부

종 별 : 긴 급

번 호 : USW-0879 일 시 : 91 0223 1749

수 신 : 장관(미북,중동1,동구 1,미안)

발 신 : 주 미 대사

제 목 : 걸프전 동향

예고문에 의거 재분류(1991.12.31) 직위 성명

검토필 91.6.30

1. 금 2.23 1600 현재 CNN 방송등 당지 언론 보도를 통해 광가된 걸프전 관련 동향을 하기 요지 보고함.

가. 현재 CAMP DAVID 별장에서 주말을 보내고 있는 부쉬 대통령은 이락군 철수 개시 시한의 경과와 관련 다음 내용의 간단한 성명을 발표함.

" 우리는 금일 정오까지도 사담 후세인이 안보리 결의안에 호응하는 여하한조치도 취하지 않은것을 유감으로 생각함. 우리는 제반 유엔 안보리 결의안을 실천할 결의를 가지고 있음. 군사 행동은 예정대로 계획에 따라(ON SCHEDULE ANDACCORDING TO PLAN)진행되고 있음"

나. 또한 동 성명 발표에 이어, FITZWATER 백악관 대변인도 다음 요지의 성명을 발표함.

"이락군이 쿠웨이트로부터 철수하고 있다는 아무런 군사적 조짐도 상금 발견되지 않고 있음.

-또한 이락측이 작일 발표된 미측 제안에 대한 동의를 유엔측에 표시 하지도 않고 있음.

-오히려,(당지 시간 금일 오전에 있었던) 대 이스라엘 스커드 미사일 공격이 현재까지 나타난 사담 후세인의 유일한 반응임.

-여사한 상황하에서, 전쟁 계속외에는 다른 대안이 없음.

다. 한편, 최근 수일전에 이미 부쉬 대통령은 슈와르츠코프 사우디 주둔 미군 사령관이 현지 상황(기후, 이락측이 매설한 지뢰 제거 정도, 보급 물자 재고등)을 고려, 임의로(AT HIS DISCRETION)대 이락 지상전 개시 일자를 결정할수 있도록 허가한바 있으며, 다국적군은 현재 지상전 개전에 대비한 만반의 준비를 갖추가 있는 상태라함.

미주국 장관 차관 1차보 2차보 미주국 구주국 중아국 청와대
안기부

PAGE 1 91.02.24 08:39
외신 2과 통제관 CH

0064

(현재 쿠웨이트내 이락군 탱크의 약 40 프로, 야포의 경우는 50 프로가 파괴된것으로 추정된다함)

라. 또한 금일 정오경 고르바쵸프 대통령이 부쉬 대통령과 의 전화 통화를 통해, 이락군 철수 개시 시한을 연기해 줄것을 요청했으나 미측은 이를 거부한것으로 알려지고 있음. 소련측은, 작일 미측 제안과 관련, 상금도 이락측이 태도의변화를 보일것으로 기대하고 있고, 또 금일 유엔 안보리 비공개 회의시 소측 대표는 이락측이 미측 제안에 대해 원칙적으로 긍정적 반응을 보였다고 발언 하기도 하였으나, 미측에서는 이를 일종의 "LAST-MINUTE FALSE ALARM"으로 보고 있다함.

마. 한편 금일 오후 발표된 이락측 혁명 평의회 부의장 명의의 성명에 따르면 미측이 제시한 철수 시한내에 이락군을 철수한다는것은 사실상 불가능할것이므로 여사한 비현실적 최후 통첩을 이락측으로서는 무시(WOULD NOT LEAD)할것이라함.

2. 관찰

가. 전기 제반 상황을 종합해볼때, 일단 당지의 분위기는 지상전 개전이 불가피하다는 쪽으로 기울어 가고 있음.

나. 즉, 부쉬 행정부로서는 지상전을 통한 금번 사태의 종결이 이락과의 교섭 보다 오히려 더 효율적인 방안인것으로 간주하고 있는것을 보이며, 당지 언론에서도 부쉬 행정부의 결의가 너무 확고하기 때문에 대이락 협상은 어려울것으로분석하고 있음.

다. 또한 1 주일 이라는 짧은 기간내에 철군을 종료한다는것이 사실상 불가능하다는것으로 잘 알면서도, 부쉬 행정부는 여사한 제안을 제시한것으로 보이는바, 미측으로서는 이락측이 이를 수락함으로서 정치적 수모와 군사적 무력화를 받아들이든가 아니면 지상전을 통해 이락 전력의 궤멸과 정권의 붕괴를 감수하든가 하는 양자 택일의 선택을 후세인 정권에게 강요하고 있는것으로 보임.

라. 한편, 각종 종전 제안과 관련, 미소 양국 수뇌부간 긴밀한 협의 채널이계속 유지되고 있고, 또한 당지 언론에서는 금번 사태와 관련, 소련측이 나름의 정치적 이득만을 추구하려는 냉전시대적 발상으로 회귀하고 있지는 않은것으로 분석하고 있는점이 주목되는바, 설사 금번 사태의 구체적 해결 방향에 대해서는 어느 정도의 이견이 존재한다 할지라도, 탈 냉전 시대 국제 관계의 초석이라 할수 있는 미소 협력 관계를 유지해 나가야 한다는데에는 양국간의 대승적 이해 관계가 일치하고 있는것으로 보임. 따라서 향후 사태 진전에는 이락측의 구체적 철수 조치 실행 여부외에 여사한 강대국 관계가 작용하게될것임.

PAGE 2

0065

(대사 박동진-차관)
예고:91.12.31 일반

PAGE 3

0066

관리 번호 91-448

원 본

외 무 부

종 별 : 초긴급

번 호 : USW-0881 일 시 : 91 0223 2220

수 신 : 장관(미북,중근동)

발 신 : 주 미 대사

제 목 : 걸프 지상전 개시-I

예고문에 의거 재분류 (1991.12.31.) 직위 성명

1. 금 2.23 저녁 9:40 국무부 DESAIX ANDERSON 동아태 부차관보는 본직에게긴급히 전화, BAKER 국무장관의 명에 따라 미군과 연합군이 금일 저녁 이락에 대한 지상 작전을 개시했음을 아측에 공식 전달한다고 하면서 이를 본국 정부에 보고 해줄것을 요청하여왔음.

2. 동 부차관보는 아국 정부가 대호 성명을 발표해준것을 높이 평가한다고 하고, 아국 정부나 연합군측의 지상 작전에 대한 지지 성명을 내준다면 금번 작전에 대한 확고한 국내적 결속 과시에 커다란 도움이 될것으로 기대한다고 말함.

3. 본직은 이에 아국 정부의 다국적군의 목표와 작전에 대한 참여와 지지르다시한번 상기 시키고, 금번 작전이 조속 성공적으로 종결되도록 기대를 표시했음.

4. 본직과 ANDERSON 부차관보와의 통화직후인 저녁 10:00 CAMP DAVID 로부터 급히 백악관에 귀환한 부쉬 대통령은 짤막한 성명을 통해 미군과 다국적 연합군은 이락군을 쿠웨이트로부터 몰아내고 쿠웨이트를 해방하기 위한 작전을 개시했다고 발표했음. 동 대통령은 연합군 정부들과의 매우 긴밀한 협의를 통해 연합군 총사령관 슈와르츠코프 장군에게 지상군을 포함한 모든 수단을 동원, 동 목표를 신속히 달성하도록 지시했다고 밝히고, 이락은 최후 통첩 시한을 무시하고 오히려 쿠워이트를 파괴하는 행동을 배가하는등, UN 안보리 결의안을 무시했다고작전 개시의 이유를 설명했음.

5. 한편, 미측은 작 2.22 철수에 대한 최후 통첩을 발하면서, 이락이 철수를 개시하지 않을것이 대비 이미 슈와르츠코프 장군으로 하여금 초동 작전의 개시를 포함한 전면 작전 개시 준비를 명하였다고 함. 금일 오후 유명환 참사관과KARTMAN 정무차관 보좌관 접촉시, 동 보좌관은 미측으로서는 이미 HUSSEIN 이 철수를 개시하지 않을것으로 판단한고, 작전 개시를 정해 놓고 있다고 언급한바 있음.

미주국	장관	차관	1차보	2차보	중아국	청와대	총리실	안기부

PAGE 1

91.02.24 13:13

외신 2과 통제관 CE

0067

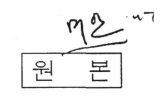

6. 전기 부쉬 대통령의 짤막한 성명발표후, CHENEY 국방장관은 국방부에서 후속 기자 회견을 갖고 연합군측이 대규모, 본격 지.해, 공 종합 작전을 개시했다고 밝히고, 가급적 상세한 작전 관련 내용에 대해서는 상세한 답변을 회피 하였음.

7. 동건 진전 사항 추보 예정임.

(대사 박동진-장관)

예고:91.12.31 일반

원 본

외 무 부

종 별 : 지 급

번 호 : USW-0883 일 시 : 91 0223 2314

수 신 : 장관(미북,중근동,미안)

발 신 : 주미대사

제 목 : 걸프 지상전- II

1.금 2.23 저녁 부쉬 대통령과 CHENEY 장관의 지상전을 포함한 전면 작전의 개시 선언 이후,당지 방송들은 전문가들의 해설과 취재를 통해 이락군이 급속히 궤멸될 가능성이 높다고 하고, 연합군측은 신속히 쿠웨이트 이락군을 포위, 항복을 받을수있을것이라고 낙관적 견해를 보도 하고있음(현지 최전선의 일부 이락군 부항 사례도보도)

2. CHENEY 장관등 국방 당국은 작전 전망과관련 언론이 지나치게 낙관적 보도를 하지 않도록이에 대한 구체적 언급을 하고 있지 않음 그러나 부쉬 대통령등 고위 인사들은 연합군이 신속하고, 결정적으로 작전을 종료할수 있을 것이라고 언급한바있고, 당지 일부 CNN 현장 기자들은 군사 당국자들이 공식적으로 표명은 않하고 있으나 일부당국자들은 내부적으로 수일내에 작전 목표의 대부분이 달성될수 있을것으로전망하고 있다고 보도하기도 하였음.

3.한편 금일 부쉬 대통령이 고르바쵸프 대통령의 전화등 소련측에 의한 철군 시한 등 구체 조건에 대한 미.소 양측안의 절충 요청을 거부하고 작전 개시를 명령한것과 관련, 당지에서는 향후 미소 관계에 관한 다각도의 분석과 전망이 제기될것으로 예상됨.

(대사 박동진-국장)

미주국	장관	차관	1차보	2차보	미주국	중아국	정문국	청와대
총리실	안기부							

PAGE 1

91.02.24 15:04 DN

외신 1과 통제관

0069

Cheney 국방장관 발표 및 질의응답 요지

(2.24(일) 12:30)

(발표 요지)

o 금번 미군 및 연합군의 지상전은 희생자를 최소화를 위해 신중히 계획되었으며 해.공군의 대규모 협동 작전이 될 것임.

o 금번 군사작전의 세부사항은 이라크측 반격에 유리한 정보가 될 것이므로 언급을 제한함.

o 국방성과 리야드에서의 정례적 브리핑도 당분간 중지할 것임.

(질의응답 요지)

문 : 금번 지상전 개시는 언제 결정했는가 ?

답 : 사담 후세인이 최후 통첩 시한을 지키지 않음으로써 오늘 지상군의 대규모 공격을 명령하게 된 것임. 금번 작전은 슈와츠코프 사령관의 판단에 기초하여 수행될 것이며, 마지막까지도 외교적.군사적 상황에 따라 변경될 수도 있음. 금번 군사 작전중에도 사담 후세인이 유엔 안보리 결의안을 준수하여 무조건적인 철군을 시작한다면 작전이 정지될 수도 있음.

문 : 금번 지상군 공격은 오직 쿠웨이트내에 한정될 것인가 ?

답 : 군사작전 세부사항에 관해서는 언급할 입장에 있지 않음.

문 : 금번 연합군(Coalition Forces)에는 몇나라가 참가하고 있는가 ?

답 : 연합군 다수국가(significant number of allies)가 참전중임.

0070

문 : 소련측 종전안과 미국측 최후 통첩 내용간에 어떠한 차이가 있는가 ?
이라크군의 철군 기간이 21일과 7일간에 큰 차이가 있는지 ?

답 : 이라크군은 불명확한 휴전기간 및 충분한 철군기간을 악용해서 군대 재편성 (regroup)과 재보급(resupply)을 통해 공격 능력을 보강할 것이 틀림없으며, 그 경우 미군과 연합군의 희생자는 더욱 늘 것임. 이는 받아들일수 없음.

문 : 미국은 사담 후세인 정부와 수뇌부를 제거(remove)할 생각인가 ?

답 : 유엔 결의안 이행을 위한 임무 수행에 있어 특정 개인을 제거하거나 이라크 정부 수뇌부를 변경시키는 것은 우리의 정책 목표가 아님.

- 끝 -

0071

미중(W보관)

원 본

외 무 부

종 별 : 지 급

번 호 : USW-0886 일 시 : 91 0224 1601

수 신 : 장 관(미북,중근동,대책반)

발 신 : 주 미 대사

제 목 : 걸프전(지상전 개막에 대한 언론 논조

작 2.23 지상전 개시에 대한 주재국 언론 주요 논조를 하기 보고함.

1. NYT 사설 '' MORE WAR-AND LESS''

0 외교적 수단의 실패에 따라 지상전이 개시되었으나, 미국은 지상전의 목표를 제한하고, 신속히 이를 종결시켜야 함.

0 그렇지 않을 경우에는 1) 이락의 극단적 위축에 따른 중동내 불안정 요인 조성, 2) 미국의이락 주둔, 3) 미.쏘 관계의 새로운 긴장 조성등이 초래 될것임.

2. NYT THOMAS FRIEDMAN (고정 기고가) 기고 '' THE UNCERTAIN TIME BEYOND HIGH NOON''

0 금번 걸프전은 중동에 잠재해왔던 많은 문제를 표면화 시키는 계기가 되었으나, 이 문제들의 해결 전망이 밝지 만은 않음.

0 친 서방 중동 정부의 정통성 문제

0 중동내 빈.부 국간의 부의 차이 해소 문제 (오히려 전쟁의 인해 나눌수 있는 재원이 고갈됨)

0 이락.이스라엘 문제 (이스라엘의 안보에 대한 우려가 더욱 심화됨)

0 금번 전쟁은 또한 미.소간에 냉전은 종식되었으나, 지정학적인 경쟁 관계는 계속되고 있음을 교훈으로 남기었음.

3. WE.P. RICHARD COHEN 기고 '' DYING FOR TIME''

0 한국전과 월남전이 남긴 귀중한 교훈의 하나는 평화 협상이 지연되면 그만큼 불필요한 인명 피해가 따르게 된다는것임.

0 후세인은 이란.이락 전쟁에서도 휴전과정에서 불성실한 태도로 일관해온바, 이러한 후세인이 내놓은 휴전안에 대해 회의적으로 대하는것은 지극히 당연한것임.

0 소련은 당사자가 아니므로 지지 부진한 휴전안을 내놓을수 있으나, 당장

미주국	장관	차관	1차보	2차보	중아국	정문국	청와대	총리실
안기부	대책반							

PAGE 1

91.02.25 08:52 WG

외신 1과 통제관

0072

사상자가 발생하는 연합국으로서는 이에 응할수가 없음.

0 부쉬 대통령이 한국전과 월남전의 이러한 교훈을 기억하고 있는 점을 평가해야함.

4. NYT PETER TARNOFF (COUNCIL ON FOREIGN RELATIONS회장) 기고

'' WE'VE WON- WHY MORE WAR ? ''

0 연합국은 이미 전쟁에 이겼음. 1) 후세인은 쿠웨이트를 포기하였고, 2) 이락의 경제, 군사 시설은 복구에 수년이 걸릴 정도로 파괴되었으며, 3) 연합국과 미국국민은 부쉬 대통령을 강력히 지지 하고있음.

0 단순히 좀더 좋은 조건으로 휴전하기 위해 지상전을 감행하는것은 큰 인명 손실의 댓가를 치루어야 함을 이해 해야함.

5.관련 기사 FAX 송부함.

(대사 박동진-국장)

報 告 畢
(서명)

報 告 事 項

1991. 2. 25.
美 洲 局
北 美 課(10)

題 目 : Washington Post紙-ABC 放送 共同 輿論調査 結果

> 미국 Washington Post지와 ABC 방송이 지상전 개시전인 2.22.(금) 저녁 미국인 성인남녀 520명을 대상으로 공동 조사한 걸프전 관련 여론조사 결과를 아래 보고드립니다.

o 이라크와의 전쟁에 대한 지지율

- 찬 성 : 81 %(1.27 조사시 67%)
- 반 대 : 18 %(1.27 조사시 33%)

o 부쉬 대통령이 평화 회복보다는 전쟁수행에 보다 관심이 있다는 주장은 ?

- 틀 린 다 : 72 %
- 맞 다 : 27 %
- 모르겠다 : 1 %

o 이라크가 2.22. 정오 미 동부 표준시각까지 쿠웨이트로부터 철수하지 않을경우 지상전 즉시 개시

- 찬 성 : 61 %
- 반 대 : 37 %
- 모르겠다 : 2 %

0074

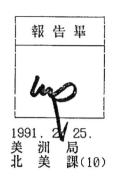

o 미국의 궁극적 전쟁목표

- 사담 후세인을 권좌로부터 제거 : 71%(1.18 조사시 65%)
- 쿠웨이트로부터 이라크의 철수 : 28%(1.18 조사시 34%)
- 모르겠다 : 1%

o 사담 후세인이 권좌로부터 제거될 때까지 전쟁 지속

- 찬 성 : 61 %
- 반 대 : 37 %
- 모르겠다 : 2 %

o 이라크가 탱크, 대포등 무기를 쿠웨이트에 남겨둔 채 쿠웨이트에서 철수할 경우에만 전쟁을 중지

- 찬 성 : 66 %
- 반 대 : 32 %
- 모르겠다 : 2 %

- 끝 -

0075

원 본

외 무 부

종 별 : 지 급

번 호 : USW-0895 일 시 : 91 0225 1702

수 신 : 장관(미북,중동1,미안)

발 신 : 주미대사

제 목 : 걸프전 전황

금 2.25. 15:30 현재 당지 CNN 방송등에 보도된걸프전 전황등을 하기 요지 보고함.

1. 금일 오전 사우디 주둔 미군 사령부의 브리핑 내용

가. 이락 포로수: 약 20,000 명

나. 지상전 개시이래 이락 탱크 파괴대수:약 270대

다. 미측 사상자: 4명 사망,21명 부상

2. 지상전 개전 직후 체니 국방장관이 밝힌바와같이 구체적 작전 내용에 관해서는 엄격한보도통제가 가해지고 있으므로, 당지 언론등도 상세한 내용에 관해서는 보도를 못하고 있는 실정이나, 금일 BLACK HISTORY MONTH 기념 연설에서부쉬 대통령이아래 요지로 언급한바와같이 다국적군은 현재 거의 파죽지세로 쿠웨이트내에서 진격을 계속하고 있음.(동연설 내용은 USW(F)-0667FAX 편 발췌 송부)

가. 전선으로 부터는 계속 좋은 소식이 들어오고 있는바, 다수의 이락군이 투항중인 반면, 다국적군사상자는 극히 경미함.

나. 쿠웨이트 해방은 예정대로 진행되고 있는바우리는 여사한 이니셔티브를 계속유지할것임.

다. 그러나 아직도 치뤄야할 전투가 많이 남아 있으므로전쟁결과에 대한 지나친낙관은 금물임.

3. 작일 실시된 갤럽 여론조사에 따르면,미국민의 84 푸로가 지상전 개전을 지지하고있고, 86푸로가 부쉬 대통령 개인의 여사한 정책 선택을지지하는등, 현재 미국내에는 낙관적 전망이팽배하고 있으나, 일부 언론등에서는 상금 이락군 정예부대인 공화국 수비대가 본격적으로 전투에 투입되지 않은점 및 쿠웨이트시 진입시치열한 시가전이 예상되는 점등을 들어 다국적군사상자수도 상당히 증가할수 있을 것으로예상하고 있음.

미주국	장관	차관	1차보	2차보	미주국	중아국	정문국	청와대
총리실	안기부	대책반						

PAGE 1

91.02.26 08:31 AQ

외신 1과 통제관

0076

원 본

외 무 부

종 별 : 긴 급

번 호 : USW-0915 일 시 : 91 0225 1942

수 신 : 장 관(미북,중동 1, 미안)

발 신 : 주 미 대사

제 목 : 걸프전 전황(이락군 철수 동향등을 하기 요지보고함)

1.금일 오후 바그다드 라디오 방송에 따르면 쿠웨이트주둔 이락군등이 90.8.1 이전 주둔 지역으로 철수 하도록 명령을 받았으며, 실제로 쿠웨이트 북부 지역등에서는 이락군이 대규모로 북진하고 있는것이 목격되고 있다함.

2. 전기 동향과 관련, 백악관 대변인실등에서는 현재의 상황이 미측의 반응을 요할 정도로 공식화되지는 않은것으로 보인다 (NOTHING OFFICIAL TORESPOND TO) 는 평가를 내리고 있는 것으로 보도 되고있는바, 미측으로서는 이락측이 대 유엔 접촉등을 통해 미측 제안의 공식 수락 의사를 밝히지 않는한 현재와 같은 대이락 공격을 계속 진행시켜 나갈 것으로 보임 (현재 다국적군의 시제 공격 진도는 당초 계획 보다도 훨씬 앞서 나가고 있다고 하며, 이락군은 거의 아무런 조직적 저항도 하지 못하고 있다함. 금일 오후 현재 이라군 포로수는 약 25,000명으로 증가 하였으며, 지상전 개시 이래 파괴된 탱크수도 약 300 대로 증가 하였다함)

3.한편 당지 언론 일각에서는 미측이 이락군은 쿠웨이트로 부터 몰아내는 것에서 한걸음 더 나아가 사담 후세인 정권의 몰락을 사실상의 전쟁목표 (DE FACTO OBJECTIVE) 로 추구하고 있기 때문에 전기 이락측의 철군 제안을 받아 들이기는 어려울것이라는 전망을 제시하고 있기도함.

(대사 박동진-국장)

미주국	장관	차관	1차보	2차보	미주국	중아국	정문국	청와대
총리실	안기부	대책반						

0077

PAGE 1

91.02.26 13:12 WG

외신 1과 통제관

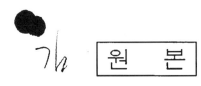

報告畢

報　告　事　項

1991. 2. 26.
美 洲 局
北 美 課(12)

題 目 : 걸프 地上戰 開始後 美 議會 및 輿論 反應

걸프 지상전 발발이후 전쟁 수행 및 후세인 정권 제거문제 등과 관련한 미 의회 및 여론 반응에 관한 미국의 언론 보도 요지를 아래 보고 드립니다.

1. 미 의회, 전쟁 수행 지지

o 걸프 지상전 개시이후 다국적군의 조속한 승리가 예견되자 미 의회는 부쉬 행정부의 전쟁 수행에 대해 전폭적인 지지 천명

- Thomas Foley 하원의장(민주, 워싱턴), Les Aspin 하원 군사위원장(민주, 위스콘신)등

o 6주전에는 부시 대통령의 무력사용에 대해 반대하던 민주당원들도 이제는 과거를 묻어두고 미국의 전후 입지 강화에 노력하여야 한다는 입장 표명

- Lee Hamilton 하원 외교위 중동소위원장(민주, 인디애나)등

2. 후세인 제거 지지

o 최근 WP-ABC 여론 조사에 의하면 70%가 후세인 축출 지지

0078

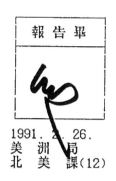

o 이러한 여론을 반영, 많은 의원들이 종전후 후세인이 정치적으로 재기 불가능하도록 하여야 한다고 주장

- Alan Dixon 상원의원(민주, 일리노이), Joseph Biden, Jr. 상원의원 (민주, 델라웨어), Joseph McDade 하원의원(공화, 펜실바니아)등

3. 후세인 제거 방법에는 이견

o Aspin 등 일부 의원은 이라크 영토 일부를 점령하고 종전후에도 경제 제재를 계속함으로써 이라크가 후세인과 Baathist 당을 축출하도록 협상하자는 의견 제시

o 그러나 일부는 미국의 전쟁 수행은 국제법 준수와 유엔 안보리 결의의 이행 수단으로서 정당화된 것이므로 그 이상의 무력행사는 삼가되, 이라크가 자체적으로 후세인을 축출할 것을 기대해야 한다는 의견

- John Kerry 상원의원(민주, 메사추세츠), Albert Gore, Jr. 상원의원 (민주, 테네시), Jim Leach 하원의원(공화, 아이오와)등

4. 전후 미군 잔류 등 반대

o 대부분 의원들은 걸프전 승리후 미국이 중동에서 주도적 역할을 수행할 것으로 기대하나, 미군의 계속 주둔에 대해서는 반대

- Hamilton 중동소위원장 등

o Foley 하원의장은 평화 유지군이 구성된다 하더라도 이는 주로 여타국 군대에 의해 구성되어야 할 것이라고 주장하고, 의회는 걸프전 승리를 위해 추경예산(150억불) 등 모든 필요한 지원을 제공할 것이나 국민들에게 재정적 부담이 되는 대규모 전쟁 피해 복구사업 참여 등은 하지 않아야 한다고 주장 끝.

0079

원 본

외 무 부

종 별 : 긴 급

번 호 : USW-0919 일 시 : 91 0226 1110

수 신 : 장관(미북,중근동)

발 신 : 주미대사

제 목 : 걸프전 (BUSH 성명)

1. 후세인의 쿠웨이트 철군 명령과 관련, BUSH 대통령은 금 2.26. 오전 9:50 백악관에서 발표한 짧은 성명을 통하여 후세인의 조치를 불성실한것으로 단정하고, 연합군이 계속 전쟁을 수행해나갈것임을 천명함.

2. BUSH 대통령은 후세인의 명령은 1) 진정한철군이 아니라 다시 싸우기 위한 군사력 유지를 위해 일단 철수하는것에 불과하며, 2) 쿠웨이트를 포기한다는 명시적 의사표시도 없을 뿐더러, 3)금번사태에 대한 후회 (REMORSE) 나 책임을 느끼지도않고, 4) UN 결의안 및 미국이 2.22. 에 제시한 휴전조건을 만족시키지 않으므로 연합군은 계속전쟁을 수행해 나갈것이라고 밝혔음.

3.한편 BUSH 대통령은 무기를 버리고 이락으로 철수하는 이락군인에 대해서는연합군이 공격을 않을것이라고 하면서, 이것만이 희생(BLOODSHED) 을 줄일수 있는방법이라고 함.

4.또한 BUSH 대통령은 현재 연합군의 공세가 예정보다 앞서나가고 있으며 쿠웨이트 해방이 곧 실현될 것이라고 하면서 연합국이 희망하는 방식으로의 사태종결이임박했다는 강한 자신감을 표시하였음.

5. BUSH 성명 전문 팩스 송부함.

(USWF-0676)

(대사 박동진- 국장)

미주국 장관 차관 1차보 2차보 중아국 정문국 청와대 총리실 안기부

PAGE 1

91.02.27 02:20 DN

외신 1과 통제관

0080

02/26/91 11:29 ☎2[redacted]7 0595 EMBASSY OF KO[redacted] → WOI ☑001/001

번호 : USW(F) - 0644

수신 : 장 관 (이북, 수신동)

발신 : 주미대사

제목 : 걸프사 (Bush 성명)

보안 통제	

배부처	장관실	차관실	1차보	2차보	기획실	의전장	아주국	미주국	구주국	중아국	국기국	경제국	통상국	정문국	영교국	총무과	감사관	공보관	외연원	청와대	총리실	안기부	문공부
	/	/	/	/				/		/			/							/	/	/	

STATEMENT OF PRESIDENT GEORGE BUSH DELIVERED IN THE ROSE GARDEN
THE WHITE HOUSE, TUESDAY, FEBRUARY 26, 1991

PRES. BUSH: I have a brief statement to make today.

Saddam's most recent speech is an outrage. He is not withdrawing. His defeated forces are retreating. He is trying to claim victory in the midst of a rout, and he is not voluntarily giving up Kuwait. He is trying to save the remnants of power and control in the Middle East by every means possible and here, too, Saddam Hussein will fail.

Saddam is not interested in peace, but only to regroup and fight another day, and he does not renounce Iraq's claim to Kuwait. To the contrary -- he makes clear that Iraq continues to claim Kuwait. Nor is there any evidence of remorse for Iraq's aggression or any indication that Saddam is prepared to accept the responsibility for the awful consequences of that aggression.

He still does not accept UN Security Council resolutions or the coalition terms of February 22, including the release of our POWs, all POWs, third country detainees, and an end to the pathological destruction of Kuwait.

The coalition will therefore continue to prosecute the war with undiminished intensity. As we announced last night, we will not attack unarmed soldiers in retreat. We have no choice but to consider retreating combat units as a threat and respond accordingly. Anything else would risk additional United States and coalition casualties.

The best way to avoid further casualties on both sides is for the Iraqi soldiers to lay down their arms, as nearly 30,000 Iraqis already have. It is time for all Iraqi forces in the theater of operation, those occupying Kuwait, those supporting the -- the occupation of Kuwait, to lay down their arms. And that will stop the bloodshed.

From the beginning of the air operation nearly six weeks ago, I have said that our efforts are on course and on schedule. This morning, I am very pleased to say that coalition efforts are ahead of schedule. The liberation of Kuwait is close at hand.

And let me just add that I share the pride of all of the American people in the magnificent, heroic performance of our armed forces. May God bless them and keep them.

(Applause.)

Q Have you changed your goals, sir? Are you trying to get Saddam Hussein?

END

0081

122 P01 LENINPROTOCOL '91-02-27 01:12

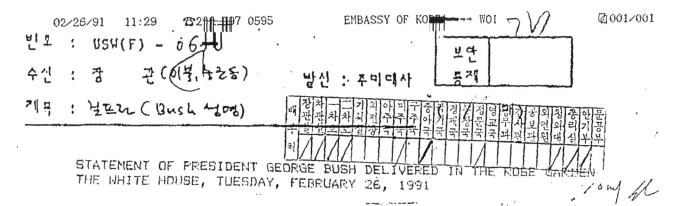

외 무 부

종 별 :

번 호 : NYW-0311　　　　　　일 시 : 91 0226 1615

수 신 : 장 관(해신.정홍)

발 신 : 주 뉴욕 총영사(문)

제 목 : 걸프논조(2.26)

1.NYT 금일자 사설은 +전쟁 참가자의 가족들을 지원할것+을 주장하였고 CSM 은 사설을 통해 미국주도 다국적군의 승리가 보이는 가운데 향후 챙겨야할 문제점들-전후 이락의 정치체제, 쿠웨이트 재건, 중동 평화장치, 신세계질서-을 언급하였음.

2.또한 NYT 와 WSJ 은 각각+전쟁의교훈+제하 논평들을 게재하였는바, NYT, 의 A.M. ROSENTHAL 기고는 중동 제후들에게 자기국민을 억압과 속박에서 해방시키라는 주장과 함께 이번 전쟁에서의 또 다른 패배자인 팔레스타인에게 각성을 촉구하였으며, WSJ 의 M.HELPRIN (유태인, 소설가이며 WSJ 기고가) 기고는 이번 전쟁으로 저급한 소련무기 체제와 전략부족의 이락을 쉽게 이겼다고 하여 쏘련에 대해 안심할수 없고 유럽에서의 재래식 방어체제는 부적합 하기 때문에 핵제한의 규정을 좀더엄격하게 해야 한다고 주장 하고 있음.

(원장-관장)

공보처	장관	차관	1차보	2차보	중아국 ②	정문국	정와대	총리실
안기부	미주국							

PAGE 1　　　　　　91.02.27　10:11 WG

외신 1과 통제관 ·

0082

외 무 부

종 별 :

번 호 : NYW-0315　　　　일 시 : 91 0227 1600

수 신 : 장 관(해신.정홍)

발 신 : 주 뉴욕 총영사(문)

제 목 : 걸프 논조(2.27)

1.NYT 2.27일자는 승전보들을 전하는 가운데 사설과 논평을 통해 신중론을편 반면, WSJ사설은 역시 강경하게 이락분쇄론을 펴고있음.

2.NYT 은 +흥분치 말고 냉정히 계산하라+제하의사설에서 이락에 새 정부를 세우려 한다든지 또는 패주하는 이락군의 무기를 철저히 파괴함으로서 생기는 결과에 대해 냉정히 검토하라는 주장을하고, LESLIE GELB 의 +걸프에서 다음 행동은?+제하기고는 이락 민주화, 사담 후세인 제거, 신세계질서, 중동의 세력균형등 장기적이며 그 실현방법이 막연한 목표들 보다는 보다 현실적이며, 미국능력 범위내의 몇가지를 우선 해결해 야 한다고주장함.

3.WSJ 사설은 +스커드은신처+제하 사설에서 스커드 미사일이 계속 위협을 주고있으므로 바그다드까지 계속 진격할것을 주장하고 있으며, CSM 사설은+쏘련과 걸프+제하로 소련이 비록 이번 전쟁에돈, 인원, 물자를 대지는 않았어도 부시가 말하는 신세계 질서의 중요 일원으로 또한 평화중재자로서의 위치를 존중하여 전쟁이 끝나면 연기되었던 2월 정상회담을 재개해야 한다고 주장함.

(원장-관장)

공보처	장관	차관	1차보	2차보	구주국	정문국	청와대	총리실
안기부	미주국	중아국						

PAGE 1　　　　91.02.28　09:47 WG

외신 1과 통제관

0083

관리 번호	91-103

원 본

외 무 부

종 별 : 긴 급

번 호 : USW-0969　　　　일 시 : 91 0227 1917

수 신 : 장관(미북,중동 1, 미안,경이,구일)

발 신 : 주 미 대사

제 목 : 국무부 정례 브리핑중 걸프 사태 관련 부분

1. 금 2.27 국무부 정례 브리핑시 TUTWILER 대변인 언급 내용중, 걸프 사태관련 주요 부분을 하기 요지 보고함(USW(F)-0706 으로 발췌 송부)

가. 주 쿠웨이트 미국 대사 임지 복귀

-현재 계획으로는 주 쿠웨이트 미국 대사가 명일중 임지 복귀토록 할 예정임(쿠웨이트 국왕등 쿠웨이트 정부 고위층의 복귀 시기는 상금 미정)

나. 쿠에이트 복구 사업 참여 문제

-미군 공병단(CORPS OF ENGINEERS)이 쿠웨이트내 교통 시설및 각종 공공 시설의 긴급 복구 수리 사업 관련, 쿠웨이트정부와 계약을 체결하였는바, 각 관련 업에체 다시 하청을 주고 있는것으로 알고 있음.

다. 미-영, 불, 독간 연쇄 외상 회담

-베이커 국무장관은 금일 HURD 영국외상과 회담을 가진데 이어, 명일은 DUMAS 불란서 외상과, 금요일은 GENSHER 독일 외상과 각각 연쇄 회담 예정인바, 전후 처리 문제 관련 4 대 부야(중동 지역 안보 장치 수립 문제, 군비 통제 문제, 아랍-이스라엘 문제, 경제 협력 문제)가 주 의제인것으로 알고 있음.

2. 한편, 금일 SCHWARZKOP 현지 사령관의 기자 회견 내용및 전기 베이커 장관의 연쇄 외상 회담 예정 사실등을 고려할때 미 행정부의 주 정책 관심 부야가 걸프 전쟁의 군사적 수행에서 전쟁 종결및 전후 처리 방안의 수립을 옮겨 가고 있는것으로 관찰되는바, 관련 동향 계속 보고 위계임.

(대사 박동진-국장)

91.12.31 까지

예고문에 의거 재분류(1991.12.31)
직위 사무관 성명 [서명]

검 토 필(1991. 6. 30.)[서명]

미주국 장관 차관 1차보 2차보 미주국 구주국 중아국 경제국
청와대 총리실 안기부

PAGE 1

91.02.28 10:52
외신 2과 통제관 BW
0084

번호 : USW(F) - 070

수신 : 장 관(미북,중동1,아2,경여(서기)) 발신 : 주미대사

제목 : 국무부 정례 브리핑 (걸프사태 관련 부분)

보 통	
통제	

(3 매)

STATE DEPARTMENT REGULAR BRIEFING
BRIEFER: MARGARET TUTWILER
12:15 P.M. (EST)/WEDNESDAY, FEBRUARY 27, 1991

MS. TUTWILER: Okay. Many of you all have been asking when the Emir and the legitimate government of Kuwait would be returned. There are still some uncertainties regarding the degree to which it is safe for senior levels of the Kuwait government and representatives of the foreign embassies to return.

The decision in this connection will be made by appropriate military commanders in consultation, obviously, with the Kuwaiti authorities.

Elements of the Kuwaiti authorities are already on the scene. They are in Kuwait City and are assisting military commanders in reestablishing orders and consulting with the Emir and his senior people.

So I don't have a time specific for you, but it is obviously something that they are very engaged in at this moment.

Concerning when our Ambassador Skip Gnehm would go back, of course we will be sending our United States Ambassador back, and we are planning to be able to return to our embassy Ambassador Skip Gnehm as early as tomorrow.

I would remind you that it is nighttime there in Kuwait City right now.

As far as who all will be going in with the Ambassador, he has assembled a -- what we refer to, as you know, a "country team." It is made up of representatives of several different agencies who have been there with him, working -- as many of you know, he's been working in Taif and in Riyadh. And they have been working for some time with their counterparts and appropriate Kuwaiti Ministers and other Kuwaiti government agencies.

The exact composition of the initial team that will be going in with the Ambassador depends to a certain extent on the Kuwaiti government having their ministers back and their government back. But, initially, we would anticipate that the American team will initially be several dozen individuals. They will obviously get the embassy up and running, and the embassy will be equipped to handle basic operations. Those, as you know, include political, economic, consular, public affairs, and administrative type of functions. And we do not have for you a thorough readout or overview of exactly what shape the embassy is in, but we do not have any information to tell us that it has been destroyed or anything like that.

0706-1

0085

02/27/91 19:32 ☎202 797 0595 EMBASSY OF KOREA ☑001

As far as yesterday I got a number of questions on what was the United States government doing in coordination with the Kuwaiti government on helping them, and as you know, our basic aim is to provide whatever technical support and advice the government of Kuwait asks of us. To do that, Ambassador Gnehm has held frequent high-level discussions with Kuwaiti officials over the past several months.

As part of our support, a task force of approximately 50 US civil affairs specialists belonging to the 352nd Civil Affairs Command have been consulting with the government of Kuwait and offering technical advice. The task force is working with military commander to restore emergency services, and will continue its efforts in support of the government of Kuwait once its senior leadership is back in place.

In addition, the Corps of Engineers has signed a contract with the government of Kuwait to perform emergency services and repairs in Kuwait for transportation facilities and public infrastructure. The 352nd Civil Affairs Command are offering advice and technical assistance, but are not involved in the actual negotiation of contracts. The Corps of Engineers group has been subcontracting under the terms of their contract with the government of Kuwait.

Contracts, it is my understanding, are negotiated and let by the government of Kuwait. US civil affairs advisors have not been involved, as I've said, with negotiations or contracts. The Corps of Engineers have solicited bids on their subcontracts from a number of international firms. I am aware that the government of Kuwait has signed a large number of contracts and I understand that a majority are with American firms, but that a large number are also with non-American firms.

AID -- several of you had asked me yesterday. There was some report that AID was preparing to send food to Kuwait. That is not a correct report. AID has been preparing contingency plans with its Office of Foreign Disaster Assistance for dealing with emergency civilian needs in the Gulf after the fighting has ceased. The projected areas of need include sanitation, public health, medical care, temporary shelter -- (clears throat) -- excuse me -- and other basic services. The full extent of these needs will obviously not be known until the war has ended and assessment teams are able to determine what type of assistance would be appropriate.

Excuse me -- (pause). On food. AID's Office of Food for Peace has also donated 29,000 metric tons of food to the United Nations

world food program to assist the refugees and displaced who have fled to Jordan and Saudi Arabia. The value of this food aid is at $12.1 million.

On another subject that we had talked about yesterday -- POWs. I'd like to direct your attention to a press release that the International Committee of the Red Cross issued yesterday in Geneva. I will be happy to make it available to you afterwards, but I would like to highlight some of the things that it says. It says the ICRC is therefore sending additional staff to its delegation in Saudi Arabia to handle, as you know, we have thousands upon thousands of POWs.

0706-2

0086

02/27/91 19:33 ☎202 797 0595 EMBASSY OF KOREA 002

The ICRC's visit to prisoners of war taking place in accordance with the provisions of the Third Geneva Convention relative to the treatment of prisoners of war. However, the ICRC has still not received any information concerning the prisoners of war captured by the Iraqi forces since August 2, 1990, and in military operations underway since January 17th, 1991. In spite of its numerous approaches, the ICRC has still not been notified by the Iraqi authorities of the identity of Kuwaiti prisoners and members of the coalition armed forces in their hands, nor has it been authorized to visit those prisoners in compliance with international humanitarian law. The ICRC hereby appeals to the authorities of the Republic of Iraq to take immediate action to remedy this serious situation, which constitutes a grave lack of respect of the third Geneva convention.

The last thing I will mention is several of you all have asked what was the purpose of Secretary Baker's meeting this afternoon with Foreign Minister Hurd, his meetings tomorrow with Foreign Minister Dumas, and Friday's meetings with Foreign Minister Genscher. Basically, it is as I stated yesterday. They will obviously be discussing the progress of the war, war termination issues, and they will obviously be consulting, beginning their consultative process on post-crisis issues.

And those four baskets, as you know, were laid out in quite some specifics by the Secretary of State in his testimony. The four baskets are arrangements -- security arrangements in the region, arms control and proliferation, Arab-Israeli issues, and economic cooperation in the region.

That's it.

0106-3

0087

관리 번호	91-102

원 본

외 무 부

종 별 : 긴 급

번 호 : USW-0970　　　　일 시 : 91 0227 1917

수 신 : 장관(미북,중동 1,미안)

발 신 : 주 미 대사

제 목 : 걸프전 전황

1. 금 2.27 NORMAN SCHWARZKOPF 사우디 현지 주둔 사령관은 기자 회견을 통해 그간의 DESERT STORM 작전 진행 상황등에 관해 리야드에서 상세한 대언론 브리핑을 가졌는바, 주요 브리핑 요지 하기 보고함(USW(F)-0707 FAX 송부함)

가. DESERT STORM 작전 개시 직전 상황

-수적인면에서 이락측에 비해 열세에 놓였었는바, 총병력에 있어서는 32 순수 전부 병력에 있어서는 21 로 미측이 열세에 처해 있었음.

-탱크 수에 있어서도, 이락측이 4,700 대를 보유한 반면, 미측은 3,500 대에 불과하였음.

나. 지상전 개시 직전 상황

검 토 필(1991.6.30.)

-대규모 집중 공습을 통해, 하기 목표 달정

. 쿠웨이트로 통하는 주요 교량등 이락군 보급로 차단

. 최전선 배치 이락군 무력화

예고문에 의거 재분류(1991.12.31.) 직위 사무관 성명

. 제공권 장악을 통해 이락측 공중 정찰 능력 무력화

-대규모 양동 상륙 작전의 계속 실시를 통해, 미군이 쿠웨이트 해안에 상륙작전을 실시할지도 모른다는 인식을 이락측에 심어줌으로서 상당 규모의 이락군 병력을 쿠웨이트 해안 부근에 계속 붙잡아둠.

-상대적으로 이락군 숫자가 적은 이락 서부 국경 지역에 대규모 병력 배치

-최전선 지역에 대규모 보급 기지 설치(약 60 일분의 식수, 탄약, 연료, 식량, 부품등 비축)

-특수 부대 요원의 적진 침부를 통해 이락군 동향 사전 탐지

-결과적으로 지상전 개시 직전까지 최전선 배치 이락군 전력은 50 프로 이하로, 제 2 전선 배치 이락군 전력은 50-75 프로 정도로 감소

미주국	장관	차관	1차보	2차보	미주국	중아국	청와대	총리실
안기부								

PAGE 1　　　　91.02.28 10:51

외신 2과 통제관 BW

0088

다. 현황

-이락군 29 개 사단 이상을 완전 무력화

-이락군 탱크 3,000 대 이상을 파괴 또는 노획(현재 진행중인 공화국 수비대와 미 제 7 군단간의 전부가 종료 되면, 동 숫자는 3,700 대로 증가 예상)

-이라군 포로 50,000 명 이상 생포

- 미해병대가 쿠웨이트 국제 공항 및 쿠웨이트시에서 외곽으로 빠지는 주요간선도로를차단한 가운데, 쿠웨이트 시내 소탕 작전 진행중

-결론적으로 쿠웨이트 영내의 이락군은 공격 능력 거의 완전 상실

2. 한편, 체니 국방장관도 금일 당지에서 개최된 미 재향 군인 협회 에서의연설을 통해 금번 DESERT STORM 작전이 종료될때 까지 며칠 남지 않은 것으로 본다는 희망적 관측을 표시하였음(AS THE PRESIDENT HAS MADE CLEAR, WE WANT TOWRAP UP THIS OPERATION JUST AS QUICKLY AS POSSIBLE. WE ARE HOPEFUL THAT TIME IS ONLY A MATTER OF A FEW DAYS AWAY.)

3. 지 G 상전 개시 당일인 2.23 체니 국방장관이 기자회견을 통해 지상 작전 현황에 관해서는 당분간 엄격한 보도 통제를 가할것이라고 언급했음에도 불구,금일 SCHWARZKOPF 사령관이 군사 비밀에 해당할 정도로 구체적인 사항을 장시간에 걸쳐 설명한점이 주목되는바, 여사한 작전 내용의 공개는 미군 지도부에서 금번 작전이 군사적으로는 사실상 마무리 단계에 접어 들었다고 판단했기 때문에가능했던것으로 보임.

(대사 박동진-국장)

91.12.31 까지

0089

31-02-28 09:18

158 P04 LENINPROTOL

번호 : USW(F) - 0707

수신 : 장 관(미북, 중동1, 미안) 발신 : 주미대사

제목 : 걸프전 전황 브리핑

보안 통제 | OL

(8 매)

DEPARTMENT OF DEFENSE UNITED STATES CENTRAL COMMAND DAILY NEWS BRIEFING
BRIEFERS: GEN. H. NORMAN SCHWARZKOPF, CINC, CENTCOM; AND LTC. MIKE GALLAGHER, CENTCOM MEDIA RELATIONS, RIYADH, SAUDI ARABIA 1:00 p.m. EST
WEDNESDAY, FEBRUARY 27, 1991

COL. GALLAGHER: Welcome, ladies and gentlemen. We will have a presentation today by the Commander in Chief of United States Central Command and the Commander of Operation Desert Storm, General H. Norman Schwarzkopf. Following the General's remarks we will have a question and answer session.

Ladies and gentlemen, General Schwarzkopf.

GEN. SCHWARZKOPF: Good evening, ladies and gentlemen, thank you for being here. I promised some of you all a few days ago that as soon as the opportunity presented itself I would give you a complete rundown on what we were doing and more importantly why we were doing it, the strategy behind what we are doing.

I've been asked by Secretary Cheney to do that this evening, and so if you will bear with me, we're going to go through a briefing. I apologize to the folks over here who won't be able to see the charts. But we're going to go through a complete briefing of the operation.

This goes back to 7 August to 17 January. As you recall, we started our deployment on the 7th of August. Basically what we started out against was a couple hundred thousand Iraqis that were in the Kuwait theatre of operation. I don't have to remind you all that we brought over initially defensive forces in the form of the 101st, the 82nd, the 24th Mechanized Infantry Division, the 3rd Armored Cavalry, and in essence we had them arrayed to the South behind the Saudi task force.

Also there were Arab forces over here in this area arrayed in defensive positions. And that, in essence, is the way we started.

In the middle of November the decision was made to increase the force because by that time huge numbers of Iraqi forces had flown into the area, and generally in the disposition as they're shown right here. And therefore we increased the forces and built up more forces.

I would tell you that at this time we made a very deliberate decision to align all of those forces within the boundary looking North towards Kuwait; this being King Khalid Military City over here. So we aligned those forces so it very much looked like they were all aligned directly on the Iraqi positions.

We also at that time had a very active naval presence out in the Gulf, and we made sure that everybody understood about that naval presence. One of the reasons why we did that is because it became very apparent to us early on that the Iraqis were quite concerned about an amphibious operation across the shores to liberate Kuwait -- this being Kuwait City. They put a very, very

0090

0707-1

02/27/91 19:35 ☎202 797 0595 EMBASSY OF KOREA 004

heavy barrier of infantry along here, and they proceeded to build an extensive barrier that went all the way across the border down and around and up the side of Kuwait.

Basically, the problem we were faced with was this. When you looked at the troop numbers, they really outnumbered us about three to two. And when you consider the number of combat service support people we had, that's logisticians and that sort of thing in our armed forces, as far as fighting troops, we were really outnumbered two to one. In addition to that, they had about 4,700 tanks versus our 3,500 when the buildup was complete, and they had a great deal more artillery than we do.

I think any student of military strategy would tell you that in order to attack a position, you should have a ratio of approximately three to one in favor of the attacker. And in order to attack a position that is heavily dug in and barracaded such as the one we had here, you should have a ratio of five to one in the way of troops in favor of the attacker. So you can see basically what our problem was at that time. We were outnumbered as a minimum three to two as far as troops were concerned, we were outnumbered as far as tanks were concerned, and we had to come up with some way to make up the difference.

Next chart, please.

I apologize for the busy nature of this chart, but I think it's very important for you to understand exactly what our strategy was. What you see here is a color coding where green is a go sign or a good sign as far as our forces are concerned, yellow would be a caution sign, and red would be a stop sign. Green represents units that have been attrited below 50 percent strength. The yellow are units that are between 50 and 75 percent strength. And of course, the red are units that are over 75 percent strength.

What we did, of course, was start an extensive air campaign, and I briefed you in quite some detail on that in the past. One of the purposes I told you at that time of that extensive air campaign was to isolate the Kuwaiti theater of operation by taking out all the bridges and supply lines that ran between the north and the southern part of Iraq. That was to prevent reinforcement and supply and coming into the southern part of Iraq and the Kuwaiti theater of operation.

We also conducted a very heavy bombing campaign and many people questioned why the extensive bombing campaign. This is the reason why. It was necessary to reduce these forces down to a strength that was -- that made them weaker, particularly on the frontline barrier that we had to go through. We continued our heavy operations out in the sea because we wanted the Iraqis to continue to believe that we were going to conduct a massive amphibious operation in this area. And I think many of you recall the number of amphibious rehearsals we had to include Imminent Thunder, that was written about quite extensively for many reasons. But we continued to have those operations because we wanted him to --

0704-2

0091

concentrate his forces, which he did.

I think this is probably one of the most important parts of the entire briefing I can talk about. As you know, very early on we took out the Iraqi air force. We knew that he had very, very limited reconnaissance means. And therefore when we took out his air force, for all intents and purposes we took out his ability to see what we were doing down here in Saudi Arabia. Once we had taken out his eyes, we did what could best be described as the "Hail Mary" play in football. I think you recall when the quarterback is desperate for a touchdown at the very end, what he does is, he steps up behind the center and all of a sudden every single one of his receivers goes way out to the -- to one flank and they all run down the field as fast as they possibly can and into the end zone and he lobs the ball.

In essence, that's what we did. When we knew that he couldn't see us any more, we did a massive movement of troops all the way out to the west, to the extreme west, because at that time we knew that he was still fixed in this area with the vast majority of his forces, and once the air campaign started he would be incapable of moving out to counter this move, even if he knew we made it.

There were some addition on troops out in this area, but they did not have the capability nor the time to put in the barrier that had been described by Saddam Hussein as an absolutely inpenetrable tank barrier that no one would ever get through. I believe those were his words. (Light laughter).

So this was absolutely an extraordinary move. I must tell you, I can't recall any time in the annals of military history when this number of forces have moved over this distance to put themselves in a position to be able to attack.

But what's more important -- and I think it's very, very important that I make this point -- and that's these logistics bases. Not only did we move the troops out there but we literally moved thousands and thousands of tons of fuel, of ammunition, of spare parts, of water, and of food out here into this area because we wanted to have enough supplies onhand so that if we launched this and we got into a slug-fest battle, which we very easily could have gotten into, we'd have enough supplies to last for 60 days. It was an absolutely gigantic accomplishment. And I can't give credit enough to the logisticians and the transporters who were able to pull this off, to the superb support we had from the Saudi government, the literally thousands and thousands of drivers really of every national origin who helped us in this move out here. And, of course, great credit goes to the commanders of these units who were also able to manouver their forces out here and put them in this position.

But as a result, by the 23rd of February what you found is this situation: The front lines had been attrited down to a point where all of these units were at 50 percent or below. The second level,

0706-3

0092

02/27/91 19:39 ☎202 797 0595 EMBASSY OF KOREA 006

basically, that we had to face -- and these were the real tough fighters that we were worried about right here -- were attrited to some place between 50 and 75 percent. Although we still had the Republican Guard located here and here, and part of the Republican Guard in this area that were very strong, and the Republican Guard up in this area is strong. And we continued to hit the bridges all across this area to make absolutely sure that no more reinforcements came into the battle. This was the situation on the 23rd of February.

(Aside) Next [chart], please. Oh, wait, I should -- I'm sorry, I shouldn't forget these fellows. That "SF" stands for Special Forces.

We put Special Forces deep into the enemy territory. They went out on strategic reconnaissance for us and they let us know what was going on out there. They were the eyes that were out there, and it's very important that I not forget those folks.

Next, please.

This, then, was the morning of the 24th. Our plan initially had been to start over here in this area and do exactly what the Iraqis thought we were going to do, and that's take them on head-on into their most heavily defended area. Also at the same time we launched amphibious feints and naval gunfire in this area so that they continued to think that we were going to be attacking along this coast and therefore fixed their forces in this position. Our hope was that by fixing the forces in this position and with this attack through here in this position, we would basically keep the forces here and they wouldn't know what was going on out in this area. And I believe we succeeded in that very well.

At 4:00 in the morning, the Marines, the 1st Marine Division and the 2nd Marine Division, launched attacks through the barrier system. They were accompanied by the 2nd -- the Tiger Brigade, US Army Tiger Brigade of the 2nd Armored Division. At the same time, over here two Saudi task forces also launched a penetration through this barrier. But while they were doing that, at 4:00 in the morning over here the 6th French Armored Division, accompanied by a brigade of the 82nd Airborne, also launched an overland attack to their objective up in this area, Al Salman (ph) airfield. And we were held up a little bit by the weather, but by 8:00 in the morning, the 101st Airborne air assault -- launched an air assault deep in the enemy territory to establish a forward operating base in this location right here.

Let me talk about each one of those moves. First of all, the Saudis over here on the east coast did a terrific job. They went up against a very, very tough barrier system. They breached the barrier very, very effectively, they moved out aggressively, and continued their attack up the coast.

I can't say enough about the two Marine divisions. The -- if I use words like brilliant it would really be an underdescription of the absolutely superb job that they did in breaching the so-called "impenetrable" barrier. It was a classic -- absolutely classic military breaching of a very, very tough mine-field-with-barbed-wire fire-trenches-type barrier. They went through the first barrier like it was water, they went across into the second barrier line.

0093

020 -1

Even though they were under artillery fire at the time, they continued to open up that breach, and then they brought both divisions streaming through that breach. Absolutely superb operation, a textbook [operation], and I think it will be studied for many, many years to come as the way to do it.

I would also like to say that the French did an absolutely superb job of moving out rapidly to take their objective out here and they were very, very succesful, as were the 101st [Airborne Division]. And again, we still had the Special Forces located in this area.

What we found was as soon as we breached these obstacles here and started bringing pressure, we started getting a large number of surrenders, and I think I talked to some of you all about that this evening when we -- when I briefed you on the evening of the 24th. We finally got a large number of surrenders, we also found that these forces right here were getting a large number of surrenders and were meeting with a great deal of success.

We were worried about the weather. The weather, it turned out was going to get pretty bad the next day and we were worried about launching this air assault, and we also started to have a huge number of atrocities -- of really the most unspeakable type -- committed in downtown Kuwait City to include reports that the desalinization had been destroyed. And when we heard that we were quite concerned about what might be going on.

Based upon that and the situation as it was developing, we made a decision that rather than wait till the following morning to launch the remainder of these forces that we would go ahead and launch those forces that afternoon. Next.

So this was the situation you saw the afternoon of the 21st. The Marines continued to make great progress going through the breach in this area and were moving rapidly north.

The Saudi task force on the east coast was also moving rapidly to the north and making very, very good progress.

We launched another Egyptian-Arab force in this location and another Saudi force in this location, again to penetrate the barrier, but once again to make the enemy continue to think that we're doing exactly what he wanted us to do and that's make a headlong assault into a very, very tough barrier system -- a very, very tough mission for these folks here.

But at the same time, what we did is continue to attack with the French. We continued -- we launched an attack on the part of the entire 7th Corps where the first infantry division went through, breached an obstacle and minefield barrier here, established quite a large breach through which we passed the 1st British Armored Division.

At the same time, we launched the 1st Armored Division, the 3rd

0706-5

0094

02/27/91 19:45 ☎202 797 0595 EMBASSY OF KOREA 008

Armored Division, and because of our deception plan and the way it worked, we didn't even have to worry about a barrier, we just went right around the enemy and were behind him in no time at all. And the 2nd Armored Cavalry Division.

And I ought to talk -- and the 24th Mechanized Division also launched out here, in the far west -- and I ought to talk about the 101st, because this is an important point. Once the 101st had their forward operating base established here, they then went ahead and launched into the Tigris and Euphrates Valley. There's a lot of people who are still saying that the object of the United States of America was to capture Iraq and cause a downfall of the entire country of Iraq.

Ladies and gentlemen, when we were here, we were 150 miles away from Baghdad and there was nobody between us and Baghdad. If it had been our intention to take Iraq, if it had been our intention to destroy the country, if it had been our intention to overrun the country, we could have done it unopposed, for all intents and purposes, from this position at that time. But that was not our intention. We had never said it was our intention. Our intention was purely to eject the Iraqis out of Kuwait and destroy the military power that had come in here.

So this was the situation at the end of February the 24th in the afternoon.

Next, please.

The next two days went exactly like we thought they would go. The Saudis continued to make great progress up on the eastern flank, keeping the pressure off the Marines on the flank here. The Special Forces went out and started operating small boat operations out in this area to help clear mines, but also to threaten the flanks and to continue to make them think that we were in fact going to conduct amphibious operations. The Saudi forces that came in and took the -- and Arab forces that came in and took these two initial objectives, turned to come in on the flank heading towards Kuwait City, located right in this area here. The British UK passed through and continued to attack up this flank. And, of course, the 7th Corps came in and attacked in this direction as shown here. The 24th Infantry Division made an unbelievable move all the way across into the Tigris and Euphrates valley and proceeded in blocking this avenue of egress out, which was the only avenue of egress left because we continued to make sure that the bridges stayed down. So there was no way out once the 24th was in this area, and the 101st continued to operate in here. The French having succeeded in acheiving all of their objectives then set up a flanking position, a flank guard position here to make sure that no forces could come in and get us from the flank. By this time we had destroyed or rendered completely ineffective over 21 Iraqi divisions.

Next [chart], please.

0709 -6

0095

And, of course that then brings us to to. Where we are today is we now have a solid wall across the north of the 18th Airborne Corps consisting of the units shown right here attacking straight to the east. We have a solid wall here again of the 7th Corps also attacking straight to the east. The forces that they are fighting right now are the forces of the Republican Guard.

Again, today we had a very significant day when the Arab forces coming from both the west and the east closed in and moved in to Kuwait City where they are now in the process of clearing Kuwait City entirely and assuring that it's absolutely secure. The First Marine Division continues to hold Kuwaiti International Airport. The Second Marine Division continues to be in a position where it blocks any egress out of the City of Kuwait so no one can leave. To date, we have destroyed over 29 -- destroyed or rendered inoperable; I don't like to say destroyed because that gives you the visions of absolutely killing everyone and that's not what we're doing. But we have renendered completely ineffective over 29 Iraqi divisions.

And the gates are closed. There is no way out of here, there is no way out of here, and the enemy is fighting us in this location right here. We continue, of course, to have overwhelming air power. The air has done a terrific job from start to finish in supporting the ground forces and we also have had great support from the Navy, both in the form of naval gunfire, and in the support of carrier air. That's the situation at the present time.

Next, please? (Referring to chart.)

Peace is not without a cost. These have been the US casualties to date. As you can see, these were casualties that we had in the air war. Then, of course, we had the terrible misfortune of the Scud attack the other night, which, again, because the weapon malfunctioned, it caused death, unfortunately, rather than in a proper function. And then, of course, these are the casualties in the ground war to date, the total being as shown here.

Next? Hold it. Hold on for one second. (Pause.)

One second is up. (Laughter.) Next, please. We'll put all these charts and have them available for you afterwards.

Now I would just like to comment briefly about that casualty chart. The loss of one human life is intolerable to any of us who are in the military. But I would tell you that casualties of that order of magnitude, considering the job that's been done and the number of forces that are involved, is almost miraculous as far as the light number of casualties. It will never be miraculous to the families of those people, but it is miraculous.

Anyhow, this is what's happened to date with the Iraqis. They started out with over 4,000 tanks. As of today, we have over 3,000 confirmed destroyed and I do mean destroyed or captured. And as a matter of fact, that number is low because you can add 700 to that as a result of the battle that's going on right now with the Republican Guard. So that number is very, very high and we've almost completely destroyed the offensive capability of the Iraqi forces in the Kuwaiti theater of operation.

0096

The armored vehicle count is also very, very high, and of course, you can see we're doing great damage to the artillery. The battle is still going on and I suspect that these numbers will mount rather considerably.

Next?

I wish I could give you a better number on this. To be very honest with you, this is just a wild guess. It's an estimate that was sent to us by the field today at noon,

but the prisoners out there are so heavy and so extensive, and obviously we're not in the business of going around counting noses at this time to determine precisely what the exact number is. But we're very, very confident that we have well over 50,000 prisoners of war at this time, and that number is mounting on a continuing basis.

I would remind you that the war is continuing to go on. Even as we speak right now, there's fighting going on out there. Even as we speak right now, there are incredible acts of bravery going on. This afternoon we had an F-16 pilot shot down. We had contact with him. He had a broken leg on the ground. Two helicopters from the 101st -- they didn't have to do it, but they went in to try and pull that pilot out. One of them was shot down, and we're still in the process of working through that. But that's the kind of thing that's going on out on that battlefield right now. It is not a Nintendo game. It is a tough battlefield where people are risking their lives at all time, and there are great heroes out there and we all ought to be very, very proud of them.

That's the campaign to date, that's the strategy to date, and I would now be very happy to take any questions anyone might have.

Yes, sir?

0707 -8

0097

걸프戰 終戰宣言 부쉬 大統領 對國民 演說要旨

(2.28. 11:00 KST 發表)

o 이라크측이 아래 조건을 수락.이행할 경우, 미국 정부는 미 동부시간 2.27. 24:00(KST 2.28. 14:00)를 기해 미군 및 다국적군의 대이라크군 공격 작전을 중지할 것임.

- 국방장관, 합참의장등의 건의 수용

o 이라크측 이행 조건

- 이라크군이 보호중인 미군, 다국적군 포로 및 모든 쿠웨이트 국민등 제3 국민의 즉각적인 석방
- 쿠웨이트 인근지역 부설 지뢰 및 어뢰의 상세 위치 통보
- 90.8. 발표 쿠웨이트 합병 의사 철회등 모든 UN 안보리 결의 준수 촉구
- 이라크의 쿠웨이트 침공으로 인한 직.간접 피해에 대해 배상 원칙 수락
- 미군 및 다국적군측과 군사적 휴전 협상에 임할 이라크군측 대표의 48시간내 지정

o Baker 장관을 다음주 걸프전 종전과 관련된 전후 평화질서, 주변국 피해 지원 문제 협의를 위해 현지에 파견 예정

0098

報告畢

長 官 報 告 事 項

1991. 3. 4.
美 洲 局
安 保 課(12)

題 目 : 美國의 새로운 戰鬪文化

Georgetown 대학 A.Cordesman 교수는 걸프전에서 나타난 美國의 새로운 戰鬪文化에 대해 아래 요지로 논평하였읍니다.(2.28자 NYT)

1. 槪 要

o 걸프전에서 美國이 거둔 신속하고 決定的인 勝利는 美軍의 완벽한 정보 能力과 尖端 高度 裝備에 기초한 월등한 軍事力에 기인한 것임

o 걸프사태 기간동안 美軍은 새로운 戰鬪文化를 보여 주었으며, 이는 포웰 合參議長, 쥬와쯔코프 司令官 및 예하 指揮官들에 의해 명백히 표현 되었음

2. 새로운 戰鬪文化 성립 背景

o 배트남 전쟁, 레바논 介入等에서 겪은 경험을 背景으로, 양적으로 우세한 蘇聯의 陸軍力에 대응키 위해 개발됨
  - 월남전 당시 병력 숫자와 화력의 중시, 경직된 戰術, 軍間 개별 작전 개념등의 비효율성 재검토

o 훈련대상 假想敵軍이 피훈련 부대보다 戰鬪力이 약한 안이한 訓練 개념 탈피

공람	안보과	년월일	담당	과장	심의관	국장	차관보	차관	장관
			김수권						

0093

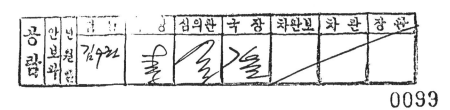

o 단기 복무로 야전에 투입되는 野戰 司令官의 指揮能力에 대한 재평가

3. 새로운 戰鬪文化의 특징

(戰術槪念의 變化)

o 野戰部隊 지휘관의 창의성, 신속성, 작전의 침투성, 4군의 연합.입체 작전 중시

o 소모전 회피, 夜間 및 악천후시에도 고도 情報裝備를 이용, 적의 취약 지역에 대한 공격 감행

o 중단없는 戰鬪를 통한 전선 유동화로 적의 교란을 유발, 戰鬪를 유리한 방향으로 誘導

(새로운 軍民關係 樹立)

o 다음과 같은 여건이 조성되지 않을 경우 戰爭 遂行회피
  - 戰爭에 대한 민간 부문으로 부터의 全幅的 支持 確保
  - 신속하고 決定的 勝利를 위해 필요한 모든 사용 가능한 資源의 동원 권한 획득
  - 漸進的 확전과 政治的 協商.거래로 인한 전투 목적 상실 사태 배제
  - 政治人의 세부 전투 행위에 대한 간섭 배제

4. 이란.이라크전과의 比較

구 분	이.이전	걸프전
공군력 및 미사일	o 이라크, 공군력과 미사일 전력에서 우위 확보 o 그러나 공대공, 유기적 작전 전개, 정밀 폭격능력 미비	o 미군, 제공권 완전 장악, 정밀 폭격으로 전투 효과 최대화 o 이라크의 지휘.통신체계를 개전 일주일이내에 무력화, 지휘체계 와해

0100

정보.정찰	o 이라크, 정보.정찰 능력 우위확보	o 미군, 이라크에 대한 완벽한 정보 정찰망 구축. 야간, 악천후시도 적의 이동 포착가능
야포화력	o 이라크, 야포의 수, 사정거리 탄약등에서 월등한 우위 확보	o 미군, 숫적 열세, 그러나 정확도 월등. 특히 공중 지원으로 적의 화력제압
방어진지	o 이라크, 지뢰매설, 철조망 부설, 보병.기갑부대용 참호 구축으로 이란의 인해 전술에 성공적 대응	o 미군, 이라크 국경일부 지역에 병력집중, 첨단 장비로 장애물 제거후 신속통과.침투 o 고도의 기동부대와 공정대 운용으로 이라크 주력을 우회.포위, 이라크 주력진지는 대규모 폭격으로 초토화

5. 美國의 國防豫算 減縮 計劃에 대한 憂慮 表明

4.

관사령

o 美國의 새로운 國防豫算 計劃에 의하면 향후 5년간 25%의 美軍 減縮 豫想

- 금번 戰爭을 승리로 이끈 人力, 技術, 裝備의 쇠퇴 예상

o 軍備減縮 趨勢가 계속될 경우, 다시는 이러한 戰爭 遂行 불가, 향후 侵略 抑制 努力이 위협 받을 우려

o 美國만이 侵略을 격퇴할 수 있는 힘을 갖고 있으며, 美國이 세계 警察 役割을 원치 않을 수도 있으나, 警察이 없는 세계에 대한 고려가 필요함

- 끝 -

0101

관리 번호	91-544

원 본

외 무 부

종 별 : 지 급

번 호 : USW-1021 일 시 : 91 0304 1841

수 신 : 장관(미북,중동일)

발 신 : 주 미 대사

제 목 : 걸프전 종전 이후 정상 회담 개최 구상

대 WUS-0792

1. 대호 1 항관련, 금 3.5 당관 임성남 서기관이 국무부 정책 기획실 STEPHEN GRUMMON 중동 담당관 및 국무부 근동국 지역 총괄과 EUGENCE DORRIS 부과장으로부터 탐문 한바에 따르면, 양인 공히 여사한 정상회담 개최 구상에 대해서 알고 있는바가 없다하며, 시간적으로도 3 월중 정상 회담 개최는 사실상 어려울것으로 보인다는 반응을 보임.

2. 또한 임 서기관이 당지 일본 대사관의 중동 담당 가와이 서기관을 접촉,전기 보도 관련 일본측이 파악하고 있는 내용을 문의한바, 동 서기관도 여사한 정상 회담 개최 구상이 금시 초문이라는 반응을 보임.

3. 한편, 시게무라 특파원 본인으로 부터의 확인한 바로는, 당초 미국측이 대호 1 항과 같은 정상 회담 개최 구상을 갖고 있었으나, 전통적으로 중동 지역에 대해 어느 정도의 영향력을 행사해 오고 있는 영국측이 금번 걸프전쟁을 계기로 미국의 대 중동 영향력이 급격히 확대 되는것을 원치 않음에 따라 동 회담 개최 구상에 반대 했으며, 이에 따라 현재는 회담 개최 가능성이 희박 해진것으로보인다함(동 특파원은 취재원을 밝힐수 없다하면서, 지난주말 개최된 연쇄 외상회담시 독일은 미측 주도의 정상 회담 개최 구상에 찬성하고, 프랑스 역시 파리개최를 조건으로 동 구상에 찬성하였으나, 영국측의 반대로 결국 무산되었다고언급함)

또한 동 특파원에 따르면, 쿠웨이트 정부가 대호 1 항과 유사한 내용의 정상 회담 개최 구상을 검토중이라는 소문도 있다함.

4. 관찰

가. 전기 내용을 종합해볼때, 대호 정상회담 개최 가능성은 희박한것으로 보임.

나. 전기와같은 회의 개최 구상은 전후의 지역 안정 문제와 관련 여러가지 대안과

미주국 장관 차관 1차보 2차보 중아국 청와대 안기부

PAGE 1 91.03.05 09:43

외신 2과 통제관 FE

0102

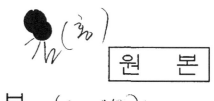

함께 검토되고 있는것으로 보이며, 베이커 장관의 주동 순방 종료 이후에나 지역 체제 정비를 위한 비교적 구체적 방안이 나올 가능성이 있는바, 관련 사항 추보 위계임.

(대사 박동진-국장)

91.12.31 일반

일반문서로 재분류(1991.12.31.)

검 토 필(1991.6.30.)

PAGE 2

0103

관리 번호 91-600

76(?) (2 copy)

원 본

외 무 부

종 별 : 지 급

번 호 : USW-1022 일 시 : 91 0304 1900

수 신 : 장관(미북,중동일,동구일)

발 신 : 주 미 대사

제 목 : 베이커 장관 중동 순방및 소련 방문 계획

대 WUS-0792

대호 3 항관련, 금 3.4 당관 임성남 서기관이 국무부 정책 기획실및 근동국담당 직원등을 접촉, 실무선 으로부터 파악한 표제 동향 요지를 우선 하기 보고함.

1. 순방 기간 금일 현재 계획 으로는 3.7(목) 당지 출발, 3.15 이나 3.16 경귀임 코자 하나 구체적인 일정은 상금 유동적임.

2. 순방국: 이스라엘, 사우디, 이집트, 시리아, 터키, 소련외에 상황이 허락한다면 쿠웨이트도 방문 예정임.

3. 순방 목적: 전후 처리 문제 관련 현재 미측이 확정적이고 구체적인 방안을 갖고 있지 않은 만큼, 주로 관련국의 복안을 청취 하는데에 주 목적이 있음.

(대사 박동진-국장)

91.12.31 일반

일반문서로 재분류(1991.12.31.)

검 토 필(1991.6.30.)

미주국	장관	차관	1차보	2차보	구주국	중아국	청와대	안기부

PAGE 1 91.03.05 09:46

외신 2과 통제관 FE

0104

관리 번호	91/968

외 무 부

종 별 : 지 급

번 호 : USW-1035　　　　　　일 시 : 91 0305 1632

수 신 : 장관(미북,동구일,국연,미안,기정)

발 신 : 주 미 대사

제 목 : 소련대사관 정무참사관 접촉

당관 유명환 참사관은 3.5(화) 당지 소련대사관 AFANSASYEV 정무참사관과 접촉, 걸프전 및 유엔 가입등에 관해 의견교환을 갖은바 동인의 발언 요지를 참고로 다음 보고함.

1. 걸프전 관련 미.소 협조

- 비록 골바쵸프의 마지막 외교적 중재노력이 미측에 의해 거부되었다고는 하지만 후세인으로하여금 쿠웨이트로부터 무조건 철수토록해야 한다는 기본적인 문제에 대해 처음부터 미측과 보조를 갈이하여왔고, 지상전 개시전에 BUSH 대통령으로부터 직접 사전 통보를 받은등 미측도 세심한 배려를 한바 있음.

- 따라서 앞으로 전후 처리 문제등과 관련 (특히 미군의 사우디.쿠웨이트 주둔문제포함)미국이 독자적인 행동을 취하지 않는한 미.소간의 관계는 걸프사태로 인해 별다른 영향을 받지 않을 것으로 봄.

-베이커 국무장관이 중동순방후 귀로에 모스크바를 비공식 방문하여 전후처리문제에 관해 협의할 예정이며, 걸프사태로 연기된 정상회담 개최에 관해서도 협의할 것으로 봄.

-정상회담 일자는 아직 구체적으로 논의된바 없으나 최소한 2 개월 정도의 준비기간이 필요하고 또한 전략무기 협상, 구주군축 문제등과 관련 아직 기술적으로 합의해야할 사항이 남아 있어 5 월하순 또는 6 월이 될것으로봄.

2. 아국의 유엔가입문제

(아측이 먼저 페트롭스키 차관 방미시 언급내용을 문의한데 대해)

- 동인은 국제기구 담당차관으로서 유엔문제를 다루고 있으나, 한국의 유엔가입 문제는 먼저 지역정책의 측면에서 검토가 이루어져야하기 때문에 로가쵸프 보다는 원칙적인 측면에서 일반적으로 언급하였을것으로 봄.

미주국	장관	차관	1차보	2차보	미주국	구주국	중아국	국기국
정문국	청와대	안기부						

PAGE 1　　　　　　　　　　　　91.03.06　07:31

외신 2과　통제관 BW

0105

- 소련은 아직 이문제에 대해 결정을 내린바 없는것으로 알고 있으며 중국이 어떠한 입장을 취할것인지도 고려에 넣고 판단하게될 것으로 봄.

(대사 박동진-국장)

예고:91.12.31 일반

부쉬 대통령 인기도

(3.5.자 NYT지 기사요약)

3.7 실국장회의시 배포. 5M 배포 자료 기술

91. 3. 7.

북 미 과

o 걸프전 승리이후, 최근 USA Today지가 조사한 부쉬 대통령의 인기도는 91%라는 놀라운 수치를 나타냄.

- 92년 대선시 민주당 후보를 제외한 전국민이 지지를 표명하고 있는 것과 마찬가지라고 Newt Gingrich(GA) 공화당 원내 부총무가 논평

o 92년 대선을 20개월을 앞둔 현 시점에서의 이와같은 높은 지지도는 차후 낮아질 것이 분명하나 일단은 92년 대선에서의 낙승이 예상됨.

- 현재 민주당측에서 George McGovern 후보만 출마 발표

o 이러한 인기도의 급격한 상승은 대내외 위기 봉착시 미국민의 단합(rally event)의 결과로 관측됨.

- 지난 1월 NYT/CBS News 합동 여론조사 결과, 부쉬 대통령 인기도는 58%

- 공중 폭격개시 이후 인기도는 86%로 급상승

0107

o 경제여건 개선 여부에 따른 대통령의 인기도 변화는 실업율 변화와도 밀접한 상관관계를 나타냄.

- 최근 경제문제 취급에 대한 부쉬 대통령 인기도는 50% 정도에 불과
- 90.6. 이래 실업율이 계속 증가 91.1. 실업율은 6.1%에 육박하고 계속 상승 예상. 끝

0108

03/05/91 14:17 [redacted]97 0595 EMBASSY OF [redacted] 001

: USW(F) - 0757

: 장 관 (미북, 미안) 발신 : 주미대사

: 미국내 정세 관련 기사

보안 통제	

(3 매)

Democrats Try to Shift Focus to Issues at Home

By RICHARD L. BERKE

Special to The New York Times

WASHINGTON, March 4 — After months as bystanders while President Bush led the country to war, the Senate and House Democratic leaders struggled today to shift some attention back to Congress, domestic affairs and partisan politics.

In separate addresses before a legislative conference of the American Federation of State, County and Municipal Employees, the Senate Democratic leader, George J. Mitchell, and the House Speaker, Thomas S. Foley, praised Mr. Bush for his leadership in the Persian Gulf crisis. But in the euphoria over the victory abroad, they said, it is no time to neglect pressing social problems at home.

The speeches were a preview of the careful balancing act facing Mr. Mitchell and Mr. Foley in the coming days: they want to show initiative among Democrats but they do not want to be accused of attacking a President whose popularity has soared to a historic high point. Conceding the wide bipartisan support for Mr. Bush's handling of the gulf crisis, the Democratic leaders have invited him to address a joint session of Congress on Wednesday night.

Mr. Foley opened his address this morning by commending the President and the American military for "a brilliant military success." But after taking note of a new "national pride," the Washington Democrat turned to domestic matters.

"We have problems here at home that are dramatic in a long-term sense, are conclusive and defining in a long-term sense, though not with the intensity or the focus of this recent war," the House Speaker said. "But if we ignore our problems at home, if we ignore the failings of our own system in this country — economic, political, educational and health — we will be inviting a time in the next century when the United States will simply not have the capacity, will not have the power, to lead the world to an undertaking such as the Desert Storm or Desert Shield operation."

Appearing later before the same friendly audience of leading union officials, Senator Mitchell was more overtly partisan, and not as effusive in his praise for the Administration. While he said Mr. Bush and his military advisers "deserve credit for the success" in the Persian Gulf, the Maine Democrat wasted no time in reciting a litany of what he views as the Administration's domestic vulnerabilities.

"In the wake of the war, the President says he seeks a new world order," Mr. Mitchell said. "We say, Join us in putting our own house in order. Our first priority must be the American people and economic growth and jobs in the United States."

The Senator condemned Mr. Bush's energy policy as "no policy at all," and dismissed Mr. Bush's recent proposal on block grants for cities and states as "ill-advised." And he vowed to champion passage of family leave and civil rights bills. Both measures were vetoed last year.

The Democratic leaders said that while the United States should play a leading diplomatic role in seeking to resolve lingering troubles in the Middle East, they were more concerned with rebuilding American cities than with rebuilding Kuwait or Iraq.

"It is not appropriate for the United States or United States taxpayers to be called upon to pay any of the cost of rebuilding of this region," Mr. Foley said, prompting applause from union leaders.

Senator Mitchell sounded a similar theme. "But what about American cities?" he asked. "They haven't been bombed. People haven't been tortured. But in many respects, there is devastation in American cities — economic devastation, psychological devastation, the loss of jobs, the loss of hope, the loss of opportunity. We've got to restore that."

Mr. Foley dwelled on a need for improvements in secondary and higher education so that students can lead the nation into the next century with the ability to "make a military achievement such as Desert Storm possible."

Unlike Senator Mitchell, the Speaker sought to give Congress a bit of credit for the military victory.

Neglecting to mention that he and two-thirds of the Democrats voted in January against using military force in the Persian Gulf, Mr. Foley told the group: "From the time the President made the decision to send forces to the gulf in August of 1990, there was strong bipartisan support for that decision. There was no significant opposition in the Congress or in the country to his determination to defend Saudi Arabia and to redeem Kuwait and to expel Saddam Hussein from Kuwait."

배부처	장관실	차관실	一차보	二차보	기획실	의전장	아주국	미주국	구주국	중아국	국기국	경제국	통상국	정문국	영교국	총무과	감사관	공보관	외연원	청와대	총리실	안기부	문공부
	/	/	/					9						/						/		/	

801124

Mar. 5, 1991
NYT

0757-1

0103

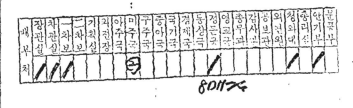

: USW(F) -

: 장 관 발신 : 주미대사

보안
통제

(매)

:

The President's Popularity

It's a stunning figure: As the Persian Gulf war ended, President Bush's popularity, in a USA Today poll, shot up to 91 percent. That prompted a gleeful Representative Newt Gingrich to say, "The number of people who don't like George Bush is almost down to the number of people running for the Democratic nomination."

A popularity figure of anything like 91 percent surely includes a fair number of fair-weather friends. For instance, only four months ago, the same Representative Gingrich ignited anger in the White House for his harsh denunciation of the President's budget deal with Congress.

But even so, 91 percent! With support like that, there's room for many fickle friends to depart and still leave the President a commanding favorite in 1992. The election is now just 20 months away and so far, apart from George McGovern, no Democrats have even declared.

Without denying President Bush an ounce of the pride and credit he has earned in the war, caution is in order. Republican glee is as exaggerated as Democratic gloom. The experience of other Presidents demonstrates a cold truth about such surges of popularity: They don't last.

•

Whenever Americans confront grave international events, they rally round the flag — and the President. After the American hostage-taking in Iran, President Carter's popularity as measured by the Gallup Poll initially shot up by 6 and then by 13 points. This is what John Mueller of the University of Rochester defines as a "rally event," and it was already evident in Mr. Bush's poll ratings. In early January, The New York Times/CBS News Poll found his approval rating to be 58 percent. A few days later — after the air war against Iraq began — it leaped to 86 percent.

The catch is that the popularity arising from such rally events is temporary. Professor Mueller and other scholars find that what creates lasting effects on a President's standing are *economic* events. And these can be appraised by correlating approval ratings with changes in the unemployment rate.

In April 1981, for instance, the unemployment rate was 7.2 percent and President Reagan's popularity stood at a strong 68 percent, in the wake of an assassination attempt. By the start of 1983, unemployment had leapt to 10.8 percent — while Mr. Reagan's popularity had plummeted to an alarming 35 percent.

There's fragility evident in Mr. Bush's present standing. Despite all the popular support for his policies in the gulf, little seems to translate into support for his other policies. In recent weeks, approval for his handling of the economy has consistently been 40 points lower than his gulf rating.

Portentously, the unemployment rate has been going up since June, rising almost a full point to 6.1 percent in January, and it's likely to keep climbing. That's sure to mean bad news for Mr. Bush. But to stop at that would be as shortsighted as it is to make too much of the present 91 percent. Between now and the next election, the President's popularity is likely to change — and change again.

Mar. 5, 1991

0757-2

0110 NYT

03/05/91 14:19 ☎[redacted]97 0595 EMBASSY OF K ☑003

: USW(F) -

: 장 관 발신 : 주미대사

보안	
통제	

: (매)

Anti-War Votes as Albatrosses

MARY McGRORY

The cast for the 1992 Georgia senatorial race is not yet assembled. But the plot is being written by Republicans who hope the Democrats can be punished severely for wimpiness—that is, for voting against the start of George Bush's smashingly successful war in the gulf.

Democratic incumbent Wyche Fowler joined his senior colleague, Sam Nunn, on Jan. 12 in voting no on the use of force, and the Republicans will not let them forget it. Georgia has always been strenuously military—it has 21 military bases and has given both houses of Congress a string of Armed Services Committee chairmen. Nunn, the present chairman, has suffered a 9-percentage-point loss in the polls for his leadership exertions to avert war. Fowler has suffered less because he is known to be liberal and less was expected of him.

Nunn, an idol in Georgia, is the subject of much angry head-shaking. In Marietta, a Democrat has purchased and set up a huge billboard that calls Nunn "Baghdad Sam, Saddam Hussein's best friend." It is signed by someone who identifies himself as "a former Nunn supporter." This to a politician who has not had a negative word addressed to him in 20 years.

National Republicans are, naturally, busy fanning the flames of disapproval. They believe that even if the president's approval rating falls below its present, astral 91 percent—as it must—the afterglow of the gulf will be strong enough for him to drag a Republican Congress home on his coattails.

The new national GOP chairman, Clayton Yeutter, said from the outset Democrats would pay the price for lack of martial spirit. Sen. Phil Gramm (Tex.), chairman of the National Republican Senatorial Committee, quipped corrosively at a recent meeting of Young Republicans that "the Democrats are like the Baath Party of Iraq—they are both working on their domestic agenda to make you forget the war."

House Minority Whip Newt Gingrich (R-Ga.) was down in his home state over the weekend making sure the Republicans understand which is the party that could prosecute efficiently a large desert war.

"The Democrats," he reminded a GOP gathering, "couldn't get eight helicopters across the desert." He was referring to the failed hostage rescue attempt undertaken by another Georgian, President Jimmy Carter. The site of the mission was called prophetically, "Desert One."

Gingrich, who has done no military service, comments contemptuously that many who voted against the war and the military buildup will be "glad to show up at the parade."

His favorite candidate is Mack Mattingly, who lost his Senate seat to Fowler in 1986. Gingrich says piously that the single vote delaying the use of force in the gulf while continuing sanctions might not be sufficient to sink a Democrat. Only those who voted against the war and the weapons that made it such a hit need beware.

Of Fowler, he says, "He is one of the most attractive liberals in the Senate"—which, of course, in certain parts of Georgia, would be like saying a man was a nice leper.

Gramm is said to favor another possible contender, Johnny Isakson, who made a strong race against the newly elected Democratic governor, Zell Miller.

George Bush, however, probably would choose Peace Corps Director Paul Coverdell, a former Georgia state GOP chairman and an early Bush supporter who carried the day in the South for him in 1988. Coverdell denies he is looking beyond his present job, but frequent trips to Georgia, some apparently at Peace Corps expense, have kept speculation alive. Gingrich says he would be "very much surprised if Coverdell didn't run."

Fowler is an incandescent campaigner. He is articulate, warm and witty. Voters enjoy the occasional vaudeville that sparks his appearances. He can clog, play the guitar and sing old tunes like, "Noah found grace in the eyes of the Lord." He tells stories about small-town characters.

In 1986, heavily outspent by Mattingly, he also bucked his constituency's military leanings by voting against the contra war and making frequent high-risk trips to Nicaragua for firsthand inspections.

But his followers wonder what good his history and his gifts will avail him if he is subject to potshots about his patriotism and facing a Bush tide.

Democratic National Committeewoman Juanelle Edwards thinks Fowler can beat back the challenge, points out that he has only lost one election, a runoff to Andrew Young, and that he has served in the military. Other Democrats say militaristic Georgians have "a sense of personality," and that Fowler, a character, may be forgiven a vote of conscience.

Mar. 5, 1991
WP

0111
0757-3 /FAIN

관리 번호	91-631

외 무 부

가 (2)

종 별 : 지 급

번 호 : USW-1082　　　　일 시 : 91 0306 1839

수 신 : 장관(미북,중동일,미안,동구일)

발 신 : 주 미 대사

제 목 : 걸프전 전후 처리 문제

대:WUS-0870

1. 당지 방문중인 이정빈 차관보는 금 3.6. KARL JACKSON 부통령 안보담당 보좌관, NSC DOUGLAS PAAL 아시아 담당 선임 보좌관 내정자 및 SANDRA CHARLES 중동담당 보좌관을 면담, 미국 주도하의 다국적 노력으로 인해 금번 걸프전쟁이 성공적으로 종료된 것을 축하하고, 아측으로서도 여사한 다국적 노력에 동참할수있었던 것을 기쁘게 생각하고 있다고 언급함.

2. 이에 대해 미측은 궁극적으로 다국적 협력이 가능했기 때문에 금번 전쟁을 승리로 이끌수 있었다고 설명하고, 아측의 지원에 대해 사의를 표명함. 이어 SANDRA CHARLES 보좌관은 약 1 시간에 걸쳐 아측과 의견 교환을 가졌는바, 요지하기 보고함.(김규현, 임성남 서기관 배석)

가. 전후 처리 문제의 대강

0 기본적으로 전후 처리문제는 현재의 정전 상태를 공식화하는 문제 및 걸프 지역 전후 질서 재편 문제의 두가지로 대별됨. 전쟁을 승리로 이끄는 일은 끝났지만 앞으로 외교적으로 중동지역에 평화를 정착시키는 일이 더욱 어려운 일임.

나. 정전 상태의 공식화 문제

동문제와 관련된 구체적 사항들은 다음과같음.

0 우선, 이락측이 억류하고 있는 다국적군 포로 및 쿠웨이트 민간인들이 석방되어야함. 다국적군측도 이락군 포로를 송환하여야하는 입장인바, 수송 수단을마련해야 하는등 이문제 자체만도 매우 복잡한 사안임.

0 이락의 쿠웨이트 합병 선언은 당초 이락국회에 의해 채택된 반면, 합병 무효선언은 이락 혁명 평의회(RCC) 에 의해 채택되었는바, 이락측의 여사한 무효조치에 법적하자가 없는지를 현재 검토중임.

미주국	장관	차관	1차보	2차보	미주국	구주국	중아국	정문국
청와대	총리실	안기부						

PAGE 1　　　　91.03.07 10:04

외신 2과 통제관 BW

0112

0 이락측이 대 쿠웨이트 배상 용의 및 이락으로 약탈해간 쿠웨이트 재산의 반환 용의를 표명하는등 정전 상태를 공식화하기 위해 적극적인 자세를 보이고 있는바, 이락측은 정전 상태의 조기 공식화를 통해 대이락 경제제재 조치가 가능한한 신속히 해제되기를 희망하고 있는것으로 보임.

현재 일부 국가들이 쿠웨이트 재산 동결조치등을 해제하고 있기는 하나, 미측으로서는 가까운 장래에 대이락 경제 제재 조치를 해제할 의사가 없음.

0 정전 공식화의 마무리 단계가 되면, 다국적군이 이락 남부로 부터 철수하는 동시에 정전협정이 서명될 것으로 보며, 그간 미결상태였던 쿠웨이트와 이락간의 국경선도 분명히 획정될것으로 봄.또한 유엔 평화 유지군도 창설되어 쿠웨이트-이락 국경 지대에 주둔할것인바, 구성을 어떻게 할것이며 구체적으로 어디에 배치할지등이 논의되어야함.

0 한편, 전기 유엔 평화 유지군이 장기적 주둔을 목적으로 창설될 예정임에반해, 쿠웨이트 정부는 자국내의 단기적 주둔을 위해 SECURITY FORCE 의 창설을 희망하고 있는바, 동 SECURITY FORCE 의 참여국 문제등이 금번 BAKER 국무장관의 중동 순방시 논의될 예정이며, 이미 이문제는 GCC 국가간에 협의되고 있음.

다. 걸프지역 전후 질서 재편 문제

1)안보 문제

0 다국적군이 금명간 철수 예정인 점을 감안한때, 쿠웨이트를 포함하는 걸프역내의 안전 보장 장치를 가능한한 빠른 시일내에 수립하는것이 긴요함.

0 미측으로서는 군사 장비의 쿠웨이트내 계속 배치, 해군력의 걸프 역내 계속 주둔및 평시 공군훈련 강화등을 통해 미국과 걸프제국간에 일정수준의 군사훈련(CONSTANT LEVEL OF MILITARY EXERCISE)을 지속적으로 유지할 생각이기는 하나지상군을 주둔시킬 계획은 없음.(지상군 주둔은 주둔국내 일부 세력의 반대를 유발함으로써 오히려 DESTABILIZING FACTOR 로 작용할 가능성이 크기 때문임.)

0 쿠웨이트와는 이란-이락 전쟁시 쿠웨이트 국적선 호위등을 통해 사실상의안보 협력관계를 발전시켜 왔으며, 사우디, 바레인과도 상호 방위 조약을 체결하고 있지는 않으나 오랫동안 안보 협력관계를 유지해 왔음.

특히, 오만에서는 미공군이 그동안 각종 훈련을 실시해 왔는바, 앞으로는 온건 아랍국들이 보다 더 적극적으로 미국 주도의 각종 합동 군사훈련에 참여할 것으로 봄.

2)정치 문제

0 금번 베이커 국무장관 중동순방시 중동지역 PEACE PROCESS 추진을 위한 방안에 관해 관련제국 의 견해를 청취예정인바, 구체적으로는 금번 걸프사태를 계기로 구축되기 시작한 이스라엘과 온건 아랍국간의 상호신뢰와 우호관계를 바탕으로 신뢰 구축 조치(CBM)를 실시하는 방안 및 이스라엘과 팔레스타인간의 대화를 재개시키는 방안등 이원적 차원에서의 평화구축방안을 추진할 예정임.

0 한편, 금번 걸프사태 기간중 PLO 측은 친이락 입장을 고수함으로서 온건 아랍국으로부터의 신뢰도가 실추된 (DISCREDITED)상황임. 종전후 무바락 대통령의 연설에서 PLO 에 대한 언급이 전혀 없는것이 이를 반영하고 있음.

3)경제 문제

0 이락이 쿠웨이트 침공을 정당화하기 위해 아랍권내 빈부국간 격차 해소를내세운점등을 감안, 금번 베이커 국무장관 중동 순방시 동문제에 대해서도 협의 예정임. 주변국에 대한 경제원조는 계속 되어야할것으로 보며 통상증진, 부자도 적극 추진되기를 기대함.

0 다만, 과거 아랍권내 국가간 원조가 현금 지원 위주로 이Y루어짐으로써 별다른 경제 개발 효과를 거두지 못했던 점을 고려, 앞으로는 경제 개발 프로젝트와 연관된 형태의 원조가 이루어져야할것으로 보는바, GCC 내부에서도 이문제에 대해 진지하게 고려하고 있는 것으로 알고 있으며 FUND 설립을 희망하고 있는것으로 알려짐.

4) 미.쏘 협력 문제

0 소련과는 걸프사태 초기부터 긴밀한 협력을 하여 왔으며 이는 전후처리에있어서도 계속 유지될것으로 생각하는바 특히 소련의 참여는 건설적인 것이 되어야할것임을 강조함.

3. 기타 질의응답시, CHARLES 보좌관의 주요 언급 요지는 다음과같음.

가. 이락 국내 정세

0 현재 이락내 약 15 개도시에서 시아파가 주동하는 반정부 시위가 진행되고 있는바, 바스라에서는 정부군이 동시위를 진압중임. 현재의 상황에서 이락이 전부행위를 재개할 가능성은 거의 없는것으로봄.

0 이락 북부에 비치되어 있던 공화국 수비대가 시위 진압에 동원되고 있고,이락내 반정부 세력이 쿠르도족, 시아파등 각종족별로 분파되어 있는 상황이기때문에 반정부 시위가 훗세인 정권의 붕괴로까지 연결될수 있을 지를 속단키 어려움.

0 다만, 이락 주변국들에게 이락내 반체제 세력에 대한 각종 지원을 계속하고

있으므로, 이락 국내 정국의 불안정 양상이 당분간 계속될 가능성도 있음.

나. 전후 정상회담 개최 문제

0 부쉬 대통령이 3.13-14 간 오타와를 방문, 멀루니 수상과 회담 예정이고 3.14. 은 마티니크에서 미테랑 대통령과 미블 정상회담 예정이기는 하나 일본언론에 보도된것과같은 대규모정상회담 개최 구상에 대해서는 아는바 없음. 메이져수상과의 미영 정상회담 시기, 장소는 상금 미정)

0 미테랑 대통령은 5 개 안보리 상임이사국 정상회담을 제의한바 있으나 의견차이로 소집하지 않기로 한바 있음.

(대사 박동진-장관)

예고:91.12.31 일반

일반문서로 재분류(1991.12.31)

검 토 필 (1991.6.30)

0115

관리번호	91-853

외 무 부

종 별 : 지 급

번 호 : USW-1087 일 시 : 91 0306 2220

수 신 : 장관(미북,미안,중근동)

발 신 : 주 미 대사

제 목 : BUSH 대통령 대의회 연설

연: USW(F)-0779

1. 금 3.6 저녁 9 시 BUSH 대통령은 GULF 전에서의 승리를 보고하기 위한 대의회 연설을 가졌음(연설 전문 연호 FAX 참조)

2. 부쉬 대통령은 금일 저녁 연설도중 민주.공화를 막론하고 의원들로부터 수많은 환호와 박수를 받았으며, 의회 연설장(하원 CHAMBER)은 미국의 승리를 자축하고 대통령의 리더쉽에 경의를 표하는 애국적 분위기로 충만되었음.

3. 최근 미국 조야는 걸프전 종전과 함께 미국이 주도하는 새로운 세계 질서의 내용과 그간 소홀히 취급되어온 국내 문제에 대해 보다 구체적인 해답이 필요하다는 의견을 제기 하였었는바, 금일 부쉬 대통령은 동 2 가지 문제에 대해 나름대로 자신감있는 답변을 제시하고 향후 국제 문제를 이용한 민주당측의 역공가능성을 사전 봉쇄하는 효과를 기였다고 관찰됨.

-유엔의 창설 당시의 취지와 기능 회복, 정의와 인권이 보장되는 세계관 제시

-미국의 승리와 저력을 계속적인 미국의 발전과 국내 문제 해결에 연결, 자신감 표시

4. 한편, 그간 미 행정부는 이락의 쿠웨이트 침공과 이스라엘-아랍분쟁의 연계를 단호히 거부 해왔으며, 중동 지역의 여타 문제는 별도로 해결되어야한다는 입장을 취해 왔는바, 금일 부쉬 대통령은 최초로 동 분쟁을 해결할 시간이 도래했다는 미국의 전향적 정책 방향을 분명히 밝혔음.

5. 현재, 부쉬 대통령은 각종 여론 조사에 90 프로를 상회하는 지지도를 얻고 있으며, 차기 선거에서 부쉬 대통령의 승산은 확고하다는것이 현지 분위기인바, 이러한 분위기는 금일 연설에 대한 의회의 반응에서 잘 보여지고 있음.

6. 본직은 금일 여타 외교단과 함께 동 연설회에 참석하였음.

미주국 장관 차관 1차보 2차보 미주국 중아국 청와대 안기부

PAGE 1 91.03.07 13:40

외신 2과 통제관 BW

0116

(대사 박동진-국장)

91.6.30 까지

91.6.30. 에 예고문에 의거 일반문서로 재 분류됨.

PAGE 2

0117

번호 : USW(F) - 0876

수신 : 장 관 (미북, 미안, 중동일, 중동이) 발신 : 주미대사

제목 : 미소외무장관 공동기자회견 (7 매)

보안 통제

PRESS CONFERENCE WITH SECRETARY OF STATE JAMES BAKER, III AND SOVIET FOREIGN MINISTER BESSMERTNYKH, MOSCOW, USSR FRIDAY, MARCH 15, 1991

MIN. BESSMERTNYKH: (In progress) -- was addressed to me, that is on Soviet attitudes toward use of military force by the United States against the Iraqi army. It is my view that military operations that were carried out against Iraq in connection with this aggression against Kuwait were based on Resolution 678 of Security Council Resolution and there were no other grounds for use of armed forces in Iraq or against Iraq.

Q (Off mike) -- a very important event in our country -- the referendum on the question, to be or not to be the Soviet Union. How would you answer this question if you vote?

SEC. BAKER: Well, I don't have a vote, and therefore I won't answer the question, because I really should not inject myself into political issues, political votes within the Soviet Union. That is a matter for the citizens of the Soviet Union and the various republics to determine.

Q What is the situation regarding the hostages --

SEC. BAKER: The situation regarding the hostages, Barry, is that we have, as the President indicated that I would, raised this issue during the course of this trip in conversations with various countries that we think might have some capacity to be helpful. And that's all I'm going to say on it.

Q You said "various countries." Syria's the only one I'm aware of. Are there other countries --

SEC. BAKER: I just said that that's all I'm going to have to say on it.

Q Well, did you raise it with Israel?

SEC. BAKER: I said "various countries."

Q Have you heard back from Iran --

SEC. BAKER: And that's all I'm going to say on it.

Q Mr. Secretary, you said that we think agreements should be honored, referring to Iraq. Are you implying that they, number one, have broken the agreement? And what does that say in terms of what the United States is prepared to do?

SEC. BAKER: Well, you heard the President speak to this. The President said we must see those undertakings respected and honored, and he did not choose to go any further than that, and I certainly am not going to go any further than that.

0876-1

0118

Q Mr. Foreign Minister, could you tell us what role the Soviet Union sees for itself in the postwar Persian Gulf situation?

MIN. BESSMERTNYKH: I feel that the main role in organizing a security system and a peaceful evolution in the Persian Gulf area belongs in the first place to the countries of the Gulf, but there is also quite an opportunity for permanent members of the Security Council to play a role in there, including the Soviet Union. And that also would include various aspects of that very difficult problem.

In the course of our discussion of the Middle East problem with the President, President Gorbachev spoke on the position of the Soviet Union concerning settlement in the Gulf on the conceptual approaches to Middle East problems. There are no ready-made plans or programs that we gave to the US side. We had a broad-ranging discussion of that issue, and I appreciate the information that Secretary Baker has shared with us on his impression about the visit to the Middle East. It helps us in our joint search of possible ways to settle the conflict.

Q (Inaudible) -- a Middle East peace conference or Israeli-Palestinian negotiations as the basis for recognizing Israel, or are you going to do an independent --

(Audio break.)

MIN. BESSMERTNYKH: It is our view that convening an international conference on the Middle East settlement still remains in the cards. It is part of our vision of how we view possible settlement in the area. But you may know, also, that we think that there are various approaches to that trouble. An international conference is a part of that multi-dimensional process. It should not rule out other approaches.

Q -- Yassir Arafat and the PLO today. Do you agree with efforts really to sidestep the PLO now that (they supported Iraq in the ?) Gulf war, or are you interested in working with the PLO?

MIN. BESSMERTNYKH: Well, the situation that has developed involving PLO and PLO leadership is a well-known fact. I don't want to make any comments on internal problems that exist in that organization. So far, PLO has remained an organization that speaks for the interests of the Palestinians, and until this remains so, I think that PLO should also be involved in the analysis of the troubles related to the Middle East settlement because at the core of that settlement we have still the Palestinian problem.

Q (Inaudible) -- in that time, did you discuss today either in the company of Mr. Gorbachev or perhaps between you and Mr. Baker the question of (scaling ?) arms flows -- conventional arms flows to the Middle East? And where is the Soviet position on continuing to sell military hardware in the Middle Eastern nations in the wake of the Gulf war?

0876-2

0119

MIN. BESSMERTNYKH: We recognize that that problem does exist and we believe that it must be addressed in a fairly particular way also in the Soviet-US dialogue, although not just the Soviet Union and the United States are the only suppliers of arms to that region. But in any event, the time is at hand for us to come to some agreement on a system whereby we would reduce arms supplies of all types to that area. We discussed that problem, but we didn't go into any specific details on that.

Q (Inaudible)

SECRETARY BAKER: Well yes, we spent a fair amount of time on that today and the President was very frank, I think, and candid in explaining to me -- the Minister was there, of course -- his view of the situation today both with respect to efforts concerning the matter of the relationship between republics and the central government and the questions surrounding the issues of economic reform and economic progress and economic problems.

And we had what I think was a very candid and frank exchange, and I don't mean frank in the diplomatic sense, in the sense that there were -- that it was adversarial in any way, but I felt that he laid the situation out very honestly and straightforwardly. That's what I mean by frank.

Q Mr. Secretary, what did he tell you exactly? You referred earlier to the prognosis for reform. What did President Gorbachev tell you about his intentions, his plans, and whether he's being hamstrung right now by forces internally --

SEC. BAKER: He -- he said that he began this process and he was committed to this process, the process of reform; that there were obvious difficulties and problems, that it didn't -- that it was easy to recognize that as a fact. But that he and the all-union government of the Soviet Union were committed to continuing on a reform course, both with respect to perestroika and democratization, political pluralism, and economic reform, reform toward a free market goal at some point.

Now, he also made it clear that the particular steps to be taken over the near term were to encourage a mixed economy, that that was -- that that was being done in order to move in the direction that he and others had originally proposed and announced.

Q Mr. Secretary, do you support that? I mean, every time we've come here, at least when Mr. Gorbachev -- (inaudible) -- perestroika, there were statements of support from the United States. I'm not sure I've heard that from you --

SEC. BAKER: Yes, well -- well, we do support his efforts to continue to reform -- to continue reform in the Soviet Union, both reform toward political pluralism and reform of the economy in order to make it more efficient, more effective and freer.

(Cross-talk.)

0876 -3

0120

Q Mr. Secretary, how do you (warrant?) ministerials -- (inaudible due to cross-talk) -- 2 percent of the CFE talks and START remaining to be resolved. Is this becoming something of a (farce?)?

SEC. BAKER: I think this is the only one we've -- that you've gone to where that was the case, if I'm not mistaken, Tom. There may have been a meeting we had, a brief meeting in Washington where that was the case, but the -- but I think this is the first meeting you might call a ministerial where that's the case. And I can't answer your question, very frankly. I would hope that we can continue on and make progress to overcome these problems in arms control to which we both alluded yesterday when we started. And I'm confident that the United States is going to make every effort to do that; I think the Soviet Union wants to make every effort to do that.

Q Mr. Secretary, did the President share with you any of the obstacles that have arisen from before in the course of perestroika and economic reform in the Soviet Union and did he tell you -- (off mike)?

SEC. BAKER: Yes, he did share that with me and he shared some other things with me that I will probably not share with you.

Q (In Russian.)

MIN. BESSMERTNYKH: The issue of the Soviet-American relationship was discussed in broad terms and in very specific terms as well and I think it's very important to say that there is a shared desire on both sides to continue to develop that relationship on a stable basis following the main directions. As to specific bilateral relationship, that was also discussed in specifics. There may be some specific agreements in the works so we're close to completion and I believe that in the course of our subsequent meetings, we may come up with some specific documents on that subject. What matters most is that Soviet-US relationship has gone through a very difficult test, passed successfully that test and thus opened reliable trust for future development.

Q Did you discuss the **Balkans** with Mr. Gorbachev and did you hear anything in your meeting today that would lead you to believe that he is going to move in the direction as promised a million times, namely negotiation and dialogue?

SEC. BAKER: The answer is yes. We did discuss that and the President pointed out that the all-Union government has appointed individuals to engage in this dialogue, that there -- it is -- it was his intention, as he expressed it to me, that these issues be resolved through dialogue and through negotiation, and his negotiators have been appointed.

0876-4

0121

Now, the point that he further made was there have to be negotiators now appointed by -- by the Baltic republics, the Baltic states, and once that is done, he expressed the hope, at least, that this matter could be resolved peacefully through dialogue and neogtiation, which is the very strong preference of the United States, as I have expressed both to the Minister, to President Gorbachev, and to all of you on numerous occasions.

Q Are you satisfied with that --

Q Mr. Secretary --

Q -- action, sir? Are those actions sufficient?

Q Minister, can you help, please, enlighten us as to what appears to be the holdup on --

Q -- followup -- he has to answer to --

Q -- (off mike) -- said earlier today, the progress -- apparently, there's been very little progress. Can you tell us what you believe to be holding things up?

MIN. BESSMERTNYKH: The problem, compared to all other problems, involves removal of concerns that the two sides have with regard to the treaty on conventional arms. This time, in the course of two sessions, the working group -- and we also discussed at the ministerial level -- additional effort was made to try and find some mutually acceptable solutions. On our side, we had Chief of General Staff Moiseyev. He headed that working group and we presented some working ideas that we thought might provide a way out, a possible solution. I have not yet heard a report from the working group on that subject, and I think they will continue working tomorrow, so we'll still have to wait and see what would be the final result. What matters most is that we have not abandoned effort to try and find solutions to the existing problems.

MIN. BESSMERTNYKH: I also must say that the subject of regional conflicts took up a lot of time in our discussion. We have a rather happy past history on efforts to finding solutions. We concentrated on Afghanistan, Central America and Cambodia, and I believe that in that area we have gained some useful experience. I believe we can use that experience in resolving the remaining regional problems -- in the first place, Middle East problem.

SEC. BAKER: And to answer the question (Doyle ?) asked earlier, let me remind you that when we met in Washington on or about the 28th or 29th of January, sometime in that time frame, we were meeting in the aftermath of the unfortunate events in Vilnius. Tensions were very high. There had been the regrettable confrontation there resulting in the loss of life. We talked at length with the minister at that time, and it was agreed that there needed to be some process or mechanism developed that would be more likely to lead to a peaceful resolution through negotiation and dialogue.

0876-5

0122

It seems to me that steps have been taken to develop such a process and mechanism. Furthermore, steps have been taken to defuse tensions by withdrawing some forces from Lithuania and, I think, some of the other -- Latvia, as well, some of the other -- at least one of the other Balitc states.

So, you asked me if this is satisfactory, and my response to you is this is a difficult issue. We are in, it seems to me, a lot better shape than the situation that existed back in January, and we can only

see that as some progress. Now, it's important that that negotiation actually take place and that the parties join in a good-faith effort to reconcile this peacefully.

Q Recently, you have said that part of our view of perestroika was that there should not be a reversal of gains for free market economics. And you even at one point told Mr. Shevardnadze not to crack down on the cooperatives and so forth. Can you stand there today and say that there has not been backsliding on that? Did you tell him -- President Gorbachev -- of your concerns about that, that -- (inaudible) -- monetary policy on such --

SEC. BAKER: The answer is "no" and "yes."

Q Mr. Secretary, you gave us, your -- you gave us an account of how you responded to the Baltics presentation, but I don't think we know how you feel about the President's description of his problems in putting through his economic program. Did he make a compelling case, did he persuade you that he's doing his best?

SEC. BAKER: Look, it's not -- it is really not my place to sit in judgment on the specifics of the economic plan. There are many, many problems. The President, the Minister, have been very candid in saying so and in explaining the manner in which they are attempting to address those problems. They are economic, and they are political, and you must weigh both. So, to answer your question specifically, David, I'm not sure that "backsliding" is the right word.

But there -- there is not -- there are some major problems in reforming an economy that for 70 years has been run pursuant to principles that are quite opposite from the principles of free market economics. And we had a very honest and candid discussion today of those problems. And the President was very -- was very honest in pointing these out. The point is, you have to look not just at the economics, but you have to look as well as the politics.

Q Mr. Secretary, do you believe the Soviet Union will remain a partner in the coalition that began with the Gulf crisis and afterwards it will be a constructive partner in the Middle East?

0876-6

0123

SEC. BAKER: That would be my hope certainly, and I don't see any reason following these talks why that would not be the case. We will have to -- obviously we will have to see. The predictions were made -- many predictions were made, particularly in the latter stages of the resolution of that crisis that somehow the Soviet Union would not remain committed to the same goals that other coalition partners were committed to, but it did.

And that's what I think the Minister meant when he said the relationship has gone through a test recently and it has, and it has survived and that is good for the Soviet Union, and that is good for the United States, and that is good for the world, and we should work to keep the relationship on that same track if we possibly can.

END

0876-7 (END)

0124

관리 번호	91-656

원 본

외 무 부

종 별 :

번 호 : USW-1101 일 시 : 91 0307 1757

수 신 : 장관(미북,중동일, 미안,기정)

발 신 : 주 미 대사

제 목 : 걸프 전후 미국의 대중동 정책

본직은 금 3.7. 백악관 ROBERT GATES 안보담당 부보좌관이 BLAIR HOUSE 에서 외교단을 위해 실시한 걸프전 종전후의 대중동 정책관련 브리핑에 참석하였는바, GATES 부보좌관의 주요 언급 요지는 다음과 같음(기본적으로는 작일 부쉬 대통령 의회 연설 내용을 부연)

1. 금번 걸프사태 수습을 위해서는 당사자인 지역내 국가들의 의견과 INITIATIVE 가 중요한바, 미국이 어떤 특정해결 방안을 강요하지 않을것임.

2. 걸프 전쟁으로 인해 사우디등에 파견된 미군 병력은 조기 철수할것이며,중동 지역내에 미 지상군을 장기적으로 주둔 시킬 계획은 없음. 중동지역 안정확보 방안의 일환으로, 미국은 역내 우방과의 합동 군사훈련 실시 및 해군력(항모 전단 포함) 계속 파견등을을 고려중임.

3. 또한 중동평화의 수립을 위해 이스라엘-팔레스타인 문제의 해결에 외교적 노력을 집중예정인바, 유엔 안보리의 관련 결의안을 기초로 이스라엘의 안전과 팔레스타인에 대한 공정한 처우를 실현하는것이 주목적임.

4. 중동지역내의 빈부 격차 및 선후진국간의 경제력 격차를 보전하기 위해 역내 경제 개발의 추진이 바람직한바, 역내 국가들이 적극 선도할 경우 미국도 제2 선에서 이를 적극 지원할것임.

5. 금번 걸프 전쟁이 다국적 연합 노력으로 성공적인 종식을 맞게 된것 처럼, 역내 평화 구축도 그와 같이 연합적 노력(COALITION) 에의해 실현되어야 하는바, 미국 단독으로 동 PROCESS 를 추진하지는 않을것임.

6. 제반 전후 처리 문제해결에 참고코자 관계국들의 의견을 청취하기 위해 베이커 국무장관이 금일 아침 중동향발 하였음.

(대사 박동진-장관)

미주국	장관	차관	1차보	2차보	미주국	중아국	청와대	안기부
국방부								

PAGE 1

91.03.08 08:57

외신 2과 통제관 CH

0125

예고:91.12.31. 일반

검토필 ('91. 6. 30.) 인

일반문서로 재분류(1991. 12. 31.)

PAGE 2

0126

외 무 부

종 별 :

번 호 : USW-1232 일 시 : 91 0315 1832

수 신 : 장 관(통일,경기원,상공부)

발 신 : 주 미 대사

제 목 : 미상무장관 쿠웨이트 방문

연: USW-1187

1. MOSBACHER 미 상무장관은 쿠웨이트 재건과 관련 현지 평가 및 협의를 위해 작 3.14. 쿠웨이트 정부초청 및 재정부담으로 쿠웨이트로 향발하였으며 래 3.17 귀임 예정이라고 함.

2. MOSBACHER 장관의 쿠웨이트 순방에는 지난 1.12 부시 대통령의 걸프전을 지지한 GALLEGLY의원 (캘리포니아)등 10명의 공화당 소속 하원의원과 LUKEN (오하이오)등 2명의 민주당 소속하원의원과 AT AND T, FLUOR, DRESSER 등 쿠웨이트재건에참여 하고 있는 주요 기업인 대표, HAIG 전 국무장관, CARLUCCI 전 국방장관등 주요 미 기업의 컨설턴트 와 ABINADER 미-아랍상공인회 회장등이 동행하였음. + Richard Allen

3.한편,금일자 WP 지는 12명의 미하원의원의 금번 여행비용은 캘리포니아 소재 FLUOR 사가 부담하였으며, FOLEY 하원의장은 민주당 소속의원에게 동여행이 미의원 윤리 규정에 어긋날것이라고 경고하였다고 보도 하였음.

4. 금 WP USW(F)-0883 팩스 송부함.

(대사-국장)

통상국 2차보 경기원 상공부 1차보 미주국 정문국 중아국 청와대 안기부

PAGE 1

91.03.16 09:09 WG

외신 1과 통제관

0127

MAR.15 '91 18:48 KOREAN EMBASSY WASHINGTON DC P.001

Lawmakers Going to Gulf Over Foley's Objections

Contractor Paying Cost at Kuwait's Request

By Gary Lee
Washington Post Staff Writer

Twelve members of Congress who supported the decision to send U.S. troops into the Persian Gulf ignored the objections of House Speaker Thomas S. Foley (D-Wash.) and left for their own visit to the region last night, their expenses paid—at Kuwait's request—by a corporation seeking to do business in Kuwait.

Foley spokesman Jeff Biggs said the speaker objected strongly to the trip during a party meeting last week. The House ethics committee had told the congressmen they could not accept a trip paid for by a foreign government, and Foley expressed concern that even U.S. corporate sponsorship might not justify the trip.

Biggs said the speaker thought corporate funding would be only superficial cover for a trip improperly financed by Kuwait. Foley "blew up," one Democrat present at the meeting said. Biggs said the speaker had "expressed his views strongly and clearly. I don't think anybody left with any doubt about how strongly he objected."

The 10 Republicans and two Democrats, who all voted Jan. 12 for a Bush administration resolution authorizing the use of force in the Persian Gulf, were invited by Kuwaiti Ambassador Saud Nasir Sabah after Kuwait was liberated from Iraqi troops. Their expenses were picked up by the Fluor Corp., based in Irvine, Calif., a spokesman there said.

Secretary of Commerce Robert A. Mosbacher also went along on the trip, representing the Bush administration. "He wants to assess the situation," department spokesman Marcie Robinson said, "and see how we can be of any further assistance."

Mosbacher's trip was paid for by the Kuwaiti government under a department rule that allows such trips if they facilitate the work of the department, Robinson said.

The four-day visit, dubbed by Sabah the "first freedom flight to Kuwait," appeared to be Kuwait's way of saying thanks to its supporters in Congress and to others assisting in rebuilding the war-torn country. Sabah traveled with the delegation and his office did not respond to telephone calls.

Fluor, a major American construction company, worked in Kuwait in the 1960s and is bidding for Kuwaiti contracts to help restore oil facilities and refineries, spokesman Deborah Land said in an interview. She said Fluor had held several discussions about the company's possible role in reconstruction with Sabah before he proposed on Tuesday that Fluor sponsor the congressmen's trip.

Others on the trip are senior business executives from American Telephone & Telegraph, Dresser Corp. and other firms involved in reconstructing Kuwait after the devastation of war. The guest list also features prominent defenders of Kuwait's cause, including Sam Zakhem, former U.S. ambassador to Bahrain, and J.R. AbiNader, chairman of the National U.S.-Arab Chamber of Commerce.

When Sabah first issued the invitation earlier this month, the ethics committee—formally named the Committee on Standards of Official Conduct—told the members that congressional rules barred travel from the United States to a foreign country under the sponsorship of a foreign government, according to a committee spokesman who asked not to be named. The exception would be a purely cultural trip, the spokesman said.

Kuwait then asked the National Council on Arab-American Relations to organize American corporate sponsorship for the trip, said Ron Cathell, a council spokesman. Several corporations agreed to contribute and the $700,000 needed was quickly raised, Cathell said. But Sabah canceled the arrangement because he did not want to invite representatives from all the companies sponsoring the trip, Cathell said. "He never envisioned this as a trade delegation," he said.

Fluor spokesman Land declined to say how much Fluor was contributing for the trip, but other sources

SPEAKER THOMAS S. FOLEY
. . . strongly advised against trip

estimated that expenses for 12 congressmen would amount to about $60,000.

Republicans included are: Elton Gallegly (Calif.), Curt Weldon (Pa.), John R. Kasich (Ohio), Helen Delich Bentley (Md.), Robert K. Dornan (Calif.), Bill Paxon (N.Y.), Ronald K. Machtley (R.I.), Michael G. Oxley (Ohio), Chalmers P. Wylie (Ohio), and James M. Inhofe (Okla.). Democrats are Charles J. Luken (Ohio) and Pete Geren (Tex.).

USW(F) - 0883
수신 : 장관 (통일, 중기원, 상공부)
발신 : 주미 대사
제목 : USW 1232 의 첨부물
(1매)

0128

관리번호	91-732

원 본

외 무 부

종 별 :

번 호 : USW-1243 일 시 : 91 0318 0726

수 신 : 장관(미북, 중동일)(사본:청와대 김종휘 외교안보 보좌관)

발 신 : 주미대사

제 목 : 전직 미 정부 관리등 쿠웨이트 방문

1. 팩스편 본부로 기송부한 3.15 자 WSJ 지의 'ALEXANDER HAIG, OTHERS, FLY TO KUWAIT IN SEARCH OF RECONSTRUCTION BENEFITS" 제하의 기사에 따르면 , 쿠웨이트 정부가 쿠웨이트 해방을 기념하기 위해 ROBERT MOSBACHER 상무장관, ROBERT DORNAN 하원의원, CHALMERS WYLIE 하원 의원, MICHAEL OXLEY 하원의원등 현직 정치인 외에 ALEXDANDER HAIG 전 국무장관, FRANK CARLUCCI 전 국방장관 및RICHARD ALLEN 전 안보보좌관등 전직 미 정부관리도 다수를 3.13. 부터 4 일간의 일정으로 초청하였다함(동기사는 USW(F)-0902 로 팩스편 재송부)

2. 원칙적으로 동 쿠웨이트 방문 관련 경비는 쿠웨이트 정부에서 부담하며,주미 쿠웨이트 대사관 및 미 상무부에서 전기 대상자를 선정했다함.

(대사 현홍주-차관)

91.6.30. 일반

예고문에 의거 일반문서로 재분류19 91 6. 30 서명

미주국 장관 차관 1차보 2차보 중아국 정문국 청와대 안기부

PAGE 1

91.03.19 08:04

외신 2과 통제관 BW

0129

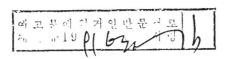

03/18/91 09:30 ☎20[redacted]7 0595 EMBASSY OF KO━━→ WOI 001/001

번호 : USW(F) - 0902 0318 0720

수신 : 장 관(미북, 중동일) 발신 : 주미대사

(사본: 청와대 김종휘 보좌관)

제목 : 전직 미 정부 관리등 쿠웨이트 방문 (첨부) (1 매)

보안 통제	

Alexander Haig, Others, Fly to Kuwait In Search of Reconstruction Benefits

By JILL ABRAMSON

Staff Reporter of THE WALL STREET JOURNAL

When the emir of Kuwait at last reclaimed his throne yesterday, a bevy of U.S. dignitaries were on hand to celebrate. But this wasn't merely a social occasion.

Among those who were flying in for the fete— on an all-expenses-paid flight that the Bush administration helped to arrange—were some of the very consultants and lobbyists now lining up to cash in on the reconstruction of the emir's war-ravaged country.

Take Alexander Haig, the former Secretary of State. He has been busily touting himself as a matchmaker between corporations eager to get a piece of the multibillion dollar reconstruction and Kuwaiti government officials, including the emir. Since leaving the government, Mr. Haig has earned millions of dollars in consulting fees from such clients as United Technologies Corp., which he once headed, and Boeing Co.

Also departing from Andrews Air Force Base Wednesday night aboard a chartered Kuwaiti Airlines 747 aircraft were former Secretary of Defense Frank Carlucci, another highly paid international business consultant; former Democratic Rep. Tony Coelho, now an investment banker in New York; and top executives from AT&T Corp., Fluor Corp. and Dresser Industries Inc. Richard Allen, an international business consultant who was Ronald Reagan's national security adviser, also was on board.

Not everyone on the plane is going gratis. Mort Zuckerman, the developer and publisher, is paying his own way, says a spokeswoman.

The Kuwaitis dubbed it the Freedom Flight. Coveted invitations for the four-day trip went out last week from Shaikh Saud Nasir al-Sabah, the Kuwaiti ambassador in Washington and a member of the ruling family. But the Bush administration had a hand in picking who would go along.

Secretary of Commerce Robert Mosbacher, who joined in the trip, spoke for the administration on which companies should receive invitations. As word of the invitation-only trip spread, both the Commerce Department and the Embassy of Kuwait were deluged by those begging for a seat on the plane.

Administration officials and some business executives wanted to play down the business aspect of the trip. "It is not a trade mission," insisted one Bush administration official knowledgeable about the trip. The group may, however, meet with Kuwait's interior minister, who will play a role in handing out contracts for the rebuilding of the country—a public works project that may approach $100 billion in value. A meeting with the emir was also tentative, according to someone familiar with the planning for the trip.

Several members of the delegation—including Mr. Carlucci, Mr. Coelho and Sam Zakhem, the former Ambassador to Bahrain—were active in the Committee for Peace and Security in the Gulf, an adhoc lobby group that supported President Bush's Gulf war policies. "Most of the people on the trip already have established strong relations with the Kuwaitis," explained Ron Cathell of the National Council of Arab-American Relations, whose president, John Duke Anthony, is on the trip.

But many of those on the excursion are hoping to exploit those ties for business. "They are all over there feeding at the trough," says Edward von Kloberg, a Washington lobbyist who once represented the government of Iraq. "They are promising the world, but I don't know what any of these consultants can really deliver."

With Kuwaitis still unable to receive incoming telephone calls, consultants such as Mr. Haig are selling themselves as emissaries to the emir and his aides. According to one person in Washington familiar with some of Mr. Haig's client contacts, the former secretary is aggressively marketing himself as someone "who can help open the right doors in Kuwait." Mr. Haig couldn't be reached in Kuwait and an associate didn't return a message left for him, although Mr. Haig's secretary confirmed that he was on the trip.

Some companies are already doing business in Kuwait without the help of Mr. Haig or other consultants. AT&T, for example, has three satellite stations and a fourth on the way that have restored some outgoing telephone service.

Not every international business consultant who made the cut was able to go along. Declining invitations for the flight were former Secretary of State Henry Kissinger and former Pentagon official Richard Perle.

The Kuwaiti government's offer to pay for the trip created an ethical minefield for some U.S. officials. While Commerce Department ethics guidelines permitted Secretary Mosbacher, for one, to accept some transportation and other gifts from a foreign government, members of Congress could not. Several alternatives were explored. Among them: a plan to join the caravan in Montreal, because a loophole in the ethics laws allows for some foreign trips to be paid for, as long as the lawmakers don't depart from the U.S.

In the end, Fluor, based in Irvine, Calif., saved the day, resolving the ethical complication by footing the bill for the 12 House members who are on the trip. Such donations from U.S. corporations are lawful for "fact finding" missions. Deborah Land, a Fluor spokesperson, said that her company received the request from the Commerce Department to pay the lawmakers' passage.

Republican congressmen outnumbered Democrats by 10 to two. They included such hawks as Robert Dornan of California and such influential committee leaders as Chalmers P. Wylie and Michael Oxley, both of Ohio. House Speaker Thomas Foley discouraged Democrats from going along. Maryland Gov. W. Donald Schaefer was also there.

For its part, Fluor also hopes to massage its relationship with the Kuwaitis. The construction giant has extensive business interests in the Middle East and has done business in Kuwait since the 1960s. "We certainly are looking for opportunities there," says Ms. Land.

—Peter Truell contributed to this article.

Mar. 15, 1991

WSJ

END

0130

관리번호	91/149

외 무 부

종 별 : 지 급

번 호 : USW-1267 일 시 : 91 0319 1557

수 신 : 장관(미북,구일,중동일,미안)

발 신 : 주 미 대사

제 목 : 부쉬 대통령 정상회담 결과 브리핑

부쉬 대통령의 영. 카나다. 불간 정상회담 결과에 대한 DAVID C.GOMPERT 특별보좌관 (SPECIAL ASSISTANT TO THE PRESIDENT FOR NATIONAL SECURITY AFFAIRS AND SENIOR DIRECTOR FOR EUROPEAN AND SOVIET AFFAIRS)의 브리핑이 국무부 주관하에 3.19(화) 11:00-12:00 간 전 주재대사를 영빈관(BLAIR HOUSE)으로 초치하여 (김공사 참석)개최되었는바, 동브리핑 내용 아래 보고함.

91.6.30. 일반

1. 개요

0 BUSH 대통령의 멀루니 카나다 수상, 미테랑 대통령, 메이저 영 수상간의 정상회담에서 GULF 전후 처리문제, 유럽 및 동구정세 변화 문제등 중요한 의제들을 심도있게 그러나 비공식 입장에서 광범하게 협의하였으나 확정적인 합의 내용은 없었음.

2. 정상회담 목적

가. GULF 전 수행기간 및 전쟁 전후를 통해 동맹국으로서 지속되어온 상호 긴밀한 협력관계를 평가하고 계속적인 협력관계 유지 필요성 재확인

나. 전후 중동정세 재조명

3. 회담 내용에 대한 관찰

가. 정상간의 중요 국제문제 해결을 위한 긴밀한 협력관계 유지 재확인의 기회

0 소련, 동구권 변화에 대한 적극 대처, 지원

0 능동적 협력관계 (DYNAMIC BASIS OF COOPERATION)의 계속 강화 기대

나. 국제 정치에서 미국의 위상이 강대국으로 부상

0 그러나 미국의 일방적 강행은 부정하고 상호 긴밀한 협력하, 문제 해결에강력하고 단호한 힘으로 대처해 가는 관례확립

0 문제 해결을 위한 사전 정보교환(LISTENING)철저

미주국 장관 차관 1차보 2차보 미주국 구주국 중아국 청와대 안기부

PAGE 1

91.03.20 08:49

외신 2과 통제관 FE

0131

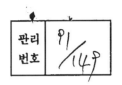

다. 각종 중요정보의 상호 개방으로 문제의 정확, 신속한 해결 도모의 계기마련

0 COALITION PARTNERSHIP 의 제 분야 확대 강화(EC, 동구, 전후 복구등)

4. 각국 정상간의 협의 내용

가. 카나다: 양국간 현안문제의 조속한 해결과 협력관계 강화

나. 불란서: 유럽문제(정치경제 통합), NATO(감군문제), 동구제국에 대한 지원, 미국의 계속적 지원, 통상문제 (GATT, UR)

다. 영국: MAJOR 수상 방소 결과 청취 및 대소지원 문제, 소련의 개방정책과 성공을 위한 확고한 지지 재확인, 경제 문제 (GATT, UR)

(대사 현홍주-국장)

예고:91.12.31 일반

관리 번호	91/181

외 무 부

종 별 : 지 급

번 호 : USW-1344 일 시 : 91 0322 1646

수 신 : 장관(미북,동구일,미안,중근동,기정)

발 신 : 주 미 대사

제 목 : 미.소 외무장관회담(미소관계)

연:USW-1331

국무부 소련과측은 미소 외무장관회담등 BAKER 국무장관의 소련방문(3.14-16)결과를 3.21 당관에 실무선에서 전달하여왔는바, 동요지 다음 보고함.(JOHN ORDWAY 소련과 부과장이 당관 김영목 서기관에게 설명)

1. 소련 방문 개요

-BAKER 장관은 베스메르트닉 장관과는 2 차례 회담을 가졌으며, 고르바쵸프와 1 차례 면담을 가졌음.

- 금번 방문시 미소 정상회담(모스크바)의 개최 일시에 대한 합의가 이루어지지 못했음. 양측은 정상회담의 개최를 위해서는 START 협상이 완결되어야 하며, START 의 완결에는 CFE 협정에 대한 미.소간의 이견 해소가 선행되어야한다는 공동 인식을 하였음.

-현재로서는 BUSH 대통령의 소련방문이 여하한 방식으로 언제 이루어질지 예측할수 없음. 다만, 금년 상반기중 개최키로한 양측간 합의는 상금까지 유효함.

- BAKER 장관은 발트 3 국 대표들과의 별도 회합, 각 공화국 지도자들과의 만찬등 소련 중앙정부이외의 지도자들과도 대화를 가졌으며, 매우 생산적이었음.

- 미.소 양측은 대부분의 시간을 걸프정세 및 BAKER 장관의 중동 순방결과협의에 소모했으며, BAKER-GORBACHEV 회담시에는 소련 국내정세, START 등 정치적 현안에 관해 주로 협의했음.(동문제외에 미소 양국관계, 군축, 지역문제등 현안전반에 대해 협의)

- 금번 방문중 캄푸챠 문제를 제외하고는 아시아 문제는 협의되지 못했음.

2. 중동정세

- 미측은 이락측과의 완전 휴전 정책 방안과 중장기적 지역안보체제 수립에관한

미주국 장관 차관 1차보 미주국 구주국 중아국 정문국 외연원
청와대 안기부 국방부

PAGE 1

91.03.23 08:30
외신 2과 통제관 BS

0133

미측 입장을 설명하였음.(종전 방안에 관해서는 3.21 유엔안보리에 제출한 미측안을 사전 설명)

가. 휴전 정착방안

. 원유와 무기의 금수계속(안보리결의 686 호의 이행)

. 미사일등 대량살상 무기의 파괴감시 체제 및 대이락 피해복구 시행을 위한 기구 수립, 유엔 휴전 감시군의 배치

. 쿠웨이트, 이락간 국경분쟁에 관한 원칙

(상세는 USW(F)-0968 참조)

나. 지역 안보체제 형성

GCC 의 강화, 이를 주축으로한 아랍군 창설

유엔 감시기구의 파견

. 미국과 각국과의 양자관계 증진 내용

- 특히 BAKER 장관은 지역안보체제에 있어 미국의 기능과 관련, 미국은 지상군의 영구주둔을 꾀하지 않을 것이나, 해군력의 배치 및 각국과의 합동 훈련실시, 장비의 사전 배치등의 정책을 추진할 것임을 설명함.

- 베스메르트닉 외상은 미국이 이락을 완전히 무력화.고립화시키려는 정책이 아닌가 우려를 표시한바, BAKER 장관은 미국의 목표는 이락의 파괴가아니라 지역안정 및 경제부흥이목표라고 답변하고 미.소가 동지역의 군비경쟁을 통제하는데 협력할것을 촉구함.(안보리 상임 이사국 5 개국이 동 지역의 무기수입의 95% 점유 지적)

-BAKER 장관은 중동은행 구상등 지역 경제개발을 위한 조직적 방안이 필요하다고 설명하고, 아랍-이스라엘 분쟁과 관련 미국은 촉매역할을 담당할 용의를 표시하였음. 동문제와 관련, BAKER 장관은 각 당사자가 모두 손해를 감수하는 어려운 결정을 해야한다고 언급함.

- 소련측은 아랍-이스라엘 분쟁과 관련, 새로운 아이디어가 보이고 있음에 만족을 표하고, 국제회의 개최등 중동평화에 관한 소련의 기존 입장을 설명함.

-미측은 중동 평화에는 TWO TRACK 접근이 필요하다고 하고, 거창한 가시적 성과의 성취이전에 우선, 쉽고, 덜가시적인 성과를 취하기 위한 작업이 필요하다는 입장을 표시함.

-소련측은 미국이 걸프전후 동지역에 군사력을 증강하려는 기도가 있다는 소련내의 우려를 표시한바, BAKER 장관은 지역안보에 있어 아랍동맹국들이 어디까지나 주역할을

하고 미국은 보조역할을 할것이며, 현재 배치된 지상군은 영. 불등과 협의 가급적 조속한 시일내 철수할 계획이라고 답변함.

- 김서기관은 소련측이 즉각적인 아랍-이스라엘 협상 개시 또는 중동국제평화회의 개최를 주장하였는지 문의한바, ORDWAY 과장은 소측은 여사한 제안을 강하게 제시하지 않고 소측의 전반적인 견해만 제시한 분위기였다고 답변함.

3. 미소 양자관계 및 소련 정세

-BAKER 장관은 보고와같이 라트비아 LIGA 에 출장소 개설을 제의한바, 베 장관은 검토하겠다고 답변함.

-BAKER-GORBACHEV 회담에서는 상당부분이 소련내 정세 협의에 소모되었음. BAKER 장관은 발트의 정치.경제정세 동향, 국민투표등에 관심을 표하고 소련의 개혁정책에 대한 미국의 지지를 재강조하였음.(소련의 계속 개혁, 시장경제로의 진행 필요성 지적)

- 이에 대해 소측은 이제는 연방분리에 관한 법이 제정되었으므로 발트 3 국이 이에 따른 절차를 밟아야한다는 입장을 강조하고, 발트측이 협상을 거부하고 있다고 불만을 표시하였음. 소측은 국민투표는 연방구성에 대한 새로운 법적 뒷바침을 하게될것이라고하고, 동조약안이 FEDERAL COUNCIL 에서 좀더 토의를 가친후 연방각 공화국간에 체결될것이라고 설명함.

-GORBACHEV 는 개혁이 계속될 것임을 강조하고, 소련은 바람직한 혼합경제(MIXED ECONOMY)를 지향하고 있다고 발언함. 베스메르트닉은 베이커장관과 회담시 일부 생필품가격 인상 계획을 소개하고, 이는 시장경제 를 향한 조치의 일환이라고 발언하였음.

4. 군축

-BAKER 장관은 베 장관과 고 대통령과의 회담시 군축에 관한 미국의 기본 입장(소련의 CFE 협정 준수등)을 개략적으로 표시하였으며, 상세는 군축 실무회의에서 별도로 협의되었음.

- CFE 의 제 3 조 해석 문제와 관련, 미측은 육상장비의 한도는 그대로 준수되어야한다는 입장을 견지한바, 소측은 연안경비대와 3 대전략 군사력은 그대로 유지하고, 여타 부문에서 한도만큼 감축하되, 우랄이동의 군사력에서 이를 보상 증가하겠다는 안을 제시함.

- 미측은 CFE 의 합의는 합의 그대로 준수되어야 한다는 입장을 강조하였음.다만

소측이 일단 합의는 그대로 준수되어야 한다는 원칙을 최초로 자인했다는점에 주목하고 있음.(연안경비대 장비는 육상장비에서 제외 되어야 한다는 당초 소측 입장에 변화)입장에 변화)

--START 에 관해서는 상금도 많은 기술적 이견이 해소되지 않고 있는바, 4-5월중 모든 군축협상이 마무리될지는 미지수임.

5. 지역문제

- 금번에는 아프가니스탄, 엘살바돌, 캄푸챠 문제가 논의되었으나 양측의 기존 입장만 교환된 정도였음.

- 한반도 문제와 일본이 북방영토 문제등은 거론되지 않았음.

6. 참고사항

- 현재 미소간 군축협상의 진전 전망이 불투명하여, BUSH 대통령이 그리스-터키 방문과 소련방문계획이 여하히 구체화될지 예측하기 어려운것으로 보임.

-다만, 미측은 금번 소련측과의 회담을 통해 소련측이 계속 안정적인 미.소관계의 유지를 희망하고 있다는 판단을 하게된것으로 감축됨.

- 현재 실무선에서는 미.소 정상회담의 개최 일자등 미소관계의 진전 전망에 대해 견해 표시를 자제하는등 매우 신중한 분위기를 보이고 있음.9 대사 현홍주-국장)

예고:91.12.31 일반

0136

외교문서 비밀해제: 걸프 사태 35

걸프 사태 미국 동향 2

초판인쇄 2024년 03월 15일
초판발행 2024년 03월 15일

지은이 한국학술정보(주)
펴낸이 채종준
펴낸곳 한국학술정보(주)
주 소 경기도 파주시 회동길 230(문발동)
전 화 031-908-3181(대표)
팩 스 031-908-3189
홈페이지 http://ebook.kstudy.com
E-mail 출판사업부 publish@kstudy.com
등 록 제일산-115호(2000. 6. 19)

ISBN 979-11-6983-995-2 94340
979-11-6983-960-0 94340 (set)

책에 대한 더 나은 생각, 끊임없는 고민, 독자를 생각하는 마음으로 보다 좋은 책을 만들어갑니다.